KOKINSHŪ

A Collection of Poems Ancient and Modern

Translated and Annotated by
Laurel Rasplica Rodd
with
Mary Catherine Henkenius

Including a study of Chinese Influences
on the *Kokinshū* Prefaces
by John Timothy Wixted
and
an Annotated Translation of
the Chinese Preface
by Leonard Grzanka

Cheng & Tsui Company

First Paperback Edition 1996
Based on original clothbound edition
published by Princeton University Press 1984

Cheng & Tsui Company
25 West Street
Boston, MA 02111-1268 USA
Fax number: (617) 426-3669

Library of Congress Catalog Number: 96-085412

ISBN 0-88727-249-5

Printed in the United States of America

PREFACE

The texts used for this translation are the one found in *Kokinwakashū* edited by Ozawa Masao (a copy of the Teika line of texts by Nijō Tameyo with a colophon by Fujiwara Teika dated the twentieth of the Eleventh Month of 1222, supplemented by the Teika texts edited by Ikeda Kikan and Nishishita Kyōichi now in the Momozono Library and the Hatsunokari Library respectively) and the edition by Kubota Utsubo in *Kokinwakashū hyōshaku*, also based on the Teika texts.

In the Heian period (794–1185), when the *Kokinshū* was compiled, Japan used the lunar calendar. Thus the new year began in late January or early February with the blossoming of the plum, the song of the mountain thrush, the appearance of green shoots through blankets of snow. The first three lunar months were considered spring, the next three summer, and so on. Occasionally an extra month, an intercalary month, had to be added to a year in order to bring the lunar calendar into accord with the solar cycle.

The names of the lunar months in pre-Heian Japan evoke the changing seasons, and when the names are used imagistically in the poems, they have been translated literally. By the Heian period, however, it was becoming more common to call the months First, Second, etc., as is done today, and generally this has been done in the translation as well as the Introduction. To feel in tune with the seasonal references, the reader need only keep in mind that these are lunar months. The First Month usually begins in February, our second month, and the lunar numbers continue to fall one or two behind our solar months.

Years were generally named in terms of year-periods, which were designated by the Japanese government beginning in the eighth century and which often corresponded with the reign of tennō (that is, the sovereign or Mikado, sometimes erroneously termed "Emperor"). The year-period designation could be changed in the course of a calendar year. The reigns and year-periods which figure most often in the *Kokinshū* or in discussion of the work include the following:

Kokinshū

Reigns		Year-periods	
Kanmu tennō	781–806	Ten-ō began	781
		Enryaku	782
Heizei	806–809	Daidō	806
Saga	809–823	Kōnin	810
Junna	823–833	Tenchō	824
Ninmyō	833–850	Shōwa	834
		Kajō	848
Montoku	850–858	Ninju	851
		Saikō	854
		Tennan	857
Seiwa	858–876	Jōgan	859
Yōzei	876(877)–884	Genkei	877
Kōkō	884–887	Ninna	885
Uda	887–897	Kanpyō	889
Daigo	897–930	Shōtai	898
		Engi	901
		Enchō	923

The Heian aristocracy were enormously status conscious, and their status was minutely graded by rank and office designations. The numerous references to rank and title in the headnotes to the poems are clarified to some extent in the notes following the poems. The reader wishing to delve into the intricacies of the system is referred to the superb notes and appendices in *A Tale of Flowering Fortunes* by William H. and Helen Craig McCullough.

In the translations in this volume, we have tried to strike a balance between literalness and pleasure for the reader of English. The only formal criterion we established for ourselves was the use of the 5/7/5/7/7 syllable pattern of Japanese waka. Whenever possible we have tried to maintain the order of the images in the original and to convey the use of pivot words, pillow words, and other rhetorical devices. The notes following many of the poems explicate rhetoric and vocabulary, comment on the circumstances of composition as described in the original headnotes, and indicate other works in which these poems occur. The annotations are based on those provided by Ozawa Masao and Kubota Utsubo in the editions mentioned above and those in *Kokinwakashū* edited by Okumura Tsuneya. The reader should refer to the Author Index for biographical information about the poets.

The Introduction, surveying the origins of the anthology, the society that produced it, the types of poetry it contains, and its overall design, is addressed to the general reader. Those who wish more than an overview are directed to the monumental study, *Japanese Court Poetry*, by Robert Brower and Earl Miner, and to other works in the Bibliography listed under Western-language sources.

The translations and studies of the two prefaces to the *Kokinshū* will interest scholars: much valuable information about the influence of Chinese poetics on Japanese criticism is found in them. I thank John Timothy Wixted and Leonard Grzanka for their contributions.

Many people have helped me during the years I have been working on this book. Robert Brower awakened my interest in waka. Mary Catherine Henkenius, my collaborator, was also the instigator of this project and the motivating force in carrying it to completion. Many students and friends have commented on translations and helped me in my thinking about the problems of translating from ninth-century Japanese into twentieth-century English. I wish particularly to thank Katsumura Yūko, Miyahara Ryōko, Saegusa Kyōko, and Doreen Maesaka for their assistance in checking and proofreading; and Julia Lin and Roy B. Teele, among many others, for reading portions of the translation and making suggestions. Earl Miner and the anonymous readers of Princeton University Press were particularly helpful. I have made use of the advice of all these people and more, and I gratefully acknowledge their assistance.

L.R.R.

P.S. I am grateful to Susan Gately, my editor at Cheng & Tsui Company, and to Jill Cheng for helping to make this paperback edition a reality.

Boulder, Colorado
1996

CONTENTS

Preface   iii

INTRODUCTION   3
By Laurel Rasplica Rodd

KANAJO, THE JAPANESE PREFACE, by Ki no Tsurayuki   35
Translated and annotated by Laurel Rasplica Rodd

TRANSLATION OF THE *Kokinshū*   49
By Laurel Rasplica Rodd and Mary Catherine Henkenius

MANAJO, THE CHINESE PREFACE, by Ki no Yoshimochi   379
Translated and annotated by Leonard Grzanka

CHINESE INFLUENCES ON THE *Kokinshū* PREFACES   387
By John Timothy Wixted

APPENDIX: Texts of the *Kokinshū*   401

Western-language Sources   403

Japanese and Chinese References   405

Author Index and Brief Biographies of *Kokinshū* Poets   407

Index of First Lines   420

Subject Index   434

INTRODUCTION

The *Kokinshū*, or *Kokinwakashū* (ca. 905), *A Collection of Ancient and Modern Poems*, was the first of twenty-one anthologies of Japanese poetry compiled at the behest of the Japanese sovereigns between 905 and 1433. It consists of 1,111 poems, all but nine in the thirty-one syllable five-line form known as tanka (short poem), which so dominates the Japanese poetic tradition that it is known also by the alternate name waka (Japanese poetry). The anthology was compiled in the early years of the tenth century, approximately one hundred years before Lady Murasaki composed her *Tale of Genji* and Sei Shōnagon her *Pillow Book*. The public writings of the early Heian period (794–1185) were in Chinese, and many of the private writings that remain to us are also in that foreign language, which the Japanese had been using since approximately the sixth century. However, in the late ninth and tenth centuries there began a steady stream of records of poetry competitions, nikki bungaku (fictionalized autobiographies), shikashū (personal poetry collections), utamonogatari (poem tales), etc., an outpouring of literature in Japanese that followed two-and-one-half centuries of fascination with things Chinese, including the Chinese language. The *Kokinshū* was the first major anthology of Japanese poetry since the great anthology, the *Man'yōshū*, compiled in the mid–eighth century, and the first since the vogue for Chinese poetry had reached its peak and resulted in the three anthologies of Chinese poetry produced at the Japanese court in the early ninth century.[1] The compilers were aware of the weight and importance of their task: they were charged with returning Japanese poetry to the public arena after a period during which it had been relegated to the bedchambers and private correspondence of the aristocracy.

The two prefaces to the *Kokinshū*, the Japanese preface (kanajo) written by Ki no Tsurayuki and the Chinese preface (manajo) attributed to Ki no Yoshimochi, make it clear with what seriousness the compilers undertook their task. They gathered poems from the previous century as well as poems

---

1 The three anthologies of poetry written in Chinese were *Ryōunshū*, 814; *Bunkashūreishū*, 818, ordered by Saga tennō; and *Keikokushū*, 827, ordered by Junna tennō.

3

they and their contemporaries had written, but their work did not stop with the task of selection. Rather than arrange their materials by date of composition or by author, they chose a thematic arrangement. The twenty books of the *Kokinshū* illustrate the topics treated in Japanese court poetry: nature and the natural progression of the seasons, love and the progress of the love affair, celebration, mourning, travel and parting, and combinations of these themes. Within the larger topics, much care was taken in the ordering of individual poems: each one is linked to those before and after by a chronological or geographical progression of natural or human affairs, by imagery, or by subtle shifts in theme. The poems in the *Kokinshū* emphasize concerns common to the entire tradition of Japanese court poetry—concern with lyrical expression, with nature, with qualities of experience rather than with moral or other absolutes, and with the social contexts of poetry rather than with social subjects.

The *Kokinshū* is, along with the records of three poetry contests of its time, our chief source of information about the early Heian waka. The two decades spanning the turn of the tenth century saw the perfection of the model waka of the court nobles, a poetic style which had begun to develop just a few decades earlier and which lasted a century after the compilation of the *Kokinshū*. Thereafter, as the economic and political stature of the aristocracy began to decline, new directions became evident in waka, too. However, the belief in the *Kokinshū* as the ideal to which poets should turn did not fade. As Helen McCullough notes, "The *Kokinshū* and the *Ise monogatari* were the indispensable literary baggage of noblemen and court ladies in the later part of the Heian period, the inexhaustible lodes mined by generations of earnest medieval commentators and the bibles of aspiring poets through the ages." [2] So thoroughly does the poetry and poetic of the *Kokinshū* pervade Japanese culture that "it may be said to be the foundation which gave its particularity to Japanese culture. It is the source of an independent Japanese culture." [3] The poetic vocabulary and the standard of elegance established in the anthology remained relatively fixed for a thousand years. It took the combined impact of Western culture and an industrial society to dethrone them in the late nineteenth century.

The society which produced this anthology was unique: it was an aristocratic society dominated by what Sir George Sansom has called "the rule of taste," a sophisticated society which demanded of each of its members competence, if not mastery, in the practice of the numerous arts that filled

[2] Helen Craig McCullough, *Tales of Ise: Lyrical Episodes from Tenth-Century Japan* (Stanford: Stanford University Press, 1968), p. 3.

[3] Ozawa Masao, *Kokinwakashū*, Nihon Koton Bungaku Zenshū, Vol. VII (Tōkyō: Shōgakukan, 1971), p. 8.

their days and nights. Although these elegant men and women also worked, behind the scenes as it were, it is their private lives that fill the literary records of the time. And among all the arts of Heian Japan—music, dance, calligraphy, the blending of incense, painting, and more—poetry was the most important. It was used for private communications with lovers and friends, and skill in poetry, as demonstrated in private messages and on such public occasions as poetry contests, was treated as a sign of both character and intelligence.

Stephen Owen has described the High T'ang period in China as "a period of transition between a view of poetry as a social gesture, represented by capital poetry with its roots in the tradition of court poetry, and poetry as an art with cultural and personal dimensions that transcended social occasion."[4] The poetry collected in the *Kokinshū* represents a similar period in Japan. In the early ninth century, Japanese poetry had served as private communication, as "social gesture" bound to the moment of its composition. Few Japanese poems from the first half of the ninth century survive. By the last decades of the century, however, waka was taking on a new role: it had been elevated to art, and new occasions for its practice and display had come into being, among them the utaawase, or poetry contest, and the composition of byōbu-uta, screen poems.

POETRY IN THE EARLY HEIAN PERIOD

Almost all the poems in the *Kokinshū* date from the early decades of the ninth century to the first decade of the tenth, one hundred years during which a change took place in Japanese literature, "a change so fundamental that the tradition was not to see another such alteration for eleven centuries."[5] By the tenth century the Japanese could read only with great difficulty the rebus-like adaptation of Chinese characters to the Japanese language in which the eighth-century *Man'yōshū* had been written. The most active poets of the early tenth century turned not to this difficult-to-read Japanese tradition for models and inspiration, but directly to Chinese poetry. As Japanese poetry lost status, poets devoted their most serious efforts to Chinese poetry, reserving Japanese writing for private or frivolous occasions.

The return to Japanese poetry that culminated in the *Kokinshū* was based

---

[4] Stephen Owen, *The Great Age of Chinese Poetry: The High T'ang* (New Haven: Yale University Press, 1981), p. xiv.

[5] Robert Brower and Earl Miner, *Japanese Court Poetry* (Stanford: Stanford University Press, 1961), p. 157.

on the Chinese models popular at court in the first half of the tenth century. At the same time, the trend was away from the admiration of a foreign culture and toward a redefinition and appreciation of the native tradition. The *Kokinshū* is the product of these two opposing trends.

The stage had been set much earlier. By the late eighth century, when Kanmu tennō determined to move his capital to Heian (modern Kyōto), the government had seen its power gradually eroded by aristocratic families and the growing Buddhist establishment. The sovereign intended his move to Heian as an escape from these powerful institutions which surrounded the court in Nara and as a return to the style of government established on the Chinese model in the previous century. The Chinese flavor of the new capital, Heian, was obvious from the beginning: the city was laid out in a grid pattern modeled after the Chinese capital of Ch'ang-an, "a T'ang-style bureaucracy operated a T'ang-style tax system," and "Chinese ideas, values, and attitudes shaped the character of court life in innumerable ways." [6]

The peak of attraction to the T'ang culture came during the reigns of Saga (809–823) and Junna (823–833), when the three Chinese poetry anthologies were compiled, but Japanese culture was not ignored during these years,[7] and the respect with which the *Man'yōshū* and its poets are treated in the *Kokinshū* is evidence for the reawakening pride in Japanese tradition and culture. Happily for waka, there was during the ninth century on the one hand an appreciation for Chinese culture and the adoption of features of Chinese poetry into waka, and on the other an appreciation of the Japanese tradition and its unique qualities which encouraged its preservation.

During the first half of the ninth century the transition from the *Man'yōshū* style to the new *Kokinshū* style thus took place at a court dominated by adaptations of Chinese culture. As Konishi Jin'ichi has demonstrated,[8] the Japanese learned a great deal from Chinese prototypes, particularly the poetry of the Six Dynasties (ca. 220–ca. 589) and early T'ang (618–ca. 713). Konishi has summarized the characteristics of the style which developed:

---

[6] McCullough, *Tales of Ise*, p. 26. For a very readable description of Chang-an in this period, see Edward H. Schafer, *The Golden Peaches of Samarkand: A Study of T'ang Exotics* (Berkeley: The University of California Press, 1963), especially Chap. I, "The Glory of T'ang."

[7] History tells of contemporary appreciation of those skilled in saibara, koto, and chōka: see Ozawa, *Kokinwakashū*, p. 8.

[8] See Konishi Jin'ichi, "The Genesis of the *Kokinshū* Style," trans. Helen C. McCullough, *Harvard Journal of Asiatic Studies*, 38 (1978), pp. 61–170, originally published as "Kokinshū-teki hyōgen no seiritsu" in *Nihon gakushūin kiyō* 7:3, pp. 163–98, and reprinted in *Kokinwakashū*, ed. Nihon bungaku kenkyū shiryō kankōkai (Tōkyō: Yūseido, 1976), pp, 151–78. See also Brower and Miner, pp. 23–26, 163–220 passim, for a discussion of the influences of Six Dynasties poetry on the *Kokinshū* style.

1. The conceptual approach is intellectual. In a typical *Kokinshū* poem, human life and the world of nature are not presented directly, but appear only after having been subjected to a process of ratiocination.
2. The boundary lines between the natural world and human experience are blurred. The poet does not focus on either a natural or a human phenomenon as such.
3. Whether the subject is nature or man, there is a strong tendency to treat it in terms of the passing of time.
4. The tone is subdued, elegant, and graceful.[9]

The Japanese were familiar with the Six Dynasties poetry collected in the *Wen hsüan* (*Literary Selections*) and probably many other Chinese anthologies,[10] and from them, as Konishi shows, they learned "obliqueness," that is, "expression of the thing perceived not in the language of the moment of perception but in different, more highly contrived terms."[11] The contrivance is found in the use of clever reasoning and in the use of decorative figurative language, dominated in the *Kokinshū* by the metaphorical interplay of the world of nature and human life.

Although Konishi feels there is less evidence of Chinese influence in the developing Japanese tendency to treat all subjects in terms of the passing of time,[12] this trait too can be seen to have grown from the variety of Chinese manners and ideas introduced in the early ninth century. Kubota Utsubo has argued that "the fusion of the natural and human worlds, and also the tendency to approach a subject within the context of eternal time, resulted from the impact of the Buddhist doctrines introduced from China by Saichō and Kūkai at the beginning of the ninth century," at a time when the political dominance of the Fujiwara families was forcing other members of the nobility to turn their energies to nonpolitical matters, such as the writing of poetry.[13]

The poetry that Japanese writers composed in Chinese during the ninth century bears a close resemblance to Six Dynasties poetry. Surely it was no great step from writing Chinese imitations to adapting some of the characteristics of these Chinese models to the Japanese waka. The craze for writing poems, at first in Chinese (kudaishi) but later also in Japanese (kudaiwaka),[14]

---

[9] Konishi, "Genesis," p. 64.

[10] The *Wen hsüan*, ca. 530 A.D., an anthology of selections from Chinese Six Dynasties prose and poetry, was used as a text at the Japanese University beginning in 798.

[11] Konishi, "Genesis," p. 79.

[12] Konishi, "Genesis," p. 107.

[13] This is Konishi's ("Genesis," p. 65) summation of Kubota's views as expressed in Kubota Utsubo, *Kokinwakashū hyōshaku*, 2nd ed., Vol. I (Tōkyō: Tōkyōdō, 1964), p. 43.

[14] Ōe no Chisato composed a personal poetry collection, *Kudaiwaka*, in 894. It was organized according to the categories of Chinese poetry and the waka were on topics formed by lines of Chinese poetry.

taking a line from a Chinese poem as a topic, reached a peak during the reign of Ninmyō tennō (833–850) and surely stimulated this trend.

This new style was accompanied by an increasing refinement of Japanese poetry. Brower and Miner write: "As it became apparent that the Chinese techniques could be successfully adapted, and that the waka could be made to express the elegant tastes and subjective experience of the age, the re-emergence of waka as a serious art form was practically assured."[15]

The highly ornate style, characterized by "elaborate metaphors, surprising conceits, subjective and sometimes apparently irrational analysis, elegant poses, and above all, a pervasive use of reasoning,"[16] proved equally congenial to Heian Japan. In many ways the two societies were similar: the poetry of Six Dynasties China and that of Heian Japan are products of hereditary aristocracies whose circumscribed lives were conducive to conservatism and sophisticated elegance. Theirs was an intellectual environment hostile to innovation. On the contrary, it fostered "a kind of 'creative imitation' similar in many ways to that found in lyric poets of the European Renaissance. Once the basic themes and forms of court poetry were set . . . poets accepted their inheritance as the absolute limits of poetry; within this inheritance poets sought novelty of expression rather than true originality. What they lost in freedom and depth, the court poets tried to compensate for in craft, style, and cleverness."[17]

The circles in which the new waka were composed were small ones. In the mid-ninth century Fujiwara no Yoshifusa (804–872), one of the master practitioners of the marriage politics that helped raise the status of women at the Japanese court, was the center of one such circle. His mansion, the Somedono, famous for cherry blossoms, was the site of numerous elegant parties during the years his daughter Meishi, the Somedono Consort, and later her son, Seiwa tennō, resided there. Other late ninth-century circles centered on Prince Koretaka, patron of Ariwara no Narihira and Ki no Aritsune, and Prince Tsuneyasu, patron of Archbishop Henjō. Many poets of the 880s and 890s were intimates of the Ki family, who were displaced in the political arena by the Fujiwaras. When Ki no Tsurayuki was appointed to compile the *Kokinshū*, he brought to the task many poetry collections by members of his family.

Court ceremonies where the courtiers had previously composed Chinese poetry now included Japanese poetry. Two waka composed by Ariwara no Yukihira on the occasion of a falconing party to the Arakawa led by Kōkō tennō in 882 are included in the *Gosenshū* (the second anthology of Japanese

---

[15] Brower and Miner, p. 168.

[16] Brower and Miner, p. 169.

[17] Stephen Owen, *The Poetry of Early T'ang* (New Haven: Yale University Press, 1977), p. 7.

poetry commissioned by a sovereign, ordered in 951 by Murakami tennō.) The succeeding reigns of Uda and Daigo provided even more such occasions. Among the excursions of Uda tennō commemorated in waka by his courtiers were a journey to Kitano, Unrin'in, and Funaoka in the intercalary First Month of 896 and one to Yamato, Kawachi, and Settsu in the Tenth Month of the same year. In 907, after his abdication, he made an excursion to the Ōi River, in which Tsurayuki and other first-rank poets participated. Forty-six poems from the excursion to the Ōi River are included in the *Kokinshū* and later commissioned collections.

Another opportunity for the display of skill in waka, the utaawase (poetry contest), also became popular in the late ninth century. Competitions were not limited to poems: "fans, shells, paintings, iris roots, chrysanthemums, songbirds, short stories, and a great variety of other living things, inanimate objects, and products of manual and verbal skill were matched," [18] but the important role these events played in the recognition of waka as an art is attested by the number of poems from such contests which are included in the *Kokinshū*. Not only did the competitions elevate the status of waka and encourage the writing of semi-public poetry, but the records that were kept ensured the preservation of the poets' efforts.

The earliest extant record of a poetry contest, the "Zai minbukyō no ie no utaawase" (The Poetry Contest at the House of the Minister of Popular Affairs [Ariwara no Yukihira]), dates from between 884 and 887. The "Kanpyō no ontoki kisai no miya no utaawase" (Poetry Contest Held by the Consort in the Kanpyō Era) dates from around 893, and the "Koresada no miko no ie no utaawase" (Poetry Contest at the House of Prince Koresada) from the fall of 898. The "Consort in the Kanpyō Era" may refer to the Consort of Uda tennō, Fujiwara Onshi, or to his mother, Princess Hanshi. Prince Koresada was Uda's elder brother. Clearly Uda and his circle stimulated the late ninth-century popularity of waka and waka competitions. All four of the *Kokinshū* compilers participated in the latter two contests, and they chose sixty-five poems from the "Poetry Contest Held by the Consort in the Kanpyō Era" and twenty-two from the "Poetry Contest at the House of Prince Koresada" for the *Kokinshū*. These two competitions also led to the compilation of a new type of anthology, one which indicates how far waka had risen in the estimation of a court which only decades before had derogated it: Sugawara no Michizane worked until his death in 903 on the *Shinsen Man'yōshū*, a translation into Chinese of the waka from these two contests.

---

[18] Edwin A. Cranston, *The Izumi Shikibu Diary* (Cambridge: Harvard University Press, 1969), p. 91.

Another occasion for the display of talent in writing waka was the composition of byōbu-uta, screen poems, commissioned by members of the sovereign's family or high-ranking courtiers to be written on screens used as decorations at ceremonies and celebrations. These screens too were modeled after Chinese examples, and it was during the reigns of Uda and Daigo that it became as common to commission screens decorated with yamato-e, Japanese-style paintings, and waka as to order screens with Chinese-style paintings and Chinese poems. The earliest extant screen poem may be the *Kokinshū* poem 930 (Book XVIII) by Sanjō no machi, who, according to the headnote, was commissioned by Montoku tennō to compose it for a screen with a painting of a waterfall which was to be used to decorate the women attendants' room at court. *Kokinshū* 293 (Book V) is from a second series of screen poems known as the "Fujiwara Takaiko gobyōbu-uta" and commissioned during the time Takaiko, as mother of the Crown Prince, held the title "tōgū no miyasundokoro," Lady of the Bedchamber.

Both of these early screens were painted for the courts of the consorts of Montoku, which were evidently the center of the development of screens with Japanese paintings and Japanese verse. There was a gradual increase in their number during the reign of Uda (887–897) and then a sudden rise early in the reign of Daigo (897–930). By the turn of the tenth century the screens no longer consisted of one panel but rather of four or six panels, which often illustrated the four seasons. These were used in birthday celebrations for members of the nobility and in the yearly festivals. There were also mono-gatari screens that presented tales of the lives of the nobility. The honor of composing the poems for the panels was divided among several poets. Because these poems were "normally written to match a painting on a screen and thus similar to poems on set topics, they are the most formal and public poems written during the early Heian period and represent the acme of recognition for a poet."[19] The popularity of the screens coincided with the development of the changing seasons as a standard topic in waka and with the establishment of uta makura, place names with imagistic associations, which came to be used in many waka. Often these were famous scenic places likely to have been depicted on screens.

COMPILATION OF THE KOKINSHŪ

Around Engi 5 (905), Daigo tennō ordered four of the well-known poets of the court, Ki no Tsurayuki, Ki no Tomonori, Ōshikōchi no Mitsune, and

---

[19] Phillip T. Harries, "Personal Poetry Collections: Their Origin and Development Through the Heian Period," *Monumenta Nipponica*, 35 (Autumn 1980), p. 312.

Mibu no Tadamine, to "gather old poems not found in the *Man'yōshū* as well as their own" into a new anthology, a collection of the best Japanese poetry. Waka were still part of court ceremony, for the *Kokinshū* includes a group of Poetry Bureau poems (Book XX). The anthology would reinject vigor into the tradition which had faltered under the weight of the passion for things Chinese in the ninth century and return the waka to the status of an art.

Whether Engi 5 is the date the *Kokinshū* was commissioned or the date it was presented to the sovereign is problematic. The Japanese preface states, "On Engi 5/4/18, [the four compilers] received the order to present to the throne old poems not found in the *Manyōshū* as well as our own." However, the dating of the Chinese preface indicates that Engi 5 was the date the anthology was presented. Fujiwara no Kiyosuke (1104–1177) was the first to call attention to the fact that poems written in Engi 7 (907), during the excursion to the Ōi River, and in Engi 13 (913), at the "Teijinoin no utaawase" (Poetry Contest of Teijinoin [former tennō Uda]), are included in the *Kokinshū*.[20] Cautiously, rather than question the traditionally accepted date of completion, he suggested that these poems were later additions. More recent studies of the ranks and titles assigned in the headnotes (for example, in poem 740, Minamoto no Noboru is called Chūnagon, an office he held from Engi 8/2 to Engi 14/8 [908–914]) suggest that the actual date of completion was after 906 and possibly as late as 917.[21]

The compilers of the *Kokinshū* have been surprisingly neglected over the years, and very little is known of their lives. Classical Japanese scholars were more inclined to criticize the poems themselves. The earliest writings about the compilers consist of brief anecdotes set down in the mid-tenth century.[22] The earliest biographies appear in the *Kokinwakashū mokuroku* (*An Index to the Kokinshū*), said to have been compiled by Fujiwara no Nakazane (d. 1118), but the four compilers receive no special attention and are treated merely as four of the many commoners whose poems are included in the *Kokinshū*.[23] Biographies of the thirty-six poetic geniuses, believed to have been written around 1183, include the four compilers, but they are based on the *Kokinwakashū mokuroku*.[24] These two works do fill in the outlines of the

[20] Nishishita Kyōichi and Sanekata Kiyoshi, *Kokinshū Shinkokinshū*, "Zōhō kokugo koku-bungaku kenkyūshi taisei," Vol. VII (Tōkyō: Sanseidō, 1977), p. 1.

[21] Nishishita and Sanekata, pp. 4–6.

[22] Nishishita and Sanekata, p. 86. Ki no Tomonori, Mibu no Tadamine, and Ōshikōchi no Mitsune are given brief mention in *Yamato Monogatari*; see Mildred Tahara, tr., *Tales of Yamato* (Honolulu: University Press of Hawaii, 1980), pp. 18, 20, 76–77, 80, 133.

[23] Nishishita and Sanekata, p. 86.

[24] Nishishita and Sanekata, p. 86.

official careers of these four middle-ranking courtiers and are valuable for that information.[25]

Ki no Tsurayuki (884?–946?) is rightly revered as the supervisor of the compilation of the *Kokinshū* and as the author of its Japanese preface, the preface to the "Waka from the Sovereign's Excursion to the Ōi River" (Ōigawa gyōkō waka no jo), and the *Tosa Diary*; but still we know almost nothing about his family, and there is considerable debate about the years of his birth and death. He is generally believed to have died in 946 or 947, at the age of eighty-four or eighty-five. He was a participant in the "Poetry Contest Held by the Consort in the Kanpyō Era" and the "Poetry Contest at the House of Prince Koresada," and was probably in his mid-forties when he was ordered to compile the *Kokinshū*.

Tsurayuki's reputation as a poet reached a peak during the compilation of the third commissioned anthology, the *Shūishū* (ca. 985–1000); 170 of his poems are included in that collection, and according to the compiler, Fujiwara no Kintō (966–1041), Tsurayuki was as skilled a poet as Hitomaro. In the fourth anthology, the *Goshūishū* (1086), whether deliberately or through oversight, Tsurayuki's three poems are attributed to another poet. The next three collections, the *Kin'yoshū* (ca. 1127), *Shikashū* (ca. 1151–1154), and *Senzaishū* (ca. 1185), contain no poems by Tsurayuki. Tastes had changed, and Tsurayuki's solution to the search for balance between kokoro (spirit) and kotoba (diction) was no longer appreciated; it lacked the overtones, the cargo of unexpressed allusion and depth of feeling that was admired in the twelfth and thirteenth centuries. By the Meiji period (1868–1912), Tsurayuki's reputation had fallen so low that Masaoka Shiki (1868–1902) could call him "a poor poet." More recently, Nishishita Kyōichi and others have reestablished Tsurayuki's proper place in the context of the *Kokinshū* era: his style was the epitome of that elegant balance sought by his generation—smooth, clever in conception yet far from shocking, original within the context of a rigidly fixed rhetoric. Tsurayuki

---

[25] During the Muromachi and Edo periods (fourteenth to mid-nineteenth centuries) the *Hyakunin isshu* compiled by Fujiwara no Teika (1162–1241), a collection of one poem each by one hundred famous poets, had the effect of deflecting interest toward the poets themselves. New information included in the commentaries on the *Hyakunin isshu*, however, is chiefly legend. The "national studies" movement of the Edo period brought a new awareness of textual evidence in scholarship, but the scholars devoted most attention to the *Man'yōshū* and introduced little new knowledge of the *Kokinshū* compilation. In the late Edo period Kagawa Keiki (d. 1844) produced the *Kokinwakashū seigi*, a study of the *Kokinshū*, the *Tsurayuki shū* (*Tsurayuki Collection*), the *Mitsune shū* (*Mitsune Collection*), *Gosenshū*, etc., in which he adduced new evidence for the date of Tsurayuki's death and his age at death. Such studies have become voluminous in the twentieth century. For a summary of the literature, see Nishishita and Sanekata, pp. 9–29.

contributed 102 poems to the *Kokinshū*, more than any other poet.

Ki no Tomonori (fl. ca. 890) was, according to the *Kokinshū mokuroku*, of "unknown ancestry." He died sometime during the compilation of the *Kokinshū*; elegies written for him by Tsurayuki and Tadamine are included in Book XVI of the *Kokinshū* (838 and 839). Although he is the author of one of the loveliest of *Kokinshū* poems (II, 84), Tomonori's poetry has received relatively little attention. He is mentioned in the *Yamato monogatari* (*Tales of Yamato*, mid-tenth century), but none of his poems are cited. The *Kokinshū* contains forty-six of his poems.

Of Ōshikōchi no Mitsune's (fl. ca. 900) family nothing is known, although a good deal has been surmised on little or no evidence. He was still alive in 921 at the time of the retired sovereign's visit to Kasuga, but neither the year he died nor his age at death are known. To judge by the anecdotes about him in the *Tales of Yamato*, Mitsune's reputation rose as Tsurayuki's fell. Nevertheless, like Tsurayuki, none of Mitsune's poems were included in the four anthologies compiled from the *Goshūishū* to the *Senzaishū*. Sixty of his poems were chosen for the *Kokinshū*.

Mibu no Tadamine (fl. ca. 910) too is of uncertain ancestry. The *Tales of Yamato* includes an anecdote about Tadamine visiting Fujiwara no Tokihira with his lord, Fujiwara no Sadakuni. Tokihira was so pleased by Tadamine's *waka* that he rewarded him with entertainment and gifts. Tadamine's poems are collected in the *Tadamine shū* (*Tadamine Collection*). He is also author of a critical work entitled *Tadamine juttei* (or *Wakatei jusshu*), *Ten Principles of Japanese Poetry*, which supplements the information found in Tsurayuki's Japanese preface about contemporary poetic practice and critical spirit. Thirty-seven of his poems are included in the *Kokinshū*.

THE AESTHETICS OF KOKINSHŪ POETRY

There are numerous unanswered questions about the two prefaces to the *Kokinshū*. Many have assumed the Chinese preface attributed to Yoshimochi to have been written first and the Japanese preface to be based on it. However, not all texts include the Chinese preface, and in most texts which do include it it appears at the end, as a sort of appendix.[26]

The Japanese preface, by Tsurayuki, has been the more influential of the two as a critical document and has received the most attention. This preface, as the introduction to a collection of poems mandated by the sovereign, tells of the nature of Japanese poetry, its origins and history, and the circumstances that have given rise to poetry in Japan; of six poets (the "six poetic

[26] Nishishita and Sanekata, pp. 74–75.

geniuses") of the generation preceding that of the compilers; and of the circumstances of compilation. The intent of the author is to define the realm and achievements of Japanese poetry and to establish it as an art equal to Chinese poetry. As Brower and Miner write:

> ... the Preface reveals the emergence of a critical consciousness, as distinguished from the earlier birth of literary awareness; it is an attempt to create a theory and prescribe a practice for Japanese poetry that would entitle it once again to social acceptance, this time as an art on a level with Chinese poetry. The effort appears to have entailed an insistence upon an established poetic language with the prestige of tradition, and a channeling of individual expression to important but subtle adjustments of the relation between the originality of the individual poet and the conventionality of his prescribed materials.[27]

In the preface Tsurayuki introduces three important critical terms: koto-ba, kokoro, and sama. By sama he seems to mean specifically those new techniques adapted from late Six Dynasties poetry: obliqueness, wit, a focusing on the poet's mental processes rather than the natural scene he describes, "elegant confusion," witty reasoning. Kotoba and kokoro refer to

> the central value in Tsurayuki's poetic ideal, an ideal that was taken up and elaborated by his contemporaries and successors, ... a strong sense of decorous elegance which involved an emphasis on style, a proper poetic diction, an accepted range of forms and themes and virtuosity. A good poem was one that responded to given situations with purity of diction and in ways sanctioned by tradition, but one that also possessed a certain originality of treatment. There was a tendency to view material, subjects, and decorum as aspects of diction, and attitude, technique, and theme as aspects of tone. Such a distinction, reflected in the Preface to the *Kokinshū* by the terms kotoba, diction, and kokoro, spirit, was to remain throughout the tradition as the central concept of the Japanese poetic; and although apprehended differently in successive ages, it may be said that the constant ideal was the achievement of balance between these two elements.[28]

Increasingly waka had come to be dominated by the rules of rhetoric and decorum. They served to make poetry "an acquired skill, a learnable art."[29] Aesthetic judgment was based not on the degree of originality or complexity, and not on the seriousness of meaning, but rather on how well the poet handled his materials and operated within the rules. As Stephen Owen has written of the High T'ang poetry, "it was an art of subtle variation in which a premium was placed on a graceful performance. There was no room here for the untutored genius."[30] Similarly Brower and Miner note that in waka, too,

[27] Brower and Miner, p. 24.
[28] Brower and Miner, p. 171.
[29] Owen, *High T'ang*, p. 8.
[30] Owen, *High T'ang*, p. 8.

the handling was required to be subtle and unobtrusive—a kind of un-metaphysical ingenuity that could be adequately appreciated only by comparison with innumerable other poems that treated the same materials in similar but significantly different ways.... Whatever other qualities of depth or meaning were necessary for great poetry, there was little room for a poet who lacked virtuosity, style, and a knowledge of this tradition. A poet was free to pursue his individual way to greatness only after he had proved he knew the rules of the game.[31]

THE RULES OF COURT POETRY

The approximately 130 poets of the *Kokinshū* range from the semi-legendary Princess Sotōri and Abe no Nakamaro through poets of the early Heian period to the poets of the generation of the compilers. It has been suggested that many of the 450 anonymous poems were known to the *Kokinshū* compilers by word of mouth as folk songs. These are believed to date mostly from the Nara period. Other poems may have been listed as anonymous to avoid possible embarrassment to the author because of the circumstances of composition, as a deliberate slight to a poet out of favor politically, or for other reasons.

Aside from an anonymous chōka, one chōka each by Tsurayuki, Mibu no Tadamine, Ōshikōchi no Mitsune, and Lady Ise, three anonymous sedōka, and another one by Tsurayuki, all the poems are waka. Both the chōka, a poetic form made up of any number of alternating five- and seven-syllable lines concluding with an extra seven-syllable line, and the sedōka, a poem of six lines in the syllable pattern 5/7/7/5/7/7, were outmoded by the ninth century. Although Yoshimochi touches on the question of form, Tsurayuki does not discuss it in his introduction: it was not a topic open to discussion in an age when waka had become the only productive form of Japanese poetry.

Readers of the *Kokinshū* may discover rules, tacit rules which this anthology established, which hold the poet to both topical and lexical decorum. Poets and contemporary readers of the *Kokinshū* normally assumed that each poem was the outgrowth of some specific occasion, and many of the poems do include headnotes telling of the circumstances in which they were composed. However, there are also many *Kokinshū* poems which were written to preset topics (daiei) at poetry contests or on other occasions. Each of these topics, which are indicated in the headnotes, had its own decorum, to which the poet had to adhere or risk ridicule. The implicit rules for diction in court poetry include the following: a vocabulary limited to native Japanese words and, of those, only those sanctioned by tradition as being poetic; metaphorical and decorative language, particularly for the expres-

---

[31] Brower and Miner, p. 178.

sion of deep emotion; occasional syntactical reversals; and expressions of wonderment, puzzlement, and confusion.

The poems of the *Kokinshū* are often divided into three periods: the early anonymous poems and poems composed in the first half of the ninth century, when the rage for things Chinese was current; poems by the "six poetic geniuses" who flourished from the 840s to the 880s; and poems by poets of the generation of the compilers, dating from around 890 to the early years of the tenth century.

The diction of the early poems resembles that of the *Man'yōshū*: the statement is direct; the rhythm of the poem is tripartite, with breaks after the second and fourth lines, rather than the two-part rhythm, with a break after the third line, which dominates the later waka; there is a balance between the subjective and the objective in description; nouns predominate rather than the adjectives, adverbs, and verbs of the typical *Kokinshū* poem; and two rhetorical techniques typical of *Man'yōshū* poetry, the makurakotoba and the jo, are employed. Ozawa suggests that the following poem is typical of the simple, direct statement of the early poetry:[32]

ōmi yori	I rose and set out
asa tachikureba	from Ōmi before daybreak—
une no no ni	as cranes cried over
tazu zo naku naru	the meadows of Une the
akenu kono yo wa	long dark night quietly dawned

The makurakotoba (pillow word) is often called a fixed epithet, but the concept of "amplification" suggested by Brower and Miner describes its function more accurately: as a five-syllable word or phrase used "for decoration or to create an effect of beauty, dignity, or even joyousness"[33] and applied to a specific place or thing, the makurakotoba can contribute a kind of stylized imagery. Many of the makurakotoba which appeared in earlier Japanese poetry, such as "hisakata no" and "ashihiki no," were no longer fully understood, although poets continued to use them to achieve an archaic flavor or to elevate the tone; others, like "asatsuyu no" (of the morning dew), "utsusemi no" (of the cicada shell), and "harugasumi" (spring mist), date from the *Kokinshū* era.[34] The presence of a makurakotoba alters the rhythm and sound pattern of a poem, and elevates the tone. Poem II, 73, in the *Kokinshū* includes the makurakotoba "utsusemi no," modifying "yo" (world), and illustrates the increasing influence of Buddhist teachings on the Heian aristocracy:

[32] Ozawa, *Kokinwakashū*, p. 398. The poem is *Kokinshū* XX, 1071.

[33] Brower and Miner, p. 136.

[34] Ozawa, *Kokinwakashū*, p. 28.

utsusemi no	like the world hollow
yo ni mo nitaru ka	as a cicada's cast-off shell—
hanazakura	oh cherry blossoms—
saku to mishi ma ni	you too will fade away just
katsu chirinikeri	as we catch sight of your beauty

The jo (preface) was a similar technique: the prefatory statement, most often two to three lines long, was joined to the rest of the poem by similarities in sound patterns or by metaphor. The opening poem in Book XIV of the *Kokinshū*, poem 677, demonstrates the linking of a jo by sound or wordplay:

michinoku no	oh flowering reeds
asaka no numa no	in the Asaka Marsh of
hanagatsumi	far Michinoku—
katsu miru hito ni	will my love for one whom I've
koi ya wataran	scarcely seen last forever

The repetition of "gatsumi," part of the word "hanagatsumi" (flowering reeds), in line 3 and "katsu mi" of "katsu miru" (rarely see) in line 4 provides the link. The later poems using the jo tend to display a tight metaphorical link between the jo and the "basic statement," a technique called ushin no jo (meaningful jo), as opposed to those linked only by wordplay or sound, which are called mushin no jo. Poem XI, 479, by Tsurayuki, illustrates the ushin no jo:

yamazakura	a fleeting glimpse
kasumi no ma yori	as of mountain cherries seen
honoka ni mo	through the thick veil of
miteshi hito koso	spring mists I scarcely saw
koishikarikere	the one who captured my heart

Lines 1 and 2, "mountain cherry blossoms from the midst of the mists," are the jo, linked to the last lines by "honoka ni mo miteshi" (even dimly seen).

A third technique derived from primitive song and poetry is the decorative or intensifying prefix such as "ma" (true) or "mi" (lovely). In the *Kokinshū* such prefixes appear most often in the anonymous poems, although occasionally one may be used with a word to which it has become conventionally attached: for example, the place name "Yoshino" very often is modified by the prefix "mi."

Another difference in diction between the poetry of the *Kokinshū* and that of the *Manyōshū* is the location of the subject-noun: in the *Kokinshū* this noun most often appears in the third line (this location is called chūjitsu), whereas in the *Man'yōshū* it more commonly occurs in the first two (jōjitsu).

By the time of the *Shinkokinshū* (1201), it had moved to the end of the poem (gejitsu). One concern of the compilers in arranging the poems in the anthology was to order the poems so as to vary the location of the subject-noun and prevent monotony.[35]

The three known poets from the early ninth century, Ono no Takamura, Ariwara no Yukihira, and Fujiwara no Sekio, show the influence of the borrowing, adaptation, and elaboration of the fashionable Six Dynasties poetic techniques which give *Kokinshū* poetry its aristocratic, subjective, and intellectual qualities. By the time of the "six poetic geniuses" these techniques were being applied naturally to Japanese poetry, and by the turn of the tenth century they had been refined and formalized in that delicate balance between conception (kokoro) and expression (kotoba) which Brower and Miner have termed the Fujiwara style. Expression in the *Kokinshū* tends to be indirect, roundabout; the intent is often comparative or metaphorical. The questioning, wonderment, and "elegant confusion" that mark the new style are illustrated in poem I, 59, by Tsurayuki:

sakurabana	now it seems that
sakinikerashi na	cherry blossoms have burst forth
ashihiki no	at last white clouds float
yama no kai yori	deep in each rocky ravine
miyuru shirakumo	in the rugged far-off mountains

Other rhetorical devices became more common in the age of the six poetic geniuses. The kakekotoba (pivot word) is a type of pun in which a series of sounds is employed in two different senses and functions as a pivot between the preceding and the following phrases. In poem XI, 531, "mirume" is a kakekotoba meaning both "seaweed" and "chance to meet":

hayaki se ni	if in the swiftly
mirume oiseba	flowing rapids seaweed could
waga sode no	grow I'd sow some in
namida no kawa ni	the river of tears that floods
uemashi mono o	my sleeves then I might see you

Because of the kakekotoba, line 2 means both "if seaweed could grow" and "if a chance to meet could develop."

Engo (word association) enabled a poet to bring out secondary meanings by creating an imagistic pattern aside from that of the surface statement of the poem. Poem XX, 1078, a ritual song which was evidently originally a love poem, includes a jo, lines 1 and 2 (catalpa bow of Adachi of the Far North), linked to "waga hikaba" (if I draw; if I invite), and a pattern of engo in the words "yumi" (bow), "sue" (tip), and "yori" (approaching):

---

[35] Ozawa, *Kokinwakashū*, p. 27.

michinoku no	from Adachi in
adachi no mayumi	far Michinoku comes this
waga hikaba	spindle bow as its
sue sae yoriko	tips draw together silently
shinobi shinobi ni	come to me now and always

The reader of the *Kokinshū* is struck by the oneness of human affairs and nature. The use of natural images as metaphors for human affairs dominates the *Man'yōshū* too, but one senses in these poems a real fusion of the two topics: one is not the tenor and the other the vehicle, neither is subservient to the other. Many *Kokinshū* poems make use of personification: it is common to find the deer or bush warbler treated as a frustrated lover. As Kubota Utsubo writes, "there is a kind of child-like state of mind required for the composition of good waka, an openness to the world, a willingness to treat it as human."[36] Yet the composition is sophisticated and the product of sharply honed minds. "The balance between the subject (the poet) and his object (nature, love or whatever), so characteristic of the generation of Hitomaro, has disappeared, and in its place we find that the subject has become the poetic center. The external world gains a reality only by virtue of its effect upon the human sensibility or by its being ordered by the mind and heart."[37]

Another characteristic of *Kokinshū* waka is concern with time: everything is treated in terms of its temporality, as though floating by on the surface of the stream of time. *Kokinshū* time is a shifting time, a time which is never static. The emotion it calls forth in the poet and the reader is an appreciation for the passing beauties of life and a poignant awareness of their brevity.

These conventions, norms, and rules of decorum constitute a narrow language, whose violable laws make up the basic language of *Kokinshū* poetry. This language is one that we can reconstruct from its multiple utterances, the individual poems.[38] Heian poets assumed their audience knew the language; it is the modern reader's task to reconstruct and understand the constraints within which these poets worked.

ARRANGEMENT OF THE ANTHOLOGY

The arrangement of the poems within the *Kokinshū* also points up the Heian poets' acute awareness of the passing of time: the organization of poetry to illustrate the changing of the seasons or the course of human affairs was established by the *Kokinshū* compilers as the model for editors of

[36] Kubota, p. 28.

[37] Brower and Miner, p. 186.

[38] This point is brought out by Owen in *High T'ang*.

anthologies. As Roy Andrew Miller writes, "We still understand very little—and we know far less than we would like to—about the ways in which the Man'yōshū was originally put together."[39] Clearly the motivation for compiling the Man'yōshū came from the Chinese anthologies; yet we do not know for certain how long the task took, who took part, or what materials they worked with. Miller summarizes the "more or less generally accepted assumptions" as follows:

(a) the Man'yōshū was compiled over a considerable period of time, and the text we have today preserves internal evidence of having passed through a fairly involved process of compilation; (b) at least five or six, and perhaps as many as ten, individuals took significant parts in its original compilation; (c) among these multiple compilers, a leading role was taken by Ōtomo Yakamochi, 718–785, who not only contributed to the work his own poetic genius, but, equally important, made available to it the Ōtomo family's treasured accumulation of earlier poetic compilations and related documentary and textual resources.[40]

The arrangement of the Kokinshū marks the first occurence of the intricate structure in which poems are arranged by formal categories within which there is a natural sense of sequence and progression,[41] but the notion of integrating sequences of poems by a single or by multiple authors, using techniques of "progression" or "association," appeared very early in Japan. Although the Man'yōshū compilers did not adopt it as the central principle of organization in their own work and evidently deliberately disrupted such sequences in reorganizing materials, there is evidence that the techniques were found within those selfsame "documentary and textual resources" at their disposal.[42]

The concept of integrating poetry into prose texts or into poetic sequences is an ancient one in Japan. Both the brevity of the waka form and its lyric tone lend themselves to the development of such compound literary forms as the nikki (diary), utamonogatari (poem tale), lyric novel, and integrated poetry anthology. The social use of poetry, a part of everyday discourse in the Heian period, meant that it was often bound to the situation and that knowledge of the circumstances of its composition was needed in order to understand what was meant. This too facilitated the use of such poems as

[39] Roy Andrew Miller, "The Lost Poetic Sequence of the Priest Manzei," *Monumenta Nipponica* 36 (Summer 1981), p. 134.

[40] Miller, "Lost Sequence," p. 136.

[41] Ozawa, *Kokinwakashū*, p. 17.

[42] Miller's article argues that the poems of the priest Manzei formed such a pre-*Man'yōshū* sequence. See also his study, *"The Footprints of the Buddha": An Eighth-Century Old Japanese Poetic Sequence* (New Haven: American Oriental Society, 1975), and Edwin A. Cranston, "Five Poetic Sequences from the *Man'yōshū*," *Journal of the Association of Teachers of Japanese*, 13 (April 1980), pp. 5–40.

building blocks for larger works of literature, wherein they could be explicated by contexts. Even formal poems, written as deliberate acts of artistic creation and designed to be read by or to a wide audience, were often prefaced by an explanatory headnote or at least an indication of topic.

The poems in the *Kokinshū* are organized by topic into twenty books, as follows:

		(number of poems)				*(number of poems)*
I.	Spring (1)	68	XI.	Love (1)		83
II.	Spring (2)	66	XII.	Love (2)		64
III.	Summer	34	XIII.	Love (3)		61
IV.	Autumn (1)	80	XIV.	Love (4)		70
V.	Autumn (2)	65	XV.	Love (5)		82
VI.	Winter	29	XVI.	Grief		34
VII.	Felicitations	22	XVII.	Miscellaneous (1)		70
VIII.	Parting	41	XVIII.	Miscellaneous (2)		68
IX.	Travel	16	XIX.	Miscellaneous Forms		68
X.	Wordplays	47	XX.	Court Poems		32

(There are minor differences in book titles and numbers of poems in variant texts.) The poems in the first nineteen books are chiefly formal, written poems meant to be read and appreciated, whereas those in book XX, Court Poems, are songs which were used in court rituals.

As is obvious from the listing of book titles, love and the seasons are the major topics of *Kokinshū* poetry. These two categories were used also in Sugawara Michizane's *Shinsen Man'yōshū* and in certain poetry contests. Among the other topics chosen by the compilers, grief (aishō) is a traditional Chinese category that appears in the *Wen hsüan* and in the three early Heian collections of Chinese poetry commissioned by the sovereigns. The first ten books contain the more formal poetry and the second ten the more informal, private compositions.

Within the books of seasonal poems, there is an orderly chronological progression beginning with the first signs of spring and moving through the year. In the books of love poems, the classic pattern of Japanese courtly love appears: the books open with poems on the first glimpses of the beloved and move on to love after meeting, fear of the loss of love, and the sadness and, ultimately, resignation that come with the end of the love affair.[43]

The first book of Spring opens with early spring imagery: there are poems about the mist, the uguisu (translated here as mountain thrush), plum blossoms, the first green herbs, the willow, geese returning north after

---

[43] Janet Walker has analyzed the pattern of courtly love narrated by the *Kokinshū* love poems in "Conventions of Love Poetry in Japan and the West," *Journal of the Association of Teachers of Japanese*, 14:1, pp. 31–65; and "Poetic Ideal and Fictional Reality in the *Izumi Shikibu Nikki*," *Harvard Journal of Asiatic Studies*, 37 (1977), pp. 135–82.

winter, and cherry blossoms. Images of lingering snow, late snowstorms, and melting ice remind us of the season past. The blossoms continue in the first fifty poems of Book II, followed by wisteria and yellow mountain roses. The book ends with regrets for the passing of spring. Of the thirty-four poems on summer, the majority treat the hototogisu (a bird admired for its song, here translated as nightingale), which is heard in the mountains from early summer to early fall. Other summer images include the mandarin orange tree, the lotus, the summer moon, dianthus.

Autumn poems outnumber winter ones, as spring poems outnumber summer. The topics treated in the Seventh Month are the winds and the festival of Tanabata; and in the Eighth Month, the moon, the dew, the insects, the wild geese and the hagi (bush clover), the ominaeshi (maiden flowers), fujibakama ("purple trousers"), pampas grass, and dianthus. Book V, Autumn II, adds images of the colored autumn leaves and fading chrysanthemum flowers. In Book VI, Winter, the poems treat the piercing cold and the sense of enclosure and retreat that come with winter: the year is brought to a close.

Almost all the poems in Book VII, Felicitations, are congratulatory pieces written for members of the sovereign's family or upper nobility on the occasion of their fortieth, fiftieth, sixtieth, or seventieth birthdays. Many are screen poems, which were written on the screens used to decorate rooms at the birthday celebrations, and as such are among the most formal and public of the *Kokinshū* poems.[44] After the four anonymous pieces which open the book, the remaining poems are arranged according to the age of the celebrant.

The poems in Book VIII, Parting, were exchanged between people leaving on journeys and those they left behind in the capital. Some are private exchanges between lovers, others were written at farewell banquets, and still others are greetings to those met along the road. Book IX, Travel Poems, is the shortest of the twenty books. This contrasts with the great number of travel poems in the *Man'yōshū*. The lives led by the Heian aristocracy had become much more sedentary than those of the seventh- and eighth-century Japanese. The poems are arranged by the length of the journey: the opening pieces are by envoys to China; next are poems by exiles; then come poems by authors whose destination is unknown and poems by those leaving for official posts in the provinces; and the book concludes with poems written on short pleasure excursions in the neighborhood of the capital.

The poems in Book X include "hidden" words, "names of things" (mono

---

[44] Ozawa, *Kokinwakashū*, p. 168.

no na); in the late Heian period they were sometimes called kakushidai (hidden-topic poems). The topics vary widely, but within each poem one or more words are hidden, the syllables often forming parts of two or more other words and frequently running over from one line to the next.

Book XI to XV trace the course of the model court love affair in Heian Japan, from first love springing up at a mere mention of the beloved or a brief glimpse of a sleeve, to secret tears and yearnings, first meeting, frustrated meetings, the spread of rumors and concern about reputations, growing distance and coldness, parting, regrets, and resignation.

The Poems of Grief in Book XVI are elegies. The first poems treat the period between death and cremation; later poems were written for commemorative ceremonies. The last poems in the book treat the respective poets' own approaching deaths. Books XVII and XVIII include poems that do not fit into the other categories, because they treat more than one topic. Book XIX, Miscellaneous Forms, opens with chōka and sedōka. These are followed by haikai poems, unconventional poems which have the waka form but which break with accepted standards in conception or in expression. An overabundance of kakekotoba or engo, a word considered too common or vulgar for waka, or a humorous conceit qualified poems for this category, but there are poems elsewhere in the anthology that seem equally "irregular." It is not always easy to define the determining factor.

The Poems in Book XX are labeled Ōutadokoro poems, poems from the Court Poetry Bureau, and are a collection of poems and songs used in court rituals and religious ceremonies. The division of the poems in this book into court poetry, Shintō ritual songs, and eastern songs (poems sung to traditional melodies, including some less courtly poetry) may be based on the division of the *Shih ching* (*Book of Songs*) into the Elegantia (ya), Eulogies (sung), and the Airs of the States (kuo-feng).[45]

The compilers gave special attention to the opening and closing poems of each book and each major division of the anthology. In the books of seasonal poems, the opening poems express joy and surprise at the beginning of each new season, and the final poems tell of regret at its passing. Where there were two poems suitable to open a book, the compilers regularly placed the anonymous poem first.

In Book XI there is a series of 69 anonymous poems, which may be a pre-*Kokinshū* collection which was incorporated into the anthology, but on the whole the compilers seem to have made an effort to avoid placing many anonymous poems in sequence in order to vary the style. The exigencies of

[45] Masuda Shigeo, "Kokinshū no chokusensei," *Kokinwakashū*, Nihon bungaku kenkyū shiryō sōsho, ed. Nihon bungaku kenkyū shiryō kankōkai (Tōkyō: Yūseidō, 1976), p. 34.

compilation frequently led the editors to separate poems composed in the same circumstances into different sequences or even different books.

Clearly the goal was an organically unified anthology having variety within the set pattern. The compilers interpreted each verse they chose and, in a sense, offered their commentary on it by its placement in the anthology, concerning themselves in ordering the poems with theme, topic, and imagery; setting, time of day, and seasonal changes; and vocabulary, rhythm, and style. The seriousness with which the selection and arrangement of the anthology were carried out and the experience of the court poets selected for the task assured the reemergence of Japanese waka as an art form, while the anthology set the standards of performance and taste for centuries to come.

THE AESTHETIC OF READING THE KOKINSHŪ

The *Kokinshū* is not a collection of outstanding poems, but a collection of poems that work together to create something larger. It is a work created through the editorial efforts of the compilers, who took a body of individual poems and, by means of selection, classification, and ordering, created a new and unique work.[46] Within the anthology individual poems function not only as discrete creations but also as part of the fabric of the whole. The context may dictate the interpretation: it may expand or limit the meaning of a poem or focus attention on a theme or image less striking when the poem is read alone or in other contexts. The notes following the translations indicate which poems of the *Kokinshū* also appear in such roughly contemporary works as *The Tales of Ise* or *The Tales of Yamato*. Excellent translations of these works are readily available, and the reader, by consulting them, may view the poems in other contexts.

The anthology has a systematic topical organization: the division of the poems into twenty books shows the fundamental intent of the compilers to group poems by topic and to augment or even change their meaning as individual poems through positioning them in new environments. Within each book of the anthology poems are further ordered by a progression of numerous subtopics. The books of seasonal, love, and miscellaneous poems in particular show an extremely complex classification and organization.

The *Kokinshū* opens with two books of poems which describe the passage of spring and, in doing so, treat the varieties of human feelings spring evokes. The flow of seasonal changes was central to the Heian aristocracy, accustomed as they were to attending to seasonal events, both natural and

---

[46] This section of the Introduction is based on Matsuda Takeo's monumental study, *Kokinshū no kōzō ni kansuru kenkyū* (Tōkyō: Kazama shobo, 1965).

man-devised, in their daily lives and in their arts. Certain images had become inextricably linked to certain times of year. The spring poems of the *Kokinshū* represent the following sequence of topics (the topics are those selected to be emphasized by the compilers and are not necessarily set topics to which the poems were originally composed):

	Number
First Month	*of Poems*
Beginning of spring	6
Spring snow	3
Mountain thrush	7
Young spring herbs	6
Mist	1
Verdure	2
Willows	2
Birds	2
Returning geese	2
Plum blossoms	17
Second Month	
Cherry blossoms	70
Third Month	
Wisteria	3
Mountain rose	5
Regrets for spring	9

An examination of the first few spring poems of the anthology will illustrate the method of organization.

1.

toshi no uchi ni	spring is here before
haru wa kinikeri	year's end when New Year's Day has
hitotose o	not yet come around
kozo to ya iwan	what should we call it is it
kotoshi to ya iwan	still last year or is it this

Ariwara no Motokata

2.

sode hijite	today long-awaited
musubishi mizu no	day when spring begins will
kōreru o	the breeze melt icebound
haru tatsu kyō no	waters in which we once dipped
kaze ya toku ran	cupped hands drenching summer robes

Ki no Tsurayuki

3.

harugasumi	where is it that the
tateru ya izuko	warm mists of spring are rising—
miyoshino no	here on the slopes
yoshino no yama ni	of lovely Mount Yoshino
yuki wa furitsutsu	the snows continue to fall

Anonymous

4.

yuki no uchi ni	spring has come amidst
haru wa kinikeri	the icy lingering snows
uguisu no	of winter surely
kōreru namida	now the frozen tears of the
ima ya toku ran	mountain thrush will melt away

Anonymous

5.

ume ga eda ni	he cries on and on—
kiiru uguisu	the mountain thrush perched on the
haru kakete	branches of the plum—
nakedomo imada	long-awaited spring has come—
yuki wa furitsutsu	still the snows of winter fall

Anonymous

6.

haru tateba	has he come to see
hana to ya miran	if those are not spring's blossoms—
shirayuki no	white snow clusters rest
kakareru eda ni	heavily on bare branches
uguisu no naku	where now the mountain thrush cries

Sosei

The first poem was composed on a set topic, the first day of spring, and it establishes the topic for the next several poems. According to the calendar, spring has arrived, but there are as yet no physical signs: snow blankets the landscape while both man and mountain thrush impatiently await the sights and sounds of the new season. The sense of anticipation is maintained in poem 2: the poet, Tsurayuki, looks back to last summer and ahead to spring. The reader is alerted to the passage of time the poems celebrate. Poem 2 introduces the image of icebound waters, an image reflected in the snows of poems 3–9 and the frozen tears of 4. Poem 3 again plays on the contradiction of calendrical and physical evidence, introducing the longed-for image of spring mist into the winter scene. Poem 4 repeats the second line of poem 1, "haru wa kinikeri" (spring has come) and introduces the image of the mountain thrush, which continues through poem 6 and is picked up again in poems 10–16.

Poem 5 repeats the images of mountain thrush and winter snow and introduces that of the plum. The line "haru kakete" is ambiguous: it may be interpreted as modifying "yuki wa furitsutsu" and meaning "from winter into spring the snow continues to fall," as translated here, or it may be taken as a modifier of "nakedomo," in which case it would be interpreted as "although he cries, anticipating spring." The ordering of the poems in the anthology suggests the first interpretation. Poem 6 repeats the images of mountain thrush, fallen snow, and blossoms (plum blossoms are suggested because of the proximity of the word in poem 5).

7.

kokorozashi	so longingly have I
fukaku someteshi	awaited the fresh flowers
orikereba	of spring that they have
kieaenu yuki no	dyed my soul and I see snow
hana to miyuran	as clustered blooms on branches

Anonymous

8.

haru no hi no	though I bask in the
hikari ni ataru	comforting warmth of spring's light
ware naredo	how melancholy
kashira no yuki to	to think that my hair now
naru zo wabishiki	wears a crown of winter snow

Funya no Yasuhide

9.

kasumi tachi	when the warm mists veil
ko no me mo haru no	all and buds swell while yet the
yuki fureba	spring snows drift downward
hana naki sato mo	even in the hibernal
hana zo chirikeru	village crystal blossoms fall

Ki no Tsurayuki

Poem 7 focuses on the elegant confusion of snow-covered branches with clusters of blossoms and expresses even more forcefully the anticipation of

spring and the passage of the seasons, while poem 8 turns to the effects of the
passage of time on human beings. The headnote to poem 8 tells us that it was
composed on the third day of the First Month and that it is allegorical: the
"comforting warmth of spring's light" in which Yasuhide basks is the favor
of the Second Ward Consort; the crown of snow (which recalls a crown of
flowers and thus echoes the blossoms of poem 7) is his white hair. Again in
poem 9 snowflakes are seen as the first blossoms of spring. The spring mist is
reintroduced and real buds appear.

10.

haru ya toki	has spring come early—
hana ya osoki to	or are the plum blossoms late—
kikiwakan	I would like to know
uguisu dani mo	but not even the song of
nakazu mo aru kana[1]	the mountain thrush trills the answer

Fujiwara no Kotonao

11.

haru kinu to	already they say
hito wa iedomo	spring is here but as for me
uguisu no	while yet there is no
nakanu kagiri wa	song from the mountain thrush I
araji to zo omou	cannot believe spring has come

Mibu no Tadamine

12.

tani kaze ni	warm breezes blowing
tokuru kōri no	down the valley slopes melt the
hima goto ni	winter's ice at each
uchiizuru nami ya	crack a foamy wave bubbles
haru no hatsu hana	upward spring's first showy blossoms

Minamoto no Masazumi

13.

hana no ka o	on the wings of the
kaze no tayori ni	wind I'll send the fragrant scent
taguete zo	of plum blossoms
uguisu sasou	a summons of spring to guide
shirube ni wa yaru	that longed-for mountain thrush to me

Ki no Tomonori

14.

uguisu no	were it not for the
tani yori izuru	song of the mountain thrush that
koe nakuba	rises from the glen
haru kuru koto o	who would even suspect that
tare ka shiramashi	spring has at long last arrived

Ōe no Chisato

15.

haru tatedo	no flowers show their
hana mo niowanu	beauties in the lonely mountain
yamazato wa	villages though spring
monoukaru ne ni	has come the very notes of
uguisu zo naku	the mountain thrush are cheerless

Ariwara no Muneyana

16.

nobe chikaku	because I make my
ie shisereba	home near the fields and meadows
uguisu no	each and every
naku naru koe wa	morning I hear the song of
asa na asa na kiku	the mountain thrush trilling spring

Anonymous

All but one of poems 10–16 treat the mountain thrush. Poems 10, 11, and 13 evoke the call of this harbinger of spring before his song has been heard, while poem 12, like a refrain, takes up the images of melting ice and spring's first blossoms, which serve again as images of spring anticipated but still unrealized. Neither the song of the mountain thrush nor the true blossoms of spring have appeared. In 13 and 14 these signs of spring begin to appear, though 15 tells us that the blossoms are not yet opening in the deep mountains. Poems 15 and 16 both treat the mountain thrush actually singing. Again time is passing.

The rest of the nature poems are similarly organized in a complex, interwoven pattern of topics, subtopics, and images that tell of the passage of the seasons and the variety of emotions they evoke, whereas the poems collected in the other books of the first half of the *Kokinshū* are arranged by topic but do not display such interwoven patterns of imagery.

The second half of the *Kokinshū* begins with another group of complexly organized poems. In the five books of love poems, the central organizing theme is the course of the love affair, from the first welling up of love through early yearning, passionate meetings, fading love, and sadness and regrets at the end of the affair. Again a detailed examination of the opening poems of this section will orient the reader to their sequencing.

469.

hototogisu
naku ya satsuki no
 ayamegusa
ayame mo shiranu
koi mo suru kana

when nightingales sing
in the sweet purple iris
 of the Fifth Month   I
am unmindful of the warp
on which we weave love's pattern

Anonymous

470.

oto ni nomi
kiku no shiratsuyu
 yoru wa okite
hiru wa omoi ni
aezu kenu beshi

the white dew settling
on the chrysanthemums   and
 I   whose nights are made
restless by these barren tidings
will vanish in the morning sun

Sosei

471.

yoshinogawa
iwanami takaku
 yuku mizu no
hayaku zo hito o
omoisomete shi

so suddenly was
my heart dyed with passion for
 you   it leapt high as
the waves in the waters of
the swift Yoshino River

Ki no Tsurayuki

472.

shiranami no
ato naki kata ni
 yuku fune mo
kaze zo tayori no
shirube narikeru

even the ship which
sails forth over white waves which
 rise and fall   leaving
no trace   can rely on the
winds to guide it safely home

Fujiwara no Kachion

Book XI opens with four poems on the topic of unexpressed, hidden love. Poem 469 describes the earliest stage, pre-love: the poet himself is all but unaware of the emotion which is to torment and delight him, although the late spring and early summer images of the nightingale's song and the iris set the stage. "Ayame" (iris) also means "reason"; the poet's sense of balance and perspective is lost as passion rises, and he is no longer able to discern the pattern (aya) of events. Poem 470 tells of the sleepless nights and restless days of the early stages of love. The image of dew on the chrysanthemums, which vanishes in the morning sun, depicts the tenuous state of the poet's feelings and already anticipates the death-wish characteristic of the end of the love affair. The auditory image of 469, the birdsong, is echoed by the longed-for tidings of 470. Poem 471 describes the sudden onset of love; it moves as swiftly as the waters of the Yoshino and the lover's heart leaps high as the waves. The water images of 470 (dew) and 471 (river waves) continue in 472, where the motion of the ship and the ocean waves echo the activity of 471. Poem 472 introduces the image of the ship, a traditional image for something on which one might rely, and contrasts it with the insecurity of the poet's love, sent forth hopefully but with little certainty of reaching its goal.

473.

otowa yama	I hear rumors of
oto ni kikitsutsu	her borne by Mount Sound of Wings
ōsaka no	and yet here on the
seki no konata ni	far side of Meeting Hill I
toshi o furu kana	pass the years in barren dreams

Ariwara no Motokata

474.

tachikaeri	I turn back to her
aware to zo omou	as the white waves roll to shore
yoso nite mo	from the offing no
hito ni kokoro o	matter the distance my heart
okitsu shiranami	is held captive by her charms

Ariwara no Motokata

Poems 473 and 474 tell of the lover distant from the beloved, unable to communicate. The longed-for tidings of 470 are reintroduced in 473, as is the auditory imagery begun in 469 and 470. The dream, an image central to Heian love poetry, appears first in 473. Poem 474 takes up again the images of white waves and of motion, and tells of the unbreakable bonds that hold the lover even against his will.

475.

yo no naka wa	such are the ways of
kaku koso arikere	this world my heart swells with love

fuku kaze no	for her and yet she
me ni minu hito mo	is invisible as the winds
koishikarikeri	which whisper of her charms

Ki no Tsurayuki

476.

mizu mo arazu	not hidden and yet
mi mo senu hito no	not disclosed was one for whom my
koishiku wa	heart leapt in new-found
ayanaku kyō ya	love must I now spend the day
nagame kurasan	in unavailing yearnings

Ariwara no Narihira

477.

shiru shiranu	why worry thus so
nani ka ayanaku	uselessly over whether
wakite iwan	you know her or not—
omoi nomi koso	love alone can introduce
shirube narikere	you to one for whom you long

Anonymous

Poems 475–477 continue the description of love for a beloved as yet unseen. Poem 475 reintroduces an image of the wind; in 472 the winds blew the ship safely home, and now in 475 they are the agent carrying the rumors that awaken the lover's passion. The lover's heart, which leapt with new emotion in 471 and was held captive in 474, now swells with longing, and in 476 is found to leap again. Poem 476 introduces the hopelessness of love; "ayanaku" (unavailing, useless) is repeated in 477. The poet's restless yearnings echo the restlessness of 470. Can this yearning serve as a go-between? Can it bring the lovers together? (477)

478.

kasuga no no	I merely glimpsed your
yuki ma o wakete	beauty barely visible—
oiide kuru	like the blades of grass
kusa no hatsuka ni	sprouting through the deep blanket
mieshi kimi wa mo	of snow on Kasuga Fields

Mibu no Tadamine

479.

yamazakura	a fleeting glimpse
kasumi no ma yori	as of mountain cherries seen

honoka ni mo	through the thick veil of
miteshi hito koso	spring mists I scarcely saw
koishikarikere	the one who captured my heart

Ki no Tsurayuki

Poems 478 and 479 describe the first fleeting glimpses of the beloved, barely visible, like blades of grass sprouting through snow (478) or cherry blossoms seen through spring mists (479). The first two syllables of the place name "Kasuga" of 478 find an echo in the word "kasumi" (mist) of 479. Poem 478 also introduces the phrase "hatsuka ni" (barely), the sounds of which are taken up again in poems 481 and 482.

480.

tayori ni mo	longing is not a
aranu omoi no	messenger and yet how strange
ayashiki wa	it is that my love
kokoro o hito ni	has carried my heart away
tsukuru narikeri	and delivered it to her

Ariwara no Motokata

481.

hatsukari no	since first I heard her
hatsuka ni koe o	voice refreshing as the first faint
kikishi yori	call of wild geese in
nakazora ni nomi	autumn I have wandered on
mono o omou kana	the heavens' enchanted paths

Ōshikōchi no Mitsune

482.

au koto wa	chance of our meeting
kumoi haruka ni	is as distant as the dark
narukami no	clouded skies where the
oto ni kikitsutsu	thunder god rumbles like the
koiwataru kana	tidings that enliven love

Ki no Tsurayuki

Poems 480 to 482 return to the auditory images introduced in 469 and 470 and describe how rumors and tidings stimulate the lover's yearning. In 480 yearning serves as a messenger, delivering the lover's heart to the beloved. The first two syllables of "ayashiki" (strange) echo the sounds of "ayame" (iris; reason) introduced in 469 and "ayanaku" (unavailing, useless) introduced in 476 and 477. The wild geese, messengers of parted lovers, call out in 481. The sounds of "hatsukari" (first wild geese) are repeated in "hatsuka ni" (faintly). The lover's restless wanderings continue in 481; the image of the heavens through which he wanders continues in 482, where the skies are spoken of as the home of the noisy thunder god.

In these few poems we have love introduced and amplified, love stimulated by physical conjunction with the lover, and love stimulated by sight and by sound. The love poems continue with the topics of first love, neverending love, the confusion of love, love unknown to others, the pain of love, nights of longing, heartless lovers, and so on.

After the books of love poems the compilers include another group of books of less intricately intertwined poems. Book XVI, Poems of Grief, begins with poems mourning others' deaths at the time of the funeral, during the period of mourning, and on anniversaries of the death, and concludes with a few poems in which the poet anticipates his own death. The Miscellaneous Poems, Books XVII and XVIII, begin with a few on a variety of topics and continue with a series on the moon—the moon awaited, the moonlight, and the waning moon—a group of poems on age, and a group on water. These are followed by poems on the Buddhist topics of weariness with life, escape from the secular word, pessimism, and the wandering life of a monk. The poems in Book XIX, Miscellaneous Forms, open with a selection of chōka and a few sedōka, and conclude with haikai on the four seasons, on love (yearning, meeting, separating), and on miscellaneous topics. The poems and songs of the last book, the Court Poems, were used in ceremonies and rituals, such as the accession of rulers to the throne, and they include poems from the "wilds" of eastern Japan.

The unique structure of the *Kokinshū*, with its integration of the individual poems and its emphasis on the whole collection rather than the individual poem or author, established a pattern which had enormous influence on subsequent Japanese literature. The concept of integrating a diverse group of poems or a body of short prose passages by means of topical and imagistic association and by the progression of seasonal change and narrative event is a fundamental one in Japanese literature. It is basic to the structure of nearly every succeeding premodern collection of poems, and it led to the development of such types of poetry as the linked-verse forms, renga and haikai. Even twentieth-century prose fiction bears the mark of this means of linking images and events.

KANAJO
THE JAPANESE PREFACE

by Ki no Tsurayuki

The seeds of Japanese poetry[1] lie in the human heart and grow into leaves of ten thousand words.[2] Many things happen to the people of this world, and all that they think and feel is given expression in description of things they see and hear.[3] When we hear the warbling of the mountain thrush in the blossoms or the voice of the frog in the water, we know every living being has its song.

It is poetry which, without effort, moves heaven and earth, stirs the feelings of the invisible gods and spirits, smooths the relations of men and women, and calms the hearts of fierce warriors.

Such songs came into being when heaven and earth first appeared.[4] However, legend has it that in the broad[5] heavens they began with Princess Shitateru,[6] and on earth[7] with the song of Susano-o no mikoto.[8]

---

[1] Yamato uta. This is the only use of this term in the *Kokinshū*, although it appears in the *Ise monogatari* 82, and in other contemporary works written in kana. The term distinguishes poetry in Japanese from poetry in Chinese.

[2] Koto no ha. This image appears in numerous poems in the *Kokinshū*; see, for example, Book XIV, poems 688, 736, and 737, and Book XV, poems 782 and 788.

[3] The majority of Japanese poems, no matter what the topic, rely heavily on images from nature.

[4] The idea that literature came into being at the same time as the universe is a Chinese one; see Yoshikawa Kōjirō, *Chūgoku bungaku hō*, Vol. 3, cited in Ozawa, *Kokinwakashū*, p. 49.

[5] "Hisakata" is a makurakotoba which modifies such words as "ame" (heavens) and "sora" (sky).

[6] When Prince Amewaka was sent to subjugate the lower world, he married Princess Shitateru, daughter of the ruler of the lower world, and did not return to the heavenly realm.

[7] Arakane no tsuchi. "Arakane no" is a makurakotoba for "tsuchi" (earth, ground).

[8] Younger brother of Amaterasu ōmikami.

This alludes to the marriage songs of the female god and the male god sung beneath the floating bridge of heaven.[9] *Princess Shitateru was the wife of Prince Amewaka. Her song was an ebisu song*[10] *praising the beauty of her elder brother's*[11] *figure as it lit up slope and valley.*

These songs do not have a fixed number of syllables or the regular form of a poem.

In the age of the awesome[12] gods,[13] songs did not have a fixed number of syllables and were difficult to understand because the poets expressed themselves directly, without polish. By the time of the age of humans, beginning with Susano-o no mikoto, poems of thirty-one syllables were composed.

Susano-o was the elder brother of Amaterasu ōmikami.[14] *When he was building a palace in Izumo Province to live in with his wife, he saw clouds of eight colors rising above the land and composed this poem:*

yakumo tatsu	in Izumo eight
izumo yaegaki	clouds rise forming an eightfold
tsumagome ni	fence that encloses
yaegaki tsukuru	husband and wife forming an
sono yaegaki o	eightfold fence that eightfold fence

Since then many poems have been composed when people were attracted by the blossoms or admired the birds, when they were moved by the haze or regretted the swift passage of the dew, and both inspiration and forms of expression have become diverse.[15] As a long journey to distant places begins with one step and is completed after many months and years, and as a high mountain is created by the accumulation of dust and mire at its skirts and gradually reaches the trailing clouds of the heavens, so too has poetry been.[16]

[9] There are many versions of Izanagi and Izanimi's wedding chants. The italicized portions of the kanajo are evidently portions of an old commentary (kochū) and do not appear in all *Kokinshū* manuscripts. They are similar to a commentary on the manajo by Fujiwara no Kintō (966–1041). (Nishishita and Sanekata, p. 80.)

[10] This may be an error in the reading of what is called a hina song in the *Nihonshoki*.

[11] This poem in praise of Shitateru's elder brother, Ajisukitakahikone, is included in both the *Kojiki* and the *Nihonshoki*.

[12] "Chihayaburu" is a makurakotoba for "kami" (gods).

[13] The age of the gods refers to the time through the seventh generation of Japanese gods; the age of human beings begins after Amaterasu ōmikami.

[14] This is an error for "younger brother."

[15] "Kokoro" (heart, inspiration, spirit) and "kotoba" (expression, diction, materials) are the central elements in the Japanese view of poetry. The *Kokinshū* ideal was a balance between the two.

[16] This is based on lines from Po Chü-i (772–846):

A journey of a thousand leagues begins with a step;
A tall mountain rises from dust and mire.
My way too is thus.
The value of this practice lies in daily renewal.

The "Naniwa Bay" poem[17] celebrates the beginning of a reign.[18]

When Ōsasagi tennō[19] was in Naniwa and was Prince, he and the Crown Prince[20] both ceded their rank and refused to take the throne for three years.[21] Because of this the man called Wani[22] became uneasy and composed a poem to present to the sovereign. The reference to blossoms of trees is probably to plum blossoms.

The Asaka Mountain poem[23] was composed by a waiting woman[24] trying to pique someone's interest.

When Prince Kazuraki was sent to the Far North, although a banquet had been arranged in his honor, he was disgruntled because he felt that the Governor of that district was not treating him well enough. Thereupon, a woman who had been a waiting woman at court offered him sake and composed this song, raising his spirits.

These two songs are considered the mother and father of poetry and are used as the first texts for calligraphy practice.

Now, there are six poetic principles.[25] This is true of Chinese poetry as well. The first type is Suasive.[26] This poem was presented to Ōsasagi tennō:

naniwazu ni	at Naniwa Bay
saku ya ko no hana	the trees are dressed in blossoms
fuyu komori	the winter-shrouded
ima wa harube to	trees are now dressed in blossoms
saku ya ko no hana	to tell the world spring has come[27]

[17] This poem is cited below as an example of soeuta, Suasive poetry.

[18] This poem celebrates the beginning of the reign of Nintoku tennō.

[19] Nintoku tennō.

[20] His younger brother Ujino Wakiiratsuko had been appointed Crown Prince.

[21] He became tennō after his brother's death.

[22] A scholar from the Korean kingdom of Kudara, who came to Japan during the reign of Ōjin (ca. 270–310), bringing copies of the *Analects* and the *Thousand Character Classic*, and thus introducing writing into Japan.

[23] *Man'yōshū* 3807.

asaka yama	Asaka Mountain
kage sae miyuru	my love was never shallow
yama no i no	as that clear mountain
asaki kokoro o	well where we two gazed upon
waga omowanaku ni	the sparkling reflection
By a waiting woman	

Asaka Mountain is in Fukushima Prefecture.

[24] Uneme, a serving woman at the court.

[25] This section is similar to the discussion of the rikugi 六義 in the manajo.

[26] Poems in which, according to Ozawa, "the surface meaning of the poem conveys an unrelated hidden meaning." "Soeuta" corresponds to the Chinese term "feng."

[27] Ostensibly a poem welcoming the beginning of spring, it also celebrates the accession of the new sovereign to the throne.

The second type of poem is Description,[28] of which this poem is an example:

saku hana ni	fascinated by
omoitsuku mi no	the opening blossoms how
ajikinasa	brief their life will be
mi ni itatsuki no	for they never notice the
iru mo shirazute	arrow which will carry ill[29]

In such poems things are described as they are without analogies. What is the meaning of this example? Why this poem belongs in this category is difficult to understand; it seems to fit into the fifth category, the Elegantia.

The third is Comparison,[30] of which one example is:

kimi ni kesa	if this morning as
ashita no shimo no	cold white frosts of dawn settle
okite inaba	you rise to leave me
koishiki goto ni	each time I yearn for you I
kie ya wataran	too will turn to melting ice[31]

Such poems present similes describing one thing as like another. This poem is not really a good example. Perhaps the following one is better:

tarachime no	*silkworms raised by*
oya no kau ko no	*my aging drooping parent*
mayu komori	*hidden in cocoons*
ibuseku mo aru ka	*shall I live only in gloom*
imo ni awazute	*unable to meet my love*[32]

The fourth principle is Evocative Imagery.[33] This is an example:

waga koi wa	though I count the ways
yomu tomo tsukiji	I love you I could never
ariso umi no	reach the end even
hama no masago wa	if I could count each grain of
yomitsukusu tomo	sand on the rough seas' shores

In such poems feeling is expressed through use of all the plants, trees, birds, and animals that exist. There is no hidden meaning. However, this is true of the first

---

[28] Kazoeuta (fu).

[29] The names of three types of birds, tsugumi, aji, and tazu, are "hidden" in this poem. "Itatsuki" (illness; a kind of arrow) and "iru" (to enter; to shoot) are kakekotoba.

[30] Nazuraeuta (pi).

[31] Lines 1 and 2 are a jo; "okite" (waking; settling) is a kakekotoba. "Kie" (vanishing) and "shimo" (frost) are engo.

[32] "Tarachime no" is a makurakotoba, usually interpreted as "droopy-breasted." Lines 1–3 are a jo.

[33] Tatoeuta (hsing).

principle, Suasion, too, so there is a slight difference in the style.[34] *Perhaps this poem is a better example:*

suma no ama no	smoke from the salt fires
shio yaku keburi	of the Suma fisherfolk
kaze o itami	buffeted by fierce
omowanu kata ni	winds sways and drifts away in
tanabikinikeri	unexpected directions[35]

Fifthly there is the Elegantia,[36] of which this is an example:

itsuwari no	if this world of ours
naki yo nariseba	were a world without falsehood
ika bakari	how greatly I would
hito no koto no ha	rejoice to hear burgeoning
ureshikaramashi	words of new love unfolding[37]

These poems tell of a world well ordered and running smoothly. The spirit of this poem is inappropriate. It should perhaps be termed a tomeuta.[38] *A better example is:*

yamazakura	I have gazed my fill
aku made iro o	at the hues of the mountain
mitsuru kana	cherry blossoms
hana chiru beku mo	in this era in which no
kaze fukanu yo ni	winds blow the petals away[39]

Sixthly there are the Eulogies.[40] For example:

kono tono wa	we knew it would be
mube mo tomikeri	as opulent as this one—
saki kusa no	this palace built with
mitsuba yotsuba ni	wings numbering three or four
tono zukuriseri	this palace like branching twigs[41]

[34] There does not seem to be any evidence that this is true; this is evidently an attempt to explain away the confusion caused by adapting Chinese classification to Japanese poetry.

[35] *Kokinshū* XIV, 708. The poem may be interpreted as a plaint that the author's lover is drifting off to another.

[36] "Tadagotouta" corresponds to the Chinese principle ya, "elegantia." To judge by the example, it was interpreted by the Japanese to refer to poems describing a world of truth, without falsehood. It seems to have been distinguished from the sixth principle by the content.

[37] *Kokinshū* XIV, 712.

[38] The meaning of "tomeuta" is unclear. Ozawa, citing Ichijō Kanera's *Kokinshū dōmōshō*, suggests that it be interpreted as a "poem of quest."

[39] The author, Taira no Kanemori, lived in the mid-tenth century, so this portion of the interpolated commentary, at least, can be dated after the mid-tenth century.

[40] "Iwaiuta" (sung) are celebratory poems.

[41] "Sakikusa no" (a plant with branches in threes) is a makurakotoba for "mitsu" (three).

These poems praise the world and are pronouncements to the gods. The poem above does not seem to belong in this category. Perhaps this is a better example:

kasugano ni	gathering young herbs
wakana tsumitsutsu	on the Plain of Kasuga
yorozuyo	we celebrate your
iwau kokoro wa	many years the awesome god
kami zo shiru ran	surely knows how I rejoice[42]

On the whole, it does not seem that there are six different principles of poetry.[43]

Nowadays because people are concerned with gorgeous appearances and their hearts admire ostentation, insipid poems, short-lived poems have appeared. Poetry has become a sunken log submerged[44] unknown to others in the homes of lovers. Poems are not things to bring out in public places as openly as the opening blossoms of the pampas grass.[45]

Japanese poetry ought not to be thus. Consider its origins: Whenever there were blossoms at dawn in spring or moonlit autumn nights, the generations of sovereigns of old summoned their attendants to compose poetry inspired by these beauties. Sometimes the poet wandered through untraveled places to use the image of the blossoms; sometimes he went to dark unknown wilderness lands to write of the moon. The sovereigns surely read these and distinguished the wise from the foolish.

Not only at such times, but on other occasions as well:

the poet might make comparison to pebbles[46]
or appeal to his lord by referring to Tsukuba Mountain;[47]
joy overflowing, his heart might be filled with delight;[48]
he could compare his smoldering love to the smoke rising from Fuji,[49]
turn his thoughts to friends when he heard the voice of the pining cricket,[50]

[42] *Kokinshū* VII, 357.

[43] This conclusion, made after study of the manajo, seems a fair one as far as the Japanese understanding of the principles goes. See John Timothy Wixted's discussion of these terms in his essay included in this volume. See also Nishishita's review of scholarship on the rikugi, pp. 80–86, and his reprints of two articles on the subject, "Kokinjo rikugi setsu ni tsuite, sono ikkaishaku" by Nakajima Kōfū, and "Kokinshūjo rikugi no saikentō" by Nose Tomotsugi, pp. 170–200.

[44] "Umoregi no" (submerged log) is a makurakotoba for "hito shirenu" (unknown to others). See *Kokinshū* XIII, 650.

[45] "Hana susuki" (flowering pampas grass) is a makurakotoba modifying "ho ni" (in ears; openly). See *Kokinshū* IV, 242 and XI, 547.

[46] *Kokinshū* VII, 343.

[47] *Kokinshū* XVIII, 966, and XX, 1095 and 1096.

[48] *Kokinshū* XVII, 865.

[49] *Kokinshū* XI, 534, and XIX, 1028.

[50] *Kokinshū* IV, 200–203.

think of the pine trees of Takasago and Suminoe as having grown up with him,[51]
recall the olden days of Otoko Mountain,[52]
or protest the swift passage of the maiden flowers' beauty;[53]
seeing the blossoms fall on a spring morn, hearing the leaves fall on an autumn
    evening, he sighed to see the drifts of snow and ripples in the mirror increase
    with each passing year;[54]
he was startled to realize the brevity of his life when he saw the dew on the grass or
    the foam on the waters;[55]
he who yesterday had prospered lost his influence;[56]
falling in the world, he became estranged from those he had loved;[57]
he might invoke the waves on Matsuyama,[58]
dip water from the meadow spring,[59]
gaze upon the underleaves of the autumn bush clover,[60]
count the flutterings of the wings of the snipe at dawn,[61]
or bemoan the sad lengths of the black bamboo;[62]
alluding to the Yoshino River, he complained of the ways of the world of love;[63]
or he might hear that there was no smoke rising from Mount Fuji[64]
or that the Nagara Bridge had been rebuilt—[65]
At such times, it was only through poetry that his heart was soothed.

This poetry has been handed down since days of old, but it is especially
since the Nara period that it has spread far and wide.[66] In that era the
sovereign must truly have appreciated poetry, and during his reign Kakino-

---

[51] *Kokinshū* XVII, 905, 906, and 909. "Aioi" means "growing together, twin."

[52] *Kokinshū* XVII, 889. "Otoko" means "man"; the poet compares his own decline to the unchanging aspect of the mountain.

[53] *Kokinshū* XIX, 1016.

[54] *Kokinshū* X, 460.

[55] *Kokinshū* XVI, 860, and XV, 827.

[56] *Kokinshū* XVII, 888.

[57] *Kokinshū* XVII, 892.

[58] *Kokinshū* XX, 1093. The image of the waves washing over Suenomatsuyama was commonly invoked to describe something that could never happen or to refer to an unfaithful lover.

[59] *Kokinshū* XVII, 887.

[60] *Kokinshū* IV, 220.

[61] *Kokinshū* XV, 761.

[62] *Kokinshū* XVIII, 958. "Ukifushi" is a kakekotoba meaning "floating and sinking," "sad happening." "Fushi" also means "joint of bamboo."

[63] *Kokinshū* XV, 828.

[64] Fuji was no longer an active volcano by the *Kokinshū* era, but poems about the rising smoke were still being written. See XI, 534, and XIX, 1028.

[65] There is a Nagara Bridge in Ōsaka today, but the location of the bridge in the Heian period is uncertain. See XV, 826; XVII, 890; and XIX, 1051. "Tsukuru" may mean either "to be rebuilt" or "to decay."

[66] The capital was located in Nara in the eighth century. The *Man'yōshū* was compiled in the mid-eighth century.

moto no Hitomaro of the Senior Third Rank was a sage of poetry.[67] Thus ruler and subjects must have been one.

On an autumn evening the crimson leaves floating on the Tatsuta River looked like brocade to the sovereign,[68] and on a spring morning the cherry blossoms on Yoshino Mountain reminded Hitomaro of clouds.[69] There was also a man named Yamabe no Akahito.[70] He was an outstanding and superior poet. Hitomaro cannot be ranked above Akahito, nor Akahito ranked below Hitomaro.

We have such examples as the Nara Mikado, Heizei's, poem:

tatsuta gawa	*a covering of*
momiji midarete	*bright scattered leaves floats on*
nagarumeri	*Tatsuta River—*
wataraba nishiki	*were I to ford the waters*
naka ya taenan	*the brocade would tear in half*[71]

Hitomaro's:

ume no hana	*the plum blossoms now*
sore to mo miezu	*are indistinguishable—*
hisakata no	*for snow mists the broad*
amagiru yuki no	*heavens and masks all below*
nabete furereba	*in a whirling world of white*[72]

the anonymous poem:

honobono to	*dimly through morning*
akashi no ura no	*mists over Akashi Bay my*
asagiri ni	*longings trace the ship*
shimagakureyuku	*vanishing from sight floating*
fune o shi zo omou	*silently behind the isle*[73]

Akahito's:

haru no no ni	*it was I who came*
sumire tsumi ni to	*to the spring green meadows to*
koshi ware so	*pluck sweet violets*

[67] Hitomaro flourished ca. 680–700.

[68] See the poem cited in the "old commentary" below and *Kokinshū* V, 283. The Nara Mikado to whom it is attributed seems to be Heizei (r. 806–809). *Yamato monogatari* 151 gives a similar attribution, but the phrase "sovereign of the Nara period" used here is less specific.

[69] The oldest poems in the *Kokinshū* on the cherry blossoms on Yoshino Mountain seem to be I, 60, and XII, 588, but these are not attributed to Hitomaro.

[70] A *Man'yōshū* poet, d. 736?

[71] *Kokinshū* V, 283.

[72] *Kokinshū* VI, 334.

[73] *Kokinshū* IX, 409.

no o natsukashimi	*and it was there I lost my*
hitoyo nenikeru	*heart and stayed to sleep one night*[74]

and the anonymous poem:

waka no ura ni	into Poetry
shio michikureba	Bay the salt tides rush leaving
kata o nami	no dry land at all
ashibe o sashite	toward the shore where rushes
tazu nakiwataru	grow the crying cranes fly[75]

Aside from these, other great poets were heard, as generations succeeded each other like the segments of the black bamboo[76] in a line unbroken as a twisted thread.[77] Earlier poems were gathered in a collection called the *Man'yōshū.*

After that there were one or two poets who knew the ancient songs and understood the heart of poetry. However, each had strengths and weaknesses. Since that time more than one hundred years and ten generations have gone by.[78] Of those who composed during this century, few have known the ancient songs and understood poetry. I would like to give some examples, but I will exclude those of poets of high rank and office, whom I cannot criticize lightly.

Among the others, one of the best known of recent times[79] was Archbishop Henjō, whose style is good but who lacks sincerity. His poetry is like a painting of a woman which stirs one's heart in vain.

asamidori	along slender threads
ito yorikakete	of delicate twisted green
shiratsuyu o	translucent dewdrops
tama ni mo nukeru	strung as small fragile jewels—
haru no yanagi ka	new willow webs in spring[80]

hachisuba no	the lotus leaves rise
nigori ni shimanu	unsullied from the muddy
kokoro mote	waters why do these

---

[74] *Man'yōshū* 424.

[75] *Man'yōshū* 919.

[76] "Kuretake no" (of the black bamboo) is a makurakotoba modifying the kakekotoba "yo" (generations; segments of a bamboo).

[77] "Kataito no" (of the single thread) is a makurakotoba for "yori" (twisting).

[78] Ten sovereigns ruled from the reign of Heizei (r. 806–809) to that of Daigo (r. 897–930).

[79] "Chikaki yo" seems to refer to the years about thirty to fifty years prior to the compilation of the *Kokinshū*. The six poets described in this section have come to be called the rokkasen, or six poetic geniuses.

[80] *Kokinshū* I, 27.

| nani ka wa tsuyu o | unblemished blooms deceive us |
| tama to azamuku | with dewdrops glowing like pearls[81] |

Written after falling off his horse in Saga Meadow.

na ni medete	I plucked you only
oreru bakari zo	because your name entranced me—
ominaeshi	oh maiden flower
ware ochiniki to	please do not tell all the world
hito ni kataru na	that I have broken my vows[82]

Ariwara no Narihira has too much feeling, too few words. His poems are like withered flowers, faded but with a lingering fragrance.[83]

tsuki ya aranu	is this not that moon—
haru ya mukashi no	is this spring not that spring we
haru naranu	shared so long ago—
waga mi hitotsu wa	it seems that I alone am
moto no mi ni shite	unaltered from what was then[84]

ōkata wa	the moon beloved
tsuki o mo medeji	by all yet my own pleasure
kore zo kono	is tinged with sadness
tsumoreba hito no	for every wax and wane
oi to naru mono	numbers the months of our lives[85]

nenuru yo no	how fleeting the dream
yume o hakanami	of the night we two slept side
madoromeba	by side trying to
iya hakana ni mo	recapture it I dozed but
narimasaru kana	it only faded faster[86]

Fun'ya no Yashuhide used words skillfully but the expression does not suit the contents. His poetry is like a tradesman attired in elegant robes.

fuku kara ni	as soon as the gales
nobe no kusaki no	begin to rage the trees and
shiorureba	field grass bend before
mube yama kaze o	them no wonder they call this
arashi to iu ran	wind from the mountains Tempest [87]

---

[81] *Kokinshū* III, 165.

[82] *Kokinshū* IV, 226. The headnote, which is not in the *Kokinshū*, may have been copied from the *Henjō shū*, the *Henjō Collection*.

[83] See note 24 to The Chinese Preface.

[84] *Kokinshū* XV, 747.

[85] *Kokinshū* XVII, 879.

[86] *Kokinshū* XIII, 644.

[87] *Kokinshū* IV, 249. The version in the text of the *Kokinshū* has "aki" (autumn) for "nobe" (fields).

44

For the anniversary of the Fukakusa Mikado's death:

kusa fukaki	the grass is deep
kasumi no tani ni	a haze dims the valley where
kage kakushi	the last reflection
teru hi no kureshi	of the sun's rays once vanished—
kyō ni ya wa aranu	is today not that sad day[88]

The poetry of Priest Kisen of Mount Uji is vague, and the logic does not run smoothly from beginning to end. Reading his poems is like looking at the autumn moon only to have it obscured by the clouds of dawn. Since few of his poems are known, we cannot make comparisons and come to understand them.

waga io wa	this is how I live
miyako no tatsumi	in my retreat southwest of
shika zo sumu	the capital though
yo o uji yama to	men call Uji Mountain a
hito wa iu nari	reminder of wordly sorrow[89]

Ono no Komachi is a modern Princess Sotōri.[90] She is full of sentiment but weak. Her poetry is like a noble lady who is suffering from a sickness, but the weakness is natural to a woman's poetry.

omoitsutsu	tormented by love
nurebaya hito no	I slept and saw him near me—
mietsuran	had I known my love's
yume to shiriseba	visit was but a dream I
samezaramashi o	should never have awakened[91]

iro miede	that which fades within
utsurou mono wa	without changing its color
yo no naka no	is the hidden bloom
hito no kokoro no	of the heart of man in
hana ni zo arikeru	this world of disillusion[92]

wabinureba	I have sunk to the
mi o ukikusa no	bottom and like the rootless
ne o taete	shifting water weeds
sasou mizu araba	should the currents summon me
inan to zo omou	I too would drift away[93]

---

[88] *Kokinshū* XVI, 846.

[89] *Kokinshū* XVIII, 983.

[90] Princess Sotōri is said to have been a consort of Ingyō tennō (r. ca. 437–454), son of Ningyō tennō. *Kokinshū* XX, 1110, is attributed to her. For a discussion of Tsurayuki's comments, see note 27 to The Chinese Preface.

[91] *Kokinshū* XII, 552.

[92] *Kokinshū* XV, 797.

[93] *Kokinshū* XVIII, 938.

waga seko ga	this is the night when
kubeki yoi nari	my beloved will come to me
sasagani no	already I know
kumo no furumai	for the spiders are weaving
kanete shirushi mo	the webs that will seize his heart[94]

Ōtomo no Kuronushi's songs are rustic in form; they are like a mountaineer with a bundle of firewood on his back resting in the shade of the blossoms.

omoi idete	when memories of
koishiki toki wa	love burn I retrace my steps
hatsu kari no	weeping as the first
nakite wataru to	geese traverse the skies with
hito wa shirazu ya	lonesome cries how can she know[95]

kagami yama	well now I'll go to
iza tachiyorite	Mirror Mountain gaze upon
mite yukan	it and then travel
toshi henuru mi wa	on for I wonder if I've
oi ya shinuru to	aged in all these years I've lived[96]

There are others as well who are known, as numerous as the leaves of the trees of the forest, as widespread as the ivy which crawls in the fields, but they think anything they compose is poetry and do not know what poems are.

In the reign of the present sovereign[97] the four seasons have unfolded nine times. The boundless waves of his benevolence flow beyond the boundaries of the Eight Islands;[98] his broad compassion provides a deeper shade than Mount Tsukuba. During his moments of leisure from the multifarious affairs of state, he does not neglect other matters: mindful of the past and desiring to revive the ancient ways, he wishes to examine them and to pass them on to future generations. On the eighteenth day of the Fourth Month of Engi 5 (905), he commanded Ki no Tomonori, Senior Secretary of the Ministry of Private Affairs, Ki no Tsurayuki, Chief of the Documents Division, Ōshikōchi no Mitsune, Former Junior Clerk of Kai Province, and Mibu no Tadamine, functionary in the Headquarters of the Palace Guards, Right Division, to present to him old poems not included in the *Man'yōshū*[99] as

---

[94] *Kokinshū* XX, 1110.

[95] *Kokinshū* XIV, 735.

[96] *Kokinshū* XVII, 899.

[97] Daigo reigned from 897 to 930, so the kanajo was written in 905.

[98] The major islands of Japan.

[99] Actually a number of *Kokinshū* poems are similar or identical to *Man'yōshū* poems (see IV, 192; IV, 247; XI, 551; and XX, 1073, 1107, and 1108). Several are included as anonymous or "topic unknown" although the *Man'yōshū* cites both author and topic. Such poems were probably known to the compilers only as oral songs.

well as our own. We have chosen poems on wearing garlands of plum blossoms, poems on hearing the nightingale, on breaking off branches of autumn leaves, on seeing the snow. We have also chosen poems on wishing one's lord the lifespan of the crane and tortoise, on congratulating someone, on yearning for one's wife when one sees the autumn bush clover or the grasses of summer, on offering prayer strips on Ōsaka Hill, on seeing someone off on a journey, and on miscellaneous topics that cannot be categorized by season. These thousand poems in twenty books are called the *Kokinwakashū*. These collected poems will last as long as the waters flowing at the foot of the mountains; they are numerous as the grains of sand on the shore. There will be no complaints that they are like the shallows of the Asuka River;[100] they will give pleasure until the pebbles grow into boulders.[101]

Now then, our[102] poems have not the fragrance of spring blossoms, but a vain reputation lingers, long as the endless autumn night.[103] Thus we fear the ear of the world and lack confidence in the heart of our poetry, but, whether going or staying like the trailing clouds, whether sleeping or rising like the belling deer,[104] we rejoice that we were born in this generation and that we were able to live in the era when this event occurred.

Hitomaro is dead, but poetry is still with us. Times may change, joy and sorrow come and go, but the words of these poems are eternal, endless as the green willow threads, unchanging as the needles of the pine, long as the trailing vines, permanent as birds' tracks.[105] Those who know poetry and who understand the heart of things will look up to the old and admire the new as they look up to and admire the moon in the broad sky.[106]

[100] The swift changes in the depth of the Asuka River are the topic of *Kokinshū* XIV, 687, and XVIII, 933 and 990.

[101] *Kokinshū* VII, 343.

[102] The word "makura" may be a scribal error or possibly a reading of the Chinese characters meaning "your servants" which occur in the manajo.

[103] "Haru no hana" (spring blossoms) is a makurakotoba for "nioi" (fragrance; beauty); "aki no yo" (autumn night) is a makurakotoba for "nagaki" (long).

[104] "Tanabiku kumo no" (of the trailing clouds) is a jo modifying "tachii" (going and staying); "naku shika no" (of the belling deer) is a jo modifying "okifushi" (rising and sleeping).

[105] "Tori no ato" (birds' tracks) also means "handwriting" and suggests the manuscript of the *Kokinshū*.

[106] The old (ko) and the new (kin) suggest the old and new poems of the *Kokinshū*.

BOOK I

Spring (1)

1 • *Written when the first day of spring came within the old year.*

toshi no uchi ni	spring is here before
haru wa kinikeri	year's end when New Year's Day has
hitotose o	not yet come around
kozo to ya iwan	what should we call it is it
kotoshi to ya iwan	still last year or is it this

Ariwara no Motokata

The new year, according to the lunar calendar, generally begins in solar February or March. Thus the first signs of spring, or the solar-calendar first day of spring, sometimes occurred before the first day of the First Lunar Month. This poem is a good example of the disingenuous reasoning that often appears in *Kokinshū* waka. Masaoka Shiki 正岡子規 (1867–1902), who glorified the *Man'yōshū* style, cited it as an example of "mere grinding away at logic" (rikutsu o koneta dake 理屈をこねただけ) in "Essay on Reading Poetry" (Utayomi ni atauru sho 歌読みに与ふる書). Poets' dates and other biographical information will be found in the Author Index.

2 • *Written on the first day of spring.*

sode hijite	today long-awaited
musubishi mizu no	day when spring begins will
kōreru o	the breeze melt icebound
haru tatsu kyō no	waters in which we once dipped
kaze ya toku ran	cupped hands drenching summer robes

Ki no Tsurayuki

This poem is based on a line from the *Li Chi* (*Book of Rites*): "In the first month of spring, the eastern wind melts the ice."

3 • *Topic unknown.*

harugasumi	where is it that the
tateru ya izuko	warm mists of spring are rising—
miyoshino no	here on the slopes
yoshino no yama ni	of lovely Mount Yoshino
yuki wa furitsutsu	the snows continue to fall

Anonymous

Yoshino in Nara Prefecture, famous for its natural beauties, often is modified by the decorative prefix "mi" (lovely, fair). The simplicity of expression of this anonymous poem contrasts with Tsurayuki's more complex treatment in poem 2. However, not all anonymous poems are necessarily of an earlier age: some poets may have wished to remain anonymous because of the private nature of their poems, whereas others may have been delberately slighted by the compilers.

4 • *Composed by the Nijō Consort on the beginning of spring.*

yuki no uchi ni	spring has come amidst
haru wa kinikeri	the icy lingering snows
uguisu no	of winter surely
kōreru namida	now the frozen tears of the
ima ya toku ran	mountain thrush will melt away

The Nijō Consort, Fujiwara Takaiko 高子, was Consort of Seiwa tennō. Because of a romantic liaison with the priest Zenyū 善祐, she was demoted in 896. She died in 898, but was posthumously reinstated as Consort [kisai 后] in 943. The uguisu, *cettia diphore*, here translated as "mountain thrush," was conventionally made to await the coming of spring in the mountain valleys and move to the villages when warm weather came. This poem is the first of a series treating "elegant confusion" as to whether plum blossoms or snow whitens the branches.

5 • *Topic unknown.*

ume ga eda ni	he cries on and on
kiiru uguisu	the mountain thrush perched on
haru kakete	branches of the plum
nakedomo imada	long-awaited spring has come
yuki wa furitsutsu	still the snows of winter fall

Anonymous

6 • *Snow on the trees.*

haru tateba	has he come to see
hana to ya miran	if those are not spring's blossoms—
shirayuki no	white snow clusters rest
kakareru eda ni	heavily on bare branches
uguisu no naku	where now the mountain thrush cries

Sosei

7 • *Topic unknown.*

kokorozashi	so longingly have I
fukaku someteshi	awaited the fresh flowers
orikereba	of spring that they have
kieaenu yuki no	dyed my soul and I see snow
hana to miyuran	as clustered blooms on branches

Some say this poem was composed by the former Chancellor.

Anonymous

The former Chancellor was Fujiwara no Yoshifusa

8 • *Ordered by the Nijō Consort (who was then known as Lady of the Bedchamber) to compose a poem about the snow falling on his head in the sunshine, as he stood in audience before her on the third of January.*

haru no hi no	though I bask in the
hikari ni ataru	comforting warmth of spring's light
ware naredo	how melancholy
kashira no yuki to	to think that my hair now
naru zo wabishiki	wears a crown of winter snow

Funya no Yasuhide

The Nijō Consort, Takaiko, was mother of Yōzei tennō, who was Crown Prince when this poem was composed. "Spring" alludes to the Spring Palace, residence of the Crown Prince. The poem expresses gratitude for the Consort's favor ("spring's light"), as was appropriate at the New Year.

9 • *On falling snow.*

kasumi tachi	when the warm mists veil
ko no me mo haru no	all and buds swell while yet

yuki fureba	spring snows drift downward
hana naki sato mo	even in the hibernal
hana zo chirikeru	village crystal blossoms fall

Ki no Tsurayuki

"Haru" here is a kakekotoba, meaning both "spring" and "to swell," serving to link the jo, the first two lines (when warm mists veil all and buds swell), to the main statement (while yet the spring snows drift downward . . .).

10 • *At the beginning of spring.*

haru ya toki	has spring come early—
hana ya osoki to	or are the plum blossoms late—
kikiwakan	I would like to know
uguisu dani mo	but not even the song of
nakazu mo aru kana	the mountain thrush trills the answer

Fujiwara no Kotonao

The song of the mountain thrush would announce the arrival of spring.

11 • *A poem on the beginning of spring.*

haru kinu to	already they say
hito wa iedomo	spring is here but as for me
uguisu no	while yet there is no
nakanu kagiri wa	song from the mountain thrush I
araji to zo omou	cannot believe spring has come

Mibu no Tadamine

12 • *A poem from the poetry contest held at the residence of the Consort in the Kanpyō era (889–898).*

tani kaze ni	warm breezes blowing
tokuru kōri no	down the valley slopes melt the
hima goto ni	winter's ice at each
uchiizuru nami ya	crack a foamy wave bubbles
haru no hatsu hana	upward spring's first showy blossoms

Minamoto no Masazumi

This poem too alludes to a line from the *Book of Rites*; see poem 2.

1 3 • *From the same contest.*

hana no ka o	on the wings of the
kaze no tayori ni	wind I'll send the fragrant scent
taguete zo	of plum blossoms
uguisu sasou	a summons of spring to guide
shirube ni wa yaru	that longed-for mountain thrush to me

Ki no Tomonori

1 4 • *From the same contest.*

uguisu no	were it not for the
tani yori izuru	song of the mountain thrush that
koe nakuba	rises from the glen
haru kuru koto o	who would even suspect that
tare ka shiramashi	spring has at long last arrived

Ōe no Chisato

This poem is based on lines from a poem in the *Shih Ching* (*Book of Songs*): "The felling of trees sounds *cheng cheng*; / The birds calling *ying ying* / Rise from the dark valleys, / And move to the tall trees."

1 5 • *From the same contest.*

haru tatedo	no flowers show their
hana mo niowanu	beauties in the lonely mountain
yamazato wa	villages though spring
monoukaru ne ni	has come the very notes of
uguisu zo naku	the mountain thrush are cheerless

Ariwara no Muneyana

1 6 • *Topic unknown.*

nobe chikaku	because I make my
iei shisereba	home near the fields and meadows
uguisu no	each and every
naku naru koe wa	morning I hear the song of
asa na asa na kiku	the mountain thrush trilling spring

Anonymous

53

17 • *Topic unknown.*

kasuga no wa
kyō wa na yaki so
  wakakusa no
tsuma mo komoreri
ware mo komoreri

not today   do not
burn the Kasuga Meadows
    now   for here amidst
the soft spring-green grasses hide
my gentle sweetheart and I

Anonymous

Kasuga Meadow is part of Kasuga Park in present-day Nara City. "Wakakusa no" (like the soft young grasses) is a makurakotoba for "tsuma" (sweetheart, spouse), and also functions as engo with Kasuga Meadows. The poem has the rhythms of a folk song, particularly in the repetitions in the last two lines, which are, literally, "my sweetheart too is hidden; I too am hidden." This poem appears in *The Tales of Ise* (*Ise Monogatari*), 12, where the first line is "Musashino wa" (the Musashi Meadows).

18 • *Topic unknown.*

kasuga no no
tobuhi no nomori
  idete miyo
ima ikuka arite
wakana tsumite

oh guardian of
the fields at Tobuhi
    on Kasuga Plain
go out to look   how many
days before we pluck new herbs

Anonymous

In 712 Tobuhi field was made the site of an installation to warn of military dangers. "Tobu hi" (leaping flames) may refer to military signal fires or to the burning of the fields by farmers. New greens plucked by women of the court on early spring outings were cooked and eaten to supplement the winter diet. It became customary to send a selection of seven or eleven herbs as a gift on the seventh day of the First Month.

19 • *Topic unknown.*

miyama ni wa
matsu no yuki dani
  kienaku ni
miyako wa nobe no
wakana tsumikeri

deep in the lovely
mountains   lingering snow weighs
    the pine boughs   while in
the fields of the capital
already they pluck young herbs

Anonymous

20 • *Topic unknown.*

azusayumi	like arrows shot from
oshite harusame	a catalpa bow raindrops
kyō furinu	stream down today
asu sae furaba	even should it rain tomorrow
wakana tsumiten	I will pluck the young spring herbs

Anonymous

The kakekotoba "haru" (spring; to draw) links the jo (bending the catalpa bow I draw) to the main statement of the poem (spring rains fall today . . .).

21 • *A poem composed to accompany a gift of young herbs presented by the Ninna Mikado when he was Crown Prince.*

kimi ga tame	for you my lord I
haru no no ni idete	pluck the tender herbs in fresh
wakana tsumu	spring-green meadows while
waga koromode ni	drifting down one by one the
yuki wa furitsutsu	snowflakes settle on my sleeves

Anonymous

The Ninna Mikado was Kōkō, here referred to by his era name.

22 • *Composed on command of the sovereign.*

kasuga no no	waving their pure white
wakana tsumi ni ya	hempen sleeves beckoning to
shirotae no	each other are these
sode furihaete	maidens bound for Kasuga
hito no yuku ran	Meadow to pluck the young herbs

Ki no Tsurayuki

In an imperial anthology (chokusenshū), when the source of the order to compose a poem is not specified, it may be assumed to be the reigning sovereign—Daigo tennō in the case of the *Kokinshū*. The first three-and-one-half lines (will they pluck the young herbs of Kasuga Meadow—waving white hempen sleeves) are a jo, connected to the main statement by the kakekotoba "furi" (to wave)/"furihaete" (expressly). This may be a screen poem, inspired by an illustration on a standing screen.

23 • *Topic unknown.*

haru no kuru	the supple robe of
kasumi no koromo	mist worn by spring is woven
nuki o usumi	on a delicate
yamakaze ni koso	weft each mountain breeze seems to
midaru beranare	tangle and unravel it

Ariwara no Yukihira

24 • *Composed for the poetry contest held at the residence of the Consort in the Kanpyō era.*

tokiwa naru	now that spring has come
matsu no midori mo	even the unchanging pine
haru kureba	is dressed in
ima hitoshio no	fresh new foliage that is
iro masarikeri	dyed a brighter shade of green

Minamoto no Muneyuki

25 • *Written on command of the sovereign.*

waga seko ga	my love's robes stretched out
koromo haru same	to dry colors bright as fields
furu goto ni	where each spring shower
nobe no midori zo	changes the velvet meadow
iro masarikeru	grasses to a richer green

Ki no Tsurayuki

The kakekotoba "haru" (to stretch out; spring) links the jo (my love's robe stretched out to dry) to the main statement (each time spring rains fall the green color of the fields deepens). The relationship between the two images is left ambiguous in the Japanese.

26 • *Written on command of the sovereign.*

aoyagi no	the soft green threads of
ito yorikakuru	disheveled willows twisted
haru shi mo zo	spun taut in spring
midarete hana no	unraveling masses of blooms
hokorobinikeru	rent open in abandon

Ki no Tsurayuki

Commentators agree that the flowers in this poem are cherry blossoms, but the imagistic focus in this sequence (24–27) of poems is on the fresh green of spring.

27 • *Willows near the Great Western Temple*

asamidori	along slender threads
ito yorikakete	of delicate twisted green
shiratsuyu o	translucent dewdrops
tama ni mo nukeru	strung as small fragile jewels—
haru no yanagi ka	new willow webs in spring

Archbishop Henjō

Nishi no Ōtera, the Great Western Temple, is the Saiji, which stood near the Rashōmon Gate in the capital, opposite the Tōji. It was built in 796 but has been destroyed.

28 • *Topic unknown.*

momochidori	the spring caroling
saezuru haru wa	of myriad chirping birds
mono goto ni	awakens each year
aratamaredomo	all is rejuvenated
ware zo furiyuku	while I alone grow older

Anonymous

Momochidori was once taken to be the name of a variety of bird and was included among the mysteries of the *Kokinshū*, the solutions to which were handed down in secret within aristocratic families. It is now interpreted to mean "all types of birds."

29 • *Topic unknown.*

ochikochi no	now far now near there
tatsuki mo shiranu	in the mountains a songbird
yama naka ni	warbles his tune
obotsukanaku mo	tentatively will she ever
yobukodori kana	hear these love notes on the wind

Anonymous

The yobukodori is a type of bird, but it is unclear which. "Yobu" also means "to call" and functions as a kakekotoba.

30 • *Hearing the returning geese and thinking of a friend in far-off Koshi.*

haru kureba	now spring is here flocks
kari kaeru nari	of geese fly northward traveling
shiragumo no	the road through white clouds—
michi yukiburi ni	would that I could send with them
koto ya tsute mashi	a message through the skies

Ōshikōchi no Mitsune

Koshi was the general term for the northern part of Honshū.

31 • *Wild geese flying north.*

harugasumi	as patches of warm
tatsu o misutete	spring mist float upward fickle
yuku kari wa	wild geese forsake us—
hana naki sato ni	are they accustomed only
sumi ya naraeru	to a village without blossoms

Ise

32 • *Topic unknown.*

oritsureba	plucking an armful
sode koso nioe	of flowers clinging fragrance
ume no hana	perfumed trailing sleeves—
ari to ya koko ni	a thrush warbles seeking plum
uguisu no naku	blossoms promised by the scent

Anonymous

This is the first of seventeen poems on the plum blossoms. The next several poems refer to the Heian custom of scenting robes with incense. Courtiers perfumed by the incense from their lovers' robes might plead that they had only been gathering blossoms.

33 • *Topic unknown.*

iro yori mo	more than the color
ka koso aware to	of the flower the fragrance
omōyure	delights my senses—
ta ga sode fureshi	whose scented sleeve brushed against
yado no ume zo mo	the plum blossoms near my house

Anonymous

34 • *Topic unknown.*

yado chikaku	never again will
ume no hana ueji	I plant a plum tree near my
ajikinaku	house for I mistook
natsu hito no ka ni	the scent for the perfumed robes
ayamatarekeri	of the one for whom I wait

Anonymous

35 • *Topic unknown.*

ume no hana	so beguiling were
tachi yoru bakari	they I could not help but draw
arishi yori	nearer their perfume
hito no no togamuru	drenched my robes in plum scent
ka ni zo shiminuru	only to draw her reproach

Anonymous

36 • *Plucking a spray of plum.*

uguisu no	they say the thrush weaves
kasa ni nuu chō	a rain hat of flowering
ume no hana	plum perhaps I too
orite kazasan	may pluck a spray and make a
oi kakuru ya to	garland to conceal my age

Minamoto no Tokiwa

The honka (a well-known poem evoked by a later one, which incorporates its words, situation, or conception into a new meaning) to which this poem alludes is poem 1081.

37 • *Topic unknown.*

yoso ni nomi	the charm of blossoms
aware to zo mishi	on the plum trees enchants me
ume no hana	but it is when I
akanu iro ka wa	pluck a spray that form and scent
orite narikeri	blend in overpowering beauty

Sosei

38 • *Plucking a spray of plum blossoms and sending it to a friend.*

kimi narade
tare ni ka misen
  ume no hana
iro o mo ka o mo
shiru hito zo shiru

my lord   if not to
you   to whom should I show these
  blossoms of the plum—
for you understand the joys
of their fragrance and splendor

Ki no Tomonori

39 • *On Mount Kurabu.*

ume no hana
niou harube wa
  kurabu yama
yami ni koyuredo
shiruku zo arikeru

  though I cross in the
darkness of night   the spring scent
  of plum blossoms on
Mount Kurabu vividly
informs us of their presence

Ki no Tsurayuki

The location of Mount Kurabu (or Kurafu) is unknown; it may be the old name of either Mount Kurama or Mount Kibune in Kyōto. It is associated with darkness (kurai) through sound similarity.

40 • *Bidden to pluck a spray of plum blossoms on a moonlit night.*

tsuki yo ni wa
sore to mo miezu
  ume no hana
ka o tazunete zo
shirubekarikeru

  on this moonlit night
phantasms in deep shadows—
  tracing that sweet scent
on the air   I may know where
the plum blossoms lie hidden

Ōshikōchi no Mitsune

41 • *Plum blossoms on a spring night.*

haru no yo no
yami wa ayanashi
  ume no hana
iro koso miene
ka ya wa kakururu

  how foolish is the
darkness on this spring night—
  though it conceals the
plum blossoms' charm and color
it cannot hide their perfume

Ōshikōchi no Mitsune

42 • *One day the poet came, after a long absence, to a house where he often lodged on his pilgrimages to Hatsuse. The host sarcastically sent a message saying there was always room at his inn. Tsurayuki plucked a branch from a flowering plum by the door and composed this poem.*

hito wa isa	the state of human
kokoro mo shirazu	hearts I cannot know and yet
furusato wa	the blossoms of this
hana zo mukashi no	familiar village still greet
ka ni nioikeru	me with the scent of years past

Ki no Tsurayuki

Hatsuse (Hase) Temple is located in Hase, Sakai City, Nara Prefecture; it was a popular temple among the aristocracy. This poem was the one poem by Tsurayuki chosen for *Hyakunin isshu* (*One Hundred Poems by One Hundred Poets*), edited by Fujiwara Teika.

43 • *Plum trees blooming near the stream.*

haru goto ni	each spring it seems I
nagaruru kawa o	shall confuse reflections in
hana to mite	the flowing stream with
orarenu mizu ni	flowers and again I'll drench
sode ya nurenan	my sleeves seeking to pluck those boughs

Ise

The waters are in a garden stream; according to the *Ise shū* (*The Ise Collection*), it was the garden in the Kyōgakuin belonging to Uda tennō.

44 • *Plum trees blooming near the stream.*

toshi o hete	are we to call them
hana no kagami to	clouded stream waters where for
naru mizu wa	many years we saw
chirikakaru o ya	the blossoms mirrored now are
kumoru to iu ran	hidden by fallen petals

Ise

"Chirikakaru" means both "scatters and rests on" and "dust settles" or "clouds over."

45 • *Seeing the petals fall from the plum tree in his garden.*

kuru to aku to
me karenu mono o
ume no hana
itsu no hitoma ni
utsuroinuran

dawn and dusk I gazed
upon the sweet plum blossoms
dazzled   unable
to turn away   when did they
find the solitude to fade

Ki no Tsurayuki

46 • *From the poetry contest held at the residence of the Consort in the Kanpyō era.*

ume ga ka o
sode ni utsushite
todometeba
haru wa sugu to mo
katami naramashi

oh that I could catch
and preserve the plums' perfume
in my gathering sleeves—
such a souvenir it would
be   of this spring's swift passing

Anonymous

It is curious that this poem and three others from the contest should be included anonymously, since this poetry contest took place less than two decades earlier and the *Kokinshū* compilers were among the participants.

47 • *From the same contest.*

chiru to mite
aru beki mono o
ume no hana
utate nioi no
sode ni tomareru

oh to watch these blooms
fall without regret   unscathed—
fragrant plum blossoms—
still their perfume lingers
on my sleeves to torment me

Sosei

48 • *Topic unknown.*

chirinu tomo
ka o dani nokose
ume no hana
koishiki toki no
omoide ni sen

although every
petal has fallen   oh plum
let your scent at least
remain   leave us a keepsake
to cling to when you are gone

Anonymous

Kokinshū

49 • *On seeing cherry blossoms blooming for the first time on a tree in someone's garden.*

kotoshi yori	oh young cherry tree—
haru shirisomuru	this year you have learned to dress
sakurabana	in spring's fresh array
chiru to iu koto wa	but may you never learn to
narawazaranan	let your soft petals scatter

Ki no Tsurayuki

In the *Kokinshū*, the word "sakura" is generally used when "cherry blossoms" are meant. It was not until the age of the *Shinkokinshū* (ca. 1206) that the unmodified word "hana" (flower) came to mean cherry blossoms. Poems 49–89 treat cherry blossoms; 90–129, spring blossoms in general.

50 • *Topic unknown.*

yama takami	high in the mountains
hito mo susamenu	with no one to admire you—
sakurabana	oh cherry blossoms—
itaku na wabi so	do not be melancholy
ware mihayasan	for I'll delight in your charms

Anonymous

51 • *Topic unknown.*

yamazakura	oh mountain cherries
waga mi ni kureba	when I come to visit you
harugasumi	the spring mist rises
mine ni mo o ni mo	rolling across both peaks and
tachikakushitsutsu	foothills concealing your beauty

Anonymous

52 • *Seeing cherry blossoms in a vase before the Somedono Consort.*

toshi fureba	as the years stream by
yowai wa oinu	my own life passes from me
shika wa aredo	still I am renewed
hana o shi mireba	when I but see the blossoms
mono omoi mo nashi	my heart's sorrows disappear

Fujiwara no Yoshifusa

Somedono no kisai, the Somedono Consort, was Consort of Montoku tennō, mother of Seiwa tennō. Her name was Akirakeiko 明子. The Somedono, a villa near the capital, was the home of her father, Fujiwara no Yoshifusa, author of this poem.

53 • *Seeing cherry blossoms at Nagisa Villa.*

yo no naka ni	if this world had never
taete sakura no	known the ephemeral charms
nakariseba	of cherry blossoms
haru no kokoro wa	then our hearts in spring might match
nodokekaramashi	nature's deep tranquility

Ariwara no Narihira

Nagisa villa, near Ōsaka, was owned by Prince Koretaka and probably used for hunting parties. This poem appears in *The Tales of Ise*, 82. "Haru no kokoro" is ambiguous: it could mean either "the heart [of man] in spring" or "the heart of spring." The translation encompasses both.

54 • *Topic unknown.*

ishi hashiru	if only the torrents
taki naku mo gana	running over the pebbles
sakurabana	would disappear I
taorite mo kon	might cross to pluck a spray of
minu hito no tame	cherry blooms for those at home

Anonymous

"Ishi hashiru" (running over rocks) is a makurakotoba for "taki" (falls).

55 • *Seeing mountain cherry blossoms.*

mite nomi ya	shall we be alone
hito ni kataran	in enjoying these delights—
sakurabana	sweet cherry blossoms—
te goto ni orite	let us gather armfuls to
iezu to ni sen	carry home as souvenirs

Sosei

56 • *Seeing the capital with the cherry blossoms in full bloom.*

miwataseba	gazing far afield
yanagi sakura o	willow green and cherry pink

kokimazete	weave a delicate
miyako zo haru no	brocade of spring so fine
nishiki narikeru	the capital may wear it

Sosei

Willows lined Suzaku Avenue in the Heian capital.

57 • *Sorrowing over his age beneath the cherry blossoms.*

iro mo ka mo	although the cherry
onaji mukashi ni	blossoms dress in the shades and
sakuramedo	scents of ages past
toshi furu hito zo	I who breathe and gaze upon
aratamarikeru	them year after year have changed

Ki no Tomonori

"Sakuramedo" (although they seem to bloom) includes the word "sakura" (cherry blossoms).

58 • *Broken cherry branches.*

tare shi ka mo	who could have come and
tomete oritsuru	stolen this spring of blossoms
harugasumi	from mountain cherries
tachikakusu ran	when they are so well hidden
yama no sakura o	by the protecting mists of spring

Ki no Tsurayuki

59 • *Commanded to compose a poem.*

sakurabana	now it seems that
sakinikerashi na	cherry blossoms have burst forth
ashihiki no	at last from here I
yama no kai yori	see white clouds floating between
miyuru shirakumo	the rugged far-off mountain slopes

Ki no Tsurayuki

"Ashihiki no" is a makurakotoba for mountains; it is now conventionally inter-preted as "foot-dragging" or "rugged," though the original meaning is unknown.

60 • *From the poetry contest held at the residence of the Consort in the Kanpyō era.*

miyoshino no	far in the distance
yamabe ni sakeru	on lovely Mount Yoshino
sakurabana	cherry blossoms must
yuki ka to nomi zo	have opened for as I gazed
ayamatarekeru	I thought I saw snowdrifts there

Ki no Tomonori

In the *Kokinshū* period, the Yoshino Mountains were renowned for deep snow; by the *Shinkokinshū* era they were better known as the site of lovely cherry blossoms.

61 • *Composed in a year with an extra Third Month.*

sakurabana	oh cherry blossoms
haru kuwawareru	in this year alone when spring
toshi dani mo	comes twice-fold to us
hito no kokoro ni	will this at last be the time
akare ya wa senu	that you satiate men's hearts

Ise

In order to keep the lunar calendar from falling too far behind the solar year, intercalary months were added when necessary. An extra Third Month had been added the year this poem was composed (904), so that spring lasted four months instead of the usual three.

62 • *On the visit of one who, after long absence, had come when the cherry blossoms were at their height.*

adanari to	these cherry blossoms
na ni koso tatere	whom men call evanescent
sakurabana	flighty patiently
toshi ni mare naru	they've awaited one who comes
hito mo machikeri	but rarely in each year

Anonymous

This poem and 63 appear in *The Tales of Ise,* 17.

63 • *In reply.*

kyō kozuba	if today I had
asu wa yuki to zo	not come tomorrow the blooms

furinamashi   would have fallen like
kiezu wa aritomo   snow   though they lay unmelted
hana to mimashi ya   would I still see them as petals

Ariwara no Narihira

64 • *Topic unknown.*

chirinureba   if the blossoms were
kouredo shirushi   all to fade and fall today
  naki mono o   my longing would turn
kyō koso sakura   to barren memory   let
oraba oriteme   me pluck a keepsake now

Anonymous

Poems 64 and 65 are linked by the repetition of forms of the verb "oru" (to break) in line 5 of 64 and line 1 of 65.

65 • *Topic unknown.*

oritoraba   to leave these branches
oshige ni mo aru ka   barren would be such a shame—
  sakurabana   sweet cherry blossoms—
iza yado karite   instead let us lodge among
chiru made wa min   them   admiring till they fall

Anonymous

66 • *Topic unknown.*

sakura iro ni   I'll dye my summer
koromo wa fukaku   garments deeply with cherry
  somete kin   blossoms' fresh color
hana no chirinan   and be cloaked in memories
nochi no katami ni   of flower clusters when they're gone

Ki no Aritomo

67 • *Sent to one who came to view the cherry blossoms.*

waga yado no   after the petals
hanami gatera ni   in my garden have fallen
  kuru hito wa   how I shall miss those

chirinan nochi zo
koishikaru beki

who came to visit   only
to view the cherry blossoms

Ōshikōchi no Mitsune

This anticipation of loneliness was much admired by later poets such as Fujiwara no Kintō (966–1041).

68 • *For the poetry party at the Teijinoin.*

   miru hito mo
naki yamazato no
   sakurabana
hoka no chirinan
nochi zo sakamashi

   oh cherry blossoms
in this mountain village far
   away where none may
see   long after the rest have
fallen   you display your charms

Ise

The Teiji villa, Teijinoin, belonged to Uda tennō. The poetry contest, the "Teijinoin no utaawase," was held in 913.

BOOK II

Spring (2)

69 • *Topic unknown.*

harugasumi
tanabiku yama no
    sakurabana
utsurowan to ya
iro kawari yuku

on distant mountains
where spring mists float and trail
    the cherry blossoms
change color   is it to tell
us of their yearly passing

Anonymous

70 • *Topic unknown.*

mate to iu ni
chirade shi tomaru
    mono naraba
nani o sakura ni
omoimasamashi

if you would but wait—
lingering on the branches
    as we admonish
each spring   what could we admire
more   oh frail cherry blossoms

Anonymous

This poem is included in *Sosei shū, The Sosei Collection.*

71 • *Topic unknown.*

nokorinaku
chiru zo medetaki
    sakurabana
arite yo no naka
hate no ukereba

so lovely   falling
saving not a single petal—
    oh cherry blossoms—
things that linger in this world
become hateful in the end

Anonymous

72 • *Topic unknown.*

kono sato ni
tabine shinu beshi
sakurabana
chiri no magai ni
ieji wasurete

tonight I must lodge
here in this village through which
I pass   surrounded
by dancing cherry blossoms
I've forgotten my way home

Anonymous

73 • *Topic unknown.*

utsusemi no
yo ni mo nitaru ka
hanazakura
saku to mishi ma ni
katsu chirinikeri

like the world   hollow
as a cicada's castoff shell—
oh cherry blossoms—
you too will fade away just
as we catch sight of your beauty

Anonymous

"Utsusemi no" (like a cicada shell) is a makurakotoba for "yo" (world).

74 • *For Archbishop Henjō.*

sakurabana
chiraba chiranan
chirazu tote
furusatobito no
kite mo minaku ni

oh cherry blossoms
if you must fall   do it now
if you cling to life
that one from my old village
will never come to see you

Prince Koretaka

75 • *Seeing cherry blossoms falling at Urin'in.*

sakura chiru
hana no tokoro wa
haru nagara
yuki zo furitsutsu
kiegate ni suru

here where the soft white
petals separate and fall
it seems spring has come—
but still snow is piled in drifts
unmelting   beneath the boughs

Sōku

The Urin'in stood in Kyōto where the Daitokuji now stands. It was built as a detached palace for Junna tennō and later became a Tendai temple that was under the control of Archbishop Henjō from 869. Prince Koretaka, author of poem 74, may have been living there.

76 • *Seeing cherry blossoms fall.*

hana chirasu	is there anyone
kaze no yadori wa	who knows where these rough winds will
tare ka shiru	lodge tonight please tell
ware ni oshieyo	me that I may go reproach
yukite uramin	them with my unhappiness

Sosei

77 • *Cherry blossoms at Urin'in.*

iza sakura	oh cherry blossoms
ware mo chirinan	may I too fall and be gone
hito sakari	for though the young can
arinaba hito ni	prosper pitiful is the
ukime mienan	sight of the man grown too old

Sōku

This poem is included in *Sosei shū.*

78 • *Attached to the flowering branches sent to a friend who had visited and returned home.*

hitome mishi	oh cherry blossoms
kimi mo ya kuru to	will he come again he who
sakurabana	cast but a single
kyō wa machimite	glance if you must fall won't you
chiraba chiranan	wait one day for his return

Ki no Tsurayuki

79 • *On mountain cherry blossoms.*

harugasumi	oh floating spring mists
nani kakusu ran	why must you conceal from me
sakurabana	those cherry blossoms
chiru ma o dani mo	I long to see them even
miru beki mono o	as they shed their soft petals

Ki no Tsurayuki

71

80 • *Seeing, as he lay ill, shut in with the curtains drawn, that the branches of cherry blossoms which had been plucked for his room were about to shed their petals.*

tarekomete	spring passed as I lay
haru no yukue no	ill heavy curtains tightly pulled
shiranu ma ni	outside the blossoms
machishi sakura mo	so eagerly awaited
utsuroinikeri	faded fell unknown to me

Fujiwara no Yoruka

81 • *Seeing, from the Crown Prince's rooms in the Gain, cherry petals falling and floating on the garden stream.*

eda yori mo	from the branches they
ada ni chirinishi	have drifted aimlessly without
hana nareba	resistance these frail
ochite mo mizu no	petals falling floating like
awa to koso nare	foam on the stream they vanish

Sugano no Takayo

Prince Yasuakira 保明 used the Gain in the Greater Imperial Palace for artistic gatherings.

82 • *Falling cherry blossoms.*

koto naraba	if it must be thus
sakazu ya wa aranu	why don't they refuse to bloom—
sakurabana	these cherry flowers—
miru ware sae ni	for even I who watch from
shizugokoro nashi	afar have no peace in spring

Ki no Tsurayuki

83 • *Composed when some said that nothing falls as quickly as the cherry blossoms.*

sakurabana	I cannot believe
toku chirinu tomo	that nothing falls as swiftly
omōezu	as the cherry blooms—
hito no kokoro zo	for man's heart does not even
kaze mo fukiaenu	await the winds to turn away

Ki no Tsurayuki

84 • *Falling cherry blossoms.*

hisakata no	the air is still and
hikari nodokeki	sun-warmed on this day of spring—
haru no hi ni	why then do cherry
shizugokoro naku	blossoms cascade to the earth
hana no chiru ran	with such restless changeful hearts

Ki no Tomonori

"Hisakata no" (broad, expansive) is a makurakotoba modifying "hikari" (light). The sound of this poem, in which fricatives and unvoiced consonants predominate, reinforces the description of the crisp spring air.

85 • *Seeing, from the Quarters of the Crown Prince's Guards, cherry blossoms fall.*

haru kaze wa	oh spring breeze please do
hana no atari o	not draw near these petals as
yogite fuke	you waft for I would
kokorozu kara ya	like to know whether it is
utsurou to min	their own wish that they should fall

Fujiwara no Yoshikaze

86 • *Falling cherry blossoms.*

yuki to nomi	although I wish the
furu dani aru o	cherry blossoms would not scatter
sakurabana	not even gently
ika ni chire to ka	as the flakes of snow with what
kaze no fuku ran	turbulence the winds toss them

Ōshikōchi no Mitsune

87 • *Returning from Mount Hiei.*

yama takami	high on mountain peaks
mitsutsu waga koshi	I gazed and longed to linger
sakurabana	admiring cherry
kaze wa kokoro ni	blossoms how the ceaseless winds
makasu beranari	must be caressing them now

Ki no Tsurayuki

Mount Hiei, site of the Enryakuji monastery, rises northeast of Kyōto on the Kyōto-Shiga Prefecture border.

88 • *Topic unknown.*

harusame no	the spring showers that
furu wa namida ka	fall must surely be teardrops—
sakurabana	even among men
chiru o oshimanu	there is none but feels regret
hito shi nakereba	when cherry petals scatter

Ōtomo no Kuronushi

Only the Teika line of texts gives Kuronushi as author; the others leave the poem anonymous.

89 • *From the contest held at the Teijinoin.*

sakurabana	the lovely petals
chirinuru kaze no	stripped from all the branches still
nagori ni wa	undulate in the
mizu naki sora ni	sky waterless waves cross the
nami zo tachikeru	heavens keepsakes of the wind

Ki no Tsurayuki

90 • *A poem by the Nara Mikado.*

furusato to	Nara the ancient
narinishi nara no	capital now deserted
miyako ni mo	by the throngs of old
iro wa kawarazu	only the blossoms visit
hana wa sakikeri	their loveliness unchanged

The Nara Mikado was Heizei, who moved back to Nara after he abdicated in favor of Saga tennō.

91 • *On spring.*

hana no iro wa	beautiful blossoms
kasumi ni komete	enshrouded by the jealous
misezu tomo	mists so warm and dense

| ka o dani nusume | oh springtime breezes of the |
| haru no yama kaze | heights   steal for us their fragrance |

Yoshimine no Munesada (Henjō)

92 • *From the poetry contest held at the residence of the Consort in the Kanpyō era.*

hana no ki mo	never again will
ima wa horiueji	I plant a blossoming tree
haru tateba	in my garden for
utsurou iro ni	in spring petals fade and fall
hito naraikeri	and teach men their faithlessness

Sosei

93 • *Topic unknown.*

haru no iro no	spring does not decide
itari itaranu	whether to appear in a
sato wa araji	village here or there—
sakeru sakazaru	yet we see flowers on one
hana no miyuran	tree but not another

Anonymous

94 • *On spring.*

miwa yama o	oh mists of spring must
shikamo kakusu ka	you hide even famous Mount
harugasumi	Miwa for surely
hito ni shirarenu	in that holy place must bloom
hana ya sakuran	flowers unknown to mankind

Ki no Tsurayuki

Mount Miwa, in Nara Prefecture, is the site of Ōmiwa Shrine. Lines 1 and 2 are quoted from the *Man'yōshū*, poem 18.

95 • *Sent to the Urin'in Crown Prince on the occasion of a trip to Kitayama to see the blossoms.*

| iza kyō wa | come then just today |
| haru no yamabe ni | let us wander deep into |

majiri nan
kurenaba nage no
hana no kage ka wa

hills of spring   should the
sun set   might we not shelter
beneath the fragile blossoms

Sosei

Prince Tsuneyasu, son of Ninmyō tennō, was known as the Urin'in Crown Prince.
Kitayama, the "northern mountains," refers to the northern part of the capital. This
poem has been interpreted as a request for shelter at the Urin'in, a palace in the capital
(see note to poem 75).

96 • *On spring.*

itsu made ka
nobe ni kokoro no
    akugaren
hana shi chirazuba
chiyo mo henu beshi

how long might my heart
enraptured   linger here in
    the meadows of spring—
if the blossoms never fell
I would stay a thousand years

Sosei

97 • *Topic unknown.*

haru goto ni
hana no sakari wa
    arinamedo
aimin koto wa
inochi narikeri

each spring the blossoms
reach their brilliance once again
    but seeing them so
we are reminded that to
watch them fall is our lot

Anonymous

98 • *Topic unknown.*

hana no goto
yo no tsune naraba
    sugushite shi
mukashi wa mata mo
kaerikinamashi

if the world of man
were as unchanging as these
    blooms   renewed each year
then the time which I have lived
would return to me once more

Anonymous

In *Kokinrokujō* this poem is attributed to Sosei, while 100 is attributed to either Sosei
or Ōshikōchi no Mitsune.

99 • *Topic unknown.*

fuku kaze ni	if these swift-blowing
atsuraetsukuru	breezes were to submit to
mono naraba	my will how quickly
kono hito moto wa	would I order them to stay
yogiyo to iwamashi	their force and spare this one tree

Anonymous

1 00 • *Topic unknown.*

matsu hito mo	awaiting my love
konu mono yue ni	he who never came I plucked
uguisu no	the spray of blossoms
nakitsuru hana o	over which the mountain thrush
oritekeru kana	had wept tears and sadly sung

Anonymous

1 0 1 • *From the poetry contest held at the residence of the Consort in the Kanpyō era.*

saku hana wa	innumerable
chigusu nagara ni	the blooms yet each must fade and
ada naredo	fall quickly changing—
tare ka wa haru o	still who can rightly think
uramihatetaru	ill thoughts of gentle spring

Fujiwara no Okikaze

1 0 2 • *From the same poetry contest.*

harugasumi	the spring mists displayed
iro no chigusa ni	a thousand colors was their
mietsuru wa	glory merely a
tanabiku yama no	reflection of the blossoms
hana no kage kamo	enveloping the mountains

Fujiwara no Okikaze

1 0 3 • *From the same contest.*

kasumi tatsu	the vernal mountains
haru no yamabe wa	where mists rise with the spring are

tōkeredo　　　　　　　far away　yet from them
fukikuru kaze wa　　　come soft breezes laden with
hana no ka zo suru　　the fragrance of the flowers

Ariwara no Motokata

The kakekotoba "tatsu" (rises; begins) links the mist (kasumi) and spring (haru) in the two opening lines.

104 • *Seeing fading flowers.*

hana mireba　　　　　seeing the flowers
kokoro sae ni zo　　　wither and fall　my heart too
　utsurikeru　　　　　changes its colors
iro ni wa ideji　　　　but I shall not display them—
hito mo koso shire　　others shall not know my weakness

Ōshikōchi no Mitsune

"Iro" (color; surface) links the images of the fading flowers and the outward expression of sorrow in this poem.

105 • *Topic unknown.*

uguisu no　　　　　　the lament of the
naku nobe goto ni　　mountain thrush fills each meadow—
　kite mireba　　　　　and as I draw near
utsurou hana ni　　　I discover the faded
kaze zo fukikeru　　　blossoms tossed upon the wind

Anonymous

This poem is linked to 106 by the repetition of "kaze" (wind) and "fuku" (to blow) in succeeding lines. The following six poems treat the sorrow of the mountain thrush at the passing of spring.

106 • *Topic unknown.*

fuku kaze o　　　　　oh mountain thrush
nakite urami yo　　　address your reproaches to
　uguisu wa　　　　　the ravaging winds—
ware ya wa hana ni　　for I would not dare even
te dani furetaru　　　brush these blossoms with my hand

Anonymous

107 • *Topic unknown.*

chiru hana no	if weeping for the
naku ni shi tomaru	falling flowers could keep them
mono naraba	securely on the
ware uguisu ni	branches my cries would rival
otoramashi ya wa	the song of the mountain thrush

Fujiwara no Amaneiko

Amaneiko was Naishi no suke, Assistant Lady-in-waiting, a post that generally carried the Junior Fourth Rank.

108 • *Composed for the poetry contest at the home of the Middle Captain Lady of the Bedchamber, in the Ninna era.*

hana no chiru	surely it is the
koto ya wabishiki	falling of the blossoms that
harugasumi	he mourns the mountain
tatsuta no yama no	thrush cries on Mount Tatsuta
uguisu no koe	where spring mists drift skyward

Fujiwara no Nochikage

Lady of the Bedchamber (miyasundokoro) was a title given ladies who had given birth to children of the sovereign. This woman had a relative who was a Middle Captain (chūjō), but she has not been identified. The Tatsuta Mountains are in Ikoma District, Nara Prefecture. Tatsu also means "to rise" and functions as a kakekotoba.

109 • *Hearing the mountain thrush sing.*

kozutaeba	fluttering now from
ono ga ha kaze ni	tree to tree the mountain thrush
chiru hana o	scatters petals as
tare ni ōsete	he passes who does he berate
kokora nakuran	crying so persistently

Sosei

110 • *Hearing the mountain thrush sing in a flowering tree.*

shirushi naki	oh mountain thrush
ne o mo naku kana	such unavailing useless
uguisu no	cries you raise—

kotoshi nomi chiru　　　　it is not this year alone that
hana naranaku ni　　　　　blossoms will wither and fall

Ōshikōchi no Mitsune

I I I • *Topic unknown.*

　　koma namete　　　　　　our many horses
iza mi ni yukan　　　　loping together　 let us
　　furusato wa　　　　　　ride to see our old
yuki to nomi koso　　town　 flower petals there
hana wa chirurame　　must now be falling like snow

Anonymous

This poem and 112 are linked by the similarity of their contiguous lines.

I I 2 • *Topic unknown.*

　　chiru hana o　　　　　why should we grieve to
nani ka uramin　　　　see the petals falling to
　　yo no naka ni　　　　　earth　 for won't we too
waga mi mo tomo ni　who share this ephemeral
aran mono ka wa　　　existence　 someday follow

Anonymous

I I 3 • *Topic unknown.*

　　hana no iro wa　　　　the colors of the
utsurinikeri na　　　blossoms have faded and passed
　　itazura ni　　　　　　as　 heedlessly　 I
waga mi yo ni furu　squandered my days in pensive
nagame seshi ma ni　gazing　 and the long rains fell

Ono no Komachi

The complex rhetoric, including two kakekotoba, "furu" (to grow old; to rain) and "nagame" (long rains; pensive gazing), and the comparison of the beauty of the blossoms and of youth mark this as a poem by Komachi, the famous poetess of love and longing.

114 • *Composed when they were to match poems at the home of the Middle Captain Lady of the Bedchamber, in the Ninna era.*

oshi to omou	would that I could twist
kokoro wa ito ni	the threads of my sorrowful
yorarenan	heart into a strand
chiru hana goto ni	that I might catch each falling
nukite todomen	bloom and tie it to the bough

Sosei

For this Lady of the Bedchamber, see 108.

115 • *Sent to the many lovely women he met as he traveled to Shiga Pass.*

azusayumi	crossing the mountains
haru no yamabe o	in spring when days grow long as
koe kureba	the catalpa bow
michi mo sariaezu	the drifts of petals deceive
hana zo chirikeru	me onto paths I should shun

Ki no Tsurayuki

The Shiga Pass refers to the road from the capital past Shiga Peak and over Shiga Mountain to modern Ōtsu City. "Azusayumi" (catalpa bow) is a makurakotoba for "haru" (to draw; spring). The azusa has not been clearly identified. It may be a type of birch.

116 • *From the poetry contest held at the residence of the Consort in the Kanpyō era.*

haru no no ni	to these spring meadows
wakana tsuman to	I came to pluck the first herbs
koshi mono o	of the year but then
chirikau hana ni	in the tumbling cascade of
michi wa madoinu	blossoms I lost the path home

Ki no Tsurayuki

117 • *Visiting a mountain temple.*

yadori shite	last night while I slept
haru no yamabe ni	here in the vernal mountains

netaru yo wa	I found that in my
yume no uchi ni mo	dreams as in my waking there
hana zo chirikeru	were fading falling petals

Ki no Tsurayuki

118 • *From the poetry contest held at the residence of the Consort in the Kanpyō era.*

fuku kaze to	if the blowing winds
tani no mizu to shi	and effervescent streams were
nakariseba	gone then I'd never
miyamagakure no	see the hidden mountain blooms
hana o mimashi ya	come drifting before my eyes

Ki no Tsurayuki

119 • *Sent to some women who had paused to admire the wisteria at Kazan on their way back from Shiga.*

yoso ni mite	another place they
kaeran hito ni	visited then turned toward home—
fuji no hana	oh wisteria
haimatsuware yo	vines intertwine and capture
eda wa oru tomo	them though fragile branches break

Henjō

On their way back from Shiga Temple (Sūfukuji in Shiga Prefecture) the women had paused to admire the wisteria at Kazan Temple (also called Gangyōji) on the outskirts of the capital, where Archbishop Henjō lived.

120 • *Seeing someone stop to view the wisteria blooming at his house.*

waga yado ni	beside my house are
sakeru fujinami	billows of wisteria—
tachikaeri	rising waves flowing—
sugikate ni nomi	one caught in the stream of blooms
hito no miru ran	turns back to eye their beauty

Ōshikōchi no Mitsune

"Tachikaeri" (rise and return) links "fujinami" (wisteria waves) and "hito" (person).

121 • *Topic unknown.*

ima mo kamo
sakiniou ran
  tachibana no
kojima no saki no
yamabuki no hana

even now the blooms
unfold and display their hue—
  wild yellow roses
on the cape of mandarin
blossom   Tachibana Isle

Anonymous

Tachibana Isle was in the Uji River near the Byōdōin. The tachibana is a mandarin
orange.

122 • *Topic unknown.*

harusame ni
nioeru iro mo
  akanaku ni
ka sae natsukashi
yamabuki no hana

never do we tire
of the glistening yellow
  of the mountain rose—
brightened by the spring showers
their fragrance ever pleases

Anonymous

123 • *Topic unknown.*

yamabuki wa
ayana na saki so
  hana min to
ueken kimi ga
koyoi konaku ni

oh mountain roses
there is no reason for you
  to bloom tonight   for
he who planted you will not
come to visit you or me

Anonymous

124 • *Seeing yellow roses in bloom by Yoshino River.*

yoshino gawa
kishi no yamabuki
  fuku kaze ni
soko no kage sae
utsuroinikeri

the blowing winds which
toss the mountain roses to
  the banks of River
Yoshino   have scattered their
bright reflection in the depths

Ki no Tsurayuki

Yoshino River runs past the Yoshino Mountains in Nara Prefecture.

125 • *Topic unknown.*

kawazu naku	the petals of the
ide no yamabuki	mountain roses of Ide
chirinikeri	have fallen and the
hana no sakari ni	frogs cry if only I had
awamashi mono o	come when they were at their peak

Some say this poem was composed by Tachibana no Kiyotomo.

Tachibana no Kiyotomo was father of the Consort of Saga tennō. The Tachibana family had a villa at Ide, a village now in Tsuzuki District in Kyōto.

126 • *A spring poem.*

omoudochi	oh that I might go
haru no yamabe ni	to spring's mountains and gather
uchimurete	with my closest friends—
soko to mo iwanu	then we might choose to remain
tabine shite shi ga	together the short swift night

Sosei

127 • *On spring's swift passing.*

azusayumi	since the first day of
haru tachishi yori	spring when the days began to
toshi tsuki no	stretch as long as the
iru ga gotoku mo	catalpa bow the hours
omōyuru kana	have passed me like swift arrows

Ōshikōchi no Mitsune

The makurakotoba "azusayumi" (catalpa bow) modifies "haru" (to draw; spring) and is imagistically tied to "iru" (to shoot) as an engo. According to the *Mitsune shū,* this was a screen poem on the topic "Twelfth Month."

128 • *Hearing, after long absence, the song of the mountain thrush in the Third Month.*

naki tomuru	no longer a
hana shi nakereba	petal clinging to the branch
uguisu mo	for the thrush to coax

84

hate wa monouku   to stay   surely that is why
narinu beranari   he's given up his useless cries

Ki no Tsurayuki

The lunar Third Month was the last month of spring—the month for blossoms to fall.

1 2 9 • *Seeing a flower-laden stream while crossing the mountains late in the Third Month.*

hana chireru   as I follow these
mizu no manimani   waters in which float petals
  tomekureba   of fallen flowers
yama ni wa haru mo   I discover at the source
nakunarinikeri   that spring has left the mountains

Kiyowara no Fukayabu

1 3 0 • *Regretting the passing of spring.*

oshimedomo   there are no regrets
todomaranakuni   that can restrain spring   when it
  harugasumi   is finally time
kaeru michi ni shi   for her to go   rising mists
tachinu to omoeba   start her on her journey home

Ariwara no Motokata

"Tachinu" has a double meaning: "risen" and "departed."

1 3 1 • *From the poetry contest held at the residence of the Consort in the Kanpyō era.*

koe taezu   oh mountain thrush   cry
nake ya uguisu   and weep   do not spare your voice
  hitotose ni   for we all know that
futatabi to dani   the beauty of spring comes but
kubeki haru ka wa   once a year   rejoice in that

Fujiwara no Okikaze

85

I 3 2 • *Seeing women returning from picking flowers at the end of the Third Month.*

todomu beki	whimsically they
mono to wa nashi ni	fall these flowers and my heart
hakanaku mo	there is nothing that
chiru hana goto ni	will keep them from drifting for
tagū kokoro ka	nature controls their motion

Ōshikōchi no Mitsune

The women have been picking altar flowers. The poem reminds us that they, as well as the blossoms, will soon fade and fall.

I 3 3 • *Sent to someone with a wisteria spray plucked in the rain on the last day of spring.*

nuretsutsu zo	although drenched and chilled
shiite oritsuru	by the late spring rains I plucked
toshi no uchi ni	a flowering bough for
haru wa iku ka mo	I know how few days of this
araji to omoeba	year's spring are left to enjoy

Ariwara no Narihira

This poem appears in *The Tales of Ise*, 80.

I 3 4 • *A poem on the end of spring from the Teijinoin poetry contest.*

kyō nomi to	even on days when
haru o omowanu	I do not feel the weight of
toki dani mo	the last day of spring
tatsu koto yasuki	how difficult it is to leave
hana no kage ka wa	the shelter of the blossoms

Ōshikōchi no Mitsune

For the Teijinoin poetry contest, see 68.

BOOK III

Summer

1 3 5 • *Topic unknown.*

waga yado no	at last they are in
ike no fujinami	bloom waves of wisteria
sakinikeri	by my garden pond
yama hototogisu	when will he come to sing his
itsu ka kinakan	song that mountain nightingale

Anonymous

Some say this poem was composed by Kakinomoto no Hitomaro.

Wisteria is a late spring flower; the hototogisu (*Cuculus poliocephalus*), a midsummer bird admired for its song. Thus this poem serves as a transition from spring to summer. The attribution to Hitomaro is doubtful.

1 3 6 • *Seeing a cherry bloom in the first month of summer.*

aware chō	to keep our lavish
koto o amata ni	praises from any other
yaraji to ya	flower surely that
haru no okurete	is why this single cherry
hitori sakuran	has bloomed now that spring is gone

Ki no Toshisada

Summer lasts from the Fourth to the Sixth Months of the lunar calendar. Cherry blossoms are out of place once summer has begun.

1 3 7 • *Topic unknown.*

satsuki matsu	oh sweet nightingale
yama hototogisu	of the mountains you who wait

87

uchi habuki
ima mo nakanan
kozo no furugoe

for midsummer's month—
flutter your wings   raise your voice
sing us your unforgotten song

Anonymous

1 3 8 • *Topic unknown.*

satsuki koba
naki mo furinan
   hototogisu
madashiki hodo no
koe o kikabaya

by midsummer the
voice of the nightingale will
   be well past its prime
oh that I might hear it sing
just once in early season

Ise

1 3 9 • *Topic unknown.*

satsuki matsu
hana tachibana no
   kao kageba
mukashi no hito no
sode no ka zo suru

when I breathe the fragrance
of the mandarin orange
   blossoms that await
the Fifth Month   it brings back the
scented sleeves of one I loved

Anonymous

This poem is included in *The Tales of Ise*, 60. The tachibana (mandarin orange) blossom is an image associated with the late Fourth Month; the hototogisu (nightingale), with the Fifth.

1 4 0 • *Topic unknown.*

itsu no ma ni
satsuki kinu ran
   ashihiki no
yama hototogisu
ima zo naku naru

the early days of
summer must already have
   passed me unawares—
just now   deep in the mountains
the nightingale sang his song

Anonymous

"Ashihiki no" is a makurakotoba for "yama" (mountains). See 59.

141 • *Topic unknown.*

kesa kinaki	he came this morning
imada tabi naru	singing his traveling song—
hototogisu	mountain nightingale—
hanatachibana ni	my mandarin orange could
yado wa karanan	be his temporary home

Anonymous

142 • *Hearing a nightingale while crossing Mount Otowa.*

otowa yama	this morning he crossed
kesa koekureba	Otowa Mountain and came
hototogisu	to visit once more
kozue karuka ni	now he warbles distant notes—
ima zo naku naru	nightingale in the treetops

Ki no Tomonori

Otowa Mountain lies to the east of Kyōto on the road to Ōsaka Barrier.

143 • *Hearing the first song of the nightingale.*

hototogisu	oh sweet nightingale
hatsukoe kikeba	your first songs of the season
ajikinaku	unleashed unbidden
nushi sadamaranu	a love without an object a
koe seraru hata	love without the hope of joy

Sosei

144 • *Hearing a nightingale at Isonokami Temple in Nara.*

isonokami	the nightingale sings
furuki miyako no	in the ancient capitol
hototogisu	Isonokami
koe bakari koso	his tunes alone recall the
mukashi narikere	past glories of these ruins

Sosei

Sosei lived at Isonokami Temple near Nara. "Isonokami," which was the capital under Ankō 安康412?–453) and Ninken 仁賢 (r. 488?–498), is a makurakotoba for "furu" (Furu [place name]; old).

145 • *Topic unknown.*

natsu yama ni	trilling nightingale
naku hototogisu	filling the summer mountains
kokoro araba	with your sweet notes if
mono omou ware ni	you have a heart take pity your
koe na kikase so	sad songs deepen my sorrow

Anonymous

146 • *Topic unknown.*

hototogisu	warbling nightingale
naku koe kikeba	each year as I hear your song
wakarenishi	even that small town
furusato sae zo	where once I lived and loved grows
koishikarikeru	dear sadly I yearn again

Anonymous

147 • *Topic unknown.*

hototogisu	oh small nightingale
na ga naku sato no	from village to village you
amata areba	sing your way never
nao utomarenu	lighting long ever keeping
omou mono kara	distant from one who loves you

Anonymous

This poem is included in *The Tales of Ise*, 43, where it is sent with a picture of a hototogisu ("nightingale") by a man to a woman he is courting.

148 • *Topic unknown.*

omoiizuru	when I remember
tokiwa no yama no	him oh nightingale high
hototogisu	on Mount Tokiwa
karakurenai no	sing forth our passions till your
furiidete zo naku	throat too is dyed Chinese red

Anonymous

Tokiwa Mountain possibly was in Kyōto, Ukyō-ku. The place name Tokiwa also means "time" and links the first line (at the time I remember) to the next four. At the same time, the first four lines are a jo, linked to the fifth by the kakekotoba "furiidete" (infusing [dye in water]; straining the voice).

149 • *Topic unknown.*

koe wa shite
namida wa mienu
hototogisu
waga koromode no
hitsu o karanan

your cries are piercing
yet no tears do you shed
lonely nightingale
please let me share with you
my flowing flood-drenched sleeves

Anonymous

150 • *Topic unknown.*

ashihiki no
yama hototogisu
orihaete
tare ka masaru to
ne o nomi zo naku

lonely nightingale
come from the rugged mountains
ceaselessly crying—
now he and I compete in
raising our cries of yearning

Anonymous

"Ashihiki no" is a makurakotoba for "yama" (mountain).

151 • *Topic unknown.*

ima sara ni
yama e kaeru na
hototogisu
koe no kagiri wa
waga yado ni nake

oh sweet nightingale
do not return to your home
in faraway hills—
as long as you can sing   please
remain here in my garden

Anonymous

152 • *Topic unknown.*

ya yo ya mate
yama hototogisu
kotozuten
ware yo no naka ni
sumiwabinu to yo

oh wait now   I cry
mountain nightingale   I have
a message to send—
tell them I weary of this
world of sorrow where we live

Mikuni no Machi

The nightingale was believed to be a messenger and guide to the afterworld.

153 • *Poems 153–158 are from the poetry contest held at the residence of the Consort in the Kanpyō era.*

samidare ni	as I sit brooding
mono omoi oreba	in the midsummer rains a
hototogisu	nightingale's cry
yobukaku nakite	pierces the deepening night—
izuchi yuku ran	where can he be going

Ki no Tomonori

154 •

yo ya kuraki	is the night too dark
michi ya madoeru	or has he wandered astray
hototogisu	lonely nightingale
waga yado o shi mo	crying as he circles the
sugikate ni naku	somber sky above my house

Ki no Tomonori

155 •

yadori seshi	the mandarin orange
hana tachibana mo	in which you spent the night still
karenaku ni	blooms in unfaded
nado hototogisu	glory why then nightingale
koe taenu ran	do we no longer hear your song

Ōe no Chisato

156 •

natsu no yo no	on a summer night
fusu ka to sureba	the first thought of sleep is pierced
hototogisu	by the brief song of
naku hitokoe ni	the nightingale summoning
akuru shinonome	the first light the break of day

Ki no Tsurayuki

157 •

kururu ka to	we watch the darkness
mireba akenuru	gather then suddenly dawn

natsu no yo o	breaks these summer nights
akazu to ya naku	the nightingale's shrill cries
yama hototogisu	must come from disappointment

Mibu no Tadamine

158 •

natsu yama ni	has the one you love
koishiki hito ya	left for a summer retreat
kiriniken	in distant mountains
koe furitatete	oh nightingale is that why
naku hototogisu	you raise your sorrowful cries

Ki no Akimine

159 • *Topic unknown.*

kozo no natsu	is this the same one
nakifurushiteshi	the same mountain nightingale
hototogisu	who sang to us so
sore ka aranu ka	prodigally last summer—
koe no kawaranu	the lonely voice has not changed

Anonymous

160 • *Hearing the song of the nightingale.*

samidare no	through the broad skies dark
sora mo todoro ni	with midsummer rains your cries
hototogisu	echo all night long
nani o ushi to ka	oh nightingale what is this
yo tadanaku ran	secret sorrow you proclaim

Ki no Tsurayuki

161 • *Summoned to write a poem on "waiting for the nightingale," by the courtiers drinking in the Attendants' Office.*

hototogisu	mountain nightingale
koe mo kikoezu	tonight your voice is silent—
yamabiko wa	could we get the far

93

| hoka ni naku ne o | off Echo of the Mountains |
| kotae ya wa senu | to sound here close beside us |

Ōshikōchi no Mitsune

Courtiers of the Fourth and Fifth Ranks were permitted in the Courtiers' Hall of the private residence of the sovereign. Mitsune was only of about the Eighth Rank at this time.

162 • *Hearing a nightingale singing in the mountains.*

hototogisu	mountain nightingale
hito matsu yama ni	your cries sound as I await
naku nareba	my love on Mount Pine
ware uchitsuke ni	and suddenly my love has
koi masarikeri	grown heavy weighting my heart

Ki no Tsurayuki

"Matsu" is a kakekotoba meaning "Matsu Mountain" and "to wait." The location of "Waiting Mountain" is unknown.

163 • *Hearing the nightingale sing in a place I lived long ago.*

mukashihe ya	even now he yearns
ima mo koishiki	for days long gone the lonely
hototogisu	mountain nightingale—
furusato ni shi mo	once more he has come back to
nakite kitsuran	his native village crying

Mibu no Tadamine

164 • *Hearing the nightingale sing.*

hototogisu	mountain nightingale
ware to wa nashi ni	you too have passed through this world
unohana no	of misery short-lived
uki yo no naka ni	as wild sunflower blossoms—
nakiwataru ran	forgetting even who you are

Ōshikōchi no Mitsune

"Unohana no" (of the deutzia) is a makurakotoba linked to "uki" (sad) by the repetition of sound. The unohana (*Deutzia scabra*) is a deciduous, sunflower-like shrub.

165 • *Seeing dew on a lotus.*

hachisuba no	the lotus leaves rise
nigori ni shimanu	unsullied from the muddy
kokoro mote	waters why do these
nani ka wa tsuyu o	unblemished blooms deceive us
tama to azamuku	with dewdrops glowing like pearls

Henjō

The first two lines of this poem are based upon a passage from the Lotus Sutra, chap. 15, "Issuing of Bodhisattvas from the Earth"; the Dharma's not becoming sullied by the world is like the lotus rising from the muddy water.

166 • *Composed one dawn when the moon was lovely.*

natsu no yo wa	on summer nights when
mada yoi nagara	the dawn comes while it is still
akenuru o	evening in which
kumo no izuko ni	of those brightening clouds does
tsuki yadoru ran	the night's moon take refuge

Kiyowara no Fukayabu

167 • *Sent in their place to a neighbor who asked for some of the wild pinks in his garden.*

chiri o dani	I never thought to
sueji to zo omou	see them sullied by a speck
sakishi yori	of dust this bed of
imo to waga nuru	wild pinks has bloomed since my love
tokonatsu no hana	and I first lay together

Ōshikōchi no Mitsune

Tokonatsu (also called nadeshiko) are pinks or wild carnations, *Dianthus superbus.* "Toko" (bed) also serves as engo for "nuru" (to sleep).

168 • *The last day of summer.*

natsu to aki to	tonight as summer
yukikau sora no	and autumn cross paths on their
kayoiji wa	journey through the sky

| katae suzushiki | half the road is cooled by the |
| kaze ya fuku ran | fresh rising breezes of fall |

Ōshikōchi no Mitsune

The last day of the lunar Sixth Month was the last day of summer.

BOOK IV

Autumn (1)

169 • *Composed on the first day of autumn.*

aki kinu to	to my eyes it is
me ni wa sayaka ni	not clear that autumn has come
mienedomo	but the chill whisper
kaze no oto ni zo	of the invisible wind
odorokarenuru	startles me to awareness

Fujiwara no Toshiyuki

170 • *Composed as he accompanied some of the court gentlemen on an excursion to the Kamo River on the first day of autumn.*

kawa kaze no	how cool the breeze
suzushiku mo aru ka	from the river I feel the
uchiyosuru	refreshing chill
nami to tomo ni ya	of near-approaching autumn
aki wa tatsu ran	roll in with each rising wave

Ki no Tsurayuki

The Kamo River flowed just east of the capital. "Tatsu" (to rise; to begin) serves to link the waves and autumn, which began with the lunar Seventh Month.

171 • *Topic unknown.*

waga seko ga	eagerly I glimpse
koromo no suso o	the splendid lining of my
fukikaeshi	love's hem blown back by
uramezurashiki	the first cool delicious breeze
aki no hatsukaze	to tell us autumn has come

Anonymous

97

The first three lines (turning back the hem of the robe of my lover) are a jo, linked by the kakekotoba "ura" (reverse)/"uramezurashiki" (enticing), as well as by the sense of the poem, to the main statement. This meaningful metaphorical link is called ushin. Poem 25 is an allusive variation (honkadori) on this.

172 • *Topic unknown.*

kinō koso	only yesterday
sanae torishika	we filled the fields with young plants
itsu no ma ni	unaware of time
inaba soyogite	and yet it has passed rice leaves
akikaze no fuku	now rustle in the autumn wind

Anonymous

173 • *Topic unknown.*

aki kaze no	since autumn's first breath
fukinishi hi yori	there has not been a single
hisakata no	day that I have not
ama no kawara ni	stood waiting for you on the
tatanu hi wa nashi	broad banks of heaven's river

Anonymous

"Hisakata no" (broad[?]) is a makurakotoba for "ama" (sky). This poem begins the sequence of Tanabata poems celebrating the yearly meeting, on the seventh day of the Seventh Month, of the celestial lovers, the herdsman (Altair) and the weaver maid (Vega), who are separated by the river of heaven, the Milky Way. The poems are arranged to form a narrative. This poem is linked to 174 by the repetition of two lines.

174 • *Topic unknown.*

hisakata no	if my love should come
ama no kawara no	to me from across the broad
watashimori	waters of heaven's
kimi watarinaba	river oh ferryman please
kaji kakushite yo	hide your oars on his return

Anonymous

175 • *Topic unknown.*

ama no kawa	the weaver maiden
momiji o hashi ni	longs for autumn's coming is

watasebaya	it because a bridge
tanabata tsu me no	of many-colored leaves will
aki o shi mo matsu	span the river of heaven

Anonymous

176 • *Topic unknown.*

koikoite	finally it is
au yo wa koyoi	our long-awaited meeting night—
ama no kawa	may the autumn mists
kiri tachiwatari	spread across the river of
akezu mo aranan	heaven that dawn may never come

Anonymous

177 • *Composed in someone's stead on the seventh of the Seventh Month during the Kanpyō era, when the Mikado commanded the gentlemen of the court to present poems.*

ama no kawa	frantically I
asase shiranami	wandered the shallow shoals of
tadoritsutsu	the great river of
watarihateneba	heaven still lost amidst the
ake zo shinikeru	white waves when dawn lit the sky

Ki no Tomonori

Uda tennō was the Mikado during the Kanpyō era, 889–898. "Shiranami" is a kakekotoba meaning "white waves" and "not knowing."

178 • *From the poetry contest held by the Consort in the same era.*

chigiriken	our one promised night
kokoro zo tsuraki	of the year will it come to
tanabata no	pass Tanabata
toshi ni hitotabi	oh too cruel is the young
au wa au ka wa	heart that would deny me this

Fujiwara no Okikaze

179 • *Composed on the night of the seventh.*

toshi goto ni	although it is true
au to wa suredo	they meet each year for the night

tanabata no   of Tanabata
neru yo no kazu zo   how few the nights they have shared
sukunakarikeru   meetings of embracing arms

Ōshikōchi no Mitsune

This poem was composed for the same contest.

1 8 0 • *Composed on the night of the seventh.*

tanabata ni   can I sustain my
kashitsuru ito no   love a long-spun year   a time
   uchihaete   that stretches far as
toshi no o nagaku   the threads offered up for love's
koi ya wataran   success on Tanabata

Ōshikōchi no Mitsune

The opening lines are a jo linked to the main statement by "uchihaete" (stretching out; lengthening), which applies to both the year between meetings and the thread offered up by young women on the occasion of this festival in hopes of becoming skillful at needle arts. "Toshi no o" (the cord of the year) is an engo for "ito" (thread).

1 8 1 • *Topic unknown.*

koyoi kon   I shall not meet the
hito ni wa awaji   one who will come tonight   for
   tanabata no   ever after   I
hisashiki hodo ni   will wait for the widely spaced
machi mo koso sure   meetings of Tanabata

Sosei

1 8 2 • *Composed at dawn on the night of the seventh.*

ima wa to te   the time to depart
wakaruru toki wa   has come   I have yet to cross
   ama no kawa   the great river of
wataranu saki ni   heaven   but already my
sode zo hichinuru   sleeves are drenched and will not dry

Minamoto no Muneyuki

183 • *Composed on the eighth.*

kyō yori wa	from today I must
ima kon toshi no	await so impatiently
kinō o zo	so anxiously the
itsu shika to nomi	coming year's celebration
machiwatarubeki	of yesterday's Tanabata

Mibu no Tadamine

This is a kinuginu ("next morning") poem, sent to a lover after a tryst.

184 • *Topic unknown.*

ko no ma yori	when I see the moon's
morikuru tsuki no	light seep down through now-barren
kage mireba	trees I realize
kokorozukushi no	how truly autumn has come
aki wa kinikeri	to vanquish my strength of heart

Anonymous

This poem is included in the *Komachi shū*, the *Komachi Collection*.

185 • *Topic unknown.*

ōkata no	when autumn has come
aki kuru kara ni	to everyone and to
waga mi koso	everything then
kanashiki mono to	I understand that it is
omoishirinure	my own self which is mournful

Anonymous

According to *Kudai waka*, by Ōe no Chisato, this is a translation of a verse by P'o Chü-i.

186 • *Topic unknown.*

waga tame ni	although autumn does
kuru aki ni shimo	not come for my sake alone—
aranaku ni	I am saddened
mushi no ne kikeba	first when I hear the lonely
mazu zo kanashiki	piping of the insects' calls

Anonymous

187 • *Topic unknown.*

monogoto ni
aki zo kanashiki
  momijitsutsu
utsuroiyuku o
kagiri to omoeba

autumn is mournful
in all its aspects   even
  the coloring and
fading of the leaves makes me
understand this is the end

Anonymous

188 • *Topic unknown.*

  hitori neru
toko wa kusaba ni
  aranedomo
aki kuru yoi wa
tsuyukekarikeri

although this bed on
which I sleep alone tonight
  is not made of grass
the mournful autumn evening
covers it with chilly dew

Anonymous

189 • *From the poetry contest held at the residence of Prince Koresada.*

  itsu wa to wa
toki wa wakanedo
  aki no yo zo
mono omou koto no
kagiri narikeru

though any season
may bring a spell of sadness
  the autumn night weights
us with the most difficult
burden of melancholy

Anonymous

Prince Koresada was the second son of Kōkō tennō. Ninety poems survive from this contest, which is also known as "The Poetry Contest of the Second Prince of the Ninna Era." It was held in 893, the same year as the "Kanpyō no ontoki kisai no utaawase," "The Poetry Contest Held at the Residence of the Consort in the Kanpyō Era."

190 • *Composed at the Kannarinotsubo when a number of courtiers were gathered to compose poems regretting the passage of the autumn night.*

  kaku bakari
oshi to omou yo o
  itazura ni

how deplorable
those who would simply pass the
  night in sleep   idly

nete akasuran   greeting the dawn   when it is
hito sae zo uki   this very night that I love

Ōshikōchi no Mitsune

The Kannarinotsubo (or Shihōsha), one of the Imperial Palace buildings, was situated northwest of the Residential Compound.

191 • *Topic unknown.*

  shiragumo ni   flying wing in wing
hane uchikawashi   across the white clouds of the
  tobu kari no   night sky   the wild geese
kazu sae miyuru   go   their very number
aki no yo no tsuki   vivid beneath the autumn moon

Anonymous

Poems 191 and 192 describe the wild geese flying across the broad harvest moon of the Eighth Month.

192 • *Topic unknown.*

  sayonaka to   as night deepens   it
yo wa fukenurashi   seems midnight must be near   for
  kari no ne no   only the cries of the
kikoyuru sora ni   wild geese are heard   and the moon
tsuki wataru miyu   has climbed high in the dark sky

Anonymous

This poem is also found in the *Man'yōshū* (701), although the Japanese Preface states that no poems from the *Man'yōshū* have been included.

193 • *Composed at the poetry contest at the residence of Prince Koresada.*

  tsuki mireba   when I gaze upon
chiji ni mono koso   that brilliant moon a thousand
  kanashikere   things burden me with
waga mi hitotsu no   sadness   though surely autumn
aki ni wa aranedo   does not come for me alone

Ōe no Chisato

194 • *Composed at the same contest.*

hisakata no	does the broad autumn
tsuki no katsura mo	moon shine so much more brightly
aki wa nao	because it wants to
momiji surebaya	cover the moon laurel too
terimasaruran	in radiant fall leaves

Mibu no Tadamine

"Hisakata no" (broad) is a makurakotoba for "tsuki" (moon). According to Chinese and Japanese legend, a katsura tree (*Cercidiphyllum japonicum*) can be seen on the moon's surface.

195 • *The moon.*

aki no yo no	is it because of
tsuki no hikari shi	the brilliance of the glowing
akakereba	autumn moon that one
kurabu no yama mo	can cross even the awesome
koenuberanari	Dark Mountain this magic night

Ariwara no Motokata

For Mount Kurabu (Dark Mountain), see 39.

196 • *Composed on a night when he had visited someone's home and heard the cry of the kirigirisu.*

kirigirisu	kirigirisu—
itaku na naki so	do not grieve so chirping
aki no yo no	crickets my prolonged
nagaki omoi wa	sorrows this long autumn night
ware zo masareru	are greater even than yours

Fujiwara no Tadafusa

The kirigirisu is a type of cicada (*Gampsocleis buergeri*). "Nagaki" (long) links "aki no yo" (autumn night) and "omoi" (longings) by zeugma.

197 • *From the poetry contest held at the residence of Prince Koresada.*

aki no yo no	on this long autumn
akuru mo shirazu	night oh crying insects not

naku mushi wa
wagagoto mono ya
kanashikaruran

even noticing
the gathering light of dawn—
can you be as sad as I

Fujiwara no Toshiyuki

198 • *Topic unknown.*

aki hagi mo
irozukinureba
　kirigirisu
waga nenu goto ya
yoru wa kanashiki

is it the autumn-
tinged bush clover whose leaves will
　soon wither　that keeps
you too　chirping cricket
from sleep　the night is so sad

Anonymous

Hagi, Japanese bush clover, or *Lespedeza bicolor*, is a plant with small purple or white flowers that bloom in autumn. For kirigirisu, see 196.

199 • *Topic unknown.*

aki no yo wa
tsuyu koso koto ni
　samukarashi
kusamura goto ni
mushi no wabureba

on autumn nights the
dew seems especially cold—
　for in each brown tuft
of grass dying insects are
murmuring their sad complaints

Anonymous

200 • *Topic unknown.*

kimi shinobu
kusa ni yatsururu
　furusato wa
matsumushi no ne zo
kanashikarikeru

in this decaying
house where I grow pale and thin
　under the grasses
of longing　how sadly sounds
the cry of the pine cricket

Anonymous

"Shinobu" is a kakekotoba meaning both "to remember" and "shinobu grass" or "hare's-foot fern" (*Polypodium lineare*). "Matsu" means "to wait" and is part of the name of the "matsumushi" (*Calytoryphus marmoratus*), a type of cicada.

201 • *Topic unknown.*

aki no no ni
michi mo madoinu
  matsu mushi no
koe suru kata ni
yado ya karamashi

        I have lost my way
        amid the fields of autumn—
           could I find shelter
        over there where the lonely
        waiting pine cricket calls out

Anonymous

202 • *Topic unknown.*

aki no no ni
hito matsu mushi no
  koesunari
ware ka to yukite
iza toburawan

        in the autumn fields
        I listen to the crying
           of the pine cricket
        as it calls across the plains—
        shall I see if it summons me

Anonymous

203 • *Topic unknown.*

momijiba no
chirite tsumoreru
  waga yado ni
tare o matsu mushi
kokora nakuran

        out in my garden
        where the autumn leaves pile high—
           I wonder for whom
        the lonely pining cricket
        waits   calling so piercingly

Anonymous

204 • *Topic unknown.*

higurashi no
nakitsuru nae ni
  hi wa kurenu
to omoeba yama no
kage ni zo arikeru

        I thought the sun set
        as the twilight cricket shrilled
           but I was quite wrong
        for in reality   it
        was only the mountain's shade

Anonymous

Higurashi is yet another variety of cicada (*Tanna japonensis*), one that cries at dusk and dawn in the autumn. The word also means "sun set."

205 • *Topic unknown.*

higurashi no	in the evening in
naku yamazato no	the mountain village where the
yuugure wa	twilight cricket cries
kaze yori hoka ni	there comes not one visitor
tou hito mo nashi	save the chilly autumn wind

Anonymous

206 • *The first geese.*

matsu hito ni	they are not the one
aranu mono kara	I await yet delightful
hatsu kari no	are the calls of the
kesa naku koe no	first wild geese whose cries I hear
mezurashiki kana	this early autumn morning

Ariwara no Motokata

207 • *From the poetry contest held at the residence of Prince Koresada.*

aki kaze ni	I hear the cries of
hatsu kari ga ne zo	the first wild geese of the year
kikoyu naru	carried on the autumn
taga tamazusa o	wind whose messages are these
kakete kitsuran	that the geese carry to me

Ki no Tomonori

"Tamazusa" originally was a makurakotoba for "tsukai" (messenger), but had come to mean "message," "letter."

208 • *Topic unknown.*

waga kado ni	the wild geese have come
inaōsedori no	back with the first autumn winds—
naku nae ni	their voices blend with
kesa fuku kaze ni	the chirping of the field birds
kari wa kinikeri	at my gate this fall morning

Anonymous

It is unclear what kind of bird the inaōsedori is; the *Kokindenjū* 古今伝集 lists it (along with yobukodori and momochidori) as one of the three *Kokinshū* birds whose identity was kept secret.

209 • *Topic unknown.*

ito haya mo	how early are the
nakinuru kari ka	cries of the wild geese this fall—
shiratsuyu no	the multicolored
irodoru kigi mo	foliage tinted by white
momiji aenakuni	dew cannot yet compete

Anonymous

210 • *Topic unknown.*

harugasumi	the voices of the
kasumite inishi	wild geese that were swallowed up
kari ga ne wa	by the mists of spring
ima zo naku naru	have returned to penetrate
aki kiri no ue ni	the autumn haze and sound again

Anonymous

211 • *Topic unknown.*

yo o samumi	the night is chilly
koromo kari ga ne	and I borrow a robe for warmth
naku nae ni	as the wild geese call
hagi no shitaba mo	even the lower boughs of
utsuroinikeri	the bush clover are autumn tinged

Anonymous

Some say this poem was composed by Kakinomoto no Hitomaro.

"Kari," meaning both "borrowing" and "geese," links the jo (the night is cold; borrowing a robe) to the main statement.

212 • *From the poetry contest held at the residence of the Consort in the Kanpyō era.*

aki kaze ni	in the autumn wind
koe o ho ni agete	with the creaking of wooden
kuru fune wa	oars the ships near shore—
ama no to wataru	it is the wild geese who cry
kari ni zo arikeru	as they cross the night's heavens

Fujiwara no Sugane

The kakekotoba "ho" (sail; aloud) links the images of honking geese flying across the sky and ships with creaking oars crossing the ocean. This may be inspired by a verse by P'o Chü-i, "Autumn geese have come with the sound of oars."

2 1 3 • *Composed on hearing the cries of the wild geese.*

uki koto o	I continue to
omoitsuranete	lament my life's miseries
karigane no	night after fall night
naki koso watare	the wild geese cry out as they
aki no yona yona	fly across celestial plains

Ōshikōchi no Mitsune

"Tsuranete" (continuing) links the series of sad thoughts and the line (tsura) of geese crossing the sky.

2 1 4 • *From the poetry contest held at the residence of Prince Koresada.*

yamazato wa	here in this mountain
aki koso koto ni	village autumn brings special
wabishikere	misery all through
shika no naku ne ni	the night the sound of the
me o samashitsutsu	belling deer awakens me

Mibu no Tadamine

The belling of the deer for their mates reminds man of his own longings and of the sorrows of autumn, the season of death and partings.

2 1 5 • *From the same contest.*

okuyama ni	treading through the
momiji fumiwake	autumn leaves in the deepest
naku shika no	mountains I hear the
koe kiku toki zo	belling of the lonely deer—
aki wa kanashiki	then it is that autumn is sad

Anonymous

This poem, attributed to Sarumaru Dayū (early Heian?), is included in *Hyakunin isshū*.

216 • *Topic unknown.*

aki hagi ni	gazing disconsolate
urabire oreba	at autumn-hued bush clover—
ashihiki no	the sad cry of the
yama shita to yomi	lonely buck echoes at the
shika no nakuran	foot of the endless mountains

Anonymous

Hagi, which bloom during the mating season of the deer, already had become the symbol of the bride the buck seeks by the time of the *Man'yōshū*. For hagi, see 198. This begins a sequence of eight poems using this image.

217 • *Topic unknown.*

aki hagi o	the belling deer that
shigarami fusete	tramples autumn bush clover
naku shika no	is invisible
me ni wa miezute	to my searching eyes but so
oto no sayakesa	vivid to my attentive ears

Anonymous

218 • *From the poetry contest held at the residence of Prince Koresada.*

aki hagi no	autumn bush clover
hana sakinikeri	has put forth its white blossoms—
takasago no	now will the buck high
onoe no shika wa	on the peak of Takasago
ima ya nakuran	Mountain cry out for his mate

Fujiwara no Toshiyuki

Takasago Peak is near Takasago City in Hyōgo Prefecture.

219 • *Composed in the fields in autumn when he happened to meet a woman he had loved.*

aki hagi no	when I see the blooms
furue ni sakeru	of the autumn bush clover
hana mireba	on last year's boughs
moto no kokoro wa	I feel that it remembers—
wasurezarikeri	it is faithful to the past

Ōshikōchi no Mitsune

220 • *Topic unknown.*

aki hagi no	the lower leaves of
shitaba irozuku	the autumn bush clover are
ima yori ya	changing their colors—
hitori aru hito no	now will they begin those long
inekate ni suru	lonely nights of sleeplessness

Anonymous

221 • *Topic unknown.*

naki wataru	are these tears shed by
kari no namida ya	the wild geese who rend the sky
ochitsuran	with cries these dew drops
mono omou yado no	fallen on the bush clover
hagi no ue no tsuyu	by my melancholy house

Anonymous

222 • *Topic unknown.*

hagi no tsuyu	bush clover's dew drops
tama ni nukamu to	disappeared as I tried to
toreba kenu	string them as jewels—
yoshi min hito wa	those who would admire them—
eda nagara miyo	do so while they're on the branch

Anonymous

Some people say this poem was composed by the Nara Mikado.

The Nara Mikado was Heizei.

223 • *Topic unknown.*

orite miba	if I tried to pluck
ochi zo shinubeki	the branches on which they rest
akihagi no	they would fall to earth—
eda mo tawawa ni	the boughs of bush clover bend
okeru shiratsuyu	under this load of dew drops

Anonymous

224 • *Topic unknown.*

   hagi ga hana
chiruran ono no
  tsuyu shimo ni
nurete o yukan
sayo wa fuku tomo

   through the fields where the
white bush clover blossoms fall
  dampened by
frost and dew   I will travel
though the dark night may grow late

Anonymous

225 • *From the poetry contest held at the residence of Prince Koresada.*

   aki no no ni
oku shiratsuyu wa
  tama nare ya
tsuranuki kakuru
kumo no itosuji

   are they all jewels—
those droplets of white dew   beads
  that have fallen on
the autumn fields   to be strung
on the threads of spider webs

Funya no Asayasu

226 • *Topic unknown.*

   na ni medete
oreru bakari zo
  ominaeshi
ware ochiniki to
hito ni kataru na

   I plucked you only
because your name entranced me
  oh maiden flower
please do not tell all the world
that I have broken my vows

Henjō

Waka poets often play on the meaning of the characters with which "ominaeshi" (*Patrinia scabiosaefolia*) is written: "maiden flower." Henjō is alluding to the vow of chastity made when he took Buddhist orders.

227 • *On seeing maiden flowers on Otoko Mountain as he traveled to Nara to Archbishop Henjō's home.*

   ominaeshi
ushi to mitsutsu zo
  yukisuguru
otoko yama ni shi
tateri to omoeba

   I passed by the sweet
maiden flowers   wretchedly
  I but looked at them
thinking that they grow in gay
array on slopes of Mount Man

Furu no Imamichi

Henjō was living at Isonokami Temple near Nara. Otoko Mountain lay near the capital, east of the Yodo River, on the way to Yamato.

228 • *From the poetry contest held at the residence of Prince Koresada.*

aki no no ni	let's sleep tonight in
yadori wa subeshi	fields of autumn's abundance—
ominaeshi	oh maiden flowers
na o mutsumashimi	your name holds us here though we've
tabi naranaku ni	not set out on a journey

Fujiwara no Toshiyuki

229 • *Topic unknown.*

ominaeshi	if we sleep tonight
ōkaru nobe ni	here in the meadow filled with
yadoriseba	sweet maiden flowers
ayanaku ata no	gossips will call us fickle
na o ya tachinan	inconstant and all for nought

Ono no Yoshiki

230 • *Poems 230 to 236 were presented at the Maiden Flower Contest at the Suzakuin.*

ominaeshi	oh maiden flowers
akino no kaze ni	you who so delicately
uchinabiki	bend and sway before
kokoro hitotsu o	the autumn wind to whom have
tare ni yosuran	you surrendered your light hearts

Fujiwara no Tokihira

The Suzakuin was the residence of former tennō Uda at the time the *Kokinshū* was compiled. This flower competition (Suzakuin no ominaeshi awase), held in the autumn of 898, is also called the "Teijinoin Maiden Flower Contest" (Teijinoin ominaeshi awase), after an alternate name for the palace.

231 •

aki narade	we never see you
au koto kataki	but in autumn sweet maiden

ominaeshi   flowers   yet it is
ama no kawara ni   not along the banks of that
oinu mono yue   river of heaven that you grow

Fujiwara no Sadakata

232 •

ta ga aki ni   maiden flowers   why
aranu mono yue   fade so openly before
   ominaeshi   your time   it's not that
nazo iro ni idete   autumn comes to you alone
madaki utsurou   or that we have tired of you

Ki no Tsurayuki

Aki means both "autumn" and "sated."

233 •

tsuma kouru   that buck crying out
shika zo naku naru   for his love mate   does he not
   ominaeshi   recognize you   oh
ono ga sumu no no   maiden flower   swaying here
hana to shirazu ya   in the meadow where he lives

Ōshikōchi no Mitsune

234 •

ominaeshi   oh maiden flowers
fukisugite kuru   the autumn wind which blows through
   aki kaze wa   rustling fields carries
me ni wa mienedo   your tantalizing fragrance
ka koso shirukere   though it is invisible

Ōshikōchi no Mitsune

235 •

hito no miru   does it pain you to
koto ya kurushiki   be on display   oh maiden

ominaeshi
akigiri ni nomi
tachikakururan

flowers   is that why
you hide your charms in meadows
enveloped in autumn mists

Mibu no Tadamine

"Tachi" is used both as an intensifying prefix and as an engo for "akigiri" (autumn mists), meaning "rising."

236 •

hitori nomi
nagamuru yori wa
   ominaeshi
waga sumu yado ni
uete mimashi o

rather than suffer
solitary reveries
   oh maiden flowers—
how I wish I could transplant
you to the place where I live

Mibu no Tadamine

237 • *Seeing maiden flowers cultivated in the garden of a house he visited.*

ominaeshi
ushirometaku mo
   miyuru kana
aretaru yado ni
hitori tatereba

oh maiden flower
how pitiful you seem to
   me   standing there
all alone and abandoned at
that dilapidated house

Prince Kanemi

238 • *Composed in the Kanpyō era on the occasion of the return of a group of courtiers from the Chamberlain's Office from flower-viewing in Saga Meadow.*

hana ni akade
nani kaeruran
   ominaeshi
ōkaru nobe ni
nenamashi mono o

oh maiden flowers
why should we return to our
   home   when we would still
admire you   oh that we could
sleep in your thick bed of bloom

Taira no Sadafun

These were Uda's courtiers from the Kurōdo-dokoro. Saga is now part of Ukyō-ku, Kyōto.

239 • *A poem from the poetry contest held at the residence of Prince Koresada.*

nanihito ka	who was it who wore
kite nugikakeshi	them here and then hung them up—
fujibakama	these purple trousers
kuru aki goto ni	each autumn when I come to
nobe o niowasu	these fields I smell their fragrance

Fujiwara no Toshiyuki

Fujibakama (*Eupatorium strechadosmum*, or Chinese agrimony) is a rather undistinguished-looking but pleasant-smelling wild flower whose name means "purple trousers."

240 • *Composed on "purple trousers" and sent to a friend.*

yadoriseshi	a remembrance
hito no katami ka	of someone who once slept here?
fujibakama	these purple trousers
wasuraregataki	perfumed with a lasting and
ka ni nioitsutsu	unforgettable fragrance

Ki no Tsurayuki

241 • *"Purple trousers."*

nushi shiranu	a sweet perfume
ka koso nioere	blended by an unknown hand blows
aki no no ni	across autumn fields—
ta ga nugikakeshi	who removed and hung them here—
fujibakama zo mo	purple trousers of the meadows

Sosei

242 • *Topic unknown.*

ima yori wa	never again will
uete dani miji	I plant it in my garden—
hanasusuki	flowering plume grass—
ho ni izuru aki wa	for autumn when it opens
wabishikarikeri	is unbearably lonesome

Taira no Sadafun

Susuki (*Miscanthus sinensis*) is a type of pampas grass. "Ho ni izuru" means "to become obvious" and "to produce ears of grain."

243 • *From the poetry contest held at the residence of the Consort in the Kanpyō era.*

aki no no no	are they the flowing
kusa no tamoto ka	sleeves of the autumn grasses
hanasusuki	in the ripening fields
ho ni idete maneku	the waving tassels appear
sode to miyuran	to be beckoning to us now

Ariwara no Muneyana

244 • *From the same poetry contest.*

ware nomi ya	am I alone in
aware to omowan	being moved in the light of
kirigirisu	the setting sun
naku yūkage no	kirigirisu cry as
yamato nadeshiko	fragile carnations nod

Sosei

For kirigirisu, see 196. The nadeshiko (*Dianthus superbus*) is a pink, or wild, carnation. The term "Yamato nadeshiko" often is used for Japanese women.

245 • *Topic unknown.*

midori naru	In spring when all the
hitotsu kusa to zo	grasses wore green I thought them
haru wa mishi	all the same autumn
aki wa iroiro no	is the season when nature
hana ni zo arikeru	clothes herself in many hues

Anonymous

The parallels and antitheses—one/various, grasses/flowers, spring/autumn—set up here are unusual in waka and give the verse a Chinese flavor.

246 • *Topic unknown.*

momo kusa no	in the autumn fields
hana no himo toku	where myriad blooms loosen
aki no no ni	the sashes of their buds

omoitawaren   how I would disport myself—
hito na togame so   onlookers   please cast no blame

Anonymous

"Himo toku" means both "to blossom" and "to untie a sash."

247 • *Topic unknown.*

   tsukigusa ni   I will print my robe
koromo wa suran   with fleeting moongrass flowers—
   asa tsuyu ni   what care I if it
nurete no nochi wa   quickly fades   when dampened by
utsuroinu tomo   the heavy dew of morning

Anonymous

Tsukigusa (*Commelina communis*) is a perennial grass used as a dyestuff. This poem is also included in the *Man'yōshū*, 351.

248 • *When the Ninna Mikado was still a prince, he stayed overnight at the home of Henjō's mother on his way to admire the Furu Waterfall and the garden was designed to resemble an autumn field. Henjō recited this poem as they conversed.*

   sato wa arete   perhaps because this
hito wa furinishi   village is desolate
   yado nare ya   its inhabitant
niwa mo magaki mo   grown old   both garden and fence
aki no no ra naru   have become autumnal fields

Henjō

The Ninna Mikado was Kōkō. The Furu Falls are in Tenri City, Nara Prefecture.

BOOK V

Autumn (2)

249 • *From the poetry contest held at the residence of Prince Koresada.*

fuku kara ni
aki no kusaki no
  shiorureba
mube yama kaze o
arashi to iu ran

as soon as the gales
begin to rage   autumn trees
and grass bend before
them   no wonder they call this
wind from the mountains Tempest

Funya no Yasuhide

The word "storm" (arashi) is written with the characters "wind" and "mountain."

250 • *From the same contest.*

kusa mo ki mo
iro kawaredomo
  watatsuumi no
nami no hana ni zo
aki nakarikeru

although the grasses
and trees have all been transformed
the white-capped blooms of
the sea-crossing waves show no
sign of impending autumn

Funya no Yashuide

251 • *Composed for an autumn poetry contest.*

momijisenu
tokiwa no yama wa
  fuku kaze no
oto ni ya aki o
kikiwataruran

no autumn colors
appear on Mount Tokiwa
  its green is constant—
is it the sound of the wind
that carries fall to my ears

Ki no Yoshimochi

For Mount Tokiwa, see 148. The name suggests "always."

252 • *Topic unknown.*

kiri tachite
kari zo nakunaru
  kataoka no
ashita no hara wa
momijishinuran

autumn haze rises
while the wild geese cry over
    Ashita Meadow
in Kataoka   surely
the leaves have turned to scarlet

Anonymous

Kataoka is in Nara Prefecture, Katsuragi District. The location of Ashita Meadow is
unknown.

253 • *Topic unknown.*

kannazuki
shigure mo imada
  furanaku ni
kanete utsurou
kannabi no mori

the early winter
rains of the godless tenth month
    have yet to fall   but
already the leaves turn bright
in the consecrated grove

Anonymous

The name of the Tenth Month (kannazuki) means "godless month." Kannabi Grove
may be a proper name; there is a Kannabi in Iruka, Ikoma District, Nara Prefecture.

254 • *Topic unknown.*

chihayaburu
kannabi yama no
  momijiba ni
omoi wa kakeji
utsurou mono o

oh awesome sacred
mountain   I will not lose my
    heart to your brightly
colored leaves   for the loveliest
things are doomed to fade and fall

Anonymous

"Chihayaburu" (awesome, mighty[?]) is a makurakotoba for "kami" (gods); the
first syllable of "kannabi" is a contraction of this word.

255 • *Composed in the Jōgan era when some of the upper court nobles were
composing poems about the branches on the west side of the plum tree in front of the
Ryōkiden beginning to change color.*

onaji e o
wakite ko no ha no

though these branches
spring from a single trunk   bright

utsurou wa	hues adorn only
nishi koso aki no	one side surely it is true
hajime narikere	that autumn rises in the west

Fujiwara no Kachion

Jōgan (859–877) was the reign period of Seiwa tennō. The Ryōkiden was one of the buildings of the Imperial Palace. Autumn is associated with west in the yin-yang system of correspondences.

256 • *On seeing the autumn leaves on Otowa Mountain on the way to Ishiyama Temple.*

aki kaze no	since that day when we
fukinishi hi yori	first heard this soughing of the
otowa yama	wind on Otowa
mine no kozue mo	Mountain even the treetops
irozukinikeri	on the peak have changed color

Ki no Tsurayuki

For Otowa Mountain, see 142. The first two syllables of Otowa also mean "sound." Ishiyama Temple is located in Ishiyama, Ōtsu City, Shiga Prefecture.

257 • *From the poetry contest held at the residence of Prince Koresada.*

shiratsuyu no	the color of dew
iro wa hitotsu o	is but an unblemished white—
ika ni shite	how is it that this
aki no ko no ha o	one hue can dye the leaves of
chiji ni somuran	autumn trees a thousand shades

Fujiwara no Toshiyuki

258 • *From the same contest.*

aki no yo no	is this merely the
tsuyu oba tsuyu to	dew of an autumn night or
okinagara	have the red tears of
kari no namida ya	the wild geese dyed the fields with
nobe o somuran	the myriad hues of fall

Mibu no Tadamine

259 • *Topic unknown.*

aki no tsuyu	it must be because
iroiro koto ni	the autumn dew settles in
okeba koso	various colors—
yama no ko no ha no	the leaves of trees on distant
chigusa narurame	mountains show a thousand hues

Anonymous

260 • *Composed near Moru Mountain.*

shiratsuyu mo	on Moru Mountain
shigure mo itaku	the white drops of dew and the
moru yama wa	cold rains have seeped through
shitaba nokorazu	to the leaves of the lowest
irozukinikeri	boughs and dyed them all fall hues

Ki no Tsurayuki

Moru Mountain is in Yasu District, Shiga Prefecture. "Moru" means "to seep through."

261 • *Composed as an autumn poem.*

ame furedo	neither rain nor dew
tsuyu mo moraji o	could pass through Kasatori
kasatori no	Mountain's sheltering
yama wa ikade ka	parasol how can those leaves
momiji someken	be dyed in bright autumn hues

Ariwara no Motokata

"Tsuyu mo" means "a little bit"; it is also an engo, meaning "the dew also," for "ame" (rain) and Kasatori (taking an umbrella) Mountain. Kasatori Mountain is near Uji City in Kyōto.

262 • *Composed on seeing autumn leaves inside the fence of a shrine as he passed by.*

chihayaburu	even the arrowroot
kami no igaki ni	climbing the sacred fences
hau kuzu mo	of the awesome gods

aki ni wa aezu   cannot hold back autumn   it
utsuroinikeri   too has donned its bright array

Ki no Tsurayuki

Kuzu is a vine, arrowroot or *Pueraria thunbergiana*. "Chihayaburu" is a makura-kotoba for "kami" (gods).

263 • *From the poetry contest held at the residence of Prince Koresada.*

ame fureba   the rain-glossed leaves of
kasatori yama no   Mount Kasatori are so
  momijiba wa   brilliant that their hues
yukikau hito no   reflect even from the sleeves
sode sae zo teru   of all the passersby

Mibu no Tadamine

264 • *From the poetry contest held at the residence of the Consort in the Kanpyō era.*

chiranedomo   they have not yet
kanete zo oshiki   begun to fall   but already
  momijiba wa   I regret their passing
ima wa kagiri no   when I see the colors of
iro to mitsureba   the autumn leaves at their peak

Anonymous

265 • *Composed when he went to Yamato Province and saw the mist rising on Saho Mountain.*

ta ga tame no   for whose pleasure is
nishiki nareba ka   this freshly woven pattern
  akigiri no   of brocade hidden—
saho no yamabe o   autumn mists slowly rise to
tachikakusuran   cover Mount Saho's bright slopes

Ki no Tomonori

Mount Saho is near Saho Village in Nara Prefecture. It appears in poems 266 and 267 also.

266 • *From the poetry contest held at the residence of Prince Koresada.*

akigiri wa
kesa wa na tachi so
  saho yama no
hahaso no momiji
yoso nite mo min

    oh mists of autumn
please   just this one morning   let
    me see from afar
the brilliant autumn-tinged leaves
of the oaks on Mount Saho

Anonymous

267 • *Composed as an autumn poem.*

saho yama no
hahaso no iro wa
  usukeredo
aki wa fukaku mo
narinikerukana

    although the colors
of the oaks on Mount Saho
    are still shallow and
faint   already we have reached
the mournful depths of autumn

Sakanoue no Korenori

268 • *A poem attached to chrysanthemum plants he sent for someone's garden.*

ueshi ueba
aki naki toki ya
  sakazaran
hana koso chirame
ne sae kareme ya

    if it has been well
planted   it will fail to bloom
    only if autumn
should not come   though the petals
scatter   the roots will not die

Ariwara no Narihira

This poem is included in *The Tales of Ise*, 51, and in *The Tales of Yamato*, 163. This is the first of thirteen poems on the chrysanthemums.

269 • *Composed in the Kanpyō era, when he was commanded to write a poem on the chrysanthemums.*

hisakata no
kumo no ue nite
  miru kiku wa
amatsu hoshi to zo
ayamatarekeru

    the chrysanthemums
seen in the clouds far above
    the common people
seemed to be clusters of
stars in the distant heavens

Fujiwara no Toshiyuki

It is said this poem was composed and presented on special imperial order before the author became a high court noble.

The poem was requested by Uda tennō. "Kumo no ue" (above the clouds) refers to the Imperial Palace; the stars are courtiers. Despite the note, Toshiyuki already was in the higher ranks of the aristocracy when this poem was written.

270 • *From the poetry contest held at the residence of Prince Koresada.*

tsuyu nagara	to wear in my hair
orite kazasan	I plucked a chrysanthemum
kiku no hana	with dew still clinging
oisenu aki no	to it oh may this present
hisashikarubeku	autumn's youth last forever

Ki no Tomonori

The Chrysanthemum Festival, held on the ninth day of the Ninth Month, was the occasion for various ceremonies promising longevity.

271 • *From the poetry contest held at the residence of the Consort in the Kanpyō era.*

ueshi toki	how impatiently
hana machidō ni	I planted and awaited
arishi kiku	you chrysanthemum
utsurou aki ni	did I ever imagine
awan to ya mishi	we would meet in fading fall

Ōe no Chisato

272 • *A poem attached to a chrysanthemum planted in the sandy beach of a tray garden for a chrysanthemum competition in the Kanpyō era. The topic is chrysanthemums on the beach at Fukiage.*

akikaze no	white chrysanthemums
fukiage ni tateru	standing in the rushing winds
shiragiku wa	on autumn beaches
hana ka aranu ka	at Fukiage are they
nami no yosuru ka	blossoms or are they breaking waves

Sugawara no Michizane

Fukiage, in Ise Province, Kaiso District, is famous for its beauties. The name means "to blow upward."

273 • *Composed on the topic "A person treading a path through chrysanthemums at the dwelling of a hermit."*

nurete hosu	on the mountain road
yamaji no kiku no	dew from the chrysanthemums
tsuyu no ma ni	drenched my hem in the
itsu ka chitose o	instant it took to dry can
ware wa heniken	a thousand years have flashed by

Sosei

"Tsuyu" means both "dew" and "brief." One day in the world of the hermits equals one thousand human years.

274 • *Composed on the topic "Awaiting someone near chrysanthemums in bloom."*

hana mitsutsu	awaiting him I
hito matsu toki wa	view the blossoms and then am
shirotae no	startled to mistake
sode ka to nomi zo	them for the white hempen sleeves
ayamatarekeru	of the robe I long to see

Ki no Tomonori

275 • *On "The chrysanthemums planted by Ōsawa Pond."*

hito moto to	I had thought there was
omoishi hana o	but a single blossom here—
ōsawa no	who could have planted
ike no soko ni mo	that other one there in the
tare ka ueken	depths of Osawa Pond

Ki no Tomonori

Ōsawa Pond is in Saga in Ukyō-ku, Kyōto.

276 • *On seeing chrysanthemums, when he was thinking of the swift passage of man's life.*

aki no kiku	while chrysanthemums
niou kagiri wa	of autumn retain their charms
kazashiten	I will decorate

hana yori saki to   my hat   I who may be gone
shiranu waga mi o   before the flowers wither

Ki no Tsurayuki

277 • *On white chrysanthemums.*

  kokoro ate ni   if you want to pluck
oraba ya oran   one   go ahead and try   white
  natsu shimo no   blossoms of autumn
okimadowaseru   chrysanthemums camouflaged
shiragiku no hana   by the first coating of frost

Ōshikōchi no Mitsune

278 • *From the poetry contest held at the residence of Prince Koresada.*

  iro kawaru   dressed now in rusty
aki no kiku oba   hues   autumn chrysanthemums
  hitotose ni   delight the viewer
futatabi niou   twice with the beauty of their
hana to koso mire   full bloom and their faded charms

Anonymous

Both 278 and 279 speak of the rusty color of withering chrysanthemums, a color admired as much as the earlier yellow or white.

279 • *Ordered to compose a poem to present with flowers to the former tennō at Ninnaji Temple.*

  aki okite   they have a time of
toki koso arikere   glory other than fall's
  kiku no hana   peak   chrysanthemums
utsurou kara ni   charm us again as they wilt—
iro no masareba   for then their colors deepen

Taira no Sadafun

Former tennō Uda was living at the Ninnaji in Omuro, now part of Ukyō-ku, Kyōto.

280 • *On transplanting chrysanthemums from someone's house.*

  sakisomeshi   it is because I
yado shi kawareba   moved it from the garden where

kiku no hana	it began to bloom
iro sae ni koso	that even the color of
utsuroinikere	this chrysanthemum is changed

Ki no Tsurayuki

281 • *Topic unknown.*

saho yama no	the deep red oak leaves
hahaso no momiji	of Saho Mountain will soon
chirinubemi	fall even at night
yoru sae miyo to	the moonlight gleams brightly to
terasu tsukikage	display their autumn beauty

Anonymous

282 • *Composed when he had retired to a mountain village and had not appeared at court for some time.*

okuyama no	within the sheer cliffs
iwagaki momiji	autumn leaves must have fallen—
chirinubeshi	there is no time when
teru hi no hikari	the sun's light touches them so
miru toki nakute	deep these mountains where they lie

Fujiwara no Sekio

Sekio retired to the Zenrinji in Higashiyama (the Eastern Mountains) and was given the nickname Gentleman of Higashiyama.

283 • *Topic unknown.*

tatsuta gawa	a covering of
momiji midarete	bright scattered leaves floats on
nagarumeri	Tatsuta River—
wataraba nishiki	were I to ford the waters
naka ya taenan	the brocade would tear in half

Anonymous

Some say this was composed by the Nara Mikado.

The source of the Tatsuta River is in the Ikoma Mountains; it flows through an area famous for autumn color in Nara Prefecture near Ikaruka and empties into the Yamato River. The Nara Mikado refers to Heizei.

284 • *Topic unknown.*

tatsuta gawa	the brilliant autumn
momijiba nagaru	leaves float by on Tatsuta
kannabi no	River freezing rains
mimuro no yama ni	must already be falling
shigure furu rashi	on holy Mount Mimuro

Anonymous

Alternatively, "asuka gawa/momijiba nagaru"
"Kannabi" and "mimuro" may be taken as common nouns referring to dwelling places of the gods. The alternative version locates the leaves on the Asuka River, which flows through Nara Prefecture, in Takaichi and Shiki Districts. A swift, winding stream, it was famous for its changeable flow.

285 • *Topic unknown.*

koishiku wa	these fallen autumn
mite mo shinoban	leaves I've come to hold so dear—
momijiba o	oh chill winds that blow
fuki na chirashi so	down from the mountains do not
yama oroshi no kaze	sweep them from my yearning gaze

Anonymous

286 • *Topic unknown.*

aki kaze ni	I whose fate so much
aezu chirinuru	resembles that of fallen
momijiba no	leaves tossed by fiercely
yukue sadamenu	blowing tempests of autumn—
ware zo kanashiki	how melancholy I am

Anonymous

287 • *Topic unknown.*

aki wa kinu	autumn has surely
momiji wa yado ni	come colored leaves carpet the
furishikinu	ground before my house—
michi fumiwakete	no visitor treads a path
tou hito wa nashi	through ever-deepening drifts

Anonymous

288 • *Topic unknown.*

fumiwakete
sara ni ya towan
  momijiba no
furikakushiteshi
michi to minagara

shall I tread a path
through them to visit again—
    even though I cannot
see the road deeply buried
beneath brilliant drifts of leaves

Anonymous

289 • *Topic unknown.*

aki no tsuki
yamabe sayaka ni
  teraseru wa
otsuru momiji no
kazu o miyo to ka

the autumn moon shines
brilliantly upon the
    mountain range   to show
us the very number of
the fallen colored leaves

Anonymous

290 • *Topic unknown.*

fuku kaze no
iro no chigusa ni
  mietsuru wa
aki no ko no ha no
chireba narikeri

the colors of autumn
visible in the thousand
    changing hues of the
blowing wind   are swirling leaves
tossed about by passing gusts

Anonymous

291 • *Topic unknown.*

shimo no tate
tsuyu no nuki koso
  yowakarashi
yama no nishiki no
oreba katsu chiru

no sooner woven
than it tears and falls to shreds—
    fragile brocade of
the mountains   a weft of dew
on a warp of autumn frost

Fujiwara no Sekio

292 • *Composed while lingering in the shelter of the trees at the Urin'in Temple.*

wabibito no
wakite tachiyoru
  ko no moto wa

there is no shelter
here beneath these trees where one
    who fled the world has

tanomu kage naku	finally made his way the
momiji chirikeri	leaves of autumn have fallen

Henjō

For Urin'in, see 75. There is irony in the use of the word "wabibito" (a person who despairs of the world) for one seeking shelter from the rain.

293 • *On the topic of autumn leaves floating down the Tatsuta River as painted on a screen seen at the residence of the Nijō Consort when she was known as Mother of the Crown Prince.*

momijiba no	there in the harbor
nagarete tomaru	where the waters come to rest
minato ni wa	deep red must be the
kurenai fukaki	waves that rise as the floating
nami ya tatsuran	autumn leaves swirl and eddy

Sosei

For the Nijō Consort, see 8. "Fukaki" (deep) links "crimson" and "waves" and relates grammatically to both. This and 294 are among the oldest screen poems (byōbu-uta).

294 • *On the same topic.*

chihayaburu	unheard of even
kami yo mo kikazu	in the stories of the age
tatsuta gawa	of the awesome gods—
karakurenai ni	the waters of Tatsuta
mizu kukuru to wa	stream dyed a Chinese red

Ariwara no Narihira

For Tatsuta River, see 283.

295 • *From the poetry contest held at the residence of Prince Koresada.*

waga kitsuru	the way I came is
kata mo shirarezu	indistinguishable now—
kurabu yama	for Mount Kurabu
kigi no ko no ha no	conceals my path with curtains
chiru to magau ni	of colorful autumn leaves

Fujiwara no Toshiyuki

For Kurabu Mountain, see 39.

296 • *From the same contest.*

kannabi no	in the autumn when
mimuro no yama o	I go to Mount Mimuro
aki yukeba	the holy place I
nishiki tachikiru	feel as though I wear a rich
kokochi koso sure	brocade cut from autumn hues

Mibu no Tadamine

For kannabi and mimuro, see 284. "Kiru" means both "to cut" and "to wear."

297 • *On going to pick autumn leaves at Kitayama.*

miru hito mo	deep in the mountains
nakute chirinuru	they have fallen with no one
okuyama no	to see their splendor—
momiji wa yoru no	these autumn leaves are a rich
nishiki narikeri	brocade spread in the dark night

Ki no Tsurayuki

Kitayama (the Northern Mountains) referred to the mountains north of the capital.

298 • *An autumn poem.*

tatsutahime	Tatsuta princess
tamukuru kami no	of autumn spreads offerings for
areba koso	a safe journey as
aki no ko no ha no	she goes like prayer strips scattering
nusa to chiruran	to the ground colored leaves fall

Prince Kanemi

Princess Tatsuta is the goddess of autumn. She scatters leaves as offerings as she departs for the west.

299 • *On seeing the autumn leaves while living at the place called Ono.*

aki no yama	imagining these
momiji o nusa to	colored leaves of autumn are
tamukureba	prayer strips offered

| sumu ware sae zo | to the gods even I who |
| tabigokochi suru | live here feel I'm traveling |

Ki no Tsurayuki

Ono is in Sakyō-ku, Kyōto.

300 • *On seeing autumn leaves floating on Tatsuta River after crossing Kannabi Mountain.*

kannabi no	because autumn is
yama o sugiyuku	returning crossing over
aki nareba	Kannabi Mountain
tasuta gawa ni zo	she offers crimson prayer
nusa wa tamukuru	strips at Tatsuta River

Kiyohara no Fukayabu

For the Tatsuta River, see 283.

301 • *From the poetry contest held at the residence of the Consort in the Kanpyō era.*

shiranami ni	the colored leaves of
aki no ko no ha no	autumn floating on the white
ukaberu o	crests of the rising
ama no nagaseru	waves look! are they not small boats
fune ka to zo miru	set sail by some fisherfolk

Fujiwara no Okikaze

302 • *Composed on the banks of the Tatsuta River.*

momijiba no	if no colored leaves
nagarezariseba	drifted downstream there who would
tatsuta gawa	know that autumn had
mizu no aki oba	come to the clear waters
tare ka shiramashi	of the Tatsuta River

Sakanoue no Korenori

For the Tatsuta River, see 283.

303 • *Composed on Shiga Pass.*

yamagawa ni	the autumn leaves are
kaze no kaketaru	unable to resist the
shigarami wa	current flowing past
nagare mo aenu	the weir built by the wind
momiji narikeri	in the deep mountain river

Harumichi no Tsuraki

For Shiga, see 115.

304 • *On seeing the autumn leaves falling near a pond.*

kaze fukeba	when the wind blows
otsuru momijiba	falling leaves embroider the
mizu kiyomi	limpid waters where
chiranu kage sae	even the leaves still clinging
soko ni mietsutsu	are reflected in the depths

Ōshikōchi no Mitsune

The limpid phrases of this poem reflect beautifully the antitheses Mitsune sets up—reflection and reality, fallen leaves and leaves still on the trees, surface and depth. The "pure water" (mizu kiyomi) serves as a pivot phrase linking the two images.

305 • *Composed after the Mikado had composed a poem on the topic of a picture on a screen in the Teijinoin, which showed a traveler leading a horse, standing beneath a tree from which autumn leaves were falling, as he prepared to cross a river.*

tachidomari	let me pause here
mite o wataran	on my journey to gaze before
momijiba wa	I ford the river—
ame to furu tomo	the autumn leaves fall like rain
mizu wa masaraji	but the waters will not rise

Ōshikōchi no Mitsune

For the Teijinoin, see 68.

306 • *From the poetry contest held at the residence of Prince Koresada.*

yama ta moru	the dew which settles
aki no kari io ni	on the temporary hut
oku tsuyu wa	guarding the rice fields

inaōsedori no　　　　　　is really tears of these
namida narikeri　　　　　field birds who would reap the grain

Mibu no Tadamine

For inaōsedori, see 208.

3 0 7　•　*Topic unknown.*

　ho ni mo idenu　　　　　guarding the mountain
yama ta o moru to　　　　fields where the grains of rice have
　fujigoromo　　　　　　　yet to ripen　not
inaba no tsuyu ni　　　　a day passes that my coarse clothes
nurenu hi zo naki　　　　are not dew-drenched by these leaves

Anonymous

3 0 8　•　*Topic unknown.*

　kareru ta ni　　　　　　they will not ripen—
ouru hizuchi no　　　　　these second-growth stalks in
　ho ni idenu wa　　　　　harvested fields　for
yo o imasara ni　　　　　it is the close of autumn
aki hatenu toka　　　　　when all the world is weary

Anonymous

"Aki" is a kakekotoba meaning "autumn" and "to tire of."

3 0 9　•　*Going to Kitayama with Archbishop Henjō to gather mushrooms.*

　momijiba wa　　　　　　we will break off these
sode ni kokiirete　　　　colored leaves and carry them
　moteidenan　　　　　　　back in our sleeves　for
aki wa kagiri to　　　　those in the capital who
min hito no tame　　　　thought autumn was at an end

Sosei

Kitayama refers to the mountains north of the capital. Henjō was Sosei's father.

3 1 0　•　*Composed in the Kanpyō era, when commanded to gather some old poems.
The intent is to convey the feeling of the poem "Colored leaves float upon the
Tatsuta River."*

miyama yori
ochikuru mizu no
iro mite zo
aki wa kagiri to
omoishirinuru

seeing the color
of the waters which tumble
down the beautiful
mountains   I know full well that
this autumn is at its end

Fujiwara no Okikaze

The poem alluded to is number 284. For Tatsutagawa, see 283.

3 I I • *Imagining the Tatsuta River near the end of autumn.*

toshi goto ni
momijiba nagasu
tatsuta gawa
minato ya aki no
tomari naruran

every year the
Tatsuta River carries
the colored leaves past—
is it that the river mouth
is the berth of autumn

Ki no Tsurayuki

3 I 2 • *Composed on the last day of autumn at Ōi.*

yūzuku yo
ogura no yama ni
naku shika no
koe no uchi ni ya
aki wa kururan

is autumn leaving
with the belling voices of
the deer   now growing
fainter on Mount Ogura
as the twilight approaches

Ki no Tsurayuki

The Ōi River was in Sakyō-ku, Kyōto, at the foot of Arashiyama. "Yūzuku yo" (approaching dusk) is a makurakotoba for "Ogura" (dusky; place name). Ogura Mountain was on the northern bank of the Ōi River, opposite Arashiyama.

3 I 3 • *Also composed on the last day of autumn.*

michi shiraba
tazune mo yukan
momijiba o
nusa to tamukete
aki wa inikeri

if I knew the road
I would go and search   having
offered up multi-
hued fallen leaves for prayers
autumn has finally gone

Ōshikōchi no Mitsune

BOOK VI

Winter

3 1 4 • *Topic unknown.*

tatsuta gawa	on the Tatsuta
nishiki orikaku	River the Godless Month weaves
kannazuki	a brocade of leaves
shigure no ame o	red and gold upon the sharp
tatenuki ni shite	silver warp and weft of sleet

Anonymous

For the Tatsuta River, see 283. The Godless Month (kannazuki) is the Tenth. The autumn leaves are an image of late autumn; sleet (shigure), of early winter.

3 1 5 • *Composed as a winter poem.*

yamazato wa	loneliness grows in
fuyu zo sabishisa	the wintry isolation of
masarikeru	this mountain village—
hitome mo kusa mo	the grasses have all withered
karenu to omoeba	no one views their summer green

Minamoto no Muneyuki

"Karenu" means both "to wither" and "to be separated."

3 1 6 • *Topic unknown.*

ōzora no	last night the moonlight
tsuki no hikari shi	in the broad skies was so bright
kiyokereba	that the waters which
kage mishi mizu zo	reflected it have frozen
mazu kōrikeru	to translucence first of all

Anonymous

317 • *Topic unknown.*

yū sareba	as evening deepens
koromode samushi	the sleeves of my robe grow cold—
miyoshino no	in fair Yoshino
yoshino no yama ni	on lovely Mount Yoshino
miyuki furu rashi	soft white snow must be falling

Anonymous

The first two lines of this poem are almost the same as those of *Man'yōshū*, 2319; the source of both poems may be a Yamato-region folk song. The repetition of the prefix "mi" (lovely, fair) reinforces the old-fashioned flavor of the direct expression.

318 • *Topic unknown.*

ima yori wa	may it continue
tsugite furanan	to fall forever lovely
waga yado no	white snow bending
susuki oshinami	the gracefully swaying stalks
fureru shirayuki	of plume grass in my garden

Anonymous

319 • *Topic unknown.*

furu yuki wa	the falling snow must
katsu zo kenu rashi	be melting as it settles for
ashihiki no	in the rugged range
yama no tagitsu se	of mountains the sound of the
oto masarunari	seething rapids grows louder

Anonymous

"Ashihiki no" is a makurakotoba for "yama" (mountain).

320 • *Topic unknown.*

kono kawa ni	here in this river
momijiba nagaru	autumn leaves so swiftly flow—
okuyama no	deep in the mountains
yukige no mizu zo	the snow drifts melt and add their
ima masaru rashi	icy waters to the stream

Anonymous

321 • *Topic unknown.*

furusato wa	here in the ancient
yoshino no yama shi	capital Mount Yoshino
chikakereba	is so near that not
hitohi mo miyuki	a single day passes when
furanu hi wa nashi	the dazzling snow does not fall

Anonymous

Two ancient capitals lay near Yoshino: Asuka and Toyora.

322 • *Topic unknown.*

waga yado wa	at my lonely home
yuki furishikite	snow falls and lies so thickly
michi mo nashi	that the path is gone
fumiwakete tou	for there is no visitor
hito shi nakereba	to tread his way to my door

Anonymous

323 • *Composed as a winter poem.*

yuki fureba	when the snow crystals
fuyugomori seru	fall on the sleeping trees and
kusa mo ki mo	grasses there bloom wild
haru ni shirarenu	flowers that are never seen
hana zo sakikeru	on branches or stems in spring

Ki no Tsurayuki

324 • *Composed on Shiga Pass.*

shirayuki no	when buried in this
tokoro mo wakazu	layer of snow that unites
furishikeba	all the white landscape
iwao ni mo saku	even the barren crags and rocks
hana to koso mire	seem to put forth blossoms

Ki no Akimine

For Shiga Pass, see 115.

325 • *Composed while stopping for the night on a journey to the Nara capital.*

miyoshino no	the white snows must be
yama no shirayuki	piling thickly on lovely
tsumoru rashi	Yoshino Mountain
furusato samuku	for in the old capital
narimasaru nari	a bitter cold penetrates

Sakanoue no Korenori

Heijō was called the Nara capital.

326 • *From the poetry contest held at the residence of the Consort in the Kanpyō era.*

ura chikaku	the swiftly driven
furikuru yuki wa	snow falling into rough drifts
shiranami no	near the shore looks like
suenomatsu yama	rows of crested waves crossing
kosu ka to zo miru	Suenomatsu Mountain

Fujiwara no Okikaze

The location of Suenomatsu Mountain is unknown. A poem from the northeast provinces evidently was the inspiration for this poem.

327 • *From the same contest.*

miyoshino no	the one who trod this
yama no shirayuki	path through the untouched snows of
fumiwakete	fair Mount Yoshino
irinishi hito no	sent not a word of greeting
otozure mo senu	before leaving in silence

Mibu no Tadamine

This and the following two poems treat feelings of isolation in winter.

328 • *From the same contest.*

shirayuki no	the white snow falls and
furite tsumoreru	drifts heavily in the hills—
yamazato wa	even the dreams of

sumu hito sae ya | those who dwell in the mountain
omoi kiyu ran | villages must melt away

Mibu no Tadamine

"Shirayuki" (white snow) and "kiyu" (melted) are engo. "Kiyu," a kakekotoba, also means "vanished."

329 • *On seeing falling snow.*

  yuki furite | the once traveled path
hito mo kayowanu | now is obscured by falling
  michi nare ya | snow   no one passes—
atohakamonaku | not a trace marks the course of
omoi kiyu ran | my fading aspirations

Ōshikōchi no Mitsune

"Atohakamonaku" means both "no trace left" and (hakanaku) "transitory." "Yuki" (snow) and "kiyu" (melted) are engo.

330 • *On seeing fallen snow.*

  fuyu nagara | still winter lingers
sora yori hana no | but from the heavens fall these
  chirikuru wa | blossoms of purest
kumo no anata wa | white   it seems that spring must wait
haru ni ya aru ran | on the far side of those clouds

Kiyohara no Fukayabu

331 • *On snow blanketing the trees.*

  fuyugomori | in winter when all's
omoikakenu o | sleeping   unexpectedly
  ko no ma yori | between the trees I
hana to miru made | glimpse new flowers glistening—
yuki zo furikeru | crystal white snow has fallen

Ki no Tsurayuki

332 • *Composed on a journey to Yamato, seeing that snow had fallen.*

  asaborake | in the first light of
ariake no tsuki to | dawn it seems a reflection

miru made ni	of the moon lingering
yoshino no sato ni	above white snow has fallen
fureru shirayuki	here in Yoshino Village

Sakanoue no Korenori

Among Korenori's writings this poem was most appreciated by Fujiwara Teika and later readers, but in the Heian period, *Kokinshū* VI, 325, was regarded more highly.

333 • *Topic unknown.*

kenu ga ue ni	fall again blanket
mata mo furishike	all once more before you melt
harugasumi	and disappear for
tachinaba miyuki	when spring mists start to rise we'll
mare ni koso mime	rarely see snowy beauty

Anonymous

334 • *Topic unknown.*

ume no hana	the plum blossoms now
sore to mo miezu	are indistinguishable—
hisakata no	for snow mists the broad
amagiru yuki no	heavens and masks all below
nabete furereba	in a whirling world of white

Anonymous

Some say this poem was composed by Kakinomoto no Hitomaro.

"Hisakata no" is a makurakotoba for "ama" (sky). The "elegant confusion" displayed by the poet is more typical of *Kokinshū*-era writers than of Hitomaro; again the attribution is dubious.

335 • *Snow fallen on the plum blossoms.*

hana no iro wa	the color of the
yuki ni majirite	flowers mingles with the snow
miezu to mo	and is lost to view—
ka o dani nioe	plum trees send us your fragrance
hito no shiru beku	that we may know your presence

Ono no Takamura

336 • *On plum blossoms in the snow.*

ume no ka no	were the fragrance of
furiokeru yuki ni	the plum blossoms imparted to
magaiseba	the blanketing snow
tare ka kotogoto	who could separate them and
wakite oramashi	pluck the thick blossoming boughs

Ki no Tsurayuki

337 • *On seeing fallen snow.*

yuki fureba	when snow has fallen
ki goto ni hana zo	flowers appear on all the
sakinikeru	trees clusters of white
izure o ume to	blooms from which of them can I
wakite oramashi	pluck the fragrant plum blossoms

Ki no Tomonori

The characters for "goto" (each)) and "ki" (tree) combine to form the character for "ume" (plum).

338 • *Composed on the last day of the year to welcome someone who had been away.*

waga matanu	unawaited comes
toshi wa kinuredo	the year's end but not a word
fuyugusa no	from one who left me
karenishi hito wa	for distant places my heart
otozure mo sezu	withers like winter grasses

Ōshikōchi no Mitsune

"Fuyugusa no" (like winter grasses) is a makurakotoba for "karenishi" (withered), which also means "gone away" and serves as a kakekotoba.

339 • *On the year's end.*

aratama no	each time the idle
toshi no owari ni	year comes to another end
naru goto ni	the snows fall ever
yuki mo waga mi mo	more deeply while the number
furi masaritsutsu	of my days piles still higher

Ariwara no Motokata

"Aratama no," often intepreted as "rough jewel's," is a makurukotoba for "toshi" (year). "Furi" (falling; aging) is a kakekotoba.

340 • *From the poetry contest held at the residence of the Consort in the Kanpyō era.*

yuki furite	at year's end when snow
toshi no kurenuru	blankets all the earth in white—
toki ni koso	then at last the pines
tsui ni momijinu	who know no autumn glory
matsu mo miekere	stand forth in all their splendor

Anonymous

This poem is based on a line from the *Lun yü* (*Analects of Confucius*): "Only when the year grows cold do we see that the pines and cypresses are the last to fade."

341 • *On the year's end.*

kinō to ii	"yesterday" we say
kyō to kurashite	and "today" we live but still
asuka gawa	months and days slip past
nagarete hayaki	as smoothly and swiftly as
tsuki hi narikeri	Tomorrow River's waters

Harumichi no Tsuraki

Tsuraki plays on the name of the Asuka (Is it tomorrow?) River and also uses it as a makurakotoba for "nagarete" (flowing). For Asuka River, see 284. This poem is an allusive variation on 933.

342 • *On being commanded to present a poem.*

yuku toshi no	the passing year too
oshiki mo aru kana	leaves regrets as it departs—
masu kagami	in the clear mirror
miru kage sae ni	the reflection dims as I
kurenu to omoeba	think of the time now gone by

Ki no Tsurayuki

This poem was requested by Daigo tennō. "Kurenu" means both "has passed" and "has darkened."

BOOK VII

Poems of Felicitation

343 • *Topic unknown.*

waga kimi wa	my lord may you live
chiyo ni ya chiyo ni	a thousand years eight thousand
sazareishi no	till pebbles grow to
iwao to narite	ancient boulders and dark
koke no musu made	green moss covers their sides

Anonymous

The first line of this poem became "kimi ga yo wa" (my lord's life) in the *Wakan roeishū* 和漢朗詠集, and that version has become the Japanese national anthem. The practice of celebrating birthdays at ten-year intervals after the fortieth was a Chinese custom adopted by the Japanese nobles of the Nara period. This poem may have been inspired by *Man'yōshū*, 228 (translation by Ian Levy):

imo ga na wa	Let my girl's name
chiyo ni nagaren	stream on through a thousand ages,
himejima no	until moss grows
komatsu ga ure ni	on the buds of the young pine
koke musu made ni	at Himejima.

344 • *Topic unknown.*

watatsu umi no	may the number of
hama no masago o	the grains of sand on beaches
kazoetsutsu	bordering the broad
kimi ga chitose no	oceans be the number of
arikazu ni sen	the centuries of your life

Anonymous

This poem seems to have been influenced by lines from *Man'yōshū*, 596:

yahoka yuku	even the grains of sand
hama no manago mo	on the eight hundred day-long shore....

345 • *Topic unknown.*

shio no yama	the plovers on the
sashide no iso ni	jutting crags beneath briny
sumu chidori	Shio Mountain cry
kimi ga miyo oba	out "May the years of your life
yachiyo to zo naku	number eight thousand and more"

Anonymous

The location of Shio Mountain is unknown. The sound of the plover's (chidori) chirp was heard as "chiyo," and these syllables are "hidden" in yachiyo (eight thousand years). The vowels of the plovers' cry, *i* and *o*, echo throughout the poem.

346 • *Topic unknown.*

waga yowai	from my allotted
kimi ga yachiyo ni	time I'll take some years for your
torisoete	life when yours are gone
todome okiteba	please live mine in remembrance
omoiide ni seyo	of one who went before you

Anonymous

347 • *Composed by the Mikado in the Ninna era for the seventieth birthday of Archbishop Henjō.*

kaku shitsutsu	may life go on like
to ni mo kaku ni mo	this flowing smoothly with no
nagaraete	ripple to mar it
kimi ga yachiyo ni	until we meet each of us
au yoshi mo gana	in our eight thousandth year

Kōkō Tennō

Kōkō tennō reigned 884–887. According to *Nihon sandai jitsuroku* 日本三代実録, this celebration took place on the eighteenth of the Twelfth Month of 885.

348 • *While the Ninna Mikado was still Crown Prince he presented his aunt with a silver staff for her eightieth birthday, and Henjō composed this poem on her behalf.*

chihayaburu	is this the handiwork
kami ya kiriken	of one of the awesome gods—

tsuku kara ni
chitose no saka mo
koenubera nari

thrusting it before
me I shall cross even the
great hill of one thousand years

Henjō

The Ninna Mikado was Kōkō. The word "oba" could refer to his aunt or his grandmother. "Chihayaburu" is a makurakotoba for "kami" (gods).

349 • *Written at a congratulatory banquet at the Kujō residence on the occasion of the fortieth birthday of the Horikawa Chancellor.*

sakurabana
chirikai kumore
  oiraku no
komu to iu naru
michi magau gani

oh cherry blossoms
flutter down and cloud the path
  where age   it is said
approaches   deceive him with
tumbling curtains of petals

Ariwara no Narihira

The Kujō residence belonged to Chancellor Fujiwara no Mototsune, whose main home was in Horikawa. This poem may be based on XVII, 895.

350 • *Composed in Ōi at a celebration of the fortieth birthday of the aunt of Prince Sadatoki.*

  kameno o no
yama no iwane o
  tomete otsuru
taki no shiratama
chiyo no kazu kamo

cascading   seeking
the rocky basin on Mount
  Kameno-o
effervescent white jewels
in the falls number your years

Ki no Koreoka

Sadatoki was the seventh son of Seiwa tennō. The Ōi River runs past Kameno-o Mountain in western Kyōto, where Sadatoki's villa was located.

351 • *On seeing the screen with a scene of people standing beneath falling cherry blossoms which was presented to the Consort by Prince Sadayasu on the occasion of her fiftieth birthday.*

  itazura ni
suguru tsukihi wa
  omōede

unthinkingly   I
pass the days and months in vain
  with not one regret—

hana mite kurasu
haru zo sukunaki

but oh how few are the spring
days spent in flower viewing

Fujiwara no Okikaze

Sadayasu was the fifth son of Seiwa tennō; the Consort was his mother, Takaiko, whose fiftieth birthday took place in 891.

3 5 2 • *Poems 352 to 354 were written on the screen which served as background to the celebration of the seventieth birthday of Prince Motoyasu.*

haru kureba
yado ni mazu saku
 ume no hana
kimi ga chitose no
kazashi to zo miru

oh plum blossoms you
who first adorn the new year
 gardens   now trim our
hats in fine celebration
of our lord's longevity

Ki no Tsurayuki

Motoyasu was the fifth son of Ninmyō tennō. This birthday celebration took place around 901.

3 5 3 •

inishie ni
ariki arazu wa
 shiranedomo
chitose no tameshi
kimi ni hajimen

whether in days of
old man lived so long I do
 not know   but you   my
lord   shall set the precedent
of one thousand years of life

Sosei

3 5 4 •

fushite omoi
okite kazouru
 yorozuyo wa
kami zo shiru ran
waga kimi no tame

the gods testify
that waking I count them and
 sleeping I dream of
them   for my lord I wish a
life of uncountable years

Sosei

3 5 5 • *Composed for the celebration of Fujiwara no Miyoshi's sixtieth birthday.*

tsuru kame mo
chitose no nochi wa

even the tortoise
and crane do not know what lies

shiranaku ni	beyond their thousand
akanu kokoro ni	year span let me whose heart shall
makase hateten	never be sated judge your years

Ariwara no Shigeharu

Some say the author was Ariwara no Tokiharu.

356 • *Composed on behalf of Yoshimine no Tsunenari's daughter for his fortieth birthday.*

yorozuyo o	the crane beneath the
matsu ni zo kimi o	pine offered in jubilee
iwaitsuru	they tell how much I
chitose no kage ni	hope to dwell eternally
suman to omoeba	in the shelter of your love

Sosei

Sosei, a master of the kakekotoba, has used three: "matsu" means "pine tree" and "to wait"; the perfective ending "-tsuru" also means "crane"; and "kage" means both "shade" and "protection."

357 • *The following seven poems were composed for the backdrop screen decorated with pictures of the four seasons used at the celebration of the fortieth birthday of the Minister of the Right, Fujiwara no Ason, held by the Principal Handmaid.*

kasuga no ni	gathering young herbs
wakana tsumitsutsu	on the Plain of Kasuga
yorozuyo o	we celebrate your
iwau kokoro wa	many years the awesome gods
kami zo shiru ran	surely know how I rejoice

Sosei

The Principal Handmaid (Naishi no kami) was Fujiwara no Michiko (Manshi), younger sister of Sadakuni, Minister of the Right. Numbers 357 and 358 are the spring poems of this set of screen poems on the seasons. The other seasons are indicated as topics.

358 •

yama takami	so high the mountains—
kumoi ni miyuru	interspersed among the clouds
sakurabana	are cherry blossoms—

kokoro no yukite
oranu hi zo naki

every day that passes
my heart goes out to pluck them

Ōshikōchi no Mitsune

3 5 9 • *Summer.*

mezurashiki
koe naranaku ni
hototogisu
kokora no toshi o
akazu mo aru kana

often his call is
heard   the sad-voiced nightingale
year after year he
sings   yet never does he tire
of singing his summer song

Ki no Tomonori

For hototogisu, see 135. The last lines might also be translated "never do we/I tire of his summer song."

3 6 0 • *Autumn.*

suminoe no
matsu o akikaze
fuku kara ni
koe uchisouru
okitsu shiranami

through the ancient pines
that line Suminoe Bay
blows the autumn wind—
its soughing carries the
echo of white waves off shore

Ōshikōchi no Mitsune

Suminoe (Sumiyoshi) is an inlet near the Sumiyoshi Shrine in Ōsaka.

3 6 1 • *Autumn.*

chidori naku
saho no kawagiri
tachinu rashi
yama no ko no ha mo
iro masariyuku

veils of mist must be
rising now over Saho
River where plovers
cry   here on the mountainside
the colors of the leaves deepen

Mibu no Tadamine

The Saho River in northern Nara City at the foot of Saho Mountain is famous for the plovers (chidori) along its banks.

362 • *Autumn.*

aki kuredo	though autumn comes to
iro mo kawaranu	evergreen Mount Tokiwa
tokiwa yama	there should be no change
yo sono momiji o	in its hues the winds borrowed
kaze zo kashikeru	brilliant leaves to carry here

Sakanoe no Korenori

For Tokiwa Mountain, see 148.

363 • *Winter.*

shirayuki no	when upon lovely
furishiku toki wa	Mount Yoshino the heavy
miyoshino no	white snows swirl to earth
yama shita kaze ni	the wind scatters the melting
hana zo chirikeru	petals down to the foothills

Ki no Tsurayuki

See poems I, 60, and XII, 588, for other examples of the "elegant confusion" of snow and cherry blossoms on Mount Yoshino.

364 • *Composed on a visit at the time of the birth of the Crown Prince.*

mine takaki	that sun which rises
kasuga no yama n.	now over the towering
izuru hi wa	Kasuga Mountain
kumoru toki naku	heights will shed its welcome light
terasuberanari	unclouded forevermore

Fujiwara no Yoruka

Yoruka was an Assistant Handmaid (Naishi no suke) when Daigo tennō's son Prince Yasuakira 保明 was born to Fujiwara Onshi 隠子. The tutelary shrine of the Fujiwara family was located at the foot of Mount Kasuga; it is now within Nara City. The poem is a paean to the ruling family.

BOOK VIII

Poems of Parting

365 • *Topic unknown.*

tachiwakare	though I must depart
inaba no yama no	I shall hurry home if I
mine ni ouru	hear you wait for me
matsu to shi kikaba	patient as the pines that grow
ima kaerikomu	on Mount Inaba where I go

Ariwara no Yukihira

Inaba (a place name, now Tottori Prefecture; if I go) and "matsu" (pine; to wait) are kakekotoba. Yukihira became Governor of Inaba Province in 855.

366 • *Topic unknown.*

sugaru naku	I shall await him
aki no hagiwara	always dreaming of his swift
asa tachite	return he who sets
tabi yuku hito o	out this autumn daybreak through
itsu to ka matan	hagi fields where hornets drone

Anonymous

367 • *Topic unknown.*

kagiri naki	though I am going
kumoi no yoso ni	to a place more distant than
wakaru to mo	your heavenly home
hito o kokoro ni	never shall I let my heart
okurasamu ya wa	outdistance your memory

Anonymous

Kokinshū

368 • *Composed by his mother when Ono no Chifuru left to become Vice-Governor of Michinoku.*

tarachine no	oh barrier guards
oya no mamori to	do not close the gates before
aisouru	this aged heart it
kokoro bakari wa	goes as a companion to
seki na todome so	guide my child on distant roads

Michinoku was the general name for Iwaki, Rikuzen, Rikuchū, Iwashiro, and Mutsu Provinces in northern Honshū. "Tarachine no" is a makurakotoba of uncertain meaning; in the *Kokinshū* generally it modifies the word "oya" (parent).

369 • *Composed the night of the farewell party held at the residence of Prince Sadatoki for Fujiwara no Kiyofu, who was newly appointed Vice-Governor of Ōmi.*

kyō wakare	today we must part
asu wa au mi to	although I think we may meet
omoedomo	again tomorrow
yo ya fukenuran	at Ōmi my sleeves are dew-
sode no tsuyukeki	drenched for the night has grown late

Ki no Toshisada

"Au mi" is a kakekotoba referring both to the place name Ōmi and "persons who will meet."

370 • *Sent to someone who had gone to the northern provinces.*

kaeru yama	I have heard that there
ari to wa kikedo	in the land for which you leave
harugasumi	Returning Mountain
tachiwakarenaba	stands still I shall long for your
koishikarubeshi	return if spring mists hide you

Ki no Toshisada

The northern provinces of Echizen, Kaga, Noto, Etchū, and Echigo were known as Koshi. Kaeru (returning) Mountain is in Fukui Prefecture. "Harugasumi" (spring haze) is a makurakotoba for the kakekotoba "tachi" (rising; departing).

371 • *Composed at a farewell banquet.*

oshimu kara	how I shall miss you
koishiki mono o	after you have disappeared

shirakumo no
tachi nan nochi wa
nanigokochi sen

like the soft white clouds
which float across the heavens—
you for whom I yearn today

Ki no Tsurayuki

"Shirakumo no" (white clouds) is a makurakotoba for the kakekotoba "tachi" (rising; departing).

372 • *For a friend leaving the capital for the country.*

wakarete wa
hodo o hedatsu to
omoeba ya
katsu minagara ni
kanete koishiki

is it that I think
of the great distance that will
separate us when
you have gone   already I
yearn   though you are still with me

Ariwara no Shigeharu

373 • *Sent to someone who had gone to the eastern provinces of Azuma.*

omoedomo
mi o shi wakeneba
me ni mienu
kokoro o kimi ni
taguete zo yaru

though I long to go
I must remain   I cannot
divide in two   instead
I'll send this heart of mine   an
unseen companion for you

Ikago no Atsuyuki

Azuma referred broadly to the eastern half of Honshū—Tōhoku, Kantō, and Tōkai.

374 • *Composed while parting from someone at Ōsaka.*

ōsaka no
seki shi masashiki
mono naraba
akazu wakaruru
kimi o todomeyo

oh barrier of
Ōsaka   if restraint
indeed you are   hold
back that one who wishes to
leave before farewells are done

Naniwa no Yorozuo

Ōsaka Barrier, originally established for military purposes on the road between Ōmi and Yamashiro at Ōtsu, had by the mid-Heian period lost its military effectiveness. However, because the name could be read as "Meeting Hill," it had attained an important place in poetry.

375 • *Topic unknown.*

kara koromo	I shall not hear that
tatsu hi wa kikaji	this is the day you set out—
asatsuyu no	cutting us apart
okite shi yukeba	like scissors through Chinese cloth—
kenubeki mono o	I shall vanish like the dew

Anonymous

A woman gave this poem, without another word, to the husband she had lived with many years when he left for a new post taking with him a new wife and only coming to give her the message, "I depart tomorrow."

"Kara koromo" (Chinese robe) is a makurakotoba for "tatsu" (to cut; to depart), and "asatsuyu no" (of the morning dew) is a makurakotoba for "okite" (settling; leaving behind). "Asatsuyu" is linked imagistically as engo with "kenu" (died; disappeared). Notes following *Kokinshū* poems may be taken as fiction.

376 • *Sent to Fujiwara no Kimitoshi when Utsuku was leaving for Hitachi.*

asa nake ni	because I have not
mibeki kimi toshi	relied on your constancy
tanomaneba	through day and night now
omoitachinuru	I can go determinedly
kusa makura nari	to pillow my head on grass

Utsuku

Kura's destination, Hitachi (modern Ibaraki Prefecture), is hidden in the phrase "omo(h)itachinuru" (have decided), and Kimitoshi, her lover's name, is woven into the second line of the poem.

377 • *When Ki no Munesada went to the eastern provinces, he spent one night at someone's house, and as he was saying his farewells at dawn, a woman sent this poem out to him.*

ezo shiranu	who knows the outcome—
ima kokoromiyo	as long as I have life I
inochi araba	will put it to the
ware ya wasururu	test shall I forget him first
hito ya towanu to	or will he not come again

Anonymous

Kubota Utsubo assumes the author to be Munesada's wife; we have followed Ozawa Masao's reading of the headnote here.

378 • *Composed for a beloved friend who was going to the eastern provinces.*

kumoi ni mo	no matter how great
kayou kokoro no	a distance you may travel
okureneba	my loving heart will
wakaru to hito ni	never lag behind though it
miyu bakari nari	may seem we have been parted

Kiyowara no Fukayabu

379 • *Composed for a friend going to the eastern provinces.*

shirakumo no	here and far away—
konata kanata ni	parted as though by white clouds
tachiwakare	rising between us—
kokoro o nusa to	how this journey tears my heart
kudaku tabi kana	into tatters of prayer strips

Yoshimine no Hideoka

For "shirakumo no," see 371. Prayer strips (nusa) were offered up to the gods for safe journeys.

380 • *Composed for someone going to the northeast provinces.*

shirakumo no	even far off where
yae ni kasanaru	cloud layers pile one upon
ochi nite mo	another do not
omowan hito ni	place a barrier before
kokoro hedatsu na	the heart of one who loves you

Ki no Tsurayuki

The northeast provinces were called Michinoku; see 368.

381 • *Parting from someone.*

wakare chō	although the thing called
koto wa iro ni mo	parting is devoid of all
aranaku ni	color somehow it
kokoro ni shimite	tortures me by dyeing my
wabishikaru ran	heart through with sorrow's hue

Ki no Tsurayuki

382 • *Written for someone of whom he was fond, who had spent some years in the capital but was returning to the northern provinces.*

kaeru yama	why should Returning
nani zo wa arite	Mountain exist although you
aru kai wa	have come back to me
kite mo tomaranu	it only summons you to
na ni koso arikere	travel far away once more

Ōshikōchi no Mitsune

For the northern provinces and Kaeru Mountain, see 370.

383 • *For someone going to the northern provinces.*

yoso ni nomi	shall I continue
koi ya wataran	loving from such a distance—
shira yama no	I who cannot go
yuki miru beku mo	to see the crisp white snows of
aranu waga mi wa	faraway Shira Mountain

Ōshikōchi no Mitsune

Shira yama (White Mountain), now called Hakusan, straddles the border between Ishikawa and Gifu Prefectures. The kakekotoba "yuki" means both "going" and "snow."

384 • *Parting from someone near Otowa Mountain.*

otowa yama	high in the treetops
kodakaku nakite	on Otowa Mountain the
hototogisu	nightingale's shrill cry
kimi ga wakare o	is echoing surely he too
oshimu beranari	drearily mourns your parting

Ki no Tsurayuki

For Otowa, see 142. The ending "-dakaku" (high, loud) refers both to the position of the bird and its piercing cry. For hototogisu, see 135.

385 • *The following two poems were composed on the occasion of a party held by the court nobles for Fujiwara no Nochikage, who was to become Import Inspector at the end of the Ninth Month.*

| morotomo ni | kirigirisu |
| nakite todomeyo | join your shrill cries to ours and |

kirigirisu
aki no wakare wa
oshiku ya wa aranu

delay the parting—
are not autumn departures
a time of grief and sorrow

Fujiwara no Kanemochi

The Import Inspector was sent to Kyūshū to examine cargo coming from China. "Nakite" means both "singing" (birds) and "weeping." For kirigirisu, see 196.

386 •

akigiri no
tomo ni tachiidete
  wakarenaba
harenu omoi ni
koi ya wataran

if now you depart—
setting off with the floating
  banners of autumn
haze   will love linger on in
the clouded depths of my heart

Taira no Motonori

"Akigiri" (autumn haze), "tachi" (rising), "harenu" (unclearing), and "wataran" (will spread) are engo.

387 • *Composed at Yamazaki when seeing off Minamoto no Sane, who was going to bathe at the hot springs of Tsukushi.*

inochi dani
kokoro ni kanau
  mono naraba
nani ka wakare no
kanashikaramashi

if even life could
be made to suit the desires
  of our frail human
hearts   I would not grieve so at
a temporary parting

Shirome

Tsukushi referred to Chikuzen and Chikugo Provinces or to Kyūshū as a whole. Yamazaki near Kyōto was the embarkation site on the Yodo River for those traveling to the western provinces.

388 • *For friends who came from Yamazaki to Kannabi to see him off and who were reluctant to return.*

hito yari no
michi naranaku ni
  ōkata wa

this journey is not
one imposed upon me   and
  like all travels in

ikiushi to iite   this world   it's hard to bear   so
iza kaerinan   then   let me now return home

Minamoto no Sane

Kannabi was near Yamazaki, on the Yodo River.

389 • *Composed when Sane told them to return home.*

shitawarete   because our yearning
kinishi kokoro no   hearts have come seeking after
   mi ni shi areba   you   our bodies   left
kaeru sama ni wa   behind   cannot discover
michi mo shirarezu   even the road that leads home

Fujiwara no Kanemochi

390 • *Composed while crossing Ōsaka when seeing off Fujiwara no Koreoka,
who was taking up the post of Vice-Governor of Musashi.*

katsu koete   while still he crosses
wakare mo yuku ka   over and journeys onward
   ōsaka wa   leaving me behind
hitodanome naru   your title   Ōsaka
na ni koso arikere   Meeting Hill   is just a name

Ki no Tsurayuki

For Ōsaka, see 374. Musashi Province is now Saitama Prefecture and Tōkyō City.

391 • *Composed at the farewell party for Ōe no Chifuru, who was going to the
northern provinces.*

kimi ga yuki   unfamiliar is
koshi no shira yama   White Mountain in Koshi   where
   shiranedomo   my lord goes   still I'll
yuki no mani mani   seek him out   following his
ato wa tazunan   path through the snows to his goal

Fujiwara no Kanesuke

For Shira yama, see 383. Here it is a makurakotoba linked to the next line by the
repetition of sounds. The kakekotoba "yuki" means both "going" and "snow."
"Ato" (tracks) is an engo for "snow."

392 • *As visitors left for the capital at dusk, after worshiping at Kazan.*

yūgure no	oh that this rough fence
magaki wa yama to	might loom in evening shadows
mienanan	like a mountain you
yoru wa koeji to	could not cross at night then you
yadori toru beku	might seek shelter here with me

Henjō

For Kazan, see 119.

393 • *Composed on parting from friends after climbing the mountain.*

wakare oba	let our departure
yama no sakura ni	be decided by these blossoms
makaseten	of mountain cherry—
tomen tomeji wa	to linger here or to go—
hana no manimani	we'll follow the flowers' whim

Yūsen

The mountain is Hiei, where Yūsen had gone presumably on ecclesiastical duties.

394 • *The following two poems were composed under the cherry blossoms on seeing Prince Urin'in leave after attending a memorial service.*

yama kaze ni	let the mountain winds
sakura fukimaki	sweep the cherry petals in
midarenan	whirling confusion
hana no magire ni	that he may lose his way in
tachitomaru beku	their wild dance and linger here

Henjō

Prince Urin'in was Tsuneyasu; see 75.

395 •

koto naraba	now that you've begun
kimi tomaru beku	to blossom oh cherries bloom
niowanan	your loveliest hold

kaesu wa hana no   him here   for his return might
uki ni ya wa aranu   betray your uncomeliness

Yūsen

The second line echoes the last line of poem 394.

396 • *Composed when the Ninna Mikado was Crown Prince and was returning from viewing Furu Falls.*

   akazu shite   longing still to stay
wakaruru namida   tears flow on parting now   and
   taki ni sou   mingle with the falls—
mizu masaru to ya   downstream they must be wide-eyed
shimo wa miru ran   to see the waters swelling

Kengei

See 21 for the Ninna Mikado and 248 for Furu Falls.

397 • *Composed at dusk, when he took up his cup before going into the heavy rain after being invited to drink with the Mikado at the Kannarinotsubo.*

   aki hagi no   the blossoms of the
hana oba ame ni   autumn bush clover were crushed
   nurasedomo   by the rainstorm   but
kimi oba mashite   my regrets are for you   my
oshi to koso omoe   lord   from whom I now must part

Ki no Tsurayuki

See 190 for Kannarinotsubo. The Mikado was Daigo tennō.

398 • *In reply to the above poem.*

   oshimu ran   you say your heart has
hito no kokoro o   been filled with love's regrets   but
   shiranu ma ni   unfathomable
aki no shigure to   has it been to one who has
mi zo furinikeru   grown old as autumn rains fell

Prince Kanemi

"Furinikeru" means both "rained" and "aged."

399 • *Composed on parting from Prince Kanemi after first conversing with him.*

wakaruredo	although we part
ureshiku mo aru ka	I am filled with happiness
koyoi yori	for now I wonder
ai minu yori	whom I might have thought I loved
nani o koimashi	before we two met tonight

Ōshikōchi no Mitsune

400 • *Topic unknown.*

akazu shite	these white jewels on
wakaruru sode no	the sleeves of my robe I shall
shiratama wa	enwrap and save as
kimi ga katami to	remembrances of one from
tsutsumite zo yuku	whom I did not wish to part

Anonymous

401 • *Topic unknown.*

kagiri naku	my sleeves are tear-drenched
omou namida ni	because unceasing thoughts of
sobochinuru	you linger in my
sode wa kawakaji	heart never shall my robes be
awan hi made ni	dry until we meet again

Anonymous

402 • *Topic unknown.*

kakikurashi	may the rains pour from
koto wa furanan	the heavens may the skies be
harusame ni	dark with spring cloudbursts
nureginu kisete	that you my lord might remain
kimi o todomen	with me and not drench your robes

Anonymous

"Harusame" (spring rains) and "nure" (drenching) are engo.

403 • *Topic unknown.*

shiite yuku	he is determined
hito o todomen	to go but I will hold him—

sakurabana
izure o michi to
madou made chire

oh cherry blossoms
scatter and erase the path
that would lead away from me

Anonymous

404 • *Composed on parting from someone with whom he had chatted at Ishii Spring on Shiga Pass.*

musubu te no
shizuku ni nigoru
  yama no i no
akade mo hito ni
wakarenuru kana

my thirst still unslaked
droplets from my cupped palms cloud
  the pure mountain spring—
still would I tarry with one
from whom I must now take leave

Ki no Tsurayuki

For Shiga, see 115. The first three lines are a jo; "aka" is a kakekotoba meaning "water offered to the Buddha" and "tiring." This poem was influenced by *Man'yōshū* 3807, quoted in the Japanese Preface, and by XV, 764.

405 • *Composed on parting from someone whose carriage he had met on the road.*

shita no obi no
michi wa katagata
  wakaru tomo
yukimegurite mo
awan to zo omou

the roads we two take
will wind to right and left   long
  as your undersash—
and yet someday it may be
that our paths will cross again

Ki no Tomonori

"Yukimegurite" (going around) is an engo for "obi" (sash).

BOOK IX

Travel Poems

406 • *On gazing at the moon in China.*

ama no hara	I gaze across the
furisake mireba	endless plains of the sky can
kasuga naru	that moon be the one
mikasa no yama ni	that comes from the rim of Mount
ideshi tsuki ka mo	Mikasa in Kasuga

Abe no Nakamaro

This story is told of this poem: Long ago Nakamaro was sent by the Mikado to China to study. For many years he was unable to return, but, when at last he was to accompany an imperial envoy back, the Chinese held a farewell banquet at a place by the sea called Mei. It is said this poem was composed when night fell and the moon rose bewitchingly.

For Kasuga, see 364. Kasuga Shrine stands at the foot of Mikasa Mountain. Before leaving for China, envoys such as Nakamaro prayed at Kasuga.

407 • *Sent to friends in the capital when his ship was setting sail for exile in Oki.*

wata no hara	oh fishing vessels
yaso shima kakete	please take this message back to
kogiidenu to	those I love over
hito ni wa tsuge yo	the vast blue ocean's expanse
ama no tsuribune	I've rowed toward endless isles

Ono no Takamura

The island of Oki was a notorious place of exile for political prisoners. Takamura was appointed envoy to China but refused to go; he was exiled in 838.

408 • *Topic unknown.*

miyako idete	today I left the
kyō mika no hara	capital Mika Meadow
izumi gawa	and the Izumi
kawa kaze samushi	River are in sight chill winds
koromo kase yama	blow Mount Kase Lend a Robe

Anonymous

Mika (here used to mean "seeing" and "third day") Meadow lies along the northern bank of the Ōtsu River near Kyōto. The Izumi River flows west through Yamashiro Province to join the Yodo and form the Kizu River near Kase (Lend) Mountain. Kase (lend; place name) functions as a kakekotoba.

409 • *Topic unknown.*

honobono to	dimly through morning
akashi no ura no	mists over Akashi Bay my
asagiri ni	longings trace the ship
shimagakure yuku	vanishing from sight floating
fune o shi zo omou	silently behind the isle

Anonymous

Some say this poem was composed by Kakinomoto no Hitomaro.

"Honobono to" (dimly) is a makurakotoba for "akashi" (dawn). Akashi Bay is in Hyōgo Prefecture, Akashi City.

410 • *Once Narihira invited one or two friends to travel east with him. When they reached a place in Mikawa Province called Yatsuhashi, they dismounted to sit in the shade of some trees, attracted by some irises blooming by the river. Narihira composed this poem expressing the feelings of a traveler, beginning each line with a syllable of the word "kakitsubata" (iris).*

kara koromo	familiar as the
kitsutsu narenishi	comfort of a well-worn robe
tsuma shi areba	is my beloved
harubaru kinuru	oh how this distant journey
tabi o shi zo omou	fills my heart with regret

Ariwara no Narihira

Mikawa Province is now Aichi Prefecture. Poems 410 and 411 are included in *The Tales of Ise*, 9. The introductions are nearly the same as the *Ise* text; presumably the source is *Narihira shū*. Poem 410, Helen McCullough has noted (*Tales of Ise*, pp. 203–4), "is a technical tour de force, much less characteristic of Narihira's best poetry than of the court style proper.... [I]t could scarcely be accused by Tsurayuki or anyone else of containing too much matter and too little art." He has complied with the rules of the game called oriku by using the syllables of "kakitsubata" to begin the lines of his poem. He has used a makurakotoba, "kara koromo" (Chinese robe) and a jo, "kara koromo kitsutsu" (continuing to wear the Chinese robe), linked to the main statement by the kakekotoba "narenishi" (having grown fond of; well worn). "Tsuma" (skirt; wife) is also a kakekotoba, and "tsuma," "kara koromo," "kitsutsu" (wearing), "nare" (long-worn), "haru" (to full) are engo.

411 • *When Narihira came to the banks of the Sumida River, which runs between Musashi Province and Shimōsa Province, he and his companions dismounted for a time, thinking longingly of the capital. "How endless the road I have come!" they thought as they gazed across the river. The ferryman urged his party to come aboard quickly for night was near, and when all were aboard and about to cross the river, there was not one who did not long for someone left in the capital. Just then they saw a white bird with a red bill and red legs splashing about at the river's edge. It was not a bird that was ever seen in the capital and so no one could identify it. When they asked the ferryman, he replied, "Why, it's a capital bird!" Narihira recited this poem.*

na ni shi owaba	oh capital bird
iza koto towan	if you are true to your name
miyakodori	you will know tell me
waga omou hito wa	if the one whom I love is
ari ya nashi ya	still in this world of partings

Ariwara no Narihira

For Musashi Province, see 390. Shimōsa is now part of Chiba Prefecture. The Sumida River ran along the boundary of Musashi and Shimōsa. The capital bird (miyakodori) is believed to be the modern yurikamome, a small gull with red bill and legs.

412 • *Topic unknown.*

kita e yuku	hauntingly they cry
kari zo naku naru	the northbound geese of the night—
tsurete koshi	one from their number
kazu wa tarade zo	who flew this way in autumn
kaeruberanaru	accompanies them not home

Anonymous

Some say this poem was composed by a woman who had gone with her husband to another province where he soon died. As she returned to the capital alone she heard the wild geese cry and wrote this poem.

Tsurayuki quotes this poem in the *Tosa Diary:* "Because one from the number who had traveled down with us was missing, I recalled the words of the old poem, 'One from their number accompanies them not home.'"

4 1 3 • *Composed on the road back to the capital from the eastern provinces.*

yama kakusu	how hateful the mists
haru no kasumi zo	of spring that hide the mountains
urameshiki	from my longing eyes—
izure miyako no	I cannot tell where lie the
sakai naru ran	contours of the capital

Oto

4 1 4 • *Composed on seeing Shira yama while in the northern provinces.*

kiehatsuru	because here there is
toki shi nakereba	no season when it can melt
koshiji naru	and disappear snow
shira yama no na wa	lends a name to towering
yuki ni zo arikeru	White Mountain on Koshi road

Ōshikōchi no Mitsune

For Koshi, the northern provinces, see 370; for Shira yama (White Mountain), 383.

4 1 5 • *Composed on the road when he was traveling in the eastern provinces.*

ito ni yoru	though life's path is not
mono naranaku ni	a tangled skein of threads which
wakareji no	ravels as we part—
kokorobosoku mo	my heart stretches thinner as
omōyuru kana	the distance between us grows

Ki no Tsurayuki

"Kokorobosoku" (forlornly) is composed of two words meaning "narrow heart."

4 1 6 • *Composed on the road when he was traveling in Kai Province.*

yo o samumi	so many times on
oku hatsushimo o	freezing nights my head rested

haraitsutsu   on pillows of grass—
kusa no makura ni   fitful in the dark I would
amata tabi nenu   brush away winter's first frosts

Ōshikōchi no Mitsune

Kai is now Yamanashi Prefecture.

4 1 7 • *When they were traveling to a hot spring in Tajima Province, Kanesuke
recited this after his companion composed a poem while they ate their evening meal
during a stop at Futami Bay.*

yūzuku yo   when night gathers   the
obotsukanaki o   waters are but dimly seen—
    tamakushige   at dawn once more I'll
futami no ura wa   view Twice-seen Bay   glittering
akete koso mime   like a jeweled box as day bursts open

Fujiwara no Kanesuke

Tajima is now part of Hyōgo Prefecture. "Tamakushige" (elegant comb box) is a
makurakotoba for "futa" (lid), the first two syllables of the place name Futami,
which also means "seeing twice." "Akete" means both "dawning" and "opening."
"Tamakushige," "futa," and "akete" are engo.

4 1 8 • *Once when Narihira was hunting with Prince Koretaka, they dismounted
on the bank of a stream called Amanogawa. As they were drinking there, the Prince
said, "Offer the sake cup with a poem on the theme 'Coming to the river of heaven
after hunting.'"*

karikurashi   hunting filled the day—
tanabatatsume ni   the night I'll spend with the maid
    yado karan   of Tanabata
ama no kawara ni   for now I have arrived at
ware wa kinikeri   the riverbed of heaven

Ariwara no Narihira

Prince Koretaka, son of Montoku tennō, is the author of two *Kokinshū* poems. The
Amanogawa (river of heaven) runs through Hirakata near Ōsaka. The name of the
river has inspired a poem about the Tanabata legend: the stars, Altair (the
herdsmann) and Vega (the weaver maid), separated by the river of heaven (the Milky
Way), are allowed one meeting a year on the seventh night of the Seventh Month.
Poems 418 and 419 are both found in *The Tales of Ise*, 82.

419 • *The Prince recited Narihira's poem several times without being able to think of a reply, so Aritsune, who was one of the party, composed this for him.*

hitotose ni	because she awaits
hitotabi kimasu	her love who visits but once
kimi mateba	each slow-passing year
yado kasu hito mo	I doubt that she will lend us
araji to zo omou	a lodging place for the night

Ki no Aritsune

420 • *The following two poems were composed on the mountain where they made offerings when Suzakuin was in Nara.*

kono tabi wa	I had no time to
nusa mo toriaezu	make prayer strips for this journey
tamuke yama	yet on the hill of
momiji no nishiki	offerings there's a bright brocade
kami no mani mani	of leaves to regale the gods

Sugawara no Michizane

Retired Mikado Uda was known by the name of his residence, the Suzakuin (see 230). The excursion took place in the fall of 898. "Tabi" means both "trip" and "occasion."

421 •

tamuke ni wa	this patched robe too I
tsuzuri no sode mo	should shred into offering
kiru beki ni	strips but mightn't the
momiji ni akeru	gods surfeited with bits of
kami ya kaesan	bright fall leaves return my gifts

Sosei

BOOK X

Wordplays

422 • *Uguisu (mountain thrush).*

kokoro kara	willingly he flits
hana no shizuku ni	among the blossoms drenched by
sobochi tsutsu	drops from the petals—
uku hizu to nomi	why then does the thrush weep to
tori no naku ran	find his plumage sadly damp

Fujiwara no Toshiyuki

The poems in Book X are products of a game in which the poet hides a given word or words within his composition. Voiced and unvoiced consonants were represented with the same symbols, and other spelling peculiarities sometimes mask the words in the transcription, but the headnotes for these poems list them and they have been italicized in the transcriptions. Often the hidden words straddle two lines; "uku hizu" (sadly not drying), representing the hidden word "uguisu," here does not, and so, functions almost as a kakekotoba. Both 422 and 423 are riddles, the answer to which is the hidden word. In some poems there is a relationship between the meaning of the poem and the hidden words; in others there is no obvious connection. For uguisu, see 4.

423 • *Hototogisu (nightingale).*

kubeki *hodo*	is it that we have
*toki su*ginure ya	awaited his coming so
machiwabite	long now that summer's
naku naru koe no	first day is past our sad cries
hito o toyomuru	echo the nightingale's song

Fujiwara no Toshiyuki

For hototogisu, see 135.

424 • *Utsusemi (cicada).*

nami no *utsu*   tumbled jewels crest
*semi*reba tama zo   the waves rising and breaking
    midarekeru   before me   like
hirowaba sode ni   cicadas' cries   they'll vanish
hakanakaran ya   in my gathering sleeves

Ariwara no Shigeharu

425 • *Reply.*

tamoto yori   could one keep precious
hanarete tama o   jewels anywhere but in
    tsutsumame ya   one's enfolding sleeves—
kore nan sore to   tell me these are gems   let me
utsuse min kashi   try to wrap them up with care

Mibu no Tadamine

426 • *Ume (plum).*

ana *u me* ni   such misery to
tsunenaru beku mo   see these blossoms   so fragile
    mienu kana   they must soon be gone—
koishikaru beki   hauntingly plum fragrance wafts—
ka wa nioi tsutsu   petals fall   still it lingers

Anonymous

427 • *Kaniwazakura (white birch).*

kazukedomo   however deep I
nami no na*ka ni wa*   dived   I could not capture the
    *sagura*rede   white gems in the waves
kaze fuku goto ni   yet with each gust of wind   pearls
ukishizumu tama   swirl into sight   then vanish

Ki no Tsurayuki

428 • *Sumomo no hana (damson plum blossoms).*

ima iku ka   how many more days
haru shi nakereba   now will spring linger   gazing

uguisu mo	listlessly he too
mono wa nagamete	laments the mountain thrush
omouberanari	cries for the faded plum boughs

Ki no Tsurayuki

429 • *Karamomo no hana (apricot blossoms).*

au kara mo	since we met beneath
mono wa nao koso	the boughs of apricot my
koishikere	sad thoughts have but grown—
wakaren koto o	for already I feel the
kanete omoeba	misery of our parting

Kiyowara no Fukayabu

430 • *Tachibana (mandarin orange).*

ashihiki no	an unsettled world
yama tachihanare	this is as changeable as
yuku kumo no	the drifting clouds which
yadori sadamenu	take leave from the steep mountains
yo ni koso arikere	where I wander homeless

Ono no Shigekage

"Ashihiki no" is a makurakotoba for "yama" (mountain). The first three lines are a jo linking the clouds and the speaker imagistically.

431 • *Ogatama no ki (an evergreen).*

miyoshino no	these bubbles of pearl
yoshino no taki ni	foaming on the rapids of
ukabi izuru	lovely Yoshino—
awa o ka tama no	did men of old too see these
kiyu to mitsuran	as fragile gems here and gone

Ki no Tomonori

The identity of the Ogatama tree was one of the mysteries listed in the *Kokindenjū*. For Yoshino, see 3. "Tama" is a kakekotoba meaning "jewel" and "spirit."

432 • *Yamagaki no ki (mountain persimmon tree).*

aki wa kinu	autumn has arrived—
ima ya magaki no	now the cicadas will cry

kirigirisu   their shrill complaints
yona yona nakan   night after night beneath the
kaze no samusa ni   bamboo fence in the chill wind

Anonymous

---

433 • *Aoi (hollyhock) and katsura (Judas tree).*

kaku bakari   how can I not think
au hi no mare ni   him cruel   that hard-hearted
naru hito o   one who came when
ika*ga tsura*shi to   hollyhocks bloomed   for now his
omowazaru beki   visits grow painfully rare

Anonymous

---

434 • *Aoi (hollyhock) and katsura (Judas tree).*

hitome yue   if   irresolute
nochi ni *au hi* no   before those watchful eyes   I
harukekuba   let the days go by
wa*ga tsura*ki ni ya   between our meetings   will she
omoi nasaren   come to think me unfeeling

Anonymous

---

435 • *Kutani (a summer flower).*

chirinureba   thoughtless butterfly—
nochi wa a*kuta ni*   it flutters and darts nearer
naru hana o   infatuated—
omoishirazu mo   never realizing that this
madou chō kana   bloom too will return to dust

Henjō

Kutani may be another name for rindō (gentian, *Gentiana scabra*).

---

436 • *Sōbi (roses).*

ware wa ke*sa*   early this morning
ui ni zo mitsuru   I first chanced to see their blooms—

hana no iro o
ada naru mono to
iu bekarikeri

how the exotic
hue of the roses deserves
to be called spectacular

Ki no Tsurayuki

"Ada" (bewitching) was a word derived from Chinese and thus appropriate to describe a flower brought from China.

437 • *Ominaeshi (maiden flowers).*

shiratsuyu o
tama ni nuku to ya
sasaga ni no
hana ni mo ha ni mo
ito *o mina heshi*

small spider spinning
your delicate threads to each
petal and leaf   do
you intend to link each dew-
drop on the maiden flowers

Ki no Tomonori

For ominaeshi, see 226.

438 • *Ominaeshi (maiden flowers).*

asa tsuyu o
wakesobochitsutsu
hana min to
ima zo no yama *o*
mina heshirinuru

while treading paths through
morning dew to see maiden
flowers glistening
I have come to know each and
every field and mountain

Ki no Tomonori

439 • *Composed for the Suzakuin Ominaeshi Contest, using the five syllables of "ominaeshi" to begin the lines.*

ogura yama
mine tachinarashi
naku shika no
heniken aki o
shiru hito zo naki

wearing down the peak
of Mount Ogura   pacing
loudly belling   no
one knows how many autumns
this deer has cried for his love

Ki no Tsurayuki

For this Ominaeshi (Maiden Flower) Contest, see 230. For Ogura Mountain, see 312. This poem is another example of oriku; see 410.

174

440 • *Kichikō no hana (bellflower blossoms).*

aki chikō	as autumn draws near
no wa narinikeri	the fields begin to dress in
shiratsuyu no	fall's brighter array—
okeru kusaba mo	even leaves where white dew clings
iro kawariyuku	redden beneath its cover

Ki no Tomonori

The kichikō, now known as kikyō, is the Chinese bellflower, *Platycodon grandiflorum.*

441 • *Shioni (aster).*

furihaete	such a distance I
iza furusato no	have come to admire the
hana min to	asters here where
koshi o nioi zo	once we lived but already
utsuroinikeru	the blooms have passed their glory

Anonymous

Shioni (shion) are asters, *Aster tataricus.*

442 • *Riutan no hana (gentian).*

waga yado no	I'll chastise these birds
hana fumishidaku	who dare to trample the blooms
tori utan	in my garden are
no wa nakeraba ya	there no gentians in the fields—
koko ni shimo kuru	why must they search for them here

Ki no Tomonori

Riutan, now called rindō, are gentians (*Gentiana scabra*).

443 • *Obana (plume grass).*

ari to mite	how difficult
tanomu zo kataki	to trust in its existence—
utsusemi no	this world fragile as
yo oba nashi to ya	a castoff cicada's shell—
omoinashiten	shall I believe it unreal

Anonymous

Obana refers to the ear of the susuki, *Miscanthus sinensis*, a pampas grass. This poem, like many others, refers to the Buddhist teaching that the seemingly real phenomena of this world are actually empty and illusory.

444 • *Kenigoshi (morning glory).*

uchitsuke *ni*	suddenly their hue
koshi to ya hana no	seems to deepen turn darker
iro o min	blue before my eyes—
oku shiratsuyu no	is it simply the cover
somuru bakari o	of crystal dew that tints them

Yatabe no Nazane

Kenigoshi, now called asagao, are morning glories, *Ipomoea purpurea*.

445 • *Yasuhide was requested to recite a poem on the carved wooden medo flowers by the Nijō Consort when she was still known as Lady of the Bedchamber.*

hana no ki ni	this is not a tree
arazara*medomo*	which blooms and yet here
sakinikeri	are the flowers oh
furinishi konomi	that there might yet be a time
naru toki mo gana	for ancient stalks to ripen

Funya no Yasuhide

The meaning of "medo" is unclear. Three explanations have been offered: that it is a type of bush clover; that it is a temporary corridor built to lead horses inside; that it is a type of paneled door. "The carved flowers of the medo" were one of the three plants about which secret explanations were passed down. For the Nijō Consort, see 8. "Ko no mi naru" means both "trees' fruit ripens" and "this body becomes."

446 • *Shinobugusa (longing grass).*

yama takami	ceaselessly the chill
tsune ni ara*shi no*	winter storms sweep down from
*fuku sa*to wa	high-peaked mountains in
nioi mo aezu	this village buds of longing
hana zo chirikeru	grass fall before they open

Ki no Toshisada

For shinobugusa, see 200.

447 • *Yamashi.*

hototogisu	oh nightingale have
mine no kumo ni *ya*	you become one with the clouds
*maji*rinishi	on the mountain peaks
ari to wa kikedo	your song floats down to my ears
miru yo shimo naki	but you are invisible

Taira no Atsuyuki

Yamashi possibly is a small purple wild flower of the lily family.

448 • *Karahagi.*

utsusemi no	within the caskets
kara wa ki goto ni	lie the bodies still here with
todomuredo	us in this world and
tama no yukue o	yet how sad that we cannot
minu zo kanashiki	see the spirit's resting place

Anonymous

Karahagi evidently means Chinese bush clover, but it is unclear which plant bore this name. "Kara" also suggests both the empty cicada shell and a human corpse (nakigara), empty of its spirit.

449 • *Kawanagusa (river grasses).*

ubatama no	jet-black gems swirl as
yume ni nani *ka wa*	in my dreams we meet comfort
*nagusa*man	still eludes me were
utsutsu ni dani mo	we to meet in daylight still
akanu kokoro o	my heart would not be sated

Kiyowara no Fukayabu

Kawanagusa, some type of river weed, was one of the "three plants" of the secret traditions of the *Kokindenjū*. "Ubatama no," often interpreted as "pitch-black" or "black as leopard-flower berries," is a makurakotoba that modifies "yume" (dream).

450 • *Sagarigoke (hanging moss).*

hana no iro wa	only briefly do
tada hito *sakari*	the autumn grasses display
*koke*redomo	their beauties yet each

kaesugaesu zo   night the dew has come to dye
tsuyu wa somekeru   the petals deeper colors

Takamuko no Toshiharu

Sagarigoke, evidently the plant now called saruogase, is a moss, *Usnea longissima*.

---

45 1 • *Nigatake (long-jointed bamboo).*

  inochi tote   difficult it is to
tsuyu o tanomu *ni*   depend upon sips of dew
  *katake*reba   to sustain one's life—
mono wabi shira ni   so anxiously they pipe long
naku nobe no mushi   lonely hours   insects of the fields

Ariwara no Shigeharu

Nigatake (medake) is a bamboo, *Arundinaria simoni*.

---

452 • *Kawatake (mushroom).*

  sayo fukete   already the moon
na*kabatake* yuku   has half climbed the celestial
  hisakata no   dome   as night grows old—
tsuki fukihaese   oh autumn wind from the peaks
aki no yamakaze   blow it backward on its course

Prince Kagenori

Kawatake may be the mushroom now called kotake. "Hisakata no" is a makura-kotoba modifying "tsuki" (moon).

---

453 • *Warabi (bracken).*

  keburi tachi   no flames blaze nor does
moyu tomo mienu   smoke ever rise from the leaves
  kusa no ha o   of this plant   why then
tare ka *warabi* to   did anyone ever name
nazuke someken   this damp black bracken "straw fire"

Shinsei

"Moyu" means both "to burn" and "to sprout." The word "warabi" (bracken) has the same sound as the words "straw fire."

454 • *Sasa (bamboo grass), matsu (pine), biwa (loquat), and bashōba (banana plant).*

isasame ni	so many days passed
toki *matsu* ma ni zo	by while I awaited this
hi wa henuru	brief encounter that
kokoro*base oba*	now together he must see
hito ni mietsutsu	how joyfully my heart leaps

Ki no Menoto

455 • *Nashi (pear), natsume (jujube), and kurumi (chestnut).*

ajiki*nashi*	how foolish is this
nageki *na tsume* so	life I have met with trials
uki koto ni	at every turn
ai*kuru mi* oba	still I did not abandon
sutenu mono kara	hope give me no more sorrow

Fujiwara no Hyōe

456 • *Composed on the first day of spring in a place called Karakoto.*

nami no oto	the very rush of
kesa *kara koto* ni	the waves resounds with the song
kikoyuru wa	of spring this morning—
haru no shirabe ya	my Chinese koto has changed
aratamaru ran	to a vernal melody

Abe no Kiyoyuki

Karakoto was along the Inland Seacoast, possibly in Okayama Prefecture. The name means "Chinese koto."

457 • *Ikagasaki (Cape Ikaga).*

kaji ni ataru	splashing droplets like
nami no shizuku o	cascading sprays of bloom oars
haru nareba	dip into the sea—
*ikaga saki*chiru	how could I miss this vision
hana to mizaramu	of spring here at Ikaga

Anonymous

Cape Ikaga may have been in Hirakata City near Ōsaka.

458 • *Karasaki (Cape Kara).*

kano kata ni	when did it travel
itsu *kara saki* ni	across our bow far on the
watariken	horizon leaving
namiji wa ato mo	not even a trace to see
nokorazarikeri	anywhere on the water paths

Abe no Tsunemi

Cape Kara is on the shore of Lake Biwa in Shiga

459 • *Karasaki (Cape Kara).*

nami no hana	from far away on
oki *kara sakite*	the horizon wave blossoms
chirikumeri	roll toward the shore—
mizu no haru to wa	is it the breeze transforming
kaze ya naruran	itself into ocean's spring

Ise

460 • *Kamiya gawa (Kamiya River).*

ubatama no	has my coal-black hair
waga kuro*kami ya*	too changed before my very
*kawa*ru ran	eyes recently white
kagami no kage ni	drifts of snow settle on that
fureru shirayuki	reflection in my mirror

Ki no Tsurayuki

The Kamiya River ran through the Heian Imperial Palace grounds and emptied into the Katsura River.

461 • *Yodo gawa (Yodo River).*

ashihiki no	at the foot of the
yamabe ni oreba	craggy mountain I make my
shirakumo no	solitary home
ika ni se*yo to ka*	white clouds hang heavily here
*haru*ru toki naki	pressing sorrow upon me

Ki no Tsurayuki

The Yodo River refers to the lower reaches of the Uji River near Ōsaka.

462 • *Katano.*

natsugusa no	like the marsh water
ue wa shigeru	pent up no outlet for its
numa mizu no	flow thickly covered
yuku *kata no* naki	with the tangle of summer
waga kokoro kana	grass my heart has no release

Mibu no Tadamine

Katano City is near Ōsaka. Kanmu tennō had a villa there. Lines 1–3, "of the marsh waters where summer grasses flourish on the surface," are a jo linked to the last lines by zeugma: "yuku" (going; to go) serves as the predicate of the jo and as part of the phrase "yuku kata no naki" (nowhere to go).

463 • *Katsura no miya.*

aki kuredo	autumn has come and
tsuki no *katsura no*	although the laurel tree of
mi ya wa naru	the moon bears no fruit
hikari o hana to	it scatters shimmering beams
chirasu bakari o	of light like falling petals

Minamoto no Hodokosu

Katsura no miya may have been the name of a villa in the capital or of a fictional character. See 194.

464 • *Hakuwakō (incense).*

hana goto ni	untiring wind
akazu chirashishi	you have scattered the petals
kaze nareba	of every bloom—
iku so*baku waga*	oh how bitterly I must
ushi to ka wa omou	regard your careless caprice

Anonymous

465 • *Suminagashi (dyeing paper by dipping it into water with ink floating on the surface).*

haruga*sumi*	if there were no path
naka shi kayoiji	through the mists of spring swirling
nakariseba	like ink on water—

| aki kuru kari wa | the wild geese that arrive in |
| kaerazaramashi | autumn could not return home |

Ariwara no Shigeharu

466 • *Okibi (blazing fire).*

nagara izuru	flowing waters not
kata dani mienu	even the source is known—
namida gawa	river of lonely
*oki*hin toki ya	tears will the depths be known at
soko wa shiraren	last when it has turned to dust

Miyako no Yoshika

467 • *Chimaki (festival rice).*

no*chimaki* no	sown late the seedlings
okurete ouru	finally sprout and yet the
nae naredo	planting of this year
ada ni wa naranu	will not be fruitless for the
tanomi to zo kiku	earth of the fields is faithful

Ōe no Chisato

Rice wrapped in miscanthus leaves was eaten during the Fifth Month festivals. "Tanomi" means both "request" and "fields' fruits."

468 • *Shōhō was told to compose a poem beginning with the syllable "ha" and ending with "ru" ("haru" means "spring"), punning on the word "nagame" (long rains; gazing), and treating the topic "spring."*

hana no *naka*	thinking my eyes would
me ni aku ya to te	never tire of their beauty
wakeyukeba	I roamed amid the
kokoro zo tomo ni	blossoms and as the petals
chirinu beranaru	fluttered my heart too wandered

Shōhō

Using the syllables of a two-syllable word to begin and end a poem was called kutsukanmuri.

BOOK XI

Love Poems (I)

469 • *Topic unknown.*

hototogisu	when nightingales sing
naku ya satsuki no	in the sweet purple iris
ayamegusa	of the Fifth Month I
ayame mo shiranu	am unmindful of the warp
koi mo suru kana	on which we weave love's pattern

Anonymous

For hototogisu, see 135. Lines 1–3 are a jo, linked to the final two lines by the similarity in sound between the words "ayamegusa" (iris, sweet flag) and "ayame" (thread of logic). "Aya" also means weave or pattern.

470 • *Topic unknown.*

oto ni nomi	the white dew settling
kiku no shiratsuyu	on the chrysanthemums and
yoru wa okite	I whose nights are made
hiru wa omoi ni	restless by these barren tidings
aezu kenu beshi	will vanish in the morning sun

Sosei

Lines 1 and 2 (only hearing rumors) are a jo ending with the kakekotoba "kiku," meaning both "to hear" and "chrysanthemum." "Okite" means both dew "settling" and "awakening." "Kenu" (die, vanish) is an engo for "tsuyu" (dew).

471 • *Topic unknown.*

yoshino gawa	so suddenly was
iwanami takaku	my heart dyed with passion for

yuku mizu no
hayaku zo hito o
omoisomete shi

you   it leapt high as
the waves in the waters of
the swift Yoshino River

Ki no Tsurayuki

For Yoshino River, see 124. The first three lines (the Yoshino River's high-standing waves) are a jo. "Hayaku" means "quickly," "early" and "high."

472 • *Topic unknown.*

shiranami no
ato naki kata ni
    yuku fune mo
kaze zo tayori no
shirube narikeru

even the ship which
sails forth over white waves which
    rise and fall   leaving
no trace   can rely on the
winds to guide it safely home

Fujiwara no Kachion

473 • *Topic unknown.*

otowa yama
oto ni kikitsutsu
    ōsaka no
seki no konata ni
toshi o furu kana

I hear rumors of
her   borne by Mount Sound of Wings
    and yet here on the
far side of Meeting Hill I
pass the years in barren dreams

Ariwara no Motokata

For Otowa (Sound of Wings) Mountain, see 142. Here the name functions as a makurakotoba for "oto" (sound; rumor) in line 2. For the Ōsaka Barrier, see 374.

474 • *Topic unknown.*

tachikaeri
aware to zo omou
    yoso nite mo
hito ni kokoro o
okitsu shiranami

I turn back to her
as the white waves roll to shore
    from the offing   no
matter the distance   my heart
is held captive by her charms

Ariwara no Motokata

"Tachikaeri" (repeatedly; rising and returning) is an engo for "nami" (waves). "Okitsu" means both "in the offing" and "giving [one's heart]."

475 • *Topic unknown.*

yo no naka wa	such are the ways of
kaku koso arikere	this world my heart swells with love
fuku kaze no	for her and yet she
me ni minu hito mo	is invisible as the winds
koishikarikeri	which whisper of her charms

Ki no Tsurayuki

476 • *On the day of an archery meet at the riding grounds of the Right Imperial Guards, Narihira glimpsed a woman's face through the hangings of the carriage opposite his. He sent her this poem.*

mizu mo arazu	not hidden and yet
mi mo senu hito no	not disclosed was one for whom my
koishiku wa	heart leapt in new-found
ayanaku kyō ya	love must I now spend the day
nagame kurasan	in unavailing yearnings

Ariwara no Narihira

An annual equestrian archery contest was held on the Imperial Palace grounds on the sixth of the Fifth Month. Carriages of the nobility were enclosed with hanging blinds and brocades through which tantalizing glimpses of the occupants might be captured. This poem appears in *The Tales of Ise*, 99, and *Yamato monogatari*, 166. The *Ise* text is almost identical to this headnote.

477 • *Reply.*

shiru shiranu	why worry thus so
nani ka ayanaku	uselessly over whether
wakite iwan	you know her or not—
omoi nomi koso	love alone can introduce
shirube narikere	you to one for whom you long

Anonymous

This reply is found also in *The Tales of Ise*, 99. In *Yamato monogatari*, the woman's reply is:

mi mo mizu mo	seen yet unseen—
tare to shirite ka	how can you know who I am—
koiraruru	unconvinced that I

obotsukanasa no   am loved   I pass the long day
kyō no nagame ya   in listless gazing.

"Omoi" (thoughts; longings) contains the word "(h)i" (fire), suggesting signal fires or fire lighting a path.

478 • *Tadamine, having asked where she lived, sent this to the home of a woman he had seen out viewing the Kasuga Festival.*

kasuga no no	I merely glimpsed your
yuki ma o wakete	beauty barely visible—
oiide kuru	like the blades of grass
kusa no hatsuka ni	sprouting through the deep blanket
mieshi kimi wa mo	of snow on Kasuga Fields

Mibu no Tadamine

Festivals were held at Kasuga Shrine in the Second and Eleventh Months. This would be the spring event. Kasuga Meadow was famous for spring greens; see poems I, 17, 18, and 22. The first three-and-one-half lines serve as a jo linked to "hatsuka" by means of the kakekotoba "ha," which is the first syllable of hatsuka (scarcely) and also means "leaf."

479 • *Tsurayuki sent this to the home of a woman he had seen plucking blossoms.*

yamazakura	a fleeting glimpse
kasumi no ma yori	as of mountain cherries seen
honoka ni mo	through the thick veil of
miteshi hito koso	spring mists I sacrcely saw
koishikarikere	the one who captured my heart

Ki no Tsurayuki

Lines 1 and 2 (mountain cherry blossoms from the midst of the mists) are a jo linked to the last lines by "honoka ni mo miteshi" (even dimly seen).

480 • *Topic unknown.*

tayori ni mo	longing is not a
aranu omoi no	messenger and yet how strange
ayashiki wa	it is that my love
kokoro o hito ni	has carried my heart away
tsukuru narikeri	and delivered it to her

Ariwara no Motokata

481 • *Topic unknown.*

hatsukari no	since first I heard her
hatsuka ni koe o	voice refreshing as the first faint
kikishi yori	call of wild geese in
nakazora ni nomi	autumn I have wandered on
mono o omou kana	the heavens' enchanted paths

Ōshikōchi no Mitsune

"Hatsukari no" (of the first wild geese) is a makurakotoba linked by sound to "hatsuka ni" (barely). "Nakazora" (up in the air) and "kari" (wild geese) are engo. Wild geese were believed to be able to carry lovers' messages, and thus this poem amplifies the sequence of images of tidings, rumors, and messages that begins in poem 470.

482 • *Topic unknown.*

au koto wa	chance of our meeting
kumoi haruka ni	is as distant as the dark
narukami no	clouded skies where
oto ni kikitsutsu	the thunder god rumbles like
koiwataru kana	tidings that enliven love

Ki no Tsurayuki

"Naru" means both "to become" and "to sound." "Narukami no" (of the thunder) is a makurakotoba for "oto" (sound; rumor).

483 • *Topic unknown.*

kataito o	if unlike these strands
konata kanata ni	braided tightly together
yorikakete	to carry jewels
awazu wa nani o	we can never meet what thread
tama no o ni sen	will hold my spirit to life

Anonymous

Lines 1–3 (single strands twisting together this way and that) are a jo linked by "awazu" (not meeting) to lines 4 and 5, which can mean either "what shall I make into the jewels' thread?" or "what shall I make [the meaning of] my life?"

484 • *Topic unknown.*

yūgure wa	at twilight I gaze
kumo no hatate ni	at the streamers of cloud stretched

mono zo omou	across the broad and
amatsu sora naru	distant skies so far above
hito o kou tote	me is the one I cherish

Anonymous

Two interpretations of "hatate" have been suggested: "edge" or "end"; and "banners." "Amatsu sora" (broad heavens) and "kumo" (clouds) are engo.

485 • *Topic unknown.*

karigomo no	can she know of my
omoimidarete	love she who scatters my thoughts
ware kou to	like reeds cut and strewn
imo shiru rame ya	about if there is no one
hito shi tsugezu wa	to tell her how can she ever know

Anonymous

"Karigomo no" (of the cut reeds) is a makurakotoba for "midarete" (scattering). This is the only instance in the *Kokinshū* of this makurakotoba which commonly is found in the *Man'yōshū.* "Imo (sister; beloved) also has an archaic flavor.

486 • *Topic unknown.*

tsure mo naki	that man unfeeling
hito o ya netaku	as the transparent dew on
shiratsuyu no	the morning grass why
oku to wa nageki	am I so plagued awake I
nu to wa shinoban	grieve asleep I yearn for him

Anonymous

"Shiratsuyu no" (of the white dew) is a makurakotoba for the kakekotoba "oku" (to settle; to awaken).

487 • *Topic unknown.*

chihayaburu	as priests bind their sleeves
kamo no yashiro no	with mulberry strands to pray
yū tasuki	to the mighty gods
hitohi mo kimi o	at Kamo Shrine my heart is
kakenu hi wa nashi	bound by thoughts of you each day

Anonymous

"Chihayaburu" is a makurakotoba of uncertain meaning which modifies words relating to the gods, here "kamo no yashiro," the Kamo Shrine in Kyōto. "Yū tasuki" (bound with mulberry cords) is a makurakotoba modifying "kakenu" (not wearing; not thinking of). Mulberry bindings were used by the priests during the Kamo Festival in the Fourth Month.

488 • *Topic unknown.*

waga koi wa	it seems my sighs of
munashiki sora ni	love have misted over all
michinurashi	the empty heavens—
omoiyaredomo	though I try to clear my thoughts
yuku kata mo nashi	there is no room to rout them

Anonymous

489 • *Topic unknown.*

suruga naru	days may pass when not
tago no ura nami	a single wave rises on
tatanu hi wa	the Bay of Tago at
aredomo kimi o	Suruga yet no day goes
koinu hi wa nashi	by without my longing for you

Anonymous

Tago Bay is in Ihara District, Shizuoka Prefecture (Suruga Province), at the mouth of the Fuji River. The repetition of the syllable "ta" at the beginning of lines 2 and 3 reflects the lapping of the waves and the repetitious passing of the days of waiting. There is an allusion to *Man'yōshū* 3670:

karatomari	days may pass when no
noko no ura nami	waves rise in the Bay of Noko
tatanu hi wa	at Karatomari
are domo ie ni	but at home no day goes by
koinu hi wa nashi	without my longing for you

490 • *Topic unknown.*

yūzuku yo	the moon at twilight
sasu ya okabe no	gleams softly on the needles
matsu no ha no	of the pines waiting
itsutomo wakanu	on the slopes as unchanging
koi mo suru kana	is the love deep in my heart

Anonymous

Lines 1–3 (the shining of the evening moon on the leaves of the pines on the slopes) are a jo linked to "itsutomo wakanu" (always unchanging). "Matsu" means both "to await" and "pine." The fifth line is the same as that of poem 469.

491 • *Topic unknown.*

ashihiki no	like the rushing
yama shita mizu no	waters of the stream beneath
kogakurete	the trees at the foot
tagitsu kokoro o	of the rugged mountains my
seki zo kanetsuru	heart leaps nothing can hold it

Anonymous

"Ashihiki no" is a makurakotoba for "yama" (mountain). Lines 1 and 2 and the first syllable of 3 (trees of the waters at the base of the "foot-dragging" mountains) are a jo linked to "gakurete tagitsu" (hiding and seething). The phrase "tagitsu kokoro" (cascading heart) echoes two *Man'yōshū* poems, 1383 and 2432.

492 • *Topic unknown.*

yoshino gawa	the bubbling waters
iwakiri toshi	of the Yoshino River
yuku mizu no	cut deep through the rocks—
oto ni wa tateji	in silence I will love you
koi wa shinu tomo	although I may die yearning

Anonymous

For Yoshino River, see 124. Lines 1–3 (of the waters flowing, cutting through the rocks—Yoshino River) are a jo modifying "oto" (sound; rumor). Compare *Man'yōshū* 2718:

takayama no	on the high mountains
iwa moto tagichi	at the foot of crags cascading
yuku mizu no	waters resound but
oto ni wa tateji	in silence I must love you
koite shinu tomo	although I may die yearning

493 • *Topic unknown.*

tagitsu se no	even in the midst
naka ni mo yodo wa	of swelling rapids there are
ari chō o	eddies they say why

nado waga koi no	in my love do neither deep
fuchise tomo naki	pools nor calm shallows exist

Anonymous

494 • *Topic unknown.*

yama takami	so high the mountains—
shita yuku mizu no	like the hidden streams flowing
shita ni nomi	far below in the
nagarete koin	secret depths I'll yearn for you
koi wa shinu tomo	though I may die of this love

Anonymous

Lines 1 and 2 (of the flowing waters below the high mountains) are a jo linked to "shita" (underneath). "Nagarete" is a kakekotoba meaning both "flowing" and "living on." The last line is the same as that of poem 492.

495 • *Topic unknown.*

omoiizuru	memories return
tokiwa no yama no	when on evergreen mountains
iwatsutsuji	wild azaleas bloom
iwaneba koso are	unspoken love burns stronger
koishiki mono o	in the silence I must keep

Anonymous

For Tokiwa Mountain, see 148. "Toki wa" also means "the time when." Lines 1-3 (when I begin to love, the azaleas of the crags on Tokiwa Mountain) are a jo linked to line 4 by the similarity in sound between "iwatsutsuji" (azaleas) and "iwaneba" (because I do not speak).

496 • *Topic unknown.*

hito shirezu	how painful it is
omoeba kurushi	to cherish one who does not
kurenai no	know my love surely
suetsumuhana no	my ardor must appear
iro ni idenan	vivid as crimson saffron

Anonymous

"Suetsumuhana" (benihana) is a safflower that has a red bloom. Lines 3 and 4 (the crimson safflower's) function as a jo modifying 'iro" (color; outward appearance). Compare *Man'yōshū* 1993:

yoso ni nomi	always from afar
mitsutsu ya koin	I shall gaze adoringly
kurenai no	although my love may
suetsumuhana no	not show itself as vividly
iro ni dezu tomo	as the crimson safflower

497 • *Topic unknown.*

aki no no no	should I reveal my
obana ni majiri	love like these bright blooms which
saku hana no	mingle with the tasseled
iro ni ya koin	grasses of the autumn fields—
au yoshi o nami	for alas we cannot meet

Anonymous

Lines 1–3 (of the flowers that bloom amid the plume grasses in the autumn fields) are a jo linked to 'iro" (color; outward appearance).

498 • *Topic unknown.*

waga sono no	there in the topmost
ume no hotsue ni	branches of the plum in my
uguisu no	garden plaintively
ne ni nakinu beki	the mountain thrush cries I too
koi mo suru kana	must cry aloud in longing

Anonymous

Lines 1–3 (of the mountain thrush in the top branches of the plum tree in my garden) are a jo linked to "ne" (sound; cries). Line 5 is the same as in 469 and 490.

499 • *Topic unknown.*

ashihiki no	mountain thrush flitting
yama hototogisu	tonight from the rugged hills—
waga goto ya	do you too find it
kimi ni koitsutsu	difficult to sleep because
inegate ni suru	of your longing for your love

Anonymous

"Ashihiki no" is a makurakotoba for "yama" (mountains).

500 • *Topic unknown.*

natsu nareba	like the mosquito
yado ni fusuburu	smudge which burns within my house
kayaribi no	when summer comes I
itsu made waga mi	too slowly char deep within—
shita moe o sen	for how long must I smolder

Anonymous

Lines 1–3 (like the smouldering mosquito smudge at my house when summer comes) is a jo linked to line 5, "shita moe" (burning underneath). "Shita" (underneath) here is the opposite of "iro" (outward appearance) in 496 and 497; it also refers to the fire burning below the rising smoke.

501 • *Topic unknown.*

koiseji to	I shall not love I
mitarashigawa ni	thought and purified myself
seshi misogi	in the river of
kami wa ukezu zo	ablutions yet it seems the
narinikerashimo	gods have refused all my prayers

Anonymous

"Mitarashigawa" refers to a stream that flows through shrine precincts and is used for ritual washing.

502 • *Topic unknown.*

aware chō	were there no word
koto dani nakuba	"alas" in this world of ours
nani o ka wa	how could I subdue
koi no midare no	my heart what ribbons could now
tsukane o ni sen	bind my scattered thoughts of love

Anonymous

503 • *Topic unknown.*

omou ni wa	burgeoning longings
shinoburu koto zo	have defeated my attempts
makenikeru	at concealment—

iro ni wa ideji to
omoishi mono o

although I had resolved
my love should never blossom

Anonymous

504 • *Topic unknown.*

waga koi wa
hito shiru rame ya
shikitae no
makura nomi koso
shiraba shiru rame

can he know   my love
that I do love him so   if
anyone could guess
my yearning it could only
be my rough hempen pillow

Anonymous

"Shikitae no" (hempen[?]) is a makurakotoba for "makura" (pillow).

505 • *Topic unknown.*

asajiu no
ono no shinohara
shinobu tomo
hito shiru rame ya
iu hito nashi ni

my love is hidden
as the bamboo grasses in
the lushly grown
meadow of reeds   how could he
know   there is none to tell him

Anonymous

"Asajiu no" (of the small reeds) is a makurakotoba for "no" (fields). Shino is a small clumping bamboo. Shinohara may be a proper noun, referring to Shinohara in Yasu, Shiga Prefecture, a place name that appears also in *Makura no sōshi*, 108. The sound repetition links lines 1 and 2 (the bamboo grass meadows of the fields of small reeds) to "shinobu" (to yearn; to bear). The use of the jo in this poem is similar to that in poems in books 11 and 12 of the *Man'yōshū*. It also breaks after lines 2 and 4, as many *Man'yōshū* poems do.

506 • *Topic unknown.*

hito shirenu
omoi ya nazo to
ashigaki no
majikakeredomo
au yoshi no naki

what could it mean   I
wondered   "a love unknown"   but
now   while we live as
near as the reeds of the rush
fence   we have no chance to meet

Anonymous

"Ashigaki no" (of the reed fence) is a makurakotoba modifying "majikakeredomo" (although closely spaced).

507 • *Topic unknown.*

omou to mo	although I yearn for
kou tomo awan	you although I long for you
mono nare ya	we can never meet—
yū te mo tayuku	my fingers tire of tying
tokuru shitahimo	my loosening undersash

Anonymous

The conceit of the undersash loosening itself as its wearer longs for a lover occurs also in XIV, 730.

508 • *Topic unknown.*

ide ware o	alas please do not
hito na togame so	chastise me though all I do
ōbune no	is dream of love I
yutanotayuta ni	drift through the days like a great
mono omou koro zo	ship pitching tossing at sea

Anonymous

"Ōbune no" (like a large ship) is a makurakotoba modifying "yutatayuta" (floating; drifting).

509 • *Topic unknown.*

ise no umi ni	restlessly drifts my
tsuri suru ama no	heart as unsettled as the
uke nare ya	bobbing buoys of the
kokoro hitotsu o	fisherfolk who cast their nets
sadamekanetsuru	into the sea at Ise

Anonymous

Ise Bay lies to the east of Kyōto, across the Kii Peninsula.

510 • *Topic unknown.*

ise no umi no	as never-ending
ama no tsurinawa	as the relentless tasks of
uchihaete	fisherfolk who cast
kurushi to nomi ya	their nets and reel them in on
omoiwataran	Ise Sea love consumes me

Anonymous

Lines 1 and 2 (the fishing nets of the fisherfolk of the sea at Ise) are a jo linked to line 3, "uchihaete" (stretched afar), which also describes the length of time the author will yearn for his love. "Kurushi" (difficult) contains the word "kuru" (to reel in), an engo for "tsurinawa" (fishing nets).

5 I I • *Topic unknown.*

namidagawa
nani minakami o
tazuneken
mono omou toki no
waga mi narikeri

where is the mouth of
this river of tears   why did
I search for its source—
surely it whelms within my
being   as I yearn for you

Anonymous

5 I 2 • *Topic unknown.*

tane shi areba
iwa ni mo matsu wa
oinikeri
kou o shi koiba
awazarame ya mo

if there is but a
seed   even on rocky cliffs
a pine may grow   dare
I not hope my steadfast love
will grow into reality

Anonymous

5 I 3 • *Topic unknown.*

asana asana
tatsu kawagiri no
sora ni nomi
ukite omoi no
aru yo narikeri

like the river mists
that float every morning
up into the skies
my yearning soul roves far from
me   such is the world of love

Anonymous

Lines 1 and 2 (of the mist that rises over the river every morning) are a jo linked to lines 3 and 4, "sora ni nomi ukite" (floating in the sky; up in the air, unsettled).

5 I 4 • *Topic unknown.*

wasuraruru
toki shi nakereba
ashi tazu no

there is never a
time when I can forget   I
can only cry for

omoimidarete   love's entanglements   loudly
ne o nomi zo naku   as the cranes among the reeds

Anonymous

"Ashi tazu no" (of the reed crane) is a makurakotoba for "ne o naku" (cry aloud).

515 • *Topic unknown.*

  kara koromo   at twilight as I
hi mo yūgure ni   tightly bind the sash of my
  naru toki wa   Chinese robe against
kaesugaesu zo   the chill night   incessantly
hito wa koishiki   my longings return to you

Anonymous

"Kara koromo" (Chinese robe) is a makurakotoba modifying "himo yū" (tying the sash), a kakekotoba that also means "day and evening." "Kaesugaesu" (repeatedly) also means "changing" and in that sense is an engo for Chinese robe.

516 • *Topic unknown.*

  yoi yoi ni   every night I
makura sadamen   try to choose a different
  kata mo nashi   direction to turn
ika ni neshi yo ka   my pillow   which way did it
yume ni mieken   face that night we met in dreams

Anonymous

517 • *Topic unknown.*

  koishiki ni   if only I could
inochi o kauru   exchange this life for love   with
  mono naraba   pleasure I would yield
shini wa yasuku zo   to death   welcome would be my
arubekarikeru   end if it meant our meeting

Anonymous

518 • *Topic unknown.*

  hito no mi mo   aren't humans too
narawashi mono o   creatures of habit   if we do

awazu shite   not meet will I die
iza kokoromin   of love   let me try   to see
koi ya shinuru to   whether death will come to me

Anonymous

519 • *Topic unknown.*

shiobureba   how painful it is
kurushiki mono o   to love and yet to keep my
   hito shirezu   longings secret   for
omou chō koto   in whom may I confide   that
tare ni kataran   the one I love will not hear

Anonymous

This poem may be based on lines from "Prose-poem on the Goddess" by Sung Yü
(290?–222? B.C.): "I yearn for her secretly, / But to whom may I speak?"

520 • *Topic unknown.*

kon yo ni mo   oh that I might soon
haya narinanan   move on to the next life   where
   me no mae ni   I could consider
tsurenaki hito o   this heartless creature before
mukashi to omowan   me   as a mere memory

Anonymous

The phrase "kon yo" (the next life) introduces the Buddhist concept of reincarnation
into this sequence of poems.

521 • *Topic unknown.*

tsure mo naki   loving a heartless
hito o kou tote   unmerciful creature   I
   yamabiko no   justly breathe laments
kotae suru made   until the mountain echo
nagekitsuru kana   answers my piteous plaints

Anonymous

522 • *Topic unknown.*

yuku mizu ni   less reliable
kazu kaku yori mo   than figures sketched upon

hakanaki wa
omowanu hito o
omou narikeri

the flowing waters
is this deep yearning for one
who does not return my love

Anonymous

This poem is found also in *The Tales of Ise*, 50. The last two lines are similar to those of *Man'yōshū* 608 and 2709.

523 • *Topic unknown.*

hito o omou
kokoro wa ware ni
araneba ya
mi no madou dani
shirarezaru ran

is it because my
yearning heart has wandered to
my love in daydreams
that it does not know that my
body is lost in darkness

Anonymous

524 • *Topic unknown.*

omoiyaru
sakai haruka ni
nari ya suru
madou yumeji ni
au hito no naki

have my longings ranged
too far in quest of my love—
even on dream roads
I wander   bewildered   alone—
no one comes to meet me there

Anonymous

"Sakai" (boundary), "madou" (to be lost), and "yumeji" (dream road) are engo.

525 • *Topic unknown.*

yume no uchi ni
aimin koto o
tanomitsutsu
kuraseru yoi wa
nenkata mo nashi

all day I consoled
my yearning heart with thoughts of
meeting in dreams   but
now I do not know how to
place my pillow to call you

Anonymous

526 • *Topic unknown.*

koishine to
suru waza narashi

it seems my love wants
me to die of this longing—

ubatama no
yoru wa sugara ni
yume ni mietsutsu

all the jet-black night
he comes to me in dreams   to
keep hopeless passion burning

Anonymous

"Ubatama no" is a makurakotoba that modifies "yoru" (night).

527 • *Topic unknown.*

namidagawa
makura nagaruru
ukine ni wa
yume mo sadaka ni
miezu zo arikeru

even in sleep the
swift currents of this river
of tears buffet my
pillow   keeping me from rest—
not even my dreams are spared

Anonymous

"Ukine" originally had the meaning "floating sleep"; that is, sleeping on a boat. It came to have a second meaning, "uneasy sleep," under the influence of the homonym "uki" (miserable, sad).

528 • *Topic unknown.*

koi sureba
waga mi wa kage to
narinikeri
sari to te hito ni
sowanu mono yue

loving so deeply
my body has wasted to
a mere shadow   yet
even this insubstantial
likeness cannot cling to him

Anonymous

529 • *Topic unknown.*

kagaribi ni
aranu waga mi no
nazo mo kaku
namida no kawa ni
ukite moyuran

my body is not
a blazing fisherman's flare—
why then does it burn
with passion even as I
float on this river of tears

Anonymous

530 • *Topic unknown.*

kagaribi no
kage to naru mi no

my body suffers
a burning fire deep within

wabishiki wa	like the reflections
nagarete shita ni	of the fishing flares that float
moyuru narikeri	beneath the river's surface

Anonymous

"Kage" (shadow) of poem 528 has here become "kagaribi no kage" (the reflection of the fishing flares).

531 • *Topic unknown.*

hayaki se ni	if in the swiftly
mirume oiseba	flowing rapids seaweed could
waga sode no	grow I'd sow some in
namida no kawa ni	the river of tears that floods
uemashi mono o	my sleeves then I might see you

Anonymous

"Mirume" is a kakekotoba meaning "seaweed" (*Codium mucronatum*) and "chance to meet."

532 • *Topic unknown.*

oki e ni mo	tossing on the waves
yoranu tamamo no	black seaweed gems have neither
nami no ue ni	offing nor shore for
midarete nomi ya	destination shall I too
koiwatarinan	drift in love's entanglements

Anonymous

The first three lines (jewel weed, approaching neither shore nor offing, above the waves) are a jo, linked to "midarete" (tangled; confused). Jewel weed (tamamo) is a poetic synonym for seaweed.

533 • *Topic unknown.*

ashigamo no	no more than do
sawagu irie no	white waves dancing across the
shiranami no	inlet where reed ducks
shirazu ya hito o	cry out noisily no more
kaku koin to wa	does my love know my yearning

Anonymous

The first three lines (like the white waves of the inlet where the reed ducks clamor) are a jo linked by the repetition of the sounds "shira" (white) in line 3 and "shirazu" (not knowing) in line 4.

534 • *Topic unknown.*

hito shirenu	like fiery Mount
omoi o tsune ni	Fuji in Suruga my
suruga naru	yearning burns within—
fuji no yama koso	an eternally smoldering
waga mi narikere	passion my love can never know

Anonymous

The last syllable of "omoi" (love) is a kakekotoba; it may be read "hi" (fire). The first two syllables of the place name Suruga (now part of Shizuoka Prefecture) are also a kakekotoba with the meaning "to do." Hi (fire) and Mount Fuji are engo.

535 • *Topic unknown.*

tobu tori no	would that my love could
koe mo kikoenu	know my yearning deep as
okuyama no	these lonely mountains
fukaki kokoro o	where not even the songs of
hito wa shiranan	soaring wild birds can be heard

Anonymous

The opening lines (of the deep mountains where even the cries of flying birds are not heard) are a jo linked to "fukaki" (deep) in line 4.

536 • *Topic unknown.*

ōsaka no	does the beribboned
yūtsukedori mo	cock of Meeting Hill share my
waga gotoku	unfulfilled longings—
hito ya koishiki	is it for love alone that
ne nomi naku ran	we raise our solemn voices

Anonymous

For Ōsaka, see 374. Kubota suggests that this poem refers to a ritual in which beribboned cocks were sent to the outreaches of the capital at times of unrest in the country.

537 • *Topic unknown.*

<table>
<tr><td>ōsaka no</td><td>the fresh spring waters</td></tr>
<tr><td>seki ni nagaruru</td><td>surge freely through the rocky</td></tr>
<tr><td>iwashimizu</td><td>crevices of the</td></tr>
<tr><td>iwade kokoro ni</td><td>Barrier at Meeting Hill   but</td></tr>
<tr><td>omoi koso sure</td><td>my words of love remain checked</td></tr>
</table>

Anonymous

Lines 1–3 (pure spring from the rocks flowing at the Barrier of Ōsaka) are a jo linked by the sound repetition of line 3, "iwashimizu" (pure spring from the rocks), and line 4, "iwade" (not speaking).

538 • *Topic unknown.*

<table>
<tr><td>ukigusa no</td><td>floating grasses must</td></tr>
<tr><td>ue wa shigereru</td><td>thickly cover the surface</td></tr>
<tr><td>fuchi nare ya</td><td>of my heart's depths   for</td></tr>
<tr><td>fukaki kokoro o</td><td>there appears to be no one</td></tr>
<tr><td>shiru hito no naki</td><td>who fathoms its mysteries</td></tr>
</table>

Anonymous

539 • *Topic unknown.*

<table>
<tr><td>uchiwabite</td><td>in my suffering</td></tr>
<tr><td>yobawan koe ni</td><td>I cry aloud   surely there</td></tr>
<tr><td>yamabiko no</td><td>can be no mountain</td></tr>
<tr><td>kotaenu yama wa</td><td>echo that remains unmoved—</td></tr>
<tr><td>araji to zo omou</td><td>my calls must summon a reply</td></tr>
</table>

Anonymous

540 • *Topic unknown.*

<table>
<tr><td>kokorogae</td><td>if only there were</td></tr>
<tr><td>suru mono ni mo ga</td><td>a way that we might exchange</td></tr>
<tr><td>katakoi wa</td><td>hearts   then I could make</td></tr>
<tr><td>kurushiki mono to</td><td>you realize   how painful</td></tr>
<tr><td>hito ni shirasen</td><td>a one-sided love can be</td></tr>
</table>

Anonymous

541 • *Topic unknown.*

  yoso ni shite
kōreba kurushi
   irehimo no
onaji kokoro ni
iza musubiten

    how difficult it
is to yearn for one who is
   so far away   I
shall fashion a love knot to
twine our two hearts into one

Anonymous

"Irehimo no" (like a braided frog fastener) is a makurakotoba for "musubi" (tying) in line 5.

542 • *Topic unknown.*

  haru tateba
kiyuru kōri no
   nokori naku
kimi ga kokoro wa
ware ni tokenan

    like ice that thaws and
disappears into flowing
   waters when spring comes
may my love's heart soften and
melt toward me without reserve

Anonymous

Lines 1 and 2 (when spring comes, the melting ice) are a jo linked to line 3, "nokori naku" (leaves no remains). "Kōri" (ice) and "tokenan" (may thaw) are engo.

543 • *Topic unknown.*

  aketateba
semi no orihae
   nakikurashi
yoru wa hotaru no
moe koso watare

    when dawn breaks   I cry
out   piercing the summer days
   like the cicadas
while the nights consume me with
flames brighter than the fireflies'

Anonymous

544 • *Topic unknown.*

  natsu mushi no
mi o itazura ni
   nasu koto mo
hitotsu omoi ni
yorite narikeri

    like summer insects
which fly too near the flame and
   burn for nought   I too
shall give my life for this blazing
but unrequited passion

Anonymous

"Omoi ni yorite" (because of love) contains the phrase "hi ni yorite" (approaching the fire) and serves as a kakekotoba.

545 • *Topic unknown.*

yū sareba	when evening comes
itodo higataki	my sleeves hang limp and heavy
waga sode ni	too moist to dry now
aki no tsuyu sae	added to my stream of tears
okisowaritsutsu	comes the dew of autumn nights

Anonymous

546 • *Topic unknown.*

itsu to te mo	there is no time when
koishikarazu wa	I do not suffer the pangs
aranedomo	of love for you but
aki no yūbe wa	miraculously yearning
ayashikarikeri	grows on autumn evenings

Anonymous

This seems to be based on these lines by Po Chü-i: "All four seasons bring sorrow to the heart, / But of them all the most poignant is autumn."

547 • *Topic unknown.*

aki no ta no	my love does not grow
ho ni koso hito o	openly like the ears of
koizarame	ripe grain in autumn
nado ka kokoro ni	fields but how can I forget
wasure shi mo sen	that it springs up within my heart

Anonymous

"Aki no ta no" (of the fields of autumn) is a makurakotoba for "ho" (ears of grain). "Ho," which also means "outward" or "visible," is a kakekotoba.

548 • *Topic unknown.*

aki no ta no	could I forget him
ho no ue o terasu	even for the brief instant

inazuma no
hikari no ma ni mo
ware ya wasururu

lightning flashes
above the ripening ears
of grain in autumn fields

Anonymous

The phrase "aki no ta no ho no ue" (upon the rice ears in the autumn fields) is quoted from *Man'yōshū*, 88. This poem repeats the rhetorical devices of 547.

549 • *Topic unknown.*

hitome moru
ware ka wa aya na
hanasusuki
nado ka ho ni idete
koizu shimo aran

is there a reason
to conceal my love from the
eyes of all   why should
I not reveal my passion
like the flowering plume grass

Anonymous

"Hanasusuki" (flowering pampas grass) is a makurakotoba for "ho" (ear) in line 4.

550 • *Topic unknown.*

awayuki no
tamareba kate ni
kudaketsutsu
waga mono omoi no
shigeki koro kana

as the burden of
soft snow snaps winter-laden
branches with its weight
so my heart crumbles beneath
the profusion of love's woes

Anonymous

Lines 1 and 2 (when the thin snow piles up unbearably) are a jo linked to "kudake-tsutsu" (continuously breaking).

551 • *Topic unknown.*

okuyama no
suga no ne shinogi
furu yuki no
kenu to ka iwan
koi no shigeki ni

the snow which drifts from
the crags to lie heavily
at the roots of the
sedge will melt away   will my
life   burdened by love   also fade

Anonymous

The first three lines (the snow that falls, pushing through to the roots of the sedge in the deep mountains) are a jo modifying "kenu" (have disappeared). There is a similar poem in the *Man'yōshū* (1655):

taka yama no	the snow which falls in
suga no ha shinogi	high mountains to rest heavily
furu yuki no	on the leaves of the
kenu to iu beku mo	sedge will melt away will my
koi no shigekeku	life burdened by love also fade

BOOK XII

Love Poems (2)

552 • *Topic unknown.*

  omoitsutsu
nureba ya hito no
  mietsuran
yume to shiriseba
samezaramashi o

     in love-tormented
sleep I saw him beside me—
     had I known my love's
visit was but a dream   I
should never have awakened

Ono no Komachi

The first two lines of *Man'yōshū* 3738 are similar to this poem.

553 • *Topic unknown.*

  utatane ni
koishiki hito o
  miteshi yori
yume chō mono wa
tanomisometeki

     since that brief sleep when
first I saw the one I love
     it is those fleeting
dreams   ephemera of the
night   on which I now rely

Ono no Komachi

554 • *Topic unknown.*

  ito semete
koishiki toki wa
  ubatama no
yoru no koromo o
kaeshite zo kiru

     when my yearning grows
unendurable   all through
     the jet-black hours of
night   I sleep with my robes turned
inside out   awaiting him

Ono no Komachi

"Ubatama" is a makurakotoba modifying "yoru" (night). The image of the reversed robe appears earlier in *Man'yōshū* 2812, 2813, and 2937.

5 5 5 • *Topic unknown.*

aki kaze no	when the autumn wind
mi ni samukereba	blows cold against my body
tsure mo naki	my cold-hearted love
hito o zo tanomu	is all the hope I have for
kururu yo goto ni	warmth each night as darkness falls

Sosei

5 5 6 • *Kiyoyuki composed this poem on the text of the sermon by the lecturer Shinsei at a memorial service at the Shimotsu Izumo Temple and sent it to Ono no Komachi.*

tsutsumedomo	although I wrap them
sode ni tamaranu	up my sleeves cannot hold them—
shiratama wa	these white jewels are
hito o minume no	teardrops falling from eyes which
namida narikeri	cannot see the one they love

Abe no Kiyoyuki

The Shimotsu Izumo Temple was by the Kamo River. The text of the sermon probably was these lines from the Lotus Sutra (chap. 8, "Receipt of Prophecy by Five Hundred Disciples"): "Meanwhile his friend, having to go forth on official duty, ties a priceless jewel within his garment as a present and departs. The man, being drunk and asleep, knows nothing of it" (Bunnō Katō et al., *The Threefold Lotus Sutra* [New York: Weatherhill/Kosei, 1975], p. 177). "Me" in line 4 means both "eyes" and "occasion."

5 5 7 • *Reply.*

oroka naru	half-hearted are tears
namida zo sode ni	that can settle as jewels in
tama wa nasu	sheltering sleeves mine
ware wa sekiaezu	burst forth tumbling rapids once
tagitsu se nareba	released nothing can hold them

Ono no Komachi

Kokinshū

558 • *Poems 558–572 are from the poetry contest held at the residence of the Consort in the Kanpyō era.*

koiwabite
uchinuru naka ni
   yukikayou
yume no tadaji wa
utsutsu naranan

all alone   weary
of yearning   I slept   oh that
   the straight clear path I
travel in my dreams might lead
to her in waking hours

Fujiwara no Toshiyuki

559 •

suminoe no
kishi ni yoru nami
   yoru sae ya
yume no kayoiji
hitome yoku ran

like the waves which dash
to shore at Sumi Bay   I
   would have you rush to
me   yet it seems you fear men's
eyes   even on the path of dreams

Fujiwara no Toshiyuki

For Suminoe, see 360. Lines 1 and 2 (waves approaching the shore at Suminoe) are a jo linked to the kakekotoba "yoru" (to approach; night).

560 •

waga koi wa
miyamagakure no
   kusa nare ya
shigesa masaredo
shiru hito no naki

is my love like
hidden grasses deep in the
   enchanting mountains
daily more luxuriant
they grow   yet no one discerns them

Ono no Yoshiki

561 •

yoi no ma mo
hakanaka miyuru
   natsu mushi ni
madoi masareru
koi mo suru kana

twilight passes   as
evanescent as the swift
   summer insects that
flit infatuated to the
fire   my rapture transcends theirs

Ki no Tomonori

210

562 •

yū sareba
hotaru yorike ni
moyuredomo
hikari mineba ya
hito no tsurenaki

when evening draws near
the fireflies glow brightly   my
heart burns more fiercely
yet to my heartless love this
flame must be invisible

Ki no Tomonori

563 •

sasa no ha ni
oku shimo yori mo
hitori nuru
waga koromode zo
sae masarikeru

the blades of bamboo
grasses   covered in crystal
frost   stand rigidly—
yet far colder is the sleeve
of one who must sleep alone

Ki no Tomonori

564 •

waga yado no
kiku no kakine ni
oku shimo no
kiekaerite zo
koishikarikeru

like the hoarfrost that
settles on the overgrown
chrysanthemum hedge
in my garden   I'll vanish
melt away   yearning for you

Ki no Tomonori

Lines 1–3 (like the frost that settles on the brushwood fence by the chrysanthemums in my garden) are a jo linked to "kie" (vanishing). This poem is not in the extant texts of the Kanpyō poetry contest.

565 •

kawa no se ni
nabiku tamamo no
migakurete
hito ni shirarenu
koi mo suru kana

like the jewel-weeds
swaying in the depths beneath
the river rapids
unseen by human eyes   my
love lies hidden   all unknown

Ki no Tomonori

Lines 1–3 (like the jewel-weeds swaying in the river rapids, hidden in the water) are a jo linked to "hito ni shirarenu" (others shall not know).

566 •

kakikurashi	like the white snow
furu shirayuki no	that falls from dark clouded skies
shita kie ni	and then melts away
kiete mono omou	secretly from underneath
koro ni mo aru kana	I too shall vanish yearning

Mibu no Tadamine

Lines 2 and 3 (melting underneath like the white snow that falls) are a jo linked to kiete (vanishing).

567 •

kimi kouru	yearning for you my
namida no toko ni	love my ceaseless weeping flooded
michinureba	my lonely chamber—
mi o tsukushi to zo	I have become but a gauge
ware wa narikeru	to mark the depths of these tides

Fujiwara no Okikaze

"Mi o tsukushi" means both "water gauge" and "exhausting the body."

568 •

shinuru inochi	can my spirit so
iki mo ya suru to	near its end be recalled to
kokoromi ni	life to test it won't
tama no o bakari	you say you'll meet me just for
awan to iwanan	the length of the jewels' thread

Fujiwara no Okikaze

"Tama" means both "spirit" and "jewel."

569 •

wabinureba	suffering I try
shiite wasuren to	resolutely to put you
omoedomo	from my mind but still
yume to iu mono zo	these things called dreams deceive me
hitodanome naru	into fresh anticipation

Fujiwara no Okikaze

The opening line is the same as that of XVIII, 938, by Ono no Komachi, while the last two lines are similar to XII, 553, also by Komachi.

570 •

warinaku mo	irrationally
nete mo samete mo	I long for my love whether
koishiki ka	asleep or awake—
kokoro o izuchi	where can I send my heart that
yaraba wasuren	it may forget you in peace

Anonymous

571 •

koishiki ni	if in my longing
wabite tamashii	my suffering soul should flee—
madoinaba	run away to hide—
munashiki kara no	what will be the stories told
na ni ya nokoran	about my lifeless body

Anonymous

"Kara" here means "corpse," but the word also has the meaning "because," and so the phrase "munashiki kara" suggests "because of empty love."

572 •

kimi kouru	but for the tears of
namida shi naku wa	unrequited love that
kara koromo	gently stream for you
mune no atari wa	my Chinese robe would burn red
iro moenamashi	over my feverish breast

Ki no Tsurayuki

This poem is not in extant texts of the Kanpyō poetry contest.

573 • *Topic unknown.*

yo to tomo ni	the river of tears
nagarete zo yuku	flowing as my life surges

namadigawa	toward its limit
fuyu mo kōranu	is ceaseless as the spume on
minawa narikeri	the free-flowing winter stream

Ki no Tsurayuki

"Yo" means both "world" and "night." "Nagarete" (flowing) may also be read "nakarete" (weeping).

574 • *Topic unknown.*

yumeji ni mo	even on the path
tsuyu ya okuran	of dreams the dewdrops must form—
yo mo sugara	for these sleeves which go
kayoeru sode no	along that road from dusk to
hijite kawakanu	dawn are soaked and never dry

Ki no Tsurayuki

575 • *Topic unknown.*

hakanakute	though fleeting were the
yume ni mo hito o	dreams in which I saw my love
mitsuru yo wa	all the lonely night
ashita no toko zo	unhappy I am to rise
okiukarikeru	from my lonely bed at dawn

Sosei

576 • *Topic unknown.*

itsuwari no	if these tears were but
namida nariseba	for show I would not wring the
kara koromo	drenched sleeves of my court
shinobi ni sode wa	robe in secret so that no
shiborazaramashi	one may share my lonely grief

Fujiwara no Tadafusa

"Kara koromo" (Chinese robe) may serve as a makurakotoba for "sode" (sleeve), but grammatically it stands alone in the poem.

577 • *Topic unknown.*

ne ni nakite	though in fact my tears
hiji ni shikadomo	soaked my sleeves while I wept in

harusame ni
nurenishi sode to
towaba kotaen

solitude   if I
am asked   I will say they were
drenched by the slow rains of spring

Ōe no Chisato

578 • *Topic unknown.*

waga gotoku
mono ya kanashiki
  hototogisu
toki zo tomo naku
yo tada naku ran

nightingale   do
you weep like me   for the sheer
  sadness of life   though
this is not your season   your
mournful notes sound the night through

Fujiwara no Toshiyuki

For hototogisu, see 135.

579 • *Topic unknown.*

satsuki yama
kozue o takami
  hototogisu
naku ne sora naru
koi mo suru kana

high in the tips of
branches on summer mountains
  the nightingale
weeps aloud   his song fills the
air where my hopeless love drifts

Ki no Tsurayuki

Lines 1–3 (nightingale high in the treetops in the mountains of the Fifth Month) are a
jo linked to "naku ne" (crying voice) in line 4. "Sora naru" is a kakekotoba meaning
"is in the sky" and "is in vain."

580 • *Topic unknown.*

akigiri no
haruru toki naki
  kokoro ni wa
tachii no sora mo
omōenaku ni

my love hangs heavy
as the drift of autumn haze
  never quite clearing
aimless as the overcast
sky   a constant restlessness

Ōshikōchi no Mitsune

"Akigiri" (autumn mist), "tachi-" (rising), and "sora" (sky) are engo. The pattern of
engo is similar to that in VIII, 386.

581 • *Topic unknown.*

mushi no goto	unlike the crying
koe ni tatete wa	insects I do not raise my
nakanedomo	voice in misery
namida nomi koso	yet within me sad tears stream—
shita ni nagarure	a constant river flowing

Kiyowara no Fukayabu

582 • *From the poetry contest held at the residence of Prince Koresada.*

aki nareba	now autumn has come
yama to yomu made	the mountains echo with the
naku shika ni	belling of the deer—
ware otorame ya	can the cries of one who sleeps
hitori nuru yo wa	alone eclipse their clamor

Anonymous

For this poetry contest, see 189.

583 • *Topic unknown.*

aki no no ni	in autumn fields
midarete sakeru	tangled flowers bloom in hues
hana no iro no	innumerable
chigusa ni mono o	as the sorrows over which
omou koro kana	I brood at this time of year

Ki no Tsurayuki

Lines 1–3 (of the colors of the flowers that have blossomed in profusion in the autumn fields) are a jo linked to "chigusa" (variety; great number) in line 4.

584 • *Topic unknown.*

hitori shite	alone I sorrow
mono o omoeba	there is no one to comfort
aki no ta no	me to speak softly
inaba no soyoto	as the gentle whisper of
iu hito no naki	the rice plants in autumn fields

Ōshikōchi no Mitsune

Kokinshū

Line 3 and half of line 4 (of the rice plants in the autumn fields) are a jo linked to "soyoto," which means "whispering" and "saying 'there, there.'"

585 • *Topic ..nknown.*

hito o omou
kokoro wa kari ni
aranedomo
kumoi ni nomi mo
naki wataru kana

my yearning heart longs
for you   crossing the cloudy
skies   crying aloud—
and yet it is not one of
the autumn flock of wild geese

Kiyowara no Fukayabu

586 • *Topic unknown.*

aki kaze ni
kaki nasu koto no
koe ni sae
hakanaku hito no
koishikaru ran

even the plaintive
voice of the koto plucked in
this chilly autumn
wind   causes me to love the
more   so unavailingly

Mibu no Tadamine

587 • *Topic unknown.*

makomo karu
yodo no sawa mizu
ame fureba
tsune yori koto ni
masaru waga koi

as the waters of
Yodo Marsh   where they reap the
true reeds   swell and flood
when the long rains fall   my heart
fills with ever-growing love

Ki no Tsurayuki

"Makomo karu" (reap the true reeds) is a makurakotoba modifying Yodo no sawa (Yodo Marsh). Yodo is in Fushimi District of present-day Kyōto. Lines 1 and 2 (waters of the Yodo Marsh where they cut true reeds) are a jo linked to lines 3, 4, and the first word of 5 (when it rains, it increases even more than usual).

588 • *Sent to someone in Yamato.*

koenu ma wa
yoshino no yama no
sakurabana

cherry blossoms of
lovely Yoshino Mountain
will be known to me

217

hitosute ni nomi   only through the words of others—
kikiwataru kana   until I too can go there

Ki no Tsurayuki

For Yoshino, see 3.

589 • *Tsurayuki sent this letter in the Third Month, when he heard that someone else was visiting and writing to a woman he had known.*

tsuyu naranu   my heart is not like
kokoro o hana ni   the dew which settles on the
  okisomete   flowers   unconcerned—
kaze fuku goto ni   each time you bend before the
mono omoi zo tsuku   wind   my torment increases

Ki no Tsurayuki

"Tsuyu" is a kakekotoba meaning both "dew" and "slight." "Tsuyu" (dew), "hana" (flower), and "oki-" (settling) are engo.

590 • *Topic unknown.*

  waga koi ni   thickly they fall to
kurabu no yama no   cover Mount Kurabu   the
  sakurabana   soft cherry petals—
ma naku chiru tomo   yet their numbers cannot grow
kazu wa masaraji   to exceed my thoughts of you

Sakanoue no Korenori

For Kurabu Mountain, see 39. Kurabu, which also means "to compare," functions as a kakekotoba.

591 • *Topic unknown.*

  fuyu kawa no   my heart is like a
ue wa kōreru   winter river frozen still
  ware nare ya   on its surface   while
shita ni nagarete   beneath the film of ice the
koiwataru ran   stream of love constantly flows

Muneoka no Ōyori

"Nagarete" (flowing) also can be read "nakarete" (weeping).

592 • *Topic unknown.*

tagitsu se ni	swept along by
nesashi tomenu	rushing rapids floating like
ukigusa no	the water grasses—
ukitaru koi mo	this love of mine drifts without
ware wa suru kana	cease unable to take root

Mibu no Tadamine

Lines 1–3 (like the floating weeds that do not take root in the bubbling rapids) are a jo linked to "uki" (floating; drifting).

593 • *Topic unknown.*

yoi yoi ni	at dusk each day I
nugite waga nuru	stretch my robe on its hanger
karigoromo	anticipating
kakete omowanu	dawn as I await the night
toki no ma mo nashi	constant in my love for you

Ki no Tomonori

Lines 1–3 (the hunting robe that I remove to sleep night after night) are a jo linked to "kakete," a kakekotoba meaning "hanging" and "extending love; pinning hopes on."

594 • *Topic unknown.*

azumaji no	why have I begun
sayanonaka yama	to love so recklessly like
nakanaka ni	one lost in the night
nani shi ka hito o	Middle Mountain of the Night
omoisomeken	on the road to Azuma

Ki no Tomonori

Sayanonaka Mountain was a rugged stretch of the Tōkaidō between Nissaka and Kiku River in Shizuoka Prefecture. Lines 1 and 2 (Sayanonaka Mountain on the eastern road) are a jo linked to "nakanaka ni" (rashly, recklessly) by the sound repetition.

595 • *Topic unknown.*

shikitae no	beneath my finely
makura no shita ni	woven pillow an ocean

ume wa aredo
hito o mirume wa
oizu zo arikeru

of tears is found   yet
we have no chance to meet   no
seaweed grows in these waters

Ki no Tomonori

"Shikitae no" (here "finely woven") is a makurakotoba that was used to modify such words as "makura" (pillow), "sode" (sleeve), "koromo" (robe), etc. "Mirume" is a kakekotoba meaning "seaweed" and "chance to meet."

596 • *Topic unknown.*

toshi o hete
kienu omoi wa
    arinagara
yoru no tamoto wa
nao kōrikeri

as years go by   my
burning passion never dies
    but still my night sleeves
grow brittle   freezing into
glistening sheets of ice

Ki no Tomonori

"Omoi" (longings) contains the word "hi" (fire), which is an engo for "kienu" (not dying out).

597 • *Topic unknown.*

waga koi wa
shiranu yamaji ni
    aranaku ni
mayou kokoro zo
wabishikarikeru

my love is not an
unfamiliar mountain road—
    still I am troubled
my wavering heart loses
its way on its wanderings

Ki no Tsurayuki

598 • *Topic unknown.*

kurenai no
furiidetsutsu naku
    namida ni wa
tamoto nomi koso
iro masarikere

not crimson dyes   but
tears   infuse their color   yet
    they transform only
my sleeves   ever-deepening
hues set by endless weeping

Ki no Tsurayuki

"Furiide" means both "infusing" and "wringing out."

599 • *Topic unknown.*

shiratama to
mieshi namida mo
  toshi fureba
karakurenai ni
utsuroinikeri

even those teardrops
which seemed like white jewels
  with the swift-passing
years   have changed to Chinese red
freshly dyed by burning hearts

Ki no Tsurayuki

600 • *Topic unknown.*

natsu mushi o
nani ka iiken
  kokoro kara
ware mo omoi ni
moenuberanari

summer insects fly
too near the flame   what name can
  I give them   I who
yearn within my heart and must
burn with a hopeless passion

Ōshikōchi no Mitsune

"Omoi" (longings) contains the word "hi" (fire), an engo for "moenu" (burned).

601 • *Topic unknown.*

kaze fukeba
mine ni wakaruru
  shirokumo no
taete tsurenaki
kimi ga kokoro ka

when the breezes blow
the white clouds take leave of
  mountain peaks without
regret   leaving not a trace
cold-hearted as my lover

Mibu no Tadamine

Lines 1–3 (like white clouds that take leave of the peaks when the wind blows) are a jo linked to the kakekotoba "taete" (disappearing; completely).

602 • *Topic unknown.*

tsuki kage ni
waga mi o kauru
  mono naraba
tsurenaki hito mo
aware to ya min

if only I could
trade my earthly form for that
  of the shining moon
surely my indifferent
love would know me too as dear

Mibu no Tadamine

603 • *Topic unknown.*

koishinaba	if I should die of
ta ga na wa tataji	unfulfilled love others will
yo no naka no	whisper only her
tsune naki mono to	name although she may talk of
ii wa nasu tomo	this world's impermanence

Kiyowara no Fukayabu

Ozawa notes that this is a particularly difficult poem to understand. Line 2, which he interprets as "others' names will not be bandied about," that is, "only your name will be on people's tongues," has been interpreted by Kubota as "your name will surely not be bandied about." We have followed Ozawa.

604 • *Topic unknown.*

tsu no kuni no	my love swells like
naniwa no ashi no	buds on the reeds that grow far
me mo haru ni	into the distance
shigeki waga koi	on Naniwa shore in Tsu
hito shiru rame ya	but can my beloved know

Ki no Tsurayuki

Tsu Province later became Settsu Province, which is part of modern Hyōgo Prefecture. Naniwa, part of modern Ōsaka, was a major port. "Me mo haru ni" (buds swelling; looking afar) is a kakekotoba linking the jo, lines 1–3 (the swelling of the buds of the reeds of Naniwa in Tsu Province), to "shigeki" (thickly; profusely) in line 4.

605 • *Topic unknown.*

te mo furede	days pass into months
tsuki hi henikeru	and still I have not touched my
shiramayumi	true white bow at night
okifushi yoru wa	drawn taut I tremble rising
i koso nerarene	resting unable to sleep

Ki no Tsurayuki

"Mayumi" means both "true bow" and "sandalwood' or spindle tree (*Euonymus sieboldianus*). Lines 1–3 (my hand not even touching—months and days have passed—the white sandalwood bow) are a jo linked to the kakekotoba "okifushi," which means both "raising and lowering" and "rising and lying down." "I" is a kakekotoba meaning "sleep" and "shooting," an engo for "yumi" (bow).

606 • *Topic unknown.*

hito shirenu
omoi nomi koso
    wabishikere
waga nageki oba
ware nomi zo shiru

my own beloved
cannot realize the pangs
    of love I suffer
only I can ever know
the searing torment I bear

Ki no Tsurayuki

The word "hi" (fire) is contained in both "hito" (person) and "omoi" (longings). "Nageki" (suffering) contains the word "ki" (wood), an engo of "hi" (fire).

607 • *Topic unknown.*

koto ni idete
iwanu bakari zo
    minase gawa
shita ni kayoite
koishiki mono o

silent am I   words
of love never pass my lips
    though deep within me
a subterranean stream
of yearning secretly flows

Ki no Tomonori

Minase River flowed through Yamashiro Province, a part of present-day Kyōto. In the *Kokinshū* the name is always used to convey the meaning "waterless" river. Here it is a makurakotoba for line 4, "shita ni kayoite," which can mean "flowing underground" or "going back and forth within my heart."

608 • *Topic unknown.*

kimi o nomi
omoine ni neshi
    yume nareba
waga kokoro kara
mitsuru narikeri

yearning for my love
I drifted into restless
    dream-filled sleep   surely
it was my own aching heart
summoned her image to me

Ōshikōchi no Mitsune

609 • *Topic unknown.*

inochi ni mo
masarite oshiku
    aru mono wa

more lamentable
even than the loss of one's
    own precious life is

mihatenu yume no
samuru narikeri

the bereavement one feels on
waking from half-finished dreams

Mibu no Tadamine

6 1 0 • *Topic unknown.*

azusayumi
hikeba moto sue
    waga kata ni
yoru koso masare
koi no kokoro wa

our hearts drawn taut as
the tips of my catalpa
    bow   and still we can't
approach one another   how
I yearn for my love at night

Harumichi no Tsuraki

Lines 1–3 (in my direction—top and bottom—when I draw my catalpa bow) are a
jo linked to the kakekotoba "yoru" (approach; night).

6 1 1 • *Topic unknown.*

    waga koi wa
yukue mo shirazu
    hate mo nashi
au o kagiri to
omou bakari zo

my heart knows not its
destination   it has no
    other goal than a
brief encounter   a single
moment alone with my love

Ōshikōchi no Mitsune

6 1 2 • *Topic unknown.*

    ware nomi zo
kanashikarikeru
    hikoboshi mo
awade suguseru
toshi shi nakereba

I alone am sad—
such suffering burdens none
    but me   for even
the Herd Boy never lives a
year without meeting his love

Ōshikōchi no Mitsune

For the Herd Boy, see 173.

6 1 3 • *Topic unknown.*

    ima wa haya
koishinamashi o

long ago I would
have died of love   yearning for

aimin to
tanomeshi koto zo
inochi narikeru

you   but your words of
promise   your vows of meeting
have become my source of life

Kiyowara no Fukayabu

614 • *Topic unknown.*

tanometsutsu
awade toshi heru
  itsuwari ni
korinu kokoro o
hito wa shiranan

though I put my trust
in love the years go by
  without our meeting
could she possibly know
I have not yet ceased to hope

Ōshikōchi no Mitsune

615 • *Topic unknown.*

inochi ya wa
nani zo wa tsuyu no
  ada mono o
au ni shi kaeba
oshikaranaku ni

what is life that I
should treasure it   it is less
  than ephemeral
dew   how little would I miss
it   could love but take its place

Ki no Tomonori

BOOK XIII

Love Poems (3)

616 • *Composed in a drizzling rain at the beginning of the Third Month and sent to a woman whom he had visited secretly.*

oki mo sezu	I am one with spring
ne mo sede yoru o	neither sleeping nor waking
akashite wa	till night turns to dawn
haru no mono tote	each day passes in pensive
nagame kurashitsu	gazing endless as the long rains

Ariwara no Narihira

"Nagame" is a kakekotoba meaning "long rains" and "gazing pensively." This poem appears, with a more detailed headnote, in *The Tales of Ise*, 2.

617 • *Sent to a woman in Narihira's household.*

tsurezure o	in idle reverie
nagame ni masaru	I weep tears that overflow like
namidagawa	the long rains of spring
sode nomi nurete	my sleeves are drenched with the stream
au yoshi mo nashi	that flows when we cannot meet

Fujiwara no Toshiyuki

Again "nagame" (long rains; gazing pensively) is used as a kakekotoba. "Kawa" or "gawa" (river), is an engo for "long rains." This poem and 618 appear in *The Tales of Ise*, 107.

618 • *A reply composed on the woman's behalf.*

asami koso	even in shallows
sode wa hizurame	sleeves may be drenched if I should

namidagawa
mi sae nagaru to
kikaba tonoman

hear that you have been
swept away by a river
of tears　then I might believe

Ariwara no Narihira

619 • *Topic unknown.*

yorube nami
mi o koso tōku
　hedate tsure
kokoro wa kimi ga
kage to nariniki

destined to remain
so far apart　never to
　be able to hold
my love　my heart has become
a shadow clinging to her

Anonymous

620 • *Topic unknown.*

itazura ni
yukite wa kinuru
　mono yue ni
mi maku hoshisa ni
iza nawaretsutsu

in vain I return
to my home　disappointed
　yet ever hopeful
of our meeting　always my
desire entices me back

Anonymous

621 • *Topic unknown.*

awanu yo no
furu shirayuki to
　tsumorinaba
ware sae tomo ni
kenu beki mono o

if the lonely nights
when we cannot meet pile up
　like the thick drifts of
white snow that falls　I too will
melt away and disappear

Anonymous

"Tsumorinaba" (if it piles up) is an engo for "yuki" (snow), as is "kenu," which means both "to melt" and "to die."

622 • *Topic unknown.*

aki no no ni
sasa wakeshi asa no

wetter than sleeves that
have pushed through fields of bamboo

sode yori mo   grass on an autumn
awade koshi yo zo   morn are mine   when I return
hiji masarikeru   on a night we did not meet

Anonymous

This poem and 623 appear in *The Tales of Ise*, 25, where they are presented as poem and reply.

623 • *Topic unknown.*

mirume naki   does he not know that
waga mi o ura to   this bay holds no seaweed   still
   shiraneba ya   comes the fisherman
karenade ama no   in search of me   though his legs
ashi tayuku kuru   grow weary on his vain quest

Ono no Komachi

"Mirume" means both "chance to meet" and a type of seaweed, *Codium mucronatum*. "Ura" is a kakekotoba meaning "buoy" and "callous"; "u" also means "sorrow." "Ura" (buoy), "mirume" (seaweed), and "ama" (fisherman) are engo. "Karu" (to reap), one meaning of the dictionary form of "karenade" (incessantly; not leaving), also may be engo.

624 • *Topic unknown.*

awazu shite   if tonight again
koyoi akenaba   dawn comes without our meeting
   haru no hi no   I will remember
nagaku ya hito o   your cruelty always   as
tsurashi to omowan   long as an endless spring day

Minamoto no Muneyuki

"Haru no hi no" (of a spring day) is a makurakotoba for "nagaku" (length).

625 • *Topic unknown.*

ariake no   since that parting when
tsurenaku mieshi   I saw the cold indifferent
   wakare yori   countenance of the
akatsuki bakari   fading moon   I have known
uki mono wa nashi   nothing so cruel as dawn

Mibu no Tadamine

Fujiwara Teika praised this poem for the quality of yōen ("voluptuous charm"). It had earlier been recognized as one of the best poems of the *Kokinshū*.

626 • *Topic unknown.*

au koto no	unable to meet
nagisa ni shi yoru	I turn back like the waves that
nami nareba	roll in to caress
uramite nomi zo	the sandy shore and return
tachikaerikeru	with but a glimpse of the bay

Ariwara no Motokata

"Nagisa" (also read nakisa) is a kakekotoba meaning "the strand" and "not being." "Uramite" is a kakekotoba meaning "reproaching" and "seeing the bay." "Tachi" (rising) is an engo for "nami" (waves).

627 • Topic unknown.

kanete yori	did these waves arise
kaze ni sakidatsu	before the breezes even
nami nare ya	began to blow still
au koto naki ni	we have not met yet on calm
madaki tatsu ran	seas ripples already swirl

Anonymous

"Naki" is a kakekotoba meaning "none" and "lull."

628 • *Topic unknown.*

michinoku ni	River of Rumors
ari to iu naru	they say that you flow through far
natori gawa	Michinoku how
naki na torite wa	painful to know that we must
kurushikarikeri	suffer from these false whispers

Mibu no Tadamine

For Michinoku, see 368. Natori (Rumor-bearing) River flows through Natori District in Miyazaki Prefecture. Lines 1–3 (Natori River, which they say is in Michinoku) are a jo linked to line 4 by the repetition of sounds.

229

629 • *Topic unknown.*

ayanakute	already rumors
madaki naki na no	swirl though as yet there is no
tatsuta gawa	truth to them can I
watarade yaman	now refrain from venturing
mono naranaku ni	forth to ford Tatsuta's course

Miharu no Arisuke

The phrases "na no tatsu" (rumors spread) and Tatsuta River are linked by the kakekotoba "tatsu." For Tatsuta River, see 283.

630 • *Topic unknown.*

hito wa isa	I cannot speak for
ware wa nakina no	her but for myself I shall
oshikereba	say I know nothing
mukashi mo ima mo	of her now nor have I known—
shirazu to o iwan	for I abhor false rumors

Ariwara no Motokata

This poem is included in the *Gosenshū*, 635, as the reply of the daughter of Ariwara no Muneyana to Prince Motoyoshi.

631 • *Topic unknown.*

korizuma ni	still I have not learned
mata mo naki na wa	my lesson now rumors will
tachinubeshi	surely fly again
hito nikukaranu	for I live in a world of
yo ni shi sumaeba	love where she is most welcome

Anonymous

632 • *Narihira was visiting a lady who lived in the vicinity of the eastern Fifth Ward. Since he was visiting secretly, he could not go in through the gate, but came and went through a broken place in the earthen wall. His visits became so frequent that the owner of the house heard about them and hid a night guard on the path. When Narihira came, he was obliged to go home without having seen the lady. He composed this poem.*

| hito shirenu | would that he might fall |
| wa ga kayoiji no | asleep   this guard posted night |

sekimori wa   after night beside
yoiyoi goto ni   the path I must travel in
uchi mo nenanan   secrecy   far from men's eyes

Ariwara no Narihira

This poem appears in *The Tales of Ise*, 5, with a similar headnote.

633 • *Topic unknown.*

shinoburedo   with difficulty
koishiki toki wa   I endure my longing   till
  ashihiki no   I must go out to
yama yori tsuki no her   as the moon leaves its home
idete koso kure   behind the rugged mountains

Ki no Tsurayuki

"Ashihiki no" is a makurakotoba for "yama" (mountains). Lines 3 and 4 (like the moon from the rugged mountains) are a jo linked to "idete" (rising; leaving).

634 • *Topic unknown.*

koikoite   I have yearned so long
mare ni koyoi zo   and at last tonight we meet—
  ōsaka no   may the beribboned
yūtsukedori wa   cock at Ōsaka never
nakazu mo aranan   announce the break of day

Anonymous

The place name Ōsaka (see 374) is a kakekotoba; it can mean "hill where we meet." In this poem it also functions as a makurakotoba for "yūtsukedori" (beribboned cock).

635 • *Topic unknown.*

aki no yo mo   the autumn night was
na nomi narikeri   long in name only   at last
  au to ieba   we met   but the blush
koto zo tomo naku of dawn parted us before
akenuru mono o   the words of love were spoken

Ono no Komachi

636 • *Topic unknown.*

    nagashi tomo
omoi zo hatenu
    mukashi yori
au hito kara no
aki no yo nareba

    I am unable
to know how long they really
    are   for men often
have said autumn nights' lengths are
decided by one's true love

Ōshikōchi no Mitsune

637 • *Topic unknown.*

    shinonome no
hogara hogara to
    akeyukeba
ono ga kinuginu
naru zo kanashiki

    beneath the faint light
of the early morning sky
    when night becomes dawn
how sadly we part the robes
that covered us in the dark

Anonymous

638 • *Topic unknown.*

    akenu tote
ima wa no kokoro
    tsuku kara ni
nado iishiranu
omoi souran

    "daybreak is here" we
say   and my heart is weighted
    with the burden of
parting   why is it coupled
with thoughts I cannot express

Fujiwara no Kunitsune

639 • *A poem from the poetry contest held at the residence of the Consort in the Kanpyō era.*

    akenu tote
kaeru michi ni wa
    kokitarete
ame mo namida mo
furisobochi tsutsu

    "daybreak is here" we
say   and I must walk the road
    away from you   all
about me torrents fall   both
teardrops and raindrops drench me

Fujiwara no Toshiyuki

640 • *Topic unknown.*

    shinonome no
wakare o oshimi

    in sorrow at our
parting with the faint flush of

ware zo masu	dawn it was I who
tori yori saki ni	first cried out before the cock
nakihajimetsuru	could announce the break of day

Utsuku

"Nakihajimetsuru" means both "have begun to cry" (of humans) and "have begun to crow, sing" (of birds).

641 • *Topic unknown.*

hototogisu	oh nightingale was
yume ka utsutsu ka	I awake or in dreams when
asatsuyu no	first I heard dawn's song
okite wakareshi	that dew-drenched morning as I
akatsuki no koe	awoke and parted from her

Anonymous

For hototogisu, see 135. "Asatsuyu no" (like the morning dew) is a makurakotoba modifying the kakekotoba "okite" (settling; rising).

642 • *Topic unknown.*

tamakushige	were I to leave when
akeba kimi ga na	night turned bright as your jeweled
tachinubemi	comb box surely they
yo fukaku koshi o	would talk did anyone see
hito miken ka mo	me fade into night's dimness

Anonymous

"Tamakushige" (jeweled comb box) is a makurakotoba modifying the kakekotoba "akeba" (when one opens; when it dawns). "Tama" is a poetic prefix used to intensify a description of a beautiful object.

643 • *Topic unknown.*

kesa wa shimo	this morning I rose
okiken kata mo	with such a heavy heart just
shirazaritsu	the memory can
omoiizuru zo	make me melt away like the
kiete kanashiki	frost in the bright noontime sun

Ōe no Chisato

"Shimo" is a kakekotoba; it is an exclamatory word and also means "frost." The kakekotoba "oki" means "settling" and "awakening," and functions as an engo for "shimo" (frost) and "kiete" (vanishing). "Omoi" (longings) contains the word "hi" (sun) and functions as a kakekotoba; the phrase "omo(h)izuru" means both "recollect" and "the sun comes out." Ozawa Masao attributes the use of such unusual kakekotoba to Chisato's background as a scholar of Chinese.

644 • *Sent to a lady on the morning after a tryst.*

nenuru yo no	how fleeting the dream
yume o hakanami	of the night we two slept side
madoromeba	by side trying to
iya hakana ni mo	recapture it I dozed but
narimasaru kana	it only faded faster

Ariwara no Narihira

This poem appears in *The Tales of Ise*, 103.

645 • *Once when Narihira was in Ise Province, he had a secret tryst with the Virgin of the Shrine. The next morning, as he was worrying about having no one to carry a message to her, this poem arrived from her.*

kimi ya koshi	did you come to me
ware ya yukiken	or did I go to you I
omōezu	cannot now recall
yume ka utsutsu ka	was it dream reality
nete ka samete ka	was I sleeping or awake

Anonymous

This poem and 646 appear in *The Tales of Ise*, 69. Ise Province is part of Mie Prefecture. Shrine Virgins (saigū) were unmarried princesses appointed to serve at the Ise Shrine.

646 • *In reply.*

kakikurasu	I am lost in the
kokoro no yami ni	total darkness of my heart—
madoiniki	people of this world
yume utsutsu to wa	you decide for me if love
yohito sadameyo	was dream or reality

Ariwara no Narihira

The vocabulary of this poem is laden with Buddhist overtones: "Kokoro no yami" (the darkness of the heart) is a phrase used to describe the blindness of the un-enlightened; "madou" (to be perplexed, lost) describes the lives of those unenlight-ened beings who live in darkness; "yume" (dream, illusion) is the state from which one must awaken, achieving life in "utsutsu" (reality).

647 • *Topic unknown.*

ubatama no	the reality
yami no utsutsu wa	of our meeting in the jet
sadaka naru	black night was no more
yume ni ikura mo	vivid than the daily dreams
masarazarikeri	in which I call you to me

Anonymous

"Ubatama no" is a makurakotoba modifying "yami" (darkness).

648 • *Topic unknown.*

sayo fukete	deep in the night as
ama no to wataru	the moon sailed across the broad
tsuki kage ni	harbor of the sky
akazu mo kimi o	we met for but a moment
aimitsuru kana	leaving desire unsatisfied

Anonymous

Poems 648–650 all contain phrases similar to *Man'yōshū* poems.

649 • *Topic unknown.*

kimi ga na mo	Naniwa in Tsu
waga na mo tateji	will never hear your name or
naniwa naru	mine on the tongues of
mitsu tomo iu na	others do not tell that we've
aiki tomo iwaji	met and I shall never speak

Anonymous

For Naniwa, see 604. "Mitsu" is a kakekotoba meaning "lovely inlet" and "met." "Aiki" (abiki) is a kakekotoba meaning "pulling the nets" and "have met." It is an engo for Naniwa. The last three lines also mean, "Do not speak of the inlet in Naniwa. I shall not speak of the nets being pulled in."

650 • *Topic unknown.*

natori gawa
seze no umoregi
arawareba
ika ni sen to ka
aimisomeken

when I began to
love you   what did I intend
to do   if hidden
logs floated to the surface
in Rumor River's shallows

Anonymous

For Natori River, see 628. The first two lines (submerged log of the shallows of Natori River) are a jo linked to "arawareba" (when it is revealed).

651 • *Topic unknown.*

yoshino gawa
mizu no kokoro wa
hayaku tomo
taki no oto ni wa
tateji to zo omou

Yoshino River
the heart of the waters flows
swiftly   but I will
never let rumors rise   loud
as the sound of the rapids

Anonymous

For Yoshino River, see 124.

652 • *Topic unknown.*

koishikuba
shita ni o omoe
murasaki no
nezuri no koromo
iro ni izu na yume

if you love me   wear
your love within   don't display
its color like a
robe printed deep purple with
the dye of violet grass

Anonymous

Lines 3 and 4 (robe dyed with the roots of the violet grass) are a jo linked to the kakekotoba "iro" (color; surface). The roots of the perennial murasaki (gromwell; *Lithospermum erythrorhizom*) were ground to extract a purple dye.

653 • *Topic unknown.*

hana susuki
ho ni idete koiba

my heart is tangled
as my knotted undersash

236

na o oshimi   for idle gossip
shita yuu himo no   stings   now our love is open
musubohoretsutsu   as the plume grass tassels

Ono no Harukaze

"Hana susuki" (flowering pampas grass) is a makurakotoba modifying the kake-kotoba "ho" (ear; surface). "Shita yuu himo no" (like a sash tied underneath) is a jo linked to "musubohoretsutsu" (is tied repeatedly).

654 • *This was sent to Tachibana no Kiyoki by a woman whom he had been secretly visiting.*

omoudochi   lovers who pretend
hitoribitori ga   to be strangers   if one should
  koishinaba   die of longing   for
tare ni yosoete   whom could the other wear rough
fujigoromo kin   wisteria mourning robes

Anonymous

"Fujigoromo" (a robe of wisteria) refers to dark clothing worn for secret trysts or for periods of mourning.

655 • *Reply.*

nakikouru   if tears stained my sleeves
namida ni sode no   with grief at the tidings of
  sobochinaba   your death I would change
nugikaegatera   to mourning robes each dark night
yoru koso wa kime   to hide my secret passion.

Tachibana no Kiyoki

656 • *Topic unknown.*

utsutsu ni wa   in waking hours   yes
sa mo koso arame   then it may be understood   but
  yume ni sae   what misery to
hitome o moru to   see myself shun watchful eyes
miru ga wabishisa   even in the world of dreams

Ono no Komachi

657 • *Topic unknown.*

kagiri naki
omoi no mama ni
　yoru mo kon
yumeji o sae ni
hito wa togameji

guided by a love
that has no bounds　I shall go
　to him by darkness—
surely no one will question
one who treads the path of dreams

Ono no Komachi

"Omo(h)i" (longings) contains the word "hi" (light; flame).

658 • *Topic unknown.*

yumeji ni wa
ashi mo yasumezu
　kayoedomo
utsutsu ni hitome
mishi goto wa arazu

though my feet never
cease running to him on the
　byways of my dreams
such meetings do not equal
one waking glimpse of my love

Ono no Komachi

659 • *Topic unknown.*

omoedomo
hitome tsutsumi no
　takakereba
kawa to minagara
e koso watarane

like the dikes of a
dangerous swollen river
　banks of watchful eyes
keep me from crossing over
to meet the one I long for

Anonymous

"Tsutsumi" is a kakekotoba meaning "shrinking from" and "embankment."
"Kawa" is a kakekotoba meaning "river" and "that, others." "Wataru" (to cross) is
an engo for "kawa" (river).

660 • *Topic unknown.*

tagitsu se no
hayaki kokoro o
　nani shi ka mo
hitome zutsumi no
seki todomu ran

a heart flooded by
turbulent cascades of love—
　how could its swollen
rapids be held in check by
embankments of watchful eyes

Anonymous

661 • *A poem from the poetry contest held at the residence of the Consort in the Kanpyō era.*

kurenai no	though the safflower
iro ni wa ideji	bud may rise crimson above
kakurenu no	the thick-grown marsh I'll
shita ni kayoite	keep my love within my heart
koi wa shinu tomo	even if it means my death

Ki no Tomonori

"Kurenai no" (crimson safflower) is a makurakotoba for the kakekotoba "iro" (color; surface). "Kakurenu no" (overgrown marsh lands) is a makurakotoba modifying "shita ni kayoite" (traveling underneath).

662 • *Topic unknown.*

fuyu no ike ni	alone the grebe glides
sumu nihodori no	over the icy waters
tsure mo naku	of the wintry pond
soko ni kayou to	unguardedly I come to
hito ni shirasu na	you do not reveal my love

Ōshikōchi no Mitsune

Lines 1 and 2 (like the grebe that lives in the winter pond) are a jo linked to the kakekotoba "tsure mo naku" (carelessly; having no companion). "Soko" is a kakekotoba meaning "over there" and "depths," and functions as an engo for "ike" (pond).

663 • *Topic unknown.*

sasa no ha ni	on the slender leaves
oku hatsushimo no	of bamboo grasses settle
yo o samumi	the first frosts of fall—
shimi wa tsuku tomo	the night chill penetrates but
iro ni idemeya	no color reveals its touch

Ōshikōchi no Mitsune

"Shimi wa tsuku" is a kakekotoba meaning both "to freeze through" and "to penetrate." "Iro ni idemeya" is a kakekotoba meaning "shall turn autumn colors" and "shall appear on the surface."

664 • *Topic unknown.*

yamashina no	would I reveal our
otowa no yama no	love would I give gossip wings
oto ni dani	send it whispering
hito no shirubeku	echoing like Sound of Wings
waga koime ka mo	Mountain in Yamashina

Anonymous

Some say that this poem was composed by a woman attendant (uneme) from Ōmi Province.

Yamashina is part of Higashiyama-ku, Kyōto. Lines 1 and 2 (of Otowa Mountain in Yamashina) are a jo linked to "oto" (sound; rumor) by the repetition of sounds. For Otowa Mountain, see 142. Ōmi Province corresponds to modern Shiga Prefecture.

665 • *Topic unknown.*

mitsu shio no	waxing tides wane but
nagare hiru ma o	we can never meet in bright
aigatami	daylight I await
mirume no ura ni	the night when floodtides carry
yoru o koso mate	seaweeds to Mirume Bay

Kiyowara no Fukayabu

The first four words, "mitsu shio no nagare" (the flowing of the waxing tides), are a jo linked to the kakekotoba "hiru" (waning; daytime). Line 4 (toward the bay where seaweed grows) is a jo linked to the kakekotoba "yoru" (approaches; night). "Mirume" is also a kakekotoba, meaning "chance to meet" as well as "seaweed."

666 • *Topic unknown.*

shira kawa no	I shall not say I
shirazu tomo iwaji	do not know you for I hope
soko kiyomi	to remain in your
nagarete yo yo ni	embrace as long as the depths
suman to omoeba	of the White River flow clear

Taira no Sadafun

"Shira kawa no" (of the Shira River) is a makurakotoba linked to "shirazu" (unknowing) by the repetition of sound. The source of the Shira River is near Shiga Pass (see 115); it flows into the Kamo River. "Soko" (depths) is an engo for "kawa" (river), as are "nagarete" (flowing) and "suman," a kakekotoba meaning both "will clear" and "will live."

667 • *Topic unknown.*

shita ni nomi	how painful is love
koureba kurushi	imprisoned in the heart do
tama no o no	not censure me if
taete midaren	my tears of anguish scatter
hito na togame so	like jewels when the thread snaps

Ki no Tomonori

"Tama no o no taete" (the jewels, their thread breaking) is a jo linked to "midaren" (will scatter, be agitated).

668 • *Topic unknown.*

waga koi o	when I no longer
shinobikanetewa	can bear to conceal my love
ashihiki no	it must be revealed
yama tachibana no	bold as mandarin blossoms
iro ni idenu beshi	deep in the rugged mountains

Ki no Tomonori

"Ashihiki no" is a makurakotoba for "yama" (mountain). Lines 3 and 4 (of the mandarin orange tree in the rugged mountains) are a jo linked to the kakekotoba "iro" (color; surface).

669 • *Topic unknown.*

ōkata wa	my reputation
waga na mo minato	sent abroad like fishing boats
kogiidenan	rowed from the harbor yet
yo o umibeta ni	our meetings are few as the
mirume sukunashi	seaweeds near the shore

Anonymous

"Umibeta" (seaside) is a kakekotoba, containing the word "umi" (misery). "Mirume" is a kakekotoba meaning "seaweed" and "chance to meet."

670 • *Topic unknown.*

makura yori	unable to hold
mata shiru hito mo	back my tears they seeped through the
naki koi o	pillow that should have

namida sekiaezu	kept our secret others should
morashitsuru kana	not have known the love we shared

Taira no Sadafun

This poem is an allusive variation on XI, 504.

671 • *Topic unknown.*

kaze fukeba	when the wind blows I
nami utsu kishi no	am like a pine on the shore
matsu nare ya	beaten by the waves—
ne ni arawarete	roots washed by the sea again
nakinu beranari	my voice rises in mournful cries

Anonymous

Some say this poem is by Kakinomoto no Hitomaro.

"Ne" (root; voice) is a kakekotoba. "Arawarete" (being washed; appearing) is a kakekotoba that, in the first meaning, also serves as an engo for "matsu" (pine) and "nami" (waves).

672 • *Topic unknown.*

ike ni sumu	the waters of the
na o oshidori no	pond are too shallow to hide
mizu o asami	the mandarin duck—
kakuru to suredo	his name tells of his unease
arawarenikeri	now that he's well known as I

Anonymous

"Oshidori" is a kakekotoba meaning "mandarin duck" and "regrets." Lines 1 and 2 (of the mandarin duck that lives in the pond) are a jo linked to "mizu o asami" (the shallowness of the waters).

673 • *Topic unknown.*

au koto wa	our meeting was as
tama no o bakari	short as the thread between the
na no tatsu wa	gems of a necklace
yoshino no kawa no	but the gossip will swell like
tagitsu se no goto	the Yoshino River waves

Anonymous

"Tama no o" (the thread between the jewels) suggests the brevity of life. "Tama" (jewel; spirit) is a kakekotoba. The place name Yoshino is also a kakekotoba: "yoshi" is an exclamation indicating resignation. For Yoshino River, see 124.

674 • *Topic unknown.*

muradori no	my reputation
tachinishi waga na	has spread like a flock of birds
ima sara ni	scattering flying
koto nashibu tomo	to the winds is it too late
shirushi arame ya	now to pretend innocence

Anonymous

"Muradori no" (of the flocking birds) is a makurakotoba modifying the kakekotoba "tachinishi" (arose; spread).

675 • *Topic unknown.*

kimi ni yori	because of you my
waga na wa hana ni	love my name spreads like spring mists
harugasumi	that hide the blossoms
no ni mo yama ni mo	floating scattering over
tachimichinikeri	mountains and through verdant fields

Anonymous

"Hana ni" means both "over the flowers" and "heavily." Lines 3 and 4 (spring mists, in the fields and in the mountains) are a jo linked to the kakekotoba "tachi" (rising; spreading). "No" (fields), "yama" (mountains), and "kasumi" (mists) are engo.

676 • *Topic unknown.*

shiru to ieba	it is said that the
makura dani sede	pillow knows so without one
neshi mono o	we slept still it seems
chiri naranu na no	my reputation drifts through
sora ni tatsu ran	the skies like dust on the wind

Anonymous

The kakekotoba "sora ni" (in the sky; at a guess) is an engo for "chiri" (dust).

BOOK XIV

Love Poems (4)

677 • *Topic unknown.*

michinoku no	oh flowering reeds
asaka no numa no	in the Asaka Marsh of
hanagatsumi	far Michinoku—
katsu miru hito ni	will my love for one whom I've
koi ya wataran	scarcely seen last forever

Anonymous

For Michinoku, see 368. Asaka Marsh is in Fukushima Prefecture. Hanagatsumi possibly is a variety of flowering reed. Lines 1–3 (the hanagatsumi of Asaka Marsh in the Far North) are a jo linked to line 4, "katsu miru" (rarely see) by the similarity of sounds.

678 • *Topic unknown.*

aimizuba	if we two never
koishiki koto mo	met and loved would I now feel
nakaran mashi	such pangs of longing
oto ni zo hito o	better I should know my love
kiku bekarikeru	only by idle gossip

Anonymous

679 • *Topic unknown.*

isonokami	ah the middle road
furu no nakamichi	that leads to Furu in far
nakanaka ni	Isonokami

244

mizuba koishi to   had I not loved rashly once
omowamashi ya wa   would I now pine so sadly

Ki no Tsurayuki

For Isonokami and Furu, see 144. Isonokami functions as a makurakotoba for Furu, and lines 1 and 2 (the middle road at Furu in Isonokami) are a jo linked to line 3, "nakanaka ni" (recklessly), by the repetition of sounds.

680 • *Topic unknown.*

kimi to ieba   whether alone or
mi mare mizu mare   together you my love keep
fuji no ne no   my passion burning
mezurashige naku   ceaselessly like smoldering
moyuru waga koi   flames deep within Mount Fuji

Fujiwara no Tadayuki

"Fuji no ne no" (like the base of Mount Fuji) is a makurakotoba modifying "moyuru" (burns). "Ko(h)i" (love) contains the word "hi" (fire), which is an engo for "moyu" (to burn).

681 • *Topic unknown.*

yume ni dani   not even in dreams
miyu to wa mieji   may I now show myself to
asa na asa na   my love with each day's
waga omokage ni   dawning I wince at the grim
hazuru mi nareba   reflection in my mirror

Ise

682 • *Topic unknown.*

ishima yuku   tirelessly I shall
mizu no shiranami   rise and come again to meet
tachikaeri   my love like the white
kaku koso wa mime   capped waves that eternally
akazu mo aru kana   surge through the rocky crevice

Anonymous

Lines 1 and 2 (white waves of the waters flowing through the rocks) are a jo linked to the kakekotoba "tachikaeri" (rising and returning; going and coming back).

245

683 • *Topic unknown.*

ise no ama no	as fisherfolk of
asa na yuu na ni	Ise dive for seaweed from
kazuku chō	morning until night—
mirume ni hito o	oh that I might see you till
aku yoshi mo gana	my longing could be sated

Anonymous

Lines 1–3 (which they say the fisherfolk of Ise dive for morning and night) are a jo linked to the kakekotoba "mirume" (chance to meet; seaweed).

684 • *Topic unknown.*

harugasumi	I never weary
tanabiku yama no	of the fragile cherry blooms
sakurabana	on the mountain where
miredomo akanu	spring mists trail though I often
kimi ni mo aru kana	gaze upon you I'll not tire

Ki no Tomonori

Lines 1–3 (cherry flowers on the mountains where spring mists trail) are a jo linked to "miredomo" (although I see; although we meet).

685 • *Topic unknown.*

kokoro o zo	dear heart I know you
warinaki mono to	are an irrational thing—
omoinuru	does longing grow with
miru mono kara ya	meetings can love deepen if
koishikaru beki	lovers often congregate

Kiyowara no Fukayabu

686 • *Topic unknown.*

karehaten	deep as grasses of
nochi oba shirade	summer grows my love for him
natsugusa no	still innocent of
fukaku mo hito no	the future when green leaves will
omōyuru kana	wither and summer depart

Ōshikōchi no Mitsune

"Kare" is a kakekotoba meaning "separating" and "withering"; it serves as an engo for "kusa" or "gusa" (grasses). "Natsugusa no" (of the summer grasses) is a makurakotoba for "fukaku" (depth).

687 • *Topic unknown.*

asuka gawa	Asuka River
fuchi wa se ni naru	the deep quiet pools may change
yo nari tomo	to rushing shallows
omoisometen	in this world but I shall not
hito wa wasureji	forget the love that's dyed my heart

Anonymous

For Asuka River, see 284. This poem may be an allusive variation on XVIII, 933.

688 • *A poem from the poetry contest held at the residence of the Consort in the Kanpyō era.*

omou chō	can it be only
koto no ha nomi ya	the leaves of my oaths of love
aki o hete	that do not change to
iro mo kawaranu	new colors once autumn comes
mono ni wa aru ran	other tendrils are transformed

Anonymous

"Ha" (leaves), "aki" (autumn), and "iro" (color) are engo.

689 • *Topic unknown.*

samushiro ni	tonight once again
koromo katashiki	does she spread but one side of
koyoi mo ya	her robe upon the
ware o matsu ran	mat bridge maiden of Uji
uji no hashihime	do your arms still await me

Anonymous

"Uji no hashihime" (maiden of Uji Bridge) refers to the goddess who guards the bridge that was first built across the Uji River in Kyōto in the seventh century.

690 • *Topic unknown.*

kimi ya kon	uncertain whether
ware ya yukan no	you would come to me or I

isayoi ni	should go to you I
maki no itado mo	fell asleep with my black pine
sasazu nenikeri	door open to the moonlight

Anonymous

"Isayoi" is a kakekotoba meaning "the moon of the sixteenth night" and "hesitating."

691 • *Topic unknown.*

ima kon to	by and by I'll come
iishi bakari ni	he said and so I waited
nagatsuki no	patiently but I
ariake no tsuki o	saw only the moon of the
machiidetsuru kana	longest month in the dawn sky

Sosei

Nagatsuki is the Ninth Month of the lunar calendar. The full moon of this month is the most famous of all, especially as it lingers in the dawn sky.

692 • *Topic unknown.*

tsuki yo yoshi	so splendid this moon
yo yoshi to hito ni	this night if I sent him a
tsuge yaraba	message would he think
ko chō ni nitari	it a summons how could
matazu shi mo	I not await him tonight

Anonymous

Man'yōshū 1011 is similar:

waga yado no	if I sent him a
ume sakitari to	message that the plum blossoms
tsuge yaraba	bloom in my garden
ko to iu ni nitari	he might think it a summons—
chirinu to mo yoshi	petals go ahead and fall

693 • *Topic unknown.*

kimi kozuba	my love if you do
neya e mo iraji	not come I'll not enter
komurasaki	my chamber alone

| waga motoyui ni | though frost falls and silvers the |
| shimo wa oku tomo | purple band that holds my hair |

Anonymous

Man'yōshū 89 has a similar phrase: "though the dew fall on my pitch-black hair."

694 • *Topic unknown.*

miyagino no	the sparsely scattered
moto ara no kohagi	leaves of bush clover weighted
tsuyu o omomi	with the heavy dew
kaze o matsu goto	yearn for winds on Miyagi
kimi o koso mate	Moor as I long for my love

Anonymous

Miyagi Moor, east of present-day Sendai City, was famous for hagi (bush clover). Ozawa notes that this is one of the loveliest and most famous of *Kokinshū* poems.

695 • *Topic unknown.*

ana koishi	oh sweet yearning if
ima mo miteshi ga	only I could meet her once
yamagatsu no	more that delicate
kakiho ni sakeru	Japanese carnation that bloomed
yamato nadeshiko	on the mountain peasant's fence

Anonymous

For nadeshiko, see 167.

696 • *Topic unknown.*

tsu no kuni no	oh Naniwa in
naniwa omowazu	Tsu Province I know not what
yamashiro no	to think for here in
towa ni aimin	Towa in Yamashiro
koto o nomi koso	I dream always of meeting

Anonymous

For Tsu and Naniwa, see 604. Yamashiro Province makes up present-day Kyōto City. "Tsu no kuni no" (of the province of Tsu) is a makurakotoba for Naniwa, a kakekotoba meaning "what" and also the name of the city. Towa is also a kakekotoba: it is the name of a district in Fushimi-ku in Kyōto and also means "perpetual."

697 • *Topic unknown.*

shikishima no	if only the days
yamato ni wa aranu	until we find a chance to
kara koromo	meet could be as few
koro mo hezu shite	as the Chinese robes here in
au yoshi mo gana	the lovely isles of Japan

Ki no Tsurayuki

"Shikishima no" is a makurakotoba for Yamato, an ancient name for Japan and specifically for the area around Nara. Lines 1–3 (Chinese robes that are not in Japan) are a jo linked to "koro mo" (time also) by the repetition of sounds.

698 • *Topic unknown.*

koishi to wa	love's "longing" that word—
ta ga nazukeken	who could it have been gave this
koto naran	feeling that false name
shinu to zo tada ni	better that they should call it
iu bekarikeru	precisely what it is "death"

Kiyowara no Fukayabu

699 • *Topic unknown.*

miyoshino no	like the waving sprays
ōkawa nobe no	of wisteria boughs near
fujinami no	the swift river at
nami ni omowaba	fair Yoshino my love flows
waga koime ya wa	to you in no common way

Anonymous

For Yoshino, see 3. Lines 1–3 (of waves of wisteria blossoms on the banks of the great   river of fair Yoshino) are a jo linked to "nami ni" (generally) by the repetition of sounds. The last two lines are almost the same as *Man'yōshū* 858.

700 • *Topic unknown.*

kaku koin	that I would suffer
mono to wa ware mo	the burning pangs of love I
omoiniki	knew from the very

| kokoro na ura zo | start my heart's clairvoyance |
| masashikarikeru | has now been proven flawless |

Anonymous

701 • *Topic unknown.*

ama no hara	the god of thunder
fumitodoro kashi	stamps his feet until the plains
narukami mo	of heaven echo—
omou naka oba	but can even he divide
sakuru mono ka wa	true lovers as close as we

Anonymous

702 • *Topic unknown.*

azusayumi	thick as the tendrils
hikino no tsuzura	of the green vines that cover
sue tsui ni	Hikino broad as
waga omou hito ni	the catalpa bow rumors
koto no shigeken	of the one I love will spread

Anonymous

Some say this poem was composed by a Mikado for a woman attendant (uneme) from Omi.

"Azusayumi" (catalpa bow) is a makurakotoba linked to the kakekotoba "hiki/no" (pulling; Hikino). The location of Hikino has not been determined. Lines 1 and 2 (the green vines of Hikino [where they] draw the catalpa bows) are a jo linked to "sue" (tips).

703 • *Topic unknown.*

natsubiki no	though gossip may spread
tebiki no ito o	thick as fibers of summer
kurikaeshi	hemp plucked by slender
koto shigeku tomo	fingers and wound upon the
taen to omou na	reel do not break off our love

Anonymous

This poem is said to be the reply.

There are two theories of the meaning of "natsubiki": silk spun by the silkworms or fibers plucked from hemp roots. Lines 1 and 2 (the fibers plucked by hand from summer plants) are a jo linked to the kakekotoba "kurikaeshi" (reeling; repeatedly).

704 • *Topic unknown.*

satobito no	though the neighbors in
koto wa natsu no no	our village spread rumors thick
shigeku tomo	as fields of summer
kareyuku kimi ni	grass though your love for me may
awazarame ya wa	wither could I live without you

Anonymous

"Kare" (withering; separating) is a kakekotoba.

705 • *This poem was composed by Narihira for a woman of his household when he heard that Fujiwara no Toshiyuki, a young man with whom she was on intimate terms, had written to her saying, "I would like to come to visit you soon, but I am worried that it will rain."*

kazukazu ni	wondering again
omoi omowazu	whether you love me or not—
toigatami	it's so hard to ask—
mi o shiru ame wa	but the rain which knows my fate
furi zo masareru	pours down in swifter torrents

Ariwara no Narihira

This poem appears in *The Tales of Ise*, 107.

706 • *Composed and sent to Narihira by a woman reproaching him for his visits to so many women.*

ōnusa no	because your life is
hiku te amata ni	filled with many beckoning
narinureba	hands as numerous
omoedo e koso	as touch the trailing votive
tanomazarikere	strips I love but cannot trust

Anonymous

Ōnusa (votive strips) were lengths of cloth attached to branches and used in the Great Purification ceremonies twice a year. This poem and 707 appear in *The Tales of Ise*, 47.

707 • *Reply.*

ōnusa to	I am reputed
na ni koso tatere	to be like the votive strips
nagarete mo	that drift and flow cast
tsui ni yoru se wa	upon the stream yet at last
ari chō mono o	they say each finds a haven

Ariwara no Narihira

"Nagarete" (flowing) and "se" (shallows) are engo.

708 • *Topic unknown.*

suma no ama no	smoke from the salt fires
shio yaku keburi	of the Suma fisherfolk
kaze o itami	buffeted by fierce
omowanu kata ni	winds sways and drifts away in
tanabikinikeri	unexpected directions

Anonymous

Suma refers to the shore near Harima in Kōbe City.

709 • *Topic unknown.*

tamakazura	as numerous as
hau ki amata ni	trees over which the jeweled
narinureba	vines creep and crawl are
taenu kokoro no	your entanglements can I
ureshige mo nashi	rejoice in your steadfastness

Anonymous

"Kazura" (vines) and "taenu" (not breaking) are engo.

710 • *Topic unknown.*

ta ga sato ni	to which villages
yogare oshite ka	have your nightime visits ceased
hototogisu	hototogisu
tada koko ni shi mo	your song tells me you will sleep
netaru koe suru	nowhere but here beside me

Anonymous

711 • *Topic unknown.*

ide hito wa
koto nomi zo yoki
  tsukigusa no
utsushigokoro wa
iro koto ni shite

Anonymous

my love is skillful
only in words of love   like
  the dye made from
moon grass   the color of his
heart lies lightly   fading soon

For tsukigusa, see 247. "Tsukigusa no" (of the moon grass) is a makurakotoba
modifying the kakekotoba "utsushi" (fading; serious).

712 • *Topic unknown.*

itsuwari no
naki yo nariseba
  ika bakari
hito no koto no ha
ureshikaramashi

Anonymous

if this world of ours
were a world without falsehood
  how greatly I would
rejoice to hear burgeoning
words of new love unfolding

713 • *Topic unknown.*

itsuwari to
omou mono kara
  ima sara ni
ta ga makoto o ka
ware wa tanoman

Anonymous

I know now your words
of love are false   yet after all
  is there anyone
whose promises I could trust
anyone who would be true

714 • *Topic unknown.*

aki kaze ni
yama no ko no ha no
  utsuroeba
hito no kokoro mo
ikaga to zo omou

Sosei

in the autumn winds
the leaves of the mountain trees
  fade and change color—
how can I not imagine
my love's heart is changing too

715 • *A poem from the poetry contest held at the residence of the Consort in the Kanpyō era.*

semi no koe	such misery the
kikeba kanashi na	piping of the cicadas
natsugoromo	brings to me for I
usuku ya hito no	wonder if his love will wear
naran to omoeba	thin as castoff summer robes

Ki no Tomonori

"Natsugoromo" (summer robe) is a makurakotoba for "usuku" (thin) and an engo for "semi" (cicadas) because of their filmy wings.

716 • *Topic unknown.*

utsusemi no	gossip flourishes
yo no hitogoto no	among the people of this
shigekereba	hollow cicada
wasurenu mono no	shell world and so it seems we
karenuberanari	must part while still love is fresh

Anonymous

"Utsusemi no" (like a hollow cicada shell) is a makurakotoba for "yo" (world). "Kare" (withering; separating) is a kakekotoba. "Kare" (withering) and "shigekereba" (because it flourishes) are engo.

717 • *Topic unknown.*

akade koso	while still he loves you
omowan naka wa	best then to part before he
hanare name	wearies and leaves you—
sō dani nochi no	in this way you'll linger
wasuregatami ni	a memory he can't forget

Anonymous

718 • *Topic unknown.*

wasurenan to	it is just when I
omou kokoro no	think I will forget him put
tsuku kara ni	him from me at last
arishi yori ke ni	that my burning love blazes
mazu zo koishiki	stronger than ever before

Anonymous

719 • *Topic unknown.*

wasurenan	I'll try to forget
ware o uramu na	you but do not be angry
hototogisu	hototogisu
hito no aki ni wa	does not await the autumn
awan to mo sezu	chill or the heedless heart

Anonymous

For hototogisu, see 135. "Aki" (autumn; tiring of) is a kakekotoba.

720 • *Topic unknown.*

taezu yuku	should the endlessly
asuka no kawa no	flowing Asuka River
yodominaba	hesitate grow still
kokoro aru to ya	onlookers would think it had
hito no omowan	a love concealed in its heart

Anonymous

Some say this poem is by Nakatomi no Azumabito.

For Asuka River, see 284. "Yodominaba" is a kakekotoba meaning "if it grows dark" and "if he stops." "Kokoro" (heart) refers both to the lover's heart and the depths of the river. This poem is similar to *Man'yōshū* 1379:

taezu yuku	should the endlessly
asuka no kawa no	flowing Asuka River
yodomeraba	hesitate grow still
yue shi mo aru goto	onlookers would come to see
hito no mimaku ni	what the reason might be

721 • *Topic unknown.*

yodo gawa no	people may think the
yodomu to hito wa	Yodo River currents stand
miruramedo	still in quiet pools
nagarete fukaki	yet deep beneath the surface
kokoro aru mono o	constant waters swiftly flow

Anonymous

For Yodo River, see 461. "Yodo gawa no" (like the Yodo River) is a makurakotoba linked to "yodomu" (slacking; stopping) by the sound repetition. The rhetorical devices here are the same as those in 720.

Kokinshū

722 • *Topic unknown.*

sokoi naki
fuchi ya wa sawagu
  yama kawa no
asaki se ni koso
ada nami wa tate

are the waters of
bottomless pools ever so
  agitated   it
is the swift shoals of mountain
streams where the restless waves rise

Sosei

723 • *Topic unknown.*

kurenai no
hatsuhanazome no
  iro fukaku
omoishi kokoro
ware wasureme ya

deep as the crimson
dye made from spring's first saffron
  blooms   could I ever
forget a love that dyed my
innocent heart so gaily

Anonymous

For kurenai, see 496. Lines 1, 2, and the first word of 3 (the color of the dye of the first blossoms of the safflower) are a jo linked to "fukaku" (deeply).

724 • *Topic unknown.*

  michinoku no
shinobu mojizuri
  tare yue ni
midaren to omou
ware naranaku ni

like the cloth printed
with ferns in far Shinobu
  of the deep north   if
not for you   for whom would I
dye my heart with tangled love

Minamoto no Tōru

For Michinoku, see 368. Shinobu is a place name in Fukushima Prefecture; the word also means "to long for" and is the names of a fern, *Davallia bullata*. Lines 1 and 2 (twisted and dyed in Shinobu in the Far North) are a jo linked to "midaren" (shall be tangled) in line 4.

725 • *Topic unknown.*

omou yori
ika ni seyo to ka
  aki kaze ni

how I long for her
what more can she ask   she who
  changes her colors

257

nabiku asaji no
iro koto ni naru

and bends this way and that like
the reeds in the autumn wind

Anonymous

Lines 3 and 4 (of the reeds that bend in the autumn wind) are a jo linked to the kakekotoba "iro" (color, surface).

726 • *Topic unknown.*

chiji no iro ni
utsurou ramedo
shiranakuni
kokoro shi aki no
momiji naraneba

it seems to go through
thousands of changes   and yet   how
can I know it   for
the human heart is not like
the leaves colored by autumn

Anonymous

"Iro ni utsurou" (to change color) and "momiji" (autumn leaves) are engo, as is "aki," a kakekotoba meaning "autumn" and "tiring of."

727 • *Topic unknown.*

ama no sumu
sato no shirube ni
aranaku ni
uramin to nomi
hito no iu ran

I am not the guide
to the villages where
     seafolk dwell   why then
does my love chastise me for
not showing him to the shore

Ono no Komachi

"Urami" is a kakekotoba meaning "grudge" and "seeing the bay" and an engo for "ama" (fisherfolk).

728 • *Topic unknown.*

kumoribi no
kage to shi nareru
ware nareba
me ni koso miene
mi oba hanarezu

I have faded like
the shadows on a cloudy
     day   wasted away—
although I may hide from his
eyes   I will not leave his side

Shimotsuke no Omune

This poem seems to have been inspired by XI, 528, and XIII, 619.

729 • *Topic unknown.*

   iro mo naki
kokoro o hito ni
  someshi yori
utsurowan to wa
omōenaku ni

    since that day when my
    innocent heart was first dyed
      with love for you   I
    never doubted the hue was
    fast   never thought it might fade

Ki no Tsurayuki

730 • *Topic unknown.*

   mezurashiki
hito o min to ya
  shika mo senu
waga shitahimo no
tokewataru ran

    shall it be that I
    will meet that one who rarely
      comes   constantly my
    undersash loosens as I
    hope to feel him in my arms

Anonymous

731 • *Topic unknown.*

   kagerō no
sore ka aranu ka
  harusame no
furu hito nareba
sode zo nurenuru

    wispy gossamer
    are you there or are you not
      the spring rains fall and
    my sleeves are drenched by thoughts of
    one I loved   so long ago

Anonymous

"Kagerō no" (like a heat shimmer) is a makurakotoba linked to line 2, "sore ka aranu ka" (Is it? Is it not?). "Harusame no" (like the spring rain) is a makurakotoba linked to the kakekotoba "furu" (to fall; to grow old). "Nurenuru" (soaked) and "harusame" (spring rain) are engo.

732 • *Topic unknown.*

   horie kogu
tana nashi obune
  kogikaeri
onaji hito ni ya
koiwatarinan

    as the tiny skiffs
    ceaselessly ply the canals
      rowing back and forth
    may my yearnings continue
    to flow toward the one I love

Anonymous

Lines 1 and 2 (as the tiny skiffs ceaselessly ply the canals) are a jo linked to "kogikaeri" (rowing back and forth).

733 • *Topic unknown.*

watatsumi to	bedding roughly tossed
arenishi toko o	and touseled as white caps on
ima sara ni	the broad sea if now
harawaba sode ya	I try to brush it smooth will
awa to ukinan	my sleeve float like fragile foam

Ise

734 • *Topic unknown.*

inishie ni	my heart leaves me and
nao tachikaeru	returns to long ago days
kokoro kana	when love was young and
koishiki koto ni	strong never shall I forget
mono wasure sede	the bonds of love that held me

Ki no Tsurayuki

735 • *Kuronushi, finding it difficult to meet a woman he had secretly been visiting, was wandering outside her house when he heard the cries of the wild geese and wrote this poem to send to her.*

omoiidete	when memories of
koishiki toki wa	love burn I retrace my steps
hatsukari no	weeping as the first
nakite wataru to	geese traverse the skies with
hito shirurame ya	lonesome cries but does she know

Ōtomo no Kuronushi

736 • *Because the Minister of the Right was no longer visiting her, Yoruka gathered together the letters he had written her during the time of their love and sent them to him with this poem.*

tanomekoshi	for so long I have
koto no ha ima wa	had faith in these sheaves of words—
kaeshiten	now I must return

waga mi furureba
oki tokoro nashi

them   for the winter of my
life has come and leaves must fall

Fujiwara no Yoruka

The Minister of the Right was Minamoto no Yoshiari, author of 737, the reply.

737 • *Reply.*

ima wa tote
kaesu koto no ha
    tamaiokite
ono ga mono kara
katami to ya min

sheaves of words returned
to me   telling my heart that
    days of love are passed—
I will always treasure these
keepsakes of my own making

Minamoto no Yoshiari

738 • *Topic unknown.*

tamaboko no
michi wa tsune ni mo
    madowanan
hito o tou tomo
ware ka to omowan

may all the roads you
travel with your jeweled staff
    lead to confusion—
may all your steps come to me
no matter their direction

Fujiwara no Yoruka

"Tamaboko no" (of the jeweled staff[?]) is a makurakotoba modifying "michi" (road).

739 • *Topic unknown.*

mate to iwaba
nete mo yukanan
    shiite yuku
koma no ashi ore
mae no tanabashi

"wait" I say to him
"sleep here and then return"   but
    if he still departs
oh plank bridge before my house
trip his horse and break its leg

Anonymous

740 • *Sent to Middle Counselor Minamoto no Noboru when he was Vice-Governor of Omi.*

ōsaka no
yūtsukedori ni

oh if I could be
the beribboned cock of the

araba koso
kimi ga yukiki o
naku naku mo mime

Ōsaka Road   how
plaintively I would cry out
as I watched you come and go

Kan'in

Ōmi Province is now Shiga Prefecture. For Ōsaka, see 374. "Naku" is a kakekotoba meaning both "to cry, to call," of animals, and "to weep," of humans.

741 • *Topic unknown.*

furusato ni
aranu mono kara
   waga tame ni
hito no kokoro no
arete miyuran

his heart is surely
not a village where I once
   dwelt   why then does it
seem to be deserted   why
have the walls of love crumbled

Ise

742 • *Topic unknown.*

yamagatsu no
kakio ni haeru
   aotsuzura
hito wa kuredomo
kotozute mo nashi

over the hedges
of the mountain cottages
   the green ivy twists
and twines   my love too comes near—
but there's no message for me

Utsuku

Lines 1–3 (the green vines growing in the hedges of the mountain dwellers) are a jo linked to the kakekotoba "kuredomo" (although he comes; although it winds) in line 4.

743 • *Topic unknown.*

aozora wa
koishiki hito no
   katami ka wa
mono omou goto ni
nagameraruran

is the broad blue sky
a keepsake left behind by the
   one I love   each time
a wave of longing rises
my empty eyes look upward

Sakai no Hitozane

744 • *Topic unknown.*

au made no	ah what shall I do
katami mo ware wa	with this keepsake left me "till
nani sen ni	we meet again" though
mite mo kokoro no	I gaze upon it there is
nagusamanaku ni	no comfort for my sad heart.

Anonymous

745 • *Once when he was dallying with a young woman whose parents were very strict and whom he had to meet with the greatest secrecy, someone came to say that the young woman's parents were calling her. As she hurried in, she left behind the overskirt she had taken off. Okikaze sent this poem when he returned the overskirt.*

au made no	this souvenir left
katami tote koso	behind "till we meet again"
todomekeme	it seems this trailing
namida ni ukabu	skirt has become a rope of
mokuzu narikeri	seaweed in a sea of tears

Fujiwara no Okikaze

The mo was a backward apron worn as an overskirt on formal occasions. Mo is also a type of seaweed.

746 • *Topic unknown.*

katami koso	ah and now at last
ima wa atanare	even this memento has
kore nakuba	become my foe if
wasururu toki mo	it did not exist there might
aranashi mono o	come a time I could forget

Anonymous

This poem appears in *The Tales of Ise*, 119.

BOOK XV

Love Poems (5)

747 • *Narihira had been secretly visiting a woman who lived in the western wing of the house of the Fifth Ward Consort, but shortly after the tenth of the First Month, she moved away. Although he asked where she was, he could not send her a message. The next spring when the plum blossoms were at their peak, on a night when the moon was at its loveliest, he went to that western wing with poignant memories of the year before. He threw himself to the bare floor of the open room, and, as he lay there until the moon sank low in the sky, composed this poem.*

tsuki ya aranu	is this not that moon
haru ya mukashi no	is this spring not that spring we
haru naranu	shared so long ago
waga mi hitotsu wa	it seems that I alone am
moto no mi ni shite	unaltered from what was then

Ariwara no Narihira

The Fifth Ward Consort was Fujiwara Junshi (d. 871), wife of Ninmyō tennō, whose home was in the Fifth Ward. This poem appears in *The Tales of Ise*, 4.

748 • *Topic unknown.*

hana susuki	I yearned within I
ware koso shita ni	who should have shown my love with
omoi shika	the splendor of the
ho ni idete hito ni	ripening plume grass tassels—
musubarenikeri	and now you are bound to him

Ariwara no Narihira

The kakekotoba "ho" (surface; ear of grain) is an engo for "hana susuki" (flowering pampas grass). "Musubu" means both "to bind" and "to ripen."

749 • *Topic unknown.*

yoso ni nomi	had I merely dreamt
kikamashi mono o	and never crossed those sounding
otowa gawa	waves of Otowa
wataru to nashi ni	River I would never have
minare someken	known the chill waters of love

Fujiwara no Kanesuke

The source of Otowa River is on Otowa Mountain, east of Kyōto. "Oto" (sound) and "kikamashi" (would that I could hear) are engo. "Minare" is a kakekotoba meaning both "accustomed to meeting" and "accustomed to the water." It functions as an engo for "gawa" (river).

750 • *Topic unknown.*

waga gotoku	if only there were
ware o omowan	someone who would love me as
hito mo gana	I know I could love
sate mo ya uki to	then would we test whether the
yo o kokoromin	world of love is misery

Ōshikōchi no Mitsune

751 • *Topic unknown.*

hisakata no	I do not make my
amatsu sora ni mo	home in the broad heavenly
sumanaku ni	skies and yet he seems
hito wa yoso ni zo	to think my heart so distant—
omou beranaru	my love unobtainable

Ariwara no Motokata

"Hisakata no" is a makurakotoba modifying "ama" (heavens). This poem is an allusive variation on XI, 484.

752 • *Topic unknown.*

mite mo mata	having met again
mata mo mimaku no	and again I would see her—
hoshikereba	how my desire grows—
naruru o hito wa	this it seems is the reason
itou beranari	she hates familiarity

Anonymous

753 • *Topic unknown.*

kumo mo naku
nagitaru asa no
ware nare ya
itowarete nomi
yo oba henuran

am I a placid
cloudless morning   do I show
no promise of storm
must I live in a world where
clouds of love never gather

Ki no Tomonori

"Itowarete" is a kakekotoba meaning "clearing greatly" and "being unloved."

754 • *Topic unknown.*

hanagatami
me narabu hito no
amata areba
wasurarenuran
kazu naranu mi wa

in rows   numerous
as the slits of a wicker
basket   are all the
women you love   I am not
worthy of being counted

Anonymous

"Hanagatami" (flower baskets woven of reeds) is a makurakotoba modifying "me" (eyes; spaces in wicker).

755 • *Topic unknown.*

ukime nomi
oite nagaruru
ura nareba
kari ni nomi koso
ama wa yorurame

as seafolk come to
reap the seaweed when it floats
thickly in the bay
he only comes to visit
when tears of misery flow

Anonymous

"Ukime" (ill fortune; floating seaweed), "oite" (bearing; growing), "nagaruru" (flowing; brought to tears), and "kari" (reaping; temporary) are all kakekotoba.

756 • *Topic unknown.*

ai ni aite
mono omou koro no
waga sode ni
yadoru tsuki sae
nururu kao naru

the moon must suit her
humor to mine   as I sit
in misery   her
rain-streaked face is reflected
in my own billowing sleeves

Ise

757 • *Topic unknown.*

aki narade
oku shiratsuyu wa
nezame suru
waga tamakura no
shizuku narikeri

not even autumn
and yet the white dew settles—
awakening I find
the crystal drops before me
on the pillow where I napped

Anonymous

758 • *Topic unknown.*

suma no ama no
shioyakigoromo
osa o arami
madō ni are ya
kimi ga kimasanu

widely spaced   woven
with a broad shuttle   are the
threads of the robes worn
by the Suma fisherfolk
and the visits of my love

Anonymous

For Suma, see 708. Lines 1–3 (the coarseness of the shuttle [used to weave] the salt-burning garments of the fisherfolk of Suma) are a jo linked to "madō ni" (widely spaced).

759 • *Topic unknown.*

yamashiro no
yodo no wakagomo
kari ni dani
konu hito tanomu
ware zo hakanaki

heedlessly as he
cuts the young reeds of Yodo
in Yamashiro
the one I love neglects me—
how fleeting my life will be

Anonymous

For Yodo, see 587. Lines 1 and 2 (young reeds of Yodo in Yamashiro) are a jo linked to the kakekotoba "kari" (reaping; temporary).

760 • *Topic unknown.*

aimineba
koi koso masare
minase gawa
nani ni fukamete
omoi someken

when we cannot meet
my love but grows the stronger—
what good to yearn
with deepening love   for one
shallow as Minase's stream

Anonymous

For Minase River, see 607. Here it functions as a makurakotoba for "nani ni fukamete" (why is it deepening?).

761 • *Topic unknown.*

akatsuki no	one hundred times or
shigi no hanegaki	more I hear the fluttering
momo hagaki	of the snipes' wings
kimi ga konu yo wa	as I count the lonely hours
ware zo kazu kaku	till dawn when you have not come

Anonymous

Lines 1 and 2 (the wing flutterings of the snipe at dawn) are a jo linked to line 3, "momo hagaki" (fluttering of hundreds of wings), by the sound repetition. "Kaku" (to write) repeats the same sound pattern.

762 • *Topic unknown.*

tamakazura	cutting us apart
ima wa tayu to ya	now like the trailing ivy—
fuku kaze no	can he mean to part
oto ni mo hito no	sending me not even a
kikoezaru ran	whisper on the blowing wind

Anonymous

"Tamakazura" (jewel-like vines) is a makurakotoba for "tayu" (to cut off, to end).

763 • *Topic unknown.*

waga sode ni	upon me falls a chill
madaki shigure no	untimely rain drenching my
furinuru wa	flowing sleeves is it
kimi ga kokoro ni	that autumn has come early
aki ya konu ran	to his heart freezing our love

Anonymous

"Aki" (autumn; satiety) is a kakekotoba.

764 • *Topic unknown.*

yama no i no	though the mountain spring
asaki kokoro mo	is shallow-hearted I am

omowanu o	not why does my love
kage bakari nomi	never visit only his
hito no miyu ran	reflection appears to me

Anonymous

765 • *Topic unknown.*

wasuregusa	I wish I had sown
tane toramashi o	grasses of forgetfulness
au koto no	when we first met if
ito kaku kataki	only I had known how hard
mono to shiriseba	it would be to see each other

Anonymous

Wasuregusa (grasses of forgetfulness) is a kind of day lily (*Hemerocallis aurantiaca*).

766 • *Topic unknown.*

kouredomo	even though I yearn
au yo no naki wa	for him there are no nights of
wasuregusa	meeting is it that
yumeji ni sae ya	even on the path of dreams
oishigeru ran	grasses of forgetting bloom

Anonymous

767 • *Topic unknown.*

yume ni dani	even in my dreams
au koto kataku	it's become difficult to
nariyuku wa	meet the one I love—
ware ya i o nenu	is it that I cannot sleep
hito ya wasururu	or has he forgotten me

Anonymous

768 • *Topic unknown.*

| morokoshi mo | even far Cathay |
| yume ni mishikaba | seemed close by in my dreams   I |

chikakariki
omowanu naka zo
harukekarikeri

know now how remote
are two who no longer love—
not even in dreams to meet

Kengei

Morokoshi (Cathay) is a poetic name for China, used here to mean "far distant."

769 • *Topic unknown.*

hitori nomi
nagame furu ya no
  tsuma nareba
hito o shinobu no
kusa zo oikeru

all alone   I pass
the days   gazing at the long
  rains falling on the
eaves of my house   where grasses
of longing for my love grow

Sada no Noboru

"Nagame" (long rains; brooding), "furu" (fall; grow old), "tsuma" (eaves; spouse),
and "shinobu" (to long for; hare's foot fern) are kakekotoba.

770 • *Topic unknown.*

waga yado wa
michi mo naki made
  arenikeri
tsurenaki hito o
matsu to seshi ma ni

around my home
weeds have grown so thick that
  the path has disappeared
during the days I've waited
for my cold-hearted lover

Henjō

771 • *Topic unknown.*

ima kon to
iite wakareshi
  ashita yori
omoikurashi no
ne o nomi zo naku

by and by I'll come
he said   and since that morning
  my cries of sorrow
have blended with the mournful
droning of the cicadas

Henjō

"Omo(h)ikurashi" means "living in reveries," while higurashi means "spending the
days" and "cicadas."

270

772 • *Topic unknown.*

kome ya to wa   won't he come   hopeless
omou mono kara   question   yet with each passing
higurashi no   night I find myself
naku yūgure wa   going out to await him
tachimataretsutsu   when cicadas drone at dusk

Anonymous

773 • *Topic unknown.*

ima shi wa to   now it is over—
wabinishi mono o   despondent   I recall our
sasaga ni no   love   but then   as an
koromo ni kakari   omen of your return   a
ware o tanomuru   lucky spider climbs my robe

Anonymous

This poem is an allusive variation on XX, 1110.

774 • *Topic unknown.*

ima wa koji to   now he will come no
omou mono kara   more   this I know   and yet each
wasuretsutsu   night I forget once
mataruru koto no   more   unthinkingly I long
mada mo yamanu ka   for him   waiting never ends

Anonymous

775 • *Topic unknown.*

tsuki yo ni wa   on such a moonlit
konu hito mataru   night I cannot help but wait
kakikumori   for one who will not
ame no furanan   come   oh that it would cloud and
wabitsutsu mo nen   rain   then   forlorn   I might sleep

Anonymous

776 • *Topic unknown.*

uete inishi   he planted   and left
aki ta karu made   and when I think he'll not come

miekoneba
kesa hatsu kari no
ne ni zo nakinuru

back till autumn fields
are reaped   my cries join those of
the first geese returning at dawn

Anonymous

777 • *Topic unknown.*

konu hito o
matsu yūgure no
aki kaze wa
ika ni fukeba ka
wabishikaru ran

how mournfully the
autumn wind must blow   to bring
me such yearning for
one who will not come   though I
still wait for him at twilight

Anonymous

778 • *Topic unknown.*

hisashiku mo
narinikeru kana
suminoe no
matsu wa kurushiki
mono ni zo arikeru

ages have passed since
last we two met   painful is
this thing called waiting
yet I am faithful as the
aged Suminoe pines

Anonymous

For Suminoe, see 360. "Suminoe no" functions as a makurakotoba for the kake-kotoba "matsu" (pine; to await) because the area was famous for the ancient pines that grew there.

779 • *Topic unknown.*

suminoe no
matsu hodo hisa ni
narinureba
ashi tazu no ne ni
nakanu hi wa nashi

gnarled roots of aged
pines of Suminoe   so
long have I waited—
now no day passes but I
cry loud as the cranes on shore

Prince Kanemi

For Suminoe, see 360. The rhetorical devices of 778 are repeated here. "Matsu" (pine), "ashi" (reeds), and "ne" (root; cry) are engo.

780 • *Ise had had a romance with Nakahira, but they had become estranged. She sent this poem to tell him that she was going to the house of her father, the Governor of Yamato.*

miwa no yama	how it awaits you—
ika ni machimin	how it longs for your coming—
toshi fu tomo	Miwa Mountain for
tazunuru hito mo	it knows there will be no
araji to omoeba	visitors though long years pass

Ise

Fujiwara no Nakahira is the author of XV, 748. Ise's father was Fujiwara no Tsugikage. She moved to Yamato Province (Nara Prefecture) in 893 or 894. Miwa Mountain in Yamato was the site of the Ōmiwa Shrine. This poem is an allusive variation on XVIII, 982.

781 • *Topic unknown.*

fukimayou	darting here and there
no kaze o samumi	the cold winds race through the fields—
aki hagi no	has my lover's heart
hito no kokoro no	changed altered like the color
utsuri mo yuku ka	of the autumn hagi's bloom

Prince Urin'in

For hagi, see 198.

782 • *Topic unknown.*

ima wa to te	it's over I know
waga mi shigure ni	for I've grown old and tiresome
furinureba	as the chill autumn
koto no ha sae ni	rains even his words of love
utsuroinikeri	fade and wither like the leaves

Ono no Komachi

"Furi" (raining; aging) is a kakekotoba, as is "koto no ha" (words)/ha (leaves).

783 • *Reply.*

hito o omou	my yearning heart if
kokoro ko no ha ni	it were those fluttering leaves

araba koso
kaze no manimani
chiri mo midareme

then only then would
it fall or drift far away
yielding to the autumn wind

Ono no Sadaki

784 • *Narihira had married the daughter of Ki no Aritsune, but because of some affront, for a time he came to visit during the day but returned home in the evening. They sent him this poem.*

ama kumo no
yoso ni mo hito no
nariyuku ka
sasuga ni me ni wa
miyuru mono kara

as distant as those
drifting clouds in the heavens
has my love become
and yet each day I see him
here before my searching eyes

Ki no Aritsuna's family

"Yoso ni" (elsewhere; estranged) is a kakekotoba, as is "me" (eyes; spouse). This poem appears in *The Tales of Ise*, 19.

785 • *Reply.*

yukikaeri
sora ni nomi shite
furu koto wa
ware ga iru yama no
kaze hayami nari

back and forth I glide
restlessly traveling the
skies only because
the wind howls so fiercely on
the mountain where I would rest

Ariwara no Narihira

"Sora ni" (in the sky; absentmindedly) is a kakekotoba. The kakekotoba "furu" (passing time; raining) is an engo for clouds (kumo), the unstated actor in this scene, to which the author is comparing himself.

786 • *Topic unknown.*

kara koromo
nareba mi ni koso
matsuwareme
kakete nomi ya wa
koin to omoishi

a Chinese robe long
worn gently embraces one
but never did I
think she would cling to me so
after one dress rehearsal

Prince Kagenori

"Kara koromo" (Chinese robe) is a makurakotoba for "nareba" (because I'm accustomed to). "Kakete" (hanging) refers to "hanging up a robe" and to "pinning one's hopes."

787 • *Topic unknown.*

aki kaze wa	the cold autumn winds
mi o wakete shi mo	encircle us but do not
fukanaku ni	blow within why then
hito no kokoro no	has her heart emptied of love
sora ni naru ran	flown off to distant vacant skies

Ki no Tomonori

"Sora" (sky; empty) is a kakekotoba.

788 • *Topic unknown.*

tsuremonaku	so cold so heartless
nariyuku hito no	has she grown the leaves of her
koto no ha zo	words have begun to
aki yori saki no	change their color they wither
momiji narikeru	even before autumn comes

Minamoto no Muneyuki

"Koto no ha" (words)/ha (leaves) is a kakekotoba.

789 • *Hyōe wrote this poem and sent it to someone she loved who had not come to visit her while she was sick but came after she had recovered.*

shide no yama	only the foothills
fumoto o mite zo	of that Mountain of Death did
kaerinishi	I see before I
tsuraki hito yori	returned I shall not cross and
mazu koeji to te	leave that heartless one behind

Hyōe

Shide Mountain was believed to lie along the road to the afterworld.

790 • *This poem was attached to a burnt reed and sent to someone whom she had loved and who was gradually growing distant.*

toki sugite	the low rushes of
kareyuku ono no	the withering meadows of

asaji ni wa	Ono have passed their
ima wa omoi zo	prime and burn ceaselessly as
taezu moekeru	memories inflame my heart

Ono no Komachi's elder sister

"Kare" (withering; separating) is a kakekotoba. The poet has woven her surname, Ono, into the poem, where it means "little meadows." "Omoi"/hi (longings; fire) and "moekeru" (burns; buds) are kakekotoba. "Moekeru" (burns) and hi (fire) are engo, as are "moe" (buds) and "asaji" (rushes).

791 • *Written when she saw fires in the fields as she traveled during a time when she was longing for someone.*

fuyugare no	my heart is like
nobe to waga mi o	lonely winter-scorched fields that
omoiseba	lie before me yet
moete mo haru o	even in burnt fields buds swell—
matamashi mono o	may I look forward to spring

Ise

"Omoi"/hi (longings; fire) is an engo for "moete" (burning; budding). "Haru" (spring; to swell) is also a kakekotoba.

792 • *Topic unknown.*

mizu no awa no	a fragile being—
kiede uki mi to	life not yet vanished like foam
iinagara	upon the water—
nagarete nao mo	while my days and tears flow on
tanomaruru kana	there is someone I would trust

Ki no Tomonori

"Uki" (floating; miserable) and "nagarete"/nakarete (flowing; weeping) are kakekotoba.

793 • *Topic unknown.*

minase gawa	"Waterless River"
arite yuku mizu	yet water flows there if none
nakuba koso	ever ran I might

| tsui ni waga mi o | feel my one-tracked hopes blocked |
| taenu to omowame | like the channel of the stream |

Anonymous

For Minase River, see 607. "Mi o" (body [object marker]; channel) is a kakekotoba.

794 • *Topic unknown.*

yoshino gawa	although you've become
yoshi ya hito koso	cold as the waters of the
tsurakarame	Yoshino River
hayaku iite shi	I shall never forget the pledge
koto va wasureji	I made when first we met

Ōshikōchi no Mitsune

For Yoshino River, see 124. Here it is a makurakotoba linked to "yoshi" (well then) by the sound repetition. "Hayaku" (swiftly) is an engo for Yoshino River.

795 • *Topic unknown.*

yo no naka no	this it is which fades
hito no kokoro wa	away as easily as
hanazome no	the dye of the moon
utsuroi yasuki	flower the heart of man in
iro ni zo arikeru	the midst of this world of love

Anonymous

Dye made from tsukigusa (see 247) faded quickly. "Iro" means both "color" and "surface"; the word appears again in 797.

796 • *Topic unknown.*

kokoro koso	how hateful a thing
utate nikukere	my heart has become had it
somezaraba	never been suffused
utsurou koto mo	with love for him would I now
oshikaramashi ya	regret his fading desire

Anonymous

797 • *Topic unknown.*

| iro miede | that which fades within |
| utsurou mono wa | without changing its color |

277

yo no naka no
hito no kokoro no
hana ni zo arikeru

is the hidden bloom
of the heart of man   in
this world of disillusion

Ono no Komachi

798 • *Topic unknown.*

ware nomi ya
yo o uguisu to
   naki wabin
hito no kokoro no
hana to chirinaba

shall I alone cry
like the mountain thrush   grieving
   over the sorrows of
this world   if the blossoms of
the heart of my love scatter

Anonymous

"Uguisu" is a kakekotoba meaning both "misery" (u) and "mountain thrush" (uguisu). "Hana" (flower) and "uguisu" are engo.

799 • *Topic unknown.*

omou tomo
karenan hito o
   ikaga sen
akazu chirinuru
hana to koso mime

no matter how I
love   he will leave   what can
   I do   I will treat
him as a flower that falls
before one tires of looking

Sosei

800 • *Topic unknown.*

ima wa to te
kimi ga karenaba
   waga yado no
hana oba hitori
mite ya shinoban

if you go away
telling me our days of love
   are past   will I gaze
alone at the flowers in
my garden and remember

Anonymous

801 • *Topic unknown.*

wasuregusa
kare mo ya suru to

ah surely this will
cause the bitter grasses of

tsuremonaki	forgetfulness to
hito no kokoro ni	wither may these biting frosts
shimo wa okanan	nip the cold heart where they grow

Minamoto no Muneyuki

For wasuregusa, see 765.

802 • *Sosei composed this poem and wrote it on a screen as ordered during the Kanpyō era.*

wasuregusa	flourishing grasses
nani o ka tane to	of forgetfulness where is
omoishi wa	the seed from which they
tsurenaki hito no	grow they seem to spring up from
kokoro narikeri	the heart of that unfeeling one

Sosei

Sosei composed this poem for a screen for Uda tennō.

803 • *Topic unknown.*

aki no ta no	I spoke nary a
ine chō koto mo	word to send him away at
kakenaku ni	rice harvest time yet
nani o ushi to ka	he's reaped displeasure for he's
hito no karu ran	marching off through autumn fields

Kengei

"Aki" (autumn; satiety), "ine" (rice plants; return), "kake" (speaking; hanging), and "karu" (reap; separate) are kakekotoba. Ozawa suggests that "ushi" may be interpreted as "ox" as well as "misery."

804 • *Topic unknown.*

hatsukari no	like the cries of these
naki koso watare	first wild geese my sobs echo
yo no naka no	through the skies for how
hito no kokoro no	sorrowful the autumn of
aki shi ukereba	man's heart in the world of love

Ki no Tsurayuki

"Aki" (autumn; satiety) is a kakekotoba.

805 • *Topic unknown.*

    aware tomo
ushi tomo mono o
    omou toki
nado ka namida no
ito nagaru ran

       although I may sigh
with joy   although I may weep
    with sorrow   why is
there never a time when no
ribbons of tears wet my cheeks

Anonymous

The last line may be read itonakaru (uninterrupted) and ito nagaru (flow in threads).

806 • *Topic unknown.*

    mi o ushi to
omou ni kienu
    mono nareba
kakute mo henuru
yo ni koso arikere

       though I am resigned
to my sad fate   I cannot
    vanish from our world—
this world in which I must live
on   in wretched misery

Anonymous

807 • *Topic unknown.*

    ama no karu
mo ni sumu mushi no
    warekara to
oto o koso nakame
yo oba uramiji

       like the insects that
live within the seaweed
    fisherfolk reap   I
weep aloud   it is my own
fault   I cannot blame the world

Fujiwara no Naoiko

Lines 1 and 2 (of the insects that live in the seaweed the seafolk reap) are a jo linked to the kakekotoba "warekara," which means "of oneself" and a kind of crustacean, the caprella. This poem appears in *The Tales of Ise*, 65.

808 • *Topic unknown.*

    aiminu mo
uki mo waga mi no
    kara koromo
omoishirazu mo
tokuru himo kana

       it is my own fault
that we no longer meet   my
    fault that I suffer—
unaware   the undersash
of my Chinese robe loosens

Anonymous

"Kara" (because of; Chinese) is a kakekotoba.

809 • *A poem from the poetry contest held at the residence of the Consort in the Kanpyō era.*

tsurenaki o	although I decide
ima wa koiji to	that I will no longer love
omoedomo	him cold-hearted one—
kokoro yowaku mo	my heart weakens and loosens
otsuru namida ka	these sad tears of love that fall

Sugano no Tadaon

810 • *Topic unknown.*

hito shirezu	if only our love
taenamashikaba	had ended before it was
wabitsutsu mo	known I might have said
naki na zo to dani	those tales were but false rumors
iwamashi mono o	and nursed my private sorrow

Ise

811 • *Topic unknown.*

sore o dani	do this at least
omou koto to te	as a sign that you care for
waga yado o	me never say you
miki to na ii so	have seen my house for others
hito no kikaku ni	will hear and gossip begin

Anonymous

812 • *Topic unknown.*

au koto no	now that our meetings
mohara taenuru	have ended now that we are
toki ni koso	parted ah now it
hito no koishiki	is that I truly know how
koto mo shirikere	it feels to love someone

Anonymous

813 • *Topic unknown.*

| wabihatsuru | even now that I |
| toki sae mono no | have reached the depths of despair |

kanashiki wa
izuko o shinobu
namida naru ran

when all my sorrow
is drained from me   tears flow   what
can I be yearning for now

Anonymous

8 1 4 • *Topic unknown.*

uramite mo
nakite mo iwan
   kata zo naki
kagami ni miyuru
kage narazu shite

although reproaches
form   and tears of grief flow   there
   is no one to whom
I can appeal   I see only
the image in my mirror

Fujiwara no Okikaze

8 1 5 • *Topic unknown.*

yū sareba
hito naki toko o
   uchiharai
nagekan tame to
nareru waga mi ka

evening draws near
and I smooth the covers where
   I must sleep alone—
is my life now given to
regrets for the love we shared

Anonymous

8 1 6 • *Topic unknown.*

watatsumi no
waga mi kosu nami
   tachikaeri
ama no sumu chō
uramitsuru kana

taller than I   waves
from the broad sea crash upon
   the shore and return
once again   I come   forlorn
to the bay where seafolk dwell

Anonymous

The first two lines (waves higher than I on the broad sea) serve as a jo linked to the kakekotoba "tachikaeri" (rising and returning; repeating). Line 4 (where the seafolk dwell, they say) is a jo linked to the kakekotoba "urami" (reproaching; seeing the coast), which also functions as an engo for "nami" (waves).

8 1 7 • *Topic unknown.*

ara ota o
ara sukikaeshi

in newly opened
fields they turn the earth again

kaeshite mo
hito no kokoro o
mite koso yamame

and again   I'll not
give up until I've seen his
heart laid open as often

Anonymous

The first two lines (newly plowed new fields) are a jo linked to line 3 by the repetition of sounds. The last two lines are the same as those of XIX, 1050, and were probably borrowed from that poem.

818 • *Topic unknown.*

ariso umi no
hama no masago to
tanomeshi wa
wasururu koto no
kazu ni zo arikeru

how he encouraged
my trust   singing of the sands
on the beach by the
rough sea   did he mean to tell
of the ways of forgetting

Anonymous

819 • *Topic unknown.*

ashibe yori
kumoi o sashite
yuku kari no
iya tōzakaru
waga mi kanashi mo

like the geese that fly
from the reeds along the shore
toward the open sky
how sad am I to travel
so far away from my love

Anonymous

Lines 1–3 (like the geese flying toward the cloudy sky from the reeds by the shore) are a jo linked to line 4 (more and more distant).

820 • *Topic unknown.*

shiguretsutsu
momizuru yori mo
koto no ha no
kokoro no aki ni
au zo wabishiki

more sorrowful to
see sear autumn touch the heart
of one who spoke words
of love   than to see the leaves
dye in the constant chill rains

Anonymous

"Koto no ha"/ha (words; leaves) and "aki" (autumn; satiety) are kakekotoba.

821 • *Topic unknown.*

aki kaze no
fuki to fukinuru
  musashino wa
nabete kusaba no
iro kawarikeri

    on Musashi Moor
where autumn winds whistle in
  cold unending blasts
no blade of grass is spared—
the color of each transformed

Anonymous

Musashi Plain extended across Mushishi Province covering modern Tōkyō City and Kanegawa and Saitama Prefectures.

822 • *Topic unknown.*

aki kaze ni
au ta no mi koso
  kanashikere
waga mi munashiku
narinu to omoeba

    lonely ears of grain
lie scattered on the field by
  chilly autumn winds
reminding me that I too
will remain unharvested

Ono no Komachi

"Aki" (autumn; satiety) and "ta no mi" (fruit of the fields; trust) are kakekotoba.

823 • *Topic unknown.*

aki kaze no
fuki uragaesu
  kuzu no ha no
ura mite mo nao
urameshiki kana

    the autumn wind turns
back the leaves of arrowroot
  for me to see   as
my thoughts turn back to the past
my regrets grow more bitter

Taira no Sadafun

The first three lines (of the leaves of the arrowroot turned back by the blowing of the autumn wind) are a jo linked to the kakekotoba "ura mite" (seeing the back; regretting).

824 • *Topic unknown.*

aki to ieba
yoso ni zo kikishi
  adabito no

    I heard them speak of
faithless autumn calmly once
  for it meant naught to

ware o furuseru
na ni koso arikere

me　but now I know it tells
of one with a frostbound heart

Anonymous

"Aki" (autumn; satiety) is a kakekotoba.

825　• *Topic unknown.*

wasuraruru
mi o ujibashi no
　naka taete
hito mo kayowanu
toshi zo henikeru

forgotten　forlorn
am I　for our love crumbled
　like the Uji Bridge—
this whole year long　there has been
no traffic across the gulf

The last two lines have an alternate:

konata kanata ni
hito mo kayowazu

Anonymous

For Uji Bridge, see 689. "Uji"/ushi is a kakekotoba, also meaning "miserable."
"Naka" means both "center" and "relationship." The alternative ending is "No one,
either on that side or this side, crosses over."

826　• *Topic unknown.*

au koto o
nagara no hashi no
　nagaraete
koiwataru ma ni
toshi zo henikeru

our meetings thwarted
so long have I yearned　that the
　days have stretched out
like the Nagara Bridge and
an entire year has gone by

Sakanoue no Korenori

Nagara Bridge crosses the Yodo River in Ōsaka. "Nargara" also functions as a
kakekotoba, the first syllable, "na," meaning "none." "Wataru" (to cross; to continue) and "hashi" (bridge) are engo.

827　• *Topic unknown.*

ukinagara
kenuru awa tomo
　nari nanamu

like foam vanishing
as it floats upon water
　I would pass away

nagarete to dani
taomarenu mi wa

for my life is as aimless
as the fragile drifting froth

Ki no Tomonori

"Uki" (miserable; floating) is a kakekotoba. "Kenuru" means both "disappeared" and "died," and "nagarete" means "flowing" and "living on."

828 • *Topic unknown.*

nagarete wa
imose no yama no
naka ni otsuru
yoshino no kawa no
yoshi ya yo no naka

like the Yoshino
River cascading between
Husband and Wife peaks
obstacles forever part
lovers in this world of ours

Anonymous

"Nagarete" means "flowing" and "living on." Yoshino River (see 124) flows between Imo (Wife) and Se (Husband) Mountains.

BOOK XVI

Poems of Grief

829 • *A poem composed when a woman he loved died.*

naku namida	may these tears fall like
ame to furanan	rain to flood that river we
watari gawa	all must cross over
mizu masarinaba	for should it overflow my
kaeri kuru ga ni	love would come to life again

Ono no Takamura

"Imo," here translated "a woman he loved," may also mean "sister." Watari River, also known as Sanzu River, is believed to flow across the road to hell. The dead crossed it on the seventh day of their journey through the afterworld.

830 • *Composed on the night of the funeral of the former Chancellor near the White River.*

chi no namida	blood red tears of grief
ochite zo tagitsu	fall rush in torrents to dye
shira kawa wa	the White River it
kimi ga yo made no	deserved that name only while
na ni koso arikere	you were in this world of ours

Sosei

The former Chancellor was Fujiwara no Tadafusa. For Shira kawa, see 666.

831 • *This and 832 were composed after the Horikawa Chancellor died and was buried at Fukakusa Mountain.*

utsusemi wa	even the lifeless form
kara o mitsutsu mo	empty as the cicada's

nagusametsu	shell comforted me
fukakusa no yama	oh Mount Fukakusa keep
keburi dani tate	the smoke spiraling skyward

Shōen

The Horikawa Chancellor was Fujiwara no Mototsune, who had a villa on the Horikawa River. he was buried in Kowada, Fushimi-ku, Kyōto, near Fukakusa Mountain. "Utsusemi" refers both to a "cicada" and "the body" in this world. "Kara" means both "empty shell" and "corpse."

832 •

fukakusa no	oh cherry trees of
nobe no sakura shi	Fukakusa Field if you
kokoro araba	truly have a heart
kotoshi bakari wa	this year at least you'll be dressed
sumizome ni sake	in blossoms dyed inky black

Kamitsuke no Mineo

833 • *Composed after the death of Fujiwara no Toshiyuki and sent to his house.*

nete mo miyu	sleeping I see him—
nede mo miekeri	awake and still I see that
ōkata wa	vision before me
utsusemi no yo zo	ah truly do they say this
yume ni wa ari	locust shell world is a dream

Ki no Tomonori

Toshiyuki's death date is variously given as 901 and 907. "Utsusemi no" (like a cicada shell) is a makurakotoba for "yo" (world).

834 • *Composed when someone he loved died.*

yume to koso	surely this must be
iu bekarikere	a dream or an illusion—
yo no naka ni	though once I thought the
utsutsu aru mono to	things in this world of ours to
omoikeru kana	exist in reality

Ki no Tsurayuki

835 • *Composed when someone he loved died.*

neru ga uchi ni	shall we give the name
miru o nomi ya wa	dream only to those visions
yume to iwan	seen in slumber this
hakanaki yo o mo	fragile world in which we live
utsutsu to wa mizu	seems equally unreal

Mibu no Tadamine

836 • *Written after the death of his elder sister.*

se o sekeba	if one stems the flow
fuchi to narite mo	of the rapids the waters form
yodomikeri	deep pools still and
wakare o tomuru	unchanging yet there is no
shigarami zo naki	weir that would hold you with me

Mibu no Tadamine

837 • *Composed and sent to express his sympathy when someone Fujiwara no Tadafusa had once loved died.*

sakidatanu	eight thousand painful
kui no yachi tabi	regrets well up why couldn't
koishiki wa	I go first like the
nagaruru mizu no	waters rushing by my love
kaeri konu nari	can never return to me

Kan'in

838 • *Composed when Ki no Tomonori died.*

asu shiranu	although I know my
waga mi to omoedo	tomorrows are uncertain—
kurenu ma no	while still I enjoy
kyō wa hito koso	my todays how I grieve for
kanashikarikere	one whose twilight has darkened

Ki no Tsurayuki

839 • *Composed when Ki no Tomonori died.*

toki shi mo are	other seasons do
aki ya wa hito no	exist should one leave life in

wakaru beki   autumn   when even
aru o miru dani   the sight of friends still with us
koishiki mono o   bring a pathetic yearning

Mibu no Tadamine

840 • *Composed in memory of his mother.*

kannazuki   glistening crimson
shigure ni nururu   leaves   soaked by the freezing rains
  momijiba wa   of the godless month
tada wabibito no   hang heavy as the sleeves of
tamoto narikeri   the sorrow-laden mourners

Ōshikōchi no Mitsune

"Kannazuki," the "godless month," is the tenth lunar month.

841 • *Composed in memory of his father.*

fujigoromo   the frayed threads of
hatsururu ito wa   the purple robes of sorrow worn
  wabibito no   by the mourners   have
namida no tama no   become the strings that carry
o to zo narikeru   shimmering teardrop jewels

Mibu no Tadamine

The fujigoromo, or mourning robe, originally was made from coarse cloth woven from the wisteria.

842 • *Composed on the way to a mountain temple in the autumn of a year in which he was in mourning.*

asa tsuyu no   come to reap late rice
okute no yamada   in mountain fields where morning
  karisome ni   dew gleams   my harvest
uki yo no naka o   is the knowledge of this sad
omoinuru kana   world's emphemerality

Ki no Tsurayuki

"Oku"/"okute" is a kakekotoba meaning "to settle" and "late rice plants." Lines 1 and 2 (mountain paddies of late rice where the morning dew settles) are a jo linked to the kakekotoba "kari"/"karisome" (reaping; temporary).

843 • *Composed in sympathy for someone who was in mourning.*

sumizome no	have those trailing ink
kimi ga tamoto wa	dyed sleeves become dark storm clouds
kumo nare ya	my lord teardrops fall
taezu namida no	as steadily as rain from
ame to nomi furu	the overcast skies above

Mibu no Tadamine

844 • *Written in reply when he was at a mountain temple mourning a parent of his wife and someone sent a messenger with condolences.*

ashihiki no	living alone now
yamabe ni ima wa	deep in the rugged mountains
sumizome no	never is there a
koromo no sode no	time when the inky black sleeves
hiru toki mo nashi	of my robes are dry of tears

Anonymous

"Ashihiki no" is a makurakotoba modifying "yamabe" (mountain slopes). "Sumizome" is a kakekotoba meaning both "beginning to live" and "ink-dyed."

845 • *On seeing blossoms by a pond during a year of mourning for the Mikado.*

mizu no omo ni	radiantly their
shizuku hana no iro	color glows deep beneath the
sayaka ni mo	surface of the pond
kimi ga mikage no	bright as the visage of my
omōyuru kana	lord reflected in my mind

Ono no Takamura

846 • *On the anniversary of the death of the Fukakusa Mikado.*

kusa fukaki	the grass is deep—
kasumi no tani ni	a haze dims the valley where
kage kakushi	the last reflection
teru hi no kureshi	of the sun's rays once vanished—
kyō ni ya wa aranu	is today not that sad day

Funya no Yasuhide

Ninmyō tennō, the Fukakusa Mikado, was buried in Fukakusa, now part of Fushimi-ku, Kyōto. The first line of the poem, "kusa fukaki" (the grass is deep), alludes to the grave site, Fukakusa (deep grass).

847 • *When the Fukakusa Mikado died, the Head Chamberlain, who had been accustomed to serving him night and day, felt he could no longer remain in society, and he climbed Mount Hiei and shaved his head. The next year, when he heard that everyone had removed their mourning robes and that some were rejoicing over promotions, he composed this poem.*

mina hito wa	everyone now is
hana no koromo ni	garbed again in robes with hues
narinu nari	of springtime blossoms—
koke no tamoto yo	oh moss-colored sleeves of mine
kawaki dani seyo	won't you at least become dry

Henjō

For the Fukakusa Mikado, see 846. Mount Hiei is the site of the Enryakuji, head temple of the Tendai Sect.

848 • *Composed and sent to the home of the Kawara Minister the autumn after his death, when the author, wandering in the vicinity of the Minister's mansion, saw that the autumn leaves had not yet colored deeply.*

uchitsuke ni	how suddenly this
sabishiku mo aru ka	desolation has settled
momijiba mo	over all even
nushi naki yado wa	the autumn leaves around his
iro nakarikeri	empty hut are colorless

Minamoto no Yoshiari

Minamoto no Tōru (d. 895), Minister of the Left, was known as the Kawara (Riverbed) Minister because his mansion was located near the Kamo River.

849 • *On hearing a nightingale the summer after Fujiwara no Takatsune died.*

hototogisu	hototogisu—
kesa naku koe ni	startled again this morning
odorokeba	by his mournful song
kimi ni wakareshi	I knew this was the day we
toki ni zo arikeru	had had to bid you goodbye

Ki no Tsurayuki

Takatsune (d. 893) was the younger brother of Mototsune; see 831. For hototogisu, see 135. It was believed to travel to the afterworld.

850 • *Composed on seeing blossoms that had bloomed only after the death of the person who had planted them.*

hana yori mo	mankind is even
hito koso ata ni	more ephemeral than the
narinikere	fragile blossoms did
izure o saki ni	I ever think there was any
koin to ka mishi	doubt which I would mourn soonest

Ki no Mochiyuki

851 • *On seeing plum blossoms in a garden whose owner had died.*

iro mo ka mo	only the blossoms
mukashi no kosa ni	retain their vivid hues
nioedomo	and perfume how I
ueken hito no	yearn for the sight of the one
kage zo koishiki	who planted them long ago

Ki no Tsurayuki

852 • *Composed after the death of the Kawara Minister of the Left, when the author went to his mansion and saw that he had designed his garden in imitation of Shiogama.*

kimi masade	now my lord is gone
keburi taenishi	how lonely is this world where
shiogama no	far across the Bay
ura sabishiku mo	of Shiogama the gray
miewataru kana	smoke disappears from our sight

Ki no Tsurayuki

For the Kawara Minister of the Left, see 848. Shiogama is in Matsushima Bay in Miyazaki Prefecture. The name also means "salt cauldron" and functions as a kakekotoba in this poem. The kakekotoba "ura" means "bay" and "heart-felt."

853 • *The apartment in which Fujiwara no Toshimoto had lived when he was Middle Captain of the Right Imperial Bodyguards was no longer used after he died. Late one autumn night when the author was on his way home, he glanced in and*

found that the garden was overgrown and desolate. Arisuke had formerly been in Toshimoto's service, and, remembering the past, he composed this poem.

kimi ga ueshi	that single clump of
hito mura susuki	waving plume grass planted by
mushi no oto no	my lord long ago
shigeki nobe tomo	is now an overgrown field
narinikeru kana	where insects pipe lonely calls

Miharu no Arisuke

854 • *Composed and appended when he wrote out and sent Prince Koretaka some poems that his father had written as the Prince had requested.*

koto naraba	if it must be so
koto no ha sae mo	may even the leaves of his
kienanan	words vanish with him
mireba namida no	for when I see these verses
taki masarikeri	tears well up and overflow

Ki no Tomonori

Tomonori's father was Ki no Aritomo, author of *Kokinshū* I, 66, and XIX, 1029.

855 • *Topic unknown.*

naki hito no	if you travel to
yado ni kayowaba	his garden in that world where
hototogisu	he now dwells tell him
kakete ne ni nomi	hototogisu how the
naku to tsugenan	sorrowful cries echo here

Anonymous

856 • *Topic unknown.*

tare miyo to	for whom have they bloomed
hana sakeru ran	who will see flowers here where
shirakumo no	carefully tended
tatsu no to hayaku	gardens have so soon become
narinishi mono o	fields only white clouds visit

Anonymous

857 • *Soon after the Prince who was Head of the Household Ministry married the fifth daughter of Kan'in, his wife died. The Prince discovered this poem, written when she was well, attached to the cord of one of the posts of her bedchamber.*

kazukazu ni	if you recall me
ware o wasurenu	fondly if you remember
mono naraba	me when I am gone
yama no kasumi o	then gaze upon the mountain
aware to wa miyo	haze in gentle reverie

The Prince was Atsunori, son of Uda tennō.

858 • *Once when a man had gone to another province, his wife suddenly became ill. Very weak, she composed this poem and then died.*

koe o dani	I must go without
kikade wakaruru	hearing your voice again more
tamayori mo	wretched even than
naki toko ni nen	my sad spirit you will sleep
kimi zo kanashiki	alone where we two once slept

Anonymous

859 • *In the autumn when he was ill and suffering, Chisato, feeling despondent, sent this poem to a friend.*

momijiba o	more fragile than
kaze ni makasete	the colored autumn leaves
miru yori mo	we see yielding to
hakanaki mono wa	the wind our lives in this world
inochi narikeri	are even more precarious

Ōe no Chisato

860 • *Composed just before he died.*

tsuyu o nado	why did I think the
adanaru mono to	dew fragile insubstantial
omoiken	for the only way
waga mi mo kusa ni	we differ is that I do
okanu bakari o	not lie upon morning grass

Fujiwara no Koremoto

861 • *Composed when he was ill and weak.*

tsui ni yuku	although I've heard
michi to wa kanete	there is a road we all must
kikishikado	travel never did
kinō kyō to wa	I think I might set out on
omowazarishi o	it yesterday or today

Ariwara no Narihira

This poem appears in *The Tales of Ise,* 125.

862 • *When he had gone to Kai Province to visit an acquaintance, he suddenly fell ill on the road. When it seemed that he might die soon, Shigeharu wrote this poem and gave it to a messenger, asking him to take it to the capital and show it to his mother.*

karisome no	I came thinking this
yukikaiji to zo	would be a simple journey
omoi koshi	along the road to
ima wa kagiri no	Kai and back but now I
kadode narikeri	have crossed the final threshold

Ariwara no Shigeharu

Kai Province corresponds to Yamanashi Prefecture. "Yukikaiji" (the road one traverses) contains the word "kaiji" (the Kai Road).

BOOK XVII

Miscellaneous Poems (I)

863 • *Topic unknown*

waga ue ni	as I slept it seems
tsuyu zo oku naru	dew settled over me could
ama no gawa	it be spray scattered
to wataru fune no	by the oars of the boat now
kai no shizuku ka	crossing the river of heaven

Anonymous

Man'yōshū 2052 also compares the rain falling on Tanabata night to the spray from the herdsman's oars as he crosses the river of heaven to visit the weaver maid.

864 • *Topic unknown.*

omoudochi	my beloved friends
matoiseru yo wa	tearing myself away from
kara nishiki	your company this
tatamaku oshiki	evening is painful as
mono ni zo arikeru	rending fine Chinese brocade

Anonymous

"Kara nishiki" (Chinese brocade) is a makurakotoba modifying "tata," a kake-kotoba meaning "cutting" and "departing."

865 • *Topic unknown.*

ureshiki o	what can I enfold
nani ni tsutsuman	this blessed happiness in—
kara koromo	if only I had

tamoto yutaka ni	asked that the sleeves in my robe
tate to iwamashi o	from Cathay be broadly cut

Anonymous

866 • *Topic unknown.*

kagiri naki	flowers I cut to
kimi ga tame ni to	celebrate the limitless
oru hana wa	years of your life my
toki shi mo wakanu	lord they too are unmindful
mono ni zo arikeru	of the progress of the years

Anonymous

Some say this poem was written by the former Chancellor.

The former Chancellor was Fujiwara no Yoshifusa, author of poem 52.

867 • *Topic unknown.*

murasaki no	a single stalk of
hito moto yue ni	royal purple upon the
musashino no	Moor of Musashi
kusa wa minagara	makes me love all the other
aware to zo miru	wild grasses all the more

Anonymous

The purple roots of the murasaki (*Lithospermum officianale* var. *erythrorhizon*), a perennial, were used for medicine and as a purple dyestuff. In summer, it has small white flowers. For Musashi Moor, see 821.

868 • *Sent with a formal cloak to the husband of his wife's younger sister.*

murasaki no	when the color of
iro koki toki wa	royal purple is deepest
me mo haru ni	it casts its glow as
no naru kusaki zo	far as I can see over
wakarezarikeru	all the plants in the meadows

Ariwara no Narihira

"Me no haru ni" means both "as far as the eye can see" and "buds swelling." Haru also has a third meaning, "spring." The poem is an allusive variation on XVII, 867. It appears with a more detailed introduction in *The Tales of Ise*, 41.

869 • *Composed and sent with a gift of undyed figured silk to be used for a formal robe when Major Counsellor Fujiwara no Kunitsune was promoted from Consultant to Middle Counsellor.*

iro nashi to	ah my lord do you
hito ya miru ran	think me as colorless as
mukashi yori	this cloth even though
fukaki kokoro ni	I have imbued it with the
someteshi mono o	love that long has dyed my heart

Minamoto no Yoshiari

Kunitsune is author of *Kokinshū* XIII, 638. "Iro nashi" means both "colorless" and "without charm."

870 • *When Isonokami no Nanmatsu had shut himself up at the place called Isonokami and was not attending court, he was suddenly promoted to the Fifth Rank. Imamichi wrote this poem and sent it to congratulate him.*

hi no hikari	the brilliant rays of
yabu shi wakeneba	the sun light up the darkest
isonokami	thicket even in
furinishi sato ni	ancient Isonokami
hana mo sakikeri	Village the flowers have bloomed

Furu no Imamichi

According to the *Sandai Jitsuroku*, Nanmatsu was promoted in 886. "Hi no hikari" (the light of the sun) is a metaphor for the imperial favor. For Isonokami, see 144. It serves as a makurakotoba for "furinishi" (grown old).

871 • *Once, when the Second Ward Consort was still known as the Lady of the Bedchamber, she made a pilgrimage to the Ōharano Shrine. Narihira composed this poem that day.*

ōhara ya	Oshio Mountain
oshio no yama mo	in Ōhara today
kyō koso wa	especially must
kami yo no koto mo	call to mind the events of
omoi izurame	the age of the awesome gods

Ariwara no Narihira

For the Second Ward Consort, see 4. For her appellation, Lady of the Bedchamber, see 8. Ōharano Shrine in Ukyō-ku, Kyōto, at the foot of Oshio Mountain in Ōharano, was established by Fujiwara no Fuyutsugu in 850.

872 • *Composed on seeing the Gosechi dancers.*

amatsu kaze	oh heavenly winds
kumo no kayoiji	close the gates across the path
fukitoji yo	they traverse through the
otome no sugata	clouds keep the fair maidens here
shibashi todomen	for just a short time longer

Yoshimine no Munesada (Henjō)

The Gosechi dancers, five highborn young girls, performed during the Thanks-giving Festival at court in the Eleventh Month.

873 • *Composed when he found a jewel that had fallen from a hair ornament on the morning after Gosechi and went to inquire whose it might be.*

nushi ya tare	although I beg to
toedo shiratama	know the owner of this white
iwanaku ni	hair jewel it gives
sareba nabete ya	no reply shall I think each
aware to omowan	of you its charming mistress

Minamoto no Tōru

874 • *In the Kanpyō era some of the men in the Courtiers' Hall had a sake jar taken to the Consort's palace to be presented to her with a request for some of the Mikado's leftover sake. The chamberlains and others in her service laughed and carried the jar before the Consort, but there was no reply. When the messenger returned and said that was the case, Toshiyuki sent this poem to the chamberlains.*

tamadare no	where has that gem-decked
kogame ya izura	flask gone into the offing
koyorogi no	parting the waves off
iso no nami wake	Koyorogi beach like a
oki ni idenikeri	tortoise returning to sea

Fujiwara no Toshiyuki

Commentators agree that this event took place during the reign of Uda tennō, although the Kanpyō era (887–898) also encompasses part of the reign of Daigo. For the Courtiers' Hall, see 161. Toshiyuki was one of the courtiers, generally gentlemen of the Fourth Rank and above. The Consort was Fujiwara Onshi. The chamberlains (kurōdo) in question are ladies in her service. "Tamadare no" (with jewels hanging) is a makurakotoba usually linked to "o" (string). Another meaning of "o" is "small," and the character "small" may have the reading ko; hence, the linking of "tamadare no" to "ko" in this poem. "Kogame" means both "jar" and "tortoise." The second and third lines are linked by the repetition of the initial syllables, "ko." Koyorogi is the stretch of shore from Kozu to Ōiso in modern Kanagawa Prefecture. "Oki" means both "offing" and "placing (the sake jar)."

875 • *Composed after some women laughed when they saw him.*

katachi koso	my appearance may
miyamagakure no	be bleak as the rotting trees
kuchiki nare	hidden deep in the
kokoro wa hana ni	mountains but within my heart
nasaba nari nan	flowers can bloom if you will it

Kengei

876 • *Once, because of a directional taboo Tomonori stayed at a friend's house and borrowed a robe belonging to the owner. He composed this poem when he returned the robe the next morning.*

semi no ha no	as delicate as
yoru no koromo wa	the filmy cicada wings
usukeredo	is my robe tonight
utsurika koku mo	yet the air about me is
nioinuru kana	thickly perfumed with your scent

Ki no Tomonori

The motions of various heavenly bodies prevented travel in their direction. The person thus halted could travel in a different direction, spend the night, and then continue his journey.

877 • *Topic unknown.*

osoku izuru	how late is the long
tsuki ni mo aru kana	awaited moon to emerge from
ashihiki no	behind the rugged
yama no anata mo	mountain crests how the other
oshimu beranari	side must long to hold it back

Anonymous

"Ashihiki no" is a makurakotoba for "yama" (mountain).

Kokinshū

878 • *Topic unknown.*

waga kokoro
nagusame kanetsu
sarashina ya
obasute yama ni
teru tsuki o mite

above the mountain—
Old Forsaken Woman of
Sarashina   the
melancholy moon shines   how
inconsolable my heart

Anonymous

Sarashina is in Nagano Prefecture, Sarashina District. Obasute Mountain, in northern Nagano, is now a famous moon-viewing site.

879 • *Topic unknown.*

ōkata wa
tsuki o mo medeji
kore zo kono
tsumoreba hito no
oi to naru mono

in the end   I find
my pleasure in the bright moon
is tinged with sadness—
for every wax and wane
numbers the months of our lives

Ariwara no Narihira

880 • *Composed when Ōshikōchi no Mitsune came to call because the moon was so lovely.*

katsu miredo
utoku mo aru kana
tsuki kage no
itaranu sato mo
araji to omoeba

I have gazed upon
the moon   but we can never
live in harmony
for I know there is no village
where the moonlight does not shine

Ki no Tsurayuki

881 • *On seeing the moon reflected in a pond.*

futatsu naki
mono o omoishi o
minasoko ni
yama no ha narade
izuru tsuki kage

I had thought it was
unique   beyond compare   yet
another has appeared
not from the mountain rim   but
rising from the water's depths

Ki no Tsurayuki

302

882 • *Topic unknown.*

ama no kawa	in heaven's river
kumo no mio nite	the tumbling rapids of clouds
hayakereba	flow so swiftly the
hikari todomezu	moonlight courses endlessly
tsuki zo nagaruru	as the moon rides the current

Anonymous

883 • *Topic unknown.*

akazu shite	before we had gazed
tsuki no kakururu	our fill the moon was hidden
yama moto wa	within the mountains—
anata omote zo	left behind in the foothills
koishikarikeru	we envy those living there

Anonymous

884 • *Once Narihira accompanied Prince Koretaka on a hunting trip. They returned to their lodgings and reminisced and drank sake all night long. Because the Prince felt drunk and prepared to retire inside just as the moon of the eleventh night was about to set, Narihira composed this poem.*

akanaku ni	though still I long to
madaki mo tsuki no	contemplate its beauty the
kakururu ka	moon goes early to
yama no ha nigete	hide oh that the mountain's crest
irezu mo aranan	might flee barring its retreat

Ariwara no Narihira

Prince Koretaka is the author of II, 74, and XVIII, 945, and he appears also in the headnote to IX, 418. The moon would have set about three in the morning on the eleventh.

885 • *During the reign of the Tamura Mikado there was talk of replacing the Princess Akirakeiko as Kamo Priestess because of a misdeed of her mother's. Kyōshin composed this poem when the matter was dropped.*

ōzora o	so brilliant the moon
teriyuku tsuki shi	that traverses the broad skies

kiyokereba	casting its soft light—
kumo kakusedomo	the clouds that try to hide it
hikari kenaku ni	cannot make it disappear

Kyōshin

The Tamura Mikado refers to Montoku, who is buried in Tamura in Ukyō-ku, Kyōto. The Kamo Priestess was chosen from the unmarried princesses; as with the Ise Priestess, she was replaced when a new sovereign came to the throne. Akirakeiko was Montoku's eighth daughter. Her mother was Fujiwara Sokushi.

886 • *Topic unknown.*

isonokami	in the meadows of
furu kara ono no	Furu in Isonokami
moto kashiwa	withered oak leaves still
moto no kokoro wa	cling to the trees so my first
wasurarenaku ni	love remains unforgotten

Anonymous

For Isonokami and Furu, see 144. "Furu kara" functions as a kakekotoba, including the place name Furu, and having the meaning "old trunk." "Moto" means "original"; "moto kashiwa" refers to an oak with the withered leaves still clinging to the branches.

887 • *Topic unknown.*

inishie no	though the waters of
nonaka no shimizu	the old spring in the meadow—
nuru keredo	once so pure and cold—
moto no kokoro o	have become tepid one who
shiru hito zo kumu	remembers still dips to drink

Anonymous

888 • *Topic unknown.*

inishie no	as the bobbin flies
shizu no odamaki	when they weave the blue striped cloth
iyashiki mo	so too do we all
yoki mo sakari wa	both the humble and the proud
arishi mono nari	have a summit in our lives

Anonymous

"Shizu" means "patterned cloth" and "humble people." Thus, lines 1 and 2 (the bobbin for the cloth [humble people] of long ago) are a jo linked to "iyashiki" (lowborn).

889 • *Topic unknown.*

ima koso are to this I have fallen
ware mo mukashi wa though once long ago I too
otoko yama knew a time of ease—
sakayuku toki mo a time when life resembled
arikoshi mono o ascent of Mount Otoko

Anonymous

Otoko yama (Man Mountain) is a makurakotoba for the kakekotoba "sakayuku" (to travel the slopes; to prosper). "Koshi" (has long been) also means "crossing" and as such is an engo for "saka" (slopes).

890 • *Topic unknown.*

yo no naka ni in this world   two things
furinuru mono wa grow old   of this I'm certain—
tsu no kuni no one is the bridge of
nagara no hashi to Nagara in Tsu Province
ware to narikeri and the second   it is I

Anonymous

For Tsu, see 604. For Nagara Bridge, see 826.

891 • *Topic unknown.*

sasa no ha ni bent are the blades of
furitsumu yuki no the bamboo grass   heavily
ure o omomi the snow weighs upon
moto kutachiyuku each leaf   my life too flourished
waga sakari wa mo but now starts the downward slope

Anonymous

The first three lines (the heaviness of the tips of the twigs where snow falls and piles up on the blades of bamboo grass) are a jo.

892 • *Topic unknown.*

ōraki no when the blades of grass
mori no shita kusa deep in Ōaraki Grove

oinureba   toughen and grow old
koma mo susamezu   no steeds will graze upon them
karu hito mo nashi   no men will come to harvest

The first two lines are also given as:

sakura asa no
ou no shita kusa

Anonymous

The location in Ōaraki Grove has not been determined. The alternative lines are "the undergrasses of the hemp fields where cherry hemp grows." Sakura asa is a variety of hemp.

893 • *Topic unknown.*

kazoureba   as I count the years
tomaranu mono o   years called nimble-footed   years
toshi to iite   which never linger
kotoshi wa itaku   ah   this year   especially
oi zo shinikeru   how sadly I feel my age

Anonymous

"Toshi" (quickly; year) is a kakekotoba.

894 • *Topic unknown.*

oshiteru ya   as salty as the
naniwa no mitsu ni   seaweed burned in Naniwa
yaku shio no   in beautiful Tsu
karaku mo ware wa   are the bitter tears I shed
oinikeru kana   so many years have I lived

Lines 1 and 2 are also given as:

ōtomo no
mitsu no hamabe ni

Anonymous

"Oshiteru ya," the meaning of which is unclear, is a makurakotoba for Naniwa. For Tsu and Naniwa, see 604. The first three lines (of the salt burnt in lovely Tsu in Naniwa) are a jo linked to "karaku" (saltily; painfully). The alternative lines are "on the beach at lovely Tsu in Ōtomo." Ōtomo refers to the Naniwa area.

895 • *Topic unknown.*

oiraku no	if only I had
kon to shiriseba	known that age was drawing near
kado sashite	I would have barred my
nashi to kotaete	gate told him I was not at home—
awazaramashi o	that we might never have met

Anonymous

It is said the previous three poems were written by three old men who lived long ago.

Poem VII, 349, is an allusive variation on this poem.

896 • *Topic unknown.*

sakasama ni	if only time could
toshi mo yukanan	travel in reverse would those
tori mo aezu	days of my life that
suguru yowai ya	escaped my grasp return to me
tomo ni keru to	with the backward passing years

Anonymous

897 • *Topic unknown.*

toritomuru	because there was no
mono ni shi araneba	way to seize and hold the swift
toshi tsuki o	moving months and years of
aware ana u to	life in delight or sorrow
sugushitsuru kana	I have passed them carelessly

Anonymous

898 • *Topic unknown.*

todomeaezu	we cannot make it
mube mo toshi to wa	linger swift-passing time is
iwarekeri	well named but sadly
shikamo tsurenaku	the years of my life too flow
suguru yowai ka	by me indifferently

Anonymous

"Toshi" means both "quickness" and "year."

899 • *Topic unknown.*

kagami yama	well now I'll go to
iza tachiyorite	Mirror Mountain gaze upon
mite yukan	it and then travel
toshi henuru mi wa	on for I wonder if I've
oi ya shinuru to	aged in all these years I've lived

Anonymous

Some say this poem was composed by Ōtomo no Kuronushi.

There are numerous Kagami mountains, but commentators, basing their choice on the birthplace of the possible author, Kuronushi, say this poem refers to the Kagami Mountain in Gamo District of Shi_ a Prefecture.

900 • *When the Princess, his mother, was living in Nagaoka, Narihira was very busy at court and was unable to visit even once in a while. Around the Twelfth Month a messenger brought a letter marked "urgent" from his mother. When he opened it, there was no message but this poem.*

oinureba	so old am I that
saranu wakare mo	inevitable time of
ari to ieba	parting draws near and
iyoiyo mimaku	my desire to see you my
hoshiki kimi kana	dear grows ever more intense

Narihira's mother

Narihira's mother was Princess Itō (d. 861), daughter of Kanmu tennō, whose court was located at Nagaoka, near Kyōto, from 784 to 794.

901 • *Reply.*

yo no naka ni	I wish there were no
saranu wakare no	inevitable partings
naku mo gana	in this world for the
chiyo mo to nageku	sake of children who pray for
hito no ko no tame	their parents' eternal life

Ariwara no Narihira

902 • *From the poetry contest held at the residence of the Consort in the Kanpyō era.*

shirayuki no	Kaeru Mountain
yae furishikeru	where the white snow mounds up in

kaeru yama	heavy eightfold drifts—
kaerugaeru mo	the years of my life too pile
oinikeru kana	up and burden my shoulders

Ariwara no Muneyana

The first three lines (Kaeru Mountain where the eightfold white snows fall and pile up) are a jo linked to "kaerugaeru" (extremely; repeatedly) by the repetition of sounds.

903 • *Composed and presented to the Mikado in the same era when the men in the Courtiers' Hall were given sake and there was poetry and music.*

oinu to te	why should I berate
nado ka waga mi o	my aging body complain
semekiken	of growing older—
oizuba kyō ni	if we did not age would I
awamashi mono ka	ever have known this blessed day

Fujiwara no Toshiyuki

The sovereign during most of the Kampyō era (889–898) was Uda. For the Courtiers' Hall, see 161.

904 • *Topic unknown.*

chihayaburu	oh once vigorous
uji no hashimori	guardian of Uji Bridge
nare o shi zo	which I've so often
aware to wa omou	crossed how pitiful to see
toshi no henureba	you bent with the passing years

Anonymous

"Chihayaburu" (awesome[?]) is a makurakotoba for Uji. The bridge across the Uji River had been built prior to the Nara period; see 689.

905 • *Topic unknown.*

ware mite mo	it has been ages
hisashiku narinu	since I first came to see you—
suminoe no	oh small twisted pines
kishi no hime matsu[2]	on Suminoe's sandy
ikuyo henu ran	shore how many years are yours

Anonymous

For Suminoe, see 360. The "hime matsu" (princess pines) are the ancient dwarfed pines along the coast.

906 • *Topic unknown.*

sumiyoshi no	were they only men
kishi no hime matsu	I would ask the youthful pines
hito naraba	that line the shores of
ikuyo ka heshi to	Sumiyoshi how many
towamashi mono o	generations they have seen

Anonymous

For Sumiyoshi, see 360.

907 • *Topic unknown*

azusayumi	smooth as a bow of
isobe no komatsu	catalpa the beach where
ta ga yo ni ka	small pines grow in whose
yorozu yo kanete	day were the seeds planted with
tane o makikeru	hopes for a thousand-year life

Anonymous

Some people say this poem was composed by Kakinomoto no Hitomaro.

"Azusayumi" (catalpa bow) is a makurakotoba for "i" (shooting), the first syllable of the kakekotoba "isobe," which also means "rocky shore."

908 • *Topic unknown.*

kakushitsutsu	hiding myself from
yo o ya tsukusan	view shall I end my days here
takasago no	at Takasago
onoe ni tateru	in Onoe though I am
matsu naranaku ni	not a pine upon the shore

Anonymous

For Takasago, mentioned in this and the next poem, see 218.

909 • *Topic unknown.*

tare o ka mo	who then shall become
shiru hito ni sen	my dear companions even

takasago no	the many pines that
matsu mo mukashi no	stand at Takasago are
tomo naranaku ni	not those friends of long ago

Fujiwara no Okikaze

910 • *Topic unknown.*

watatsumi no	the bubbles that drift
oki tsu shio ai ni	where the currents of the broad
ukabu awa no	ocean converge float
kienu mono kara	quietly and linger there
yoru kata mo nashi	though they too know no shelter

Anonymous

"Watatsumi no" (of the broad seas) is a makurakotoba for "oki" (offing). The first three lines (like the bubbles that float where the currents meet in the offing of the broad sea) are a jo linked to "kienu" (do not disappear; do not die).

911 • *Topic unknown.*

watatsumi no	Awaji Island
kazashi ni saseru	rising like a mountain from
shirotae no	the midst of the sea
nami mote yuheru	crowned with fine hair ornaments—
awaji shima yama	waves with crests as white as hemp

Anonymous

Awaji Island is in the Inland Sea, Hyōgo Prefecture.

912 • *Topic unknown.*

wata no hara	as often as those
yosekuru nami no	rolling waves cross the broad
shibashiba mo	sea to strike the shore—
mimaku no hoshiki	so often would I see this
tamatsushima kamo	mountain Tamatsushima

Anonymous

"Wata no hara" (wide fields; expanse) refers to the ocean. Lines 1 and 2 (like the waves approaching on the expanse) are a jo linked to "shibashiba" (repeatedly). Tamatsushima Mountain is in Wakayama City, Wakanoura, near the Tamatsushima Shrine. It was, in the *Man'yōshū* era, an island.

913 • *Topic unknown.*

naniwagata	it seems the tide is
shio michikurashi	now flooding in Naniwa
amagoromo	Bay crying the cranes
tamino no shima ni	fly toward Tamino Isle
tazu naki wataru	seeking fields of straw rain-cloaks

Anonymous

For Naniwa, see 604. Amagoromo (rain-cloak) is a makurakotoba for Tamino (Field Straw Raincoat) Island, a sandbar that lay along the shore in Ōsaka City near Tennōji. This poem may be based on *Man'yōshū* 919, which begins, "when the tide waxes in Waka Bay."

914 • *Composed and sent to Tsurayuki in Izumi Province as Tadafusa crossed into that province from Yamato.*

kimi o omoi	I think longingly
okitsu no hama ni	of you where cranes cry upon
naku tazu no	the Okitsu shore—
tazunekureba zo	their visit to me has told
ari to dani kiku	me that you are still alive

Fujiwara no Tadafusa

Izumi Province corresponds to southern Ōsaka City. Okitsu is near Ōsaka. The name functions as a kakekotoba, "oki" also meaning "placing." Lines 1–3 (like the cranes crying along the Okitsu shore, where I think longingly of you) are a jo linked to line 4 by the repetition of sounds in "tazu" (crane) and "tazune" (visiting).

915 • *Reply.*

okitsu nami	tall as the waves that
takashi no hama no	surge in the offing beyond
hama matsu no	the Takashi Shore
na ni koso kimi o	are the beach pines their name tells
machiwataritsure	how I yearned for you my old friend

Ki no Tsurayuki

"Okitsu nami" (waves of the offing) is a makurakotoba modifying Takashi, another stretch of the shore near Ōsaka, which functions as a kakekotoba also meaning "tall." "Matsu" means both "pine" and "to wait."

916 • *Composed when he had traveled to Naniwa.*

naniwagata	for a while it seems
ouru tamamo o	a fisherman I must be
karisome no	reaping the harvest
ama to zo ware wa	of jeweled seaweed that grows
narinuberanaru	deep beneath Naniwa Bay

Ki no Tsurayuki

For Naniwa, see 604. The first two lines (the jewel-like seaweed growing in Naniwa Bay) are a jo linked to the kakekotoba "kari" (reaping)/"karisome" (temporary).

917 • *Composed and sent to a friend who had gone on a pilgrimage to Sumiyoshi.*

sumiyoshi to	though fisherfolk say
ama wa tsugu tomo	Sumiyoshi is a good
nagaisu na	place to live do not
hito wasuregusa	remain long for grasses of
ou to iu nari	forgetfulness thrive there too

Mibu no Tadamine

For Sumiyoshi, see 360. In this poem the name serves as a kakekotoba also meaning "pleasant to live." For wasuregusa, see 765.

918 • *Composed on encountering rain at Tamino Island when he had traveled to Naniwa.*

ame ni yori	caught in the rain I
tamino no shima o	went today to Tamino
kyō yukedo	Island but I
na ni wa kakurenu	found no shelter in its name—
mono ni zo arikeru	straw raincoat of the rice fields

Ki no Tsurayuki

For Tamino Island, see 913. For Naniwa, see 604.

919 • *On the day the retired Mikado went to the west river, Tsurayuki was ordered to compose this poem on the topic, "cranes standing in the shallows."*

ashitazu no	to my eyes it seems
tateru kawabe o	the waves driven by the wind

fuku kaze ni
yosete kaeranu
nami ka to zo miru

to the river banks
approach but do not return—
cranes standing among the reeds

Ki no Tsurayuki

The retired Mikado was Uda. The Ōi and its lower reaches, the Katsura River, were known as the west river. This excursion took place in the Ninth Month of 907.

920 • *The retired Mikado attended the first party held at the residence of Prince Nakatsukasa, when a boat had been built and was to be set afloat on the garden pond. Toward evening, the Mikado prepared to withdraw, and Ise composed and presented this poem.*

mizu no ue ni
ukaberu fune no
  kimi naraba
koko zo tomari to
iwamashi mono o

were you only a
boat drifting on the waters
  of my pond   then I
could order you to rest here
weighing anchor for the night

Ise

For the retired Mikado, see 919. Nakatsukasa was Prince Atsuyoshi, son of Uda tennō. Ise, Consort (kōi) of Uda tennō, later bore a daughter, known as the poet Nakatsukasa, by Atsuyoshi.

921 • *Composed at the place called Karakoto.*

miyako made
hibiki kayoeru
  karakoto wa
nami no o sugete
kaze zo hikikeru

echoing as far
as the capital   whispers
  of Chinese Lute Bay
travel as though the wind played
upon taut strings of the waves

Shinsei

For Karakoto, see 456.

922 • *Composed at Nunohiki Falls.*

kokichirasu
taki no shiratama
  hiroiokite

scattered white jewels
broadcast by the waterfall
  I will gather them

| yo no uki toki no | up   to use as borrowed tears |
| namida ni zo karu | in times of lonely sorrow |

Ariwara no Yukihira

Nunohiki Falls, mentioned in this and the next headnote, are located on the upper Ikuta River in Kōbe City.

923 • *Composed when a group had gathered near Nunohiki Falls to compose poetry.*

nukimidaru	surely someone is
hito koso aru rashi	plucking these white jewels from
shiratama no	their string for they fall
manaku mo chiru ka	without a moment's pause to
sode no sebaki ni	overflow my narrow sleeves

Ariwara no Narihira

This poem appears in *The Tales of Ise*, 87.

924 • *Composed on seeing the falls on Yoshino River.*

ta ga tame ni	for whose sake is this
hikite saraseru	fabric stretched to bleach upon
nuno nare ya	the river waters—
yo o hete miredo	though I watch as years pass by
toru hito mo naki	no one comes to gather it

Zōku

For Yoshino, see 124.

925 • *Topic unknown.*

kiyotaki no	would that I could spin
seze no shiraito	the white threads of the rushing
kuritamete	torrents of Kiyo
yamawakegoromo	Falls and weave a rustic robe
orite kimashi o	to wear to my mountain retreat

Shintai

There is a Kiyotaki River that runs through Saga, west of Kyōto. However, Ozawa suggests this is a common noun, "pure falls," referring to the Yoshino Falls. The robe would be one worn on a Buddhist retreat in the Yoshino Mountains.

926 • *Composed on a pilgrimage to Ryūmon near the falls.*

tachinuwanu	there is no one here
kinu kishi hito mo	to wear the "garment which is
naki mono o	neither cut nor sewn"—
nani yama hime no	why then does the mountain sprite
nuno sarasu ran	rinse and bleach the pure white cloth

Ise

Ryūmon Temple was in Ryūmon Village. Yoshino District, Nara Prefecture, near the Rymon Falls. Ascetic sorcerers were believed to wear robes of cloth that could not be cut or sewn. The foam on the water is compared to cloth that the mountain goddess has spread on the grass to bleach.

927 • *On the seventh of the Seventh Month the Suzakuin Mikado went to see Nunohiki Falls and ordered those accompanying him to compose poems.*

nushi nakute	oh that I might take
saraseru nuno o	that ownerless cloth bleaching
tanabata ni	in the stream and give
waga kokoro to ya	it as an offering to
kyō wa kasamashi	the Maid of Tanabata

Tachibana no Nagamori

The seventh of the Seventh Month is the Tanabata Festival; see 173. For Suzakuin, see 230. For Nunohiki Falls, see 922.

928 • *On seeing Otowa Falls on Mount Hiei.*

ochitagitsu	ah upper reaches
taki no minakami	of these tumbling seething falls
toshi tsumori	the years have piled up
oinikerashi na	and you've grown elderly—
kuroki suji nashi	not one strand of black remains

Mibu no Tadamine

Otowa Falls are on the western slope of Mount Hiei within the Kyōto City limits.

929 • *On the same falls.*

kaze fukedo	the wind blows them yet
tokoro mo saranu	these white clouds never scatter
shirakumo wa	never leave this place—

yo o hete otsuru
mizu ni zo arikeru

Ōshikōchi no Mitsune

through the ages they fall   for
they are but tumbling waters

930 • *During his reign, the Tamura Mikado went to the Hall of the Ladies-in-waiting to see a screen painting. On seeing it, he exclaimed at the beauty of the waterfall painted there and ordered those accompanying him to compose poems with the painting as topic.*

omoiseku
kokoro no uchi no
  taki nare ya
otsu to wa miredo
oto no kikoenu

do these falls exist
only within my heart where
  miseries are
dammed up   although I see
the waters   I hear no sound

Sanjō no Machi

Tamura refers to Montoku tennō; see 885. Sanjō no Machi was one of his Ladies-in-waiting. "Seku" (dammed up) is an engo for "taki" (waterfalls).

931 • *On flowers painted on a screen.*

sakisomeshi
toki yori nochi wa
  uchihaete
yo wa haru nare ya
iro no tsune naru

since first these flowers
blossomed   unchanging color
has delighted us—
can it be that springtime has
lingered in the world so long

Ki no Tsurayuki

932 • *Composed to add to a screen painting.*

karite hosu
yamada no ine no
  kokitarete
naki koso watare
aki no ukereba

new cut rice   hung to
dry in mountain fields   a line
of geese fly across
the sky crying   for autumn
is the season of sadness

Sakanoue no Korenori

"Karite" (cutting) contains the word "kari" (geese). Lines 1 and 2 (like the rice of the mountain fields, reaped and dried) are a jo linked to the kakekotoba "kokitarete" (reaping and hanging)/"tarete" (dripping). "Naki" refers both to human crying and the honking of the geese.

BOOK XVIII

Miscellaneous Poems (2)

933 • *Topic unknown.*

yo no naka wa	in this world of ours
nani ka tsune naru	what is there that does not change
asuka gawa	Tomorrow River—
kinō no fuchi zo	the deep pools of yesterday
kyō wa se ni naru	have become today's shallows

Anonymous

For Asuka River, see 284. "Asu" (tomorrow) is an engo for "kinō" (yesterday).

934 • *Topic unknown.*

iku yo shi mo	I do not know how
araji waga mi o	much longer this life will last—
nazo mo kaku	why then do my thoughts
ama no karu mo ni	drift aimlessly tangled as
omoi midaruru	seaweed the fisherfolk reap

Anonymous

935 • *Topic unknown.*

kari no kuru	over the peaks where
mine no asagiri	the wild geese now come flying
harezu nomi	morning mists hang low
omoitsukisenu	cloudy as my troubled thoughts
yo no naka no usa	of the sorrow of this world

Anonymous

The first two lines (morning mist of the peaks where the geese approach) are a jo linked to "harezu" (not clearing).

936 • *Topic unknown.*

shikari tote	although my life is
somukare naku ni	sad I cannot turn my back
koto shi areba	on it whenever
mazu nagekarenu	times of misery come I
ano yo no naka	grieve ah this unhappy world

Ono no Takamura

937 • *Composed when he was Governor of Kai Province, for someone who was returning to the capital.*

miyakobito	in the capital
ika ni to towaba	if any should ask after
yama takami	me tell them that here
harenu kumoi ni	where mountains loom above me
wabu to kotaeyo	and clouds never clear I grieve

Ono no Sadaki

Kai Province corresponds to Yamanashi Prefecture.

938 • *When Funya no Yasuhide was appointed Secretary of Mikawa, he wrote, "Won't you come for a tour of the provinces?" and Komachi replied with this poem.*

wabinureba	I have sunk to the
mi o ukigusa no	bottom and like the rootless
ne o taete	shifting water weeds
sasou mizu araba	should the currents summon me
inan to zo omou	I too would drift away

Ono no Komachi

Mikawa Province corresponds to Aichi Prefecture. The office of Secretary (jō) was the third highest in the provincial hierarchy. "Uki" (misery; floating) is a kakekotoba.

939 • *Topic unknown.*

aware chō	each murmur of joy
koto koso utate	and sorrow agitates my

yo no naka o
omoihanarenu
hodashi narikere

heart and binds me more
tightly   shackles me to this
sad life I had hoped to leave

Ono no Komachi

940 • *Topic unknown.*

aware chō
koto no ha goto ni
oku tsuyu wa
mukashi o kouru
namida narikeri

murmurs of joy
and sorrow   on each sheaf of
words   on each small leaf
settles a drop of dew   tears
of regret for times now past

Anonymous

941 • *Topic unknown.*

yo no naka no
uki mo tsuraki mo
tsugenaku ni
mazu shiru mono wa   ·
namida narikeri

although I never
tell them of the misery
and pain of this world
they are always the first to
know   these tears that overflow

Anonymous

942 • *Topic unknown.*

yo no naka wa
yume ka utsutsu ka
utsutsu tomo
yume tomo shirazu
arite nakereba

is this world of ours
a dream or reality—
whether it be dream
or real I cannot say   for
it exists yet is not there

Anonymous

943 • *Topic unknown.*

yo no naka ni
izura waga mi no
arite nashi
aware to ya iwan
ana u to ya iwan

where am I   I who
exist in this world and yet
do not   I know not
if I am fascinated
or distressed by this deceit

Anonymous

944 • *Topic unknown.*

yamazato wa
mono no kanashiki
koto koso are
yo no uki yori wa
sumiyokarikeri

truly one knows the
loneliness of life here in
this mountain village
yet how much better to live
here than midst the world's sorrows

Anonymous

945 • *Topic unknown.*

shirakumo no
taezu tanabiku
mine ni dani
sumeba suminuru
yo ni koso ari

where the white clouds trail
endlessly across the peaks
high above   only
by dwelling here can I live
in this world of misery

Prince Koretaka

Koretaka had taken Buddhist orders and lived at Ono, now part of Sakyō-ku, Kyōto, at the foot of Mount Hiei.

946 • *Topic unknown.*

shiriniken
kikite mo itoe
yo no naka wa
nami no sawagi ni
kaze zo shikumeru

you must already
know this   but hear me now and
feel horror for this
world   where tumultuous winds
and riotous waves are constant

Furu no Imamichi

947 • *Topic unknown.*

izuku ni ka
yo oba itowan
kokoro koso
no ni mo yama ni mo
madou beranare

where shall I go to
renounce this sorrowful world
whether in mountains
or in fields my heart surely
will be distracted and stray

Sosei

948 • *Topic unknown.*

yo no naka wa
mukashi yori ya wa
   ukariken
waga mi hitotsu no
tame ni nareru ka

has this wretched world
been filled with desolation
   since days of old   or
was it for my sake alone
that it became so woeful

Anonymous

949 • *Topic unknown.*

yo no naka o
itou yamabe no
   kusaki to ya
ana u no hana no
iro ni ideniken

is it because the
deutzia thrives on mountain
   slopes where I hide from
the world   that its blossoms tell
of the misery we must know

Anonymous

"Ana u" (ah, misery)/"u no hana" (deutzia) is a kakekotoba.

950 • *Topic unknown.*

miyoshino no
yama no anata ni
   yado mo gana
yo no uki toki no
kakure ga ni sen

if only I had
a home on the far side of
   fair Mount Yoshino
I would make it my refuge
in times of worldly sorrow

Anonymous

For Yoshino, mentioned in this and the next poem, see 3.

951 • *Topic unknown.*

yo ni fureba
usa koso masare
   miyoshino no
iwa no kakemichi
fuminarashiten

as I grow older
afflictions alone increase—
   I will walk onward
treading the narrow pathways
through the crags of Yoshino

Anonymous

952 • *Topic unknown.*

ika naran
iwao no naka ni
    sumaba ka wa
yo no uki koto no
kikoekozaran

in what sort of cave
amidst the crags and boulders
    must I dwell   so that
no whisper of the sorrows
of this world can reach my ears

Anonymous

953 • *Topic unknown.*

ashihiki no
yama no manimani
    kakurenan
uki yo no naka wa
aru kai mo nashi

somewhere within those
rugged lonely mountains I
    will seek seclusion—
for existence within this
sad world is of no avail

Anonymous

"Ashihiki no" is a makurakotoba for "yama" (mountain). "Kai" means both "result" and "ravine"; in the latter sense it is an engo for "yama."

954 • *Topic unknown.*

yo no naka no
ukeku ni akinu
    okuyama no
ko no ha ni fureru
yuki ya kenamashi

overburdened with
the misery of this world
    I long to go where
snow falls on the tree leaves   deep
in the mountains   vanishing

Anonymous

Lines 3 and 4 (fallen on the tree leaves in the deep mountains) are a jo linked to the kakekotoba "yuki" (snow; going).

955 • *A poem in which no syllable appears twice.*

yo no ukime
mienu yamaji e
    iran ni wa
omou hito koso
hodashi narikere

trying to set forth
for mountain paths where the world's
    miseries do not
exist   thoughts of my love are
the fetters that hold me fast

Mononobe no Yoshina

None of the characters of the Japanese syllabary is repeated in this poem. The mountain paths, implying retreat from secular life, are a metaphor for the Buddhist way of life.

956 • *Sent to a monk in the mountains.*

yo o sutete	you who renounce the
yama ni iru hito	world wandering deep into
yama nite mo	the mountains where can
nao uki toki wa	you go when miseries still
izuchi yuku ran	assail you in your refuge

Ōshikōchi no Mitsune

957 • *On seeing a child at a time when he was filled with cares.*

ima sara ni	why this renewed life
nani oiizuran	for what reason do you grow—
take no ko no	infant bamboos now
uki fushi shigeki	flourish thick as life's sorrows—
yo to wa shirazu ya	do you not perceive this world

Ōshikōchi no Mitsune

"Take no ko no" (of the bamboo shoots) means literally "bamboo children," and is a makurakotoba modifying the kakekotoba "uki fushi" (time of grief)/"fushi" (node of bamboo). The kakekotoba "yo" means both "world" and "joint of bamboo," and functions as engo.

958 • *Topic unknown.*

yo ni fureba	as we pass through this
koto no ha shigeki	world our laments are many
kuretake no	as the leaves of the
ukifushi goto ni	black bamboo where wood thrush cry—
uguisu zo naku	one upon each swaying stalk

Anonymous

"Kuretake no" (of the black bamboo) is a makurakotoba for the kakekotoba "fushi" (node; time).

959 • *Topic unknown.*

ki ni mo arazu	neither a tree nor
kusa ni mo aranu	yet a grass is the bamboo

take no yo no	and like it have I
hashi ni waga mi wa	become a being somewhere
narinu beranari	between joint and node half-formed

Anonymous

Some say this poem was composed by Princess Takatsu.

The first two-and-one-half lines (of the bamboo, which is neither grass nor tree) are a jo linked to the kakekotoba "yo" (joint; world). "Hashi" (center) is an engo for "yo" (joint). This poem is based on lines from the Chin-dynasty writer Tai K'ai-chih: "Among the plants, there is one called bamboo; it is neither hard nor soft, neither tree nor grass." Princess Takatsu (d. 841) was a daughter of Kanmu tennō and a consort of Saga tennō.

960 • *Topic unknown.*

waga mi kara	it is because of
uki yo no naka to	me that this world we live in
nazuketsutsu	is called the world of
hito no tame sae	sorrow why do others too
kanashikaru ran	feel burdened with such sadness

Anonymous

961 • *composed when he was exiled to Oki Province.*

omoiki ya	did ever I think
hina no wakare ni	one day I might be sent far
otoroete	from our capital
ama no nawataki	where worn with grief I'd pull hand
isarisen to wa	over hand on fishing nets

Anonymous

For Oki, see 407.

962 • *Sent to someone at court during the time Yukihira was staying away at the place called Suma in Tsu Province after some incident in the reign of Tamura.*

wakuraba ni	if from time to time
tou hito araba	anyone should ask after
suma no ura ni	me answer them this

| moshiotaretsutsu | on Suma Bay with tear-drenched |
| wabu to kotaeyo | sleeves I gather seaweed salt |

Ariwara no Yukihira

For Tamura, see 885; for Tsu, see 604; for Suma, 708. "Shiotaru" means "to weep" and is an engo for Suma, a place famous for salt-making. Saltwater was poured over the seaweed gathered there and boiled dry to collect the salt.

963 • *Sent in reply to his wife's letter of commiseration when he was dismissed from the office of Lieutenant in the Left Imperial Guards.*

amabiko no	for now I shall not
otozureji to zo	visit not even the far
ima wa omou	away echo will
ware ka hito ka to	you hear for this world does not
mi o tadoru yo ni	distinguish me from others

Ono no Harukaze

Harukaze was dismissed from the post of shōgen, third in command of the Imperial Guards, because of slander. "Amabiko no" (of the mountain echo) is a makura-kotoba modifying the kakekotoba "oto" (sound)/"otozureji" (shall not visit).

964 • *Composed when he was dismissed from office.*

ukiyo ni wa	the gateway leading
kado saseri tomo	from this world of misery
mienaku ni	is not shut and barred—
nado ka waga mi no	why then do I find it so
idegate ni suru	difficult to take my leave

Taira no Sadafun

965 • *Composed when he was dismissed from office.*

arihatenu	I await the end
inochi matsu ma no	of my life it cannot be
hodo bakari	far off so for this
uki koto shigeku	brief moment alone I pray
omowazu mo gana	that sorrows might not flourish

Taira no Sadafun

966 • *Composed when he was told he was derelict in his duties and dismissed from the Crown Prince's Guards.*

tsukubane no	I seek shade beneath
ko no moto goto ni	each leafy springtime bough on
tachi zo yoru	Mount Tsukubane
haru no miyama no	just as I long for shelter
kage o koitsutsu	within my Prince's favor

Miyaji no Kiyoki

The Crown Prince was Yasuakira. Tsukuba Peak is in Ibaraki Prefecture. The Crown Prince's Quarters were known as the Spring Palace; thus there is a veiled reference to him in line 4, "haru no miyama" (the lovely mountains of spring). This poem is an allusive variation on 1095.

967 • *Composed when he saw that those who prosper soon grieve over reversals, but that he himself had neither occasion for sorrow nor cause for rejoicing.*

hikari naki	spring too is unknown
tani ni wa haru mo	in this valley which the sun
yoso nareba	never brightens here
sakite toku chiru	I am not troubled by thoughts of
mono omoi mo nashi	blossoms' glory and swift fall

Kiyohara no Fukayabu

Light (hikari) is a metaphor for imperial favor; spring (haru), a metaphor for worldly prosperity.

968 • *Sent in reply to a letter from the Seventh Ward Consort when Ise was in Katsura.*

hisakata no	because I dwell in
naka ni oitaru	the village of Katsura
sato nareba	tree of the broad skies
hikari o nomi zo	I shall bask only in that
tanomu beranaru	glorious light from above

Ise

The Seventh Ward Consort was Fujiwara Onshi, Consort of Uda. Katsura village is in present-day Ukyō-ku, Kyōto. "Hisakata no" is a common makurakotoba for "tsuki" (moon); here the phrase is used to mean "moon." It was believed that a katsura tree (*Cercidiphyllum japonicum*) was visible on the moon. Light (hikari) is a metaphor for the favor of the Consort.

969 • *When Ki no Toshisada was going to Awa Province as Vice-Governor,*
Narihira wanted to have a farewell party and went to Toshisada's house to tell him it
would be that day. However, Toshisada was out gadding about here and there.
When he still had not returned late that night, Narihira sent him this poem.

ima zo shiru	now I know what it
kurushiki mono to	is to wait how painful it
hito matan	must have been for her—
sato oba karezu	I should never have left our
tou bekarikeri	home I should have stayed with her

Ariwara no Narihira

Awa Province corresponds to Tokushima Prefecture. This poem appears in *The*
Tales of Ise, 48.

970 • *During the time he was frequenting the palace of Prince Koretaka, the*
Prince shaved his head and moved to the place called Ono, and Narihira went to visit
him in the First Month. Because it was at the foot of Mount Hiei, the snow was very
deep. With difficulty Narihira made his way to the hermitage and found the Prince
looking bored and unhappy. When he returned to the capital, he sent this poem.

wasurete wa	I had forgotten—
yume ka to zo omou	was it all a dream I wonder—
omoiki ya	did I ever think
yuki fumiwakete	that one day I would trudge through
kimi o min to wa	drifts of snow to see my lord

Ariwara no Narihira

For Koretaka and Ono, see 945. This poem appears in *The Tales of Ise*, 83.

971 • *When he had been living in Fukakusa, Narihira sent this to someone there*
to tell her he was going to the capital.

toshi o hete	oh Fukakusa
sumikoshi sato o	if I go now leaving this
idete inaba	village I've known so
itodo fukakusa	long will the deep grass become
no to ya narinan	a dense and tangled field

Ariwara no Narihira

Fukakusa (Deep Grass) is now in Fushimi-ku within the Kyōto city limits, but during
the *Kokinshū* era it was a small, quiet village. This poem and 972 appear in *The Tales*
of Ise, 123.

972 • *Reply.*

no to naraba	if all becomes dense
uzura to nakite	fields I will pass my years
toshi wa hen	crying like the quail—
kari ni dani ya wa	for surely you will come if
kimi wa kozaran	only for a few days' hunt

Anonymous

"Uzura" (quail) and "kari" (hunting) are engo. "Kari" (hunting: temporary) is a kakekotoba..

973 • *Topic unknown.*

ware o kimi	at Naniwa Bay
naniwa no ura ni	you scorned me my lord and in
arishikaba	sorrow I drifted
ukime o mitsu no	to Mitsu Temple where the
ama to nariniki	fisherfolk gather seaweed

Anonymous

Some say this poem was composed long ago when a woman whose husband had stopped visiting her went to the Mitsu Temple in Naniwa to become a nun and sent this poem to her husband.

For Naniwa, see 604. The name, also meaning "what," is a kakekotoba, as are "ura" (bay; resentment; back), "ukime" (painful event; floating seaweed), "mitsu" (Mitsu Temple; seen; imperial harbor), and "ama" (nun; fisherfolk). These words also form a pattern of engo.

974 • *Reply.*

naniwagata	I cannot think where
uramu beki ma mo	you saw this scorn that vexed you
omoezu	and sent you off to
izuko o mitsu no	Naniwa Bay to become a
ama to ka wa naru	seeker at Mitsu Temple

Anonymous

Naniwagata (Naniwa Bay) is a makurakotoba for the kakekotoba "ura" (bay)/"uramu" (to resent). "Mitsu" (Mitsu Temple; seen; imperial harbor) is a kakekotoba.

975 • *Topic unknown.*

ima sara ni
tou beki hito mo
　omōezu
yaemugura shite
kado saserite e

I cannot think that
now　after so long　any would
　come to visit me—
tell them the tangled grass has
grown too thick and bars my gate

Anonymous

Yaemugura (*Humulus japonicus*) is a wild grass.

976 • *Sent to a friend who had not come to visit for a long time.*

mizu no omo ni
ouru satsuki no
　ukikusa no
uki koto are ya
ne o taete konu

is his resentment
thick as rootless grasses on
　the surface of the
Fifth Month pond　he has cut our
ties　no more do I hear his voice

Ōshikōchi no Mitsune

The first three lines (of the floating grasses of the Fifth Month growing on the surface of the water) are a jo linked to the kakekotoba "uki" (miserable; floating). "Ne" (sound; root) and "taete" (completely; cutting) are also kakekotoba.

977 • *Composed when he met someone whom he had not visited for a long time and that person reproached him.*

mi o sutete
yuki ya shiniken
　omou yori
hoka naru mono wa
kokoro narikeri

forsaking my body
it seems my heart has wandered
　away on its own—
I cannot rule it with thoughts—
it is a stranger to them

Ōshikōchi no Mitsune

978 • *Composed when Muneoka no Ōyori, who had come to the capital from the northern provinces, saw the snow falling and said, "I remember the snow piling up like this."*

kimi ga omoi
yuki to tsumoraba

if your thoughts of me
"gather thick as snow"　I should

tanomarezu
haru yori nochi wa
araji to omoeba

not rely on them
for once spring has come I know
the drifts will vanish from sight

Ōshikōchi no Mitsune

979 • *Reply.*

kimi o nomi
omoi koshiji no
shira yama wa
itsu ka wa yuki no
kiyuru toki aru

as I walked along
the road to Koshi   I thought
only of you   when
do the snows ever disappear
on glistening Shira Mountain

Muneoka no Ōyori

"Koshi" is a kakekotoba meaning "far north" and "have come"; see 370. For Shira yama, see 383.

980 • *Sent to someone in the northern provinces.*

omoiyaru
koshi no shira yama
shiranedomo
hito yo mo yume ni
koenu yo zo naki

my thoughts turn to you
and though I do not yet know
Shira Mountain in
Koshi   each and every
night   I cross it in my dreams

Ki no Tsurayuki

For Koshi, see 370; for Shira yama, 383. "Shiraredomo" (although I do not know) repeats the syllables "shira."

981 • *Topic unknown.*

iza koko ni
waga yo wa henan
sugawara ya
fushimi no sato no
aremaku mo oshi

well then   it is here
that I shall spend my life   in
Sugawara   though
it will bring me grief to see
Fushimi village crumble

Anonymous

Sugawara District is a part of Nara City; Fushimi is located in Sugawara, within the boundaries of the old capital Heijō.

982 • *Topic unknown.*

waga io wa
miwa no yama moto
  koishikuba
toburai kimase
sugitateru kado

my hut stands at the
foot of Miwa Mountain   so
if you long to see
me once more   come and visit
at the gate where cedars stand

Anonymous

For Miwa Mountain, see 780.

983 • *Topic unknown.*

waga io wa
miyako no tatsumi
  shika zo sumu
yo o uji yama to
hito wa iu nari

this is how I live
in my retreat southeast of
the capital   though
men call Uji Mountain a
reminder of worldly sorrow

Kisen

"Shika" (thus) may be functioning as a kakekotoba with the second meaning of "deer." Ushi (misery)/Uji is a kakekotoba. The Uji Mountains lie east of Uji City near Kyōto.

984 • *Topic unknown.*

arenikeri
aware iku yo no
  yado nare ya
sumiken hito no
otozure mo senu

desolate it is—
how many generations
have lived in this house—
now   it seems   not even those
who dwelt here come to visit

Anonymous

This poem appears in *The Tales of Ise*, 58.

985 • *Written and sent into a dilapidated house in Nara where he heard a woman playing the lute.*

wabibito no
sumubeki yado to

to my eyes it seemed
the secret refuge of a

mirunabe ni	world weary soul and the
nageki kuwawaru	plaintive notes of the koto
koto no oto zo suru	deepened my heartfelt sorrow

Yoshimine no Munesada (Henjō)

The kin (lute) is a thirteen-stringed instrument. Ozawa suggests the term "koto" used in the poem may be a general term for stringed instruments or that Henjō chose koto in order to exclude Chinese vocabulary from the poem.

986 • *Composed when she had stopped overnight in the Nara capital on a pilgrimage to Hatsuse.*

hito furusu	weary of the town
sato o itoite	where people had turned from me
koshika domo	I came to Nara
nara no miyako mo	but the "old capital" too
uki na narikeri	told me of my misery

Nijō

For Hatsuse, see 42. Commentators agree that "sato" (town) refers to Heian (Kyōto), the new capital, contrasting with Nara, the old.

987 • *Topic unknown.*

yo no naka wa	in this world of ours
izure ka sashite	what place should I single out
waga naran	as my home that spot
yuki tomaru o zo	where I find rest at journey's
yado to sadamuru	end will become my haven

Anonymous

988 • *Topic unknown.*

ōsaka no	in Ōsaka
arashi no kaze wa	the howling tempests rage and
samukeredo	winds lash cold but still
yukue shiraneba	I know no place to go so
wabitsutsu zo neru	I'll sleep here in misery

Anonymous

For Ōsaka, see 374.

989 • *Topic unknown.*

kaze no ue ni	I have become a
ari ka sadamenu	speck of the dust carried in
chiri no mi wa	helpless flurries by
yukue mo shirazu	the dancing winds I who know
narinu beranari	no destination no home

Anonymous

990 • *Composed when she sold her house.*

asuka gawa	not a deep pool of
fuchi ni mo aranu	the Asuka River yet
waga yado mo	my house has turned to
se ni kaeriyuku	tumbling coins flowing like the
mono ni zo arikeru	bubbling shallows of the stream

Ise

For Asuka River, see 284. "Fuchi" may be a kakekotoba meaning "deep pools" and "support." "Se ni" (into shallows; coins) is a kakekotoba.

991 • *When he was in Tsukushi, Tomonori sent this to the home of a friend where he had often gone to play go, telling him that he would be returning to the capital.*

furusato wa	home at last and yet
mishi goto mo arazu	it is not what it once was
ono no e no	to me now that I
kuchishi tokoro zo	long for that place of exile
koishikarikeru	where the ax handle crumbled

Ki no Tomonori

For Tsukushi, see 387. This poem is based upon a Chinese Rip Van Winkle legend: a man played go with the gods, returning to find that he had been gone so long the handle of his ax had rotted. The syllable go in "goto" (as) may be a reference to the game played in the legend.

992 • *Composed on parting with a woman friend after talking over old times.*

akazarishi	was I so sorry
sode no naka ni ya	to separate our sleeves that
iriniken	I left my spirit

334

waga tamashii no   wrapped in yours now I feel
naki kokochi suru   I have no life within me

Michinoku

993 • *Composed when the courtiers in the Courtiers' Hall of the Crown Prince's palace were given sake on Tadafusa's being appointed Secretary of a mission to China in the Kanpyō era.*

nayotake no   on elongated
yo nagaki ue ni   stalks of slender bamboo the
 hatsu yuki no   first snows settled all
okiite mono o   the long night as heavy as
omou koro kana   the thoughts on my wakeful mind

Fujiwara no Tadafusa

For the Kanpyō era, see 177. This mission left in 894. "Yo" (joint of bamboo; night) is a kakekotoba. Lines 1–3 (of the first snow [at night] on top of the long joints of lithe bamboo) are a jo linked to the kakekotoba "oki" (settling; awakening).

994 • *Topic unknown.*

kaze fukeba   as the howling winds
okitsu shiranami   keep white waves rising in the
 tatsuta yama   offing in the deep
yowa ni ya kimi ga of night is my lord crossing
hitori koyu ran   Tatsuta Mountain alone

Anonymous

Someone told this story about this poem: Long ago in Yamato Province, the daughter of a certain man had lived with someone as his wife. Because her parents had died and her family was becoming poorer, the man took to visiting someone in Kōchi Province and became estranged from his first wife. However, she showed no resentment and allowed her husband to go as he wished whenever he said he was going to Kōchi, so he began to suspect she had a lover. One moonlit night, pretending to set off for Kōchi, he hid in the shrubbery in the garden and watched. Late into the night she sat, playing the koto and sighing, and at last she composed this poem and went to bed. Hearing this, the man never again went visiting elsewhere.

Lines 1 and 2 (white waves of the offing, when the wind blows) are a jo linked to the kakekotoba "tatsu" (rise)/"tatsuta." Tatsuta Mountain is in the Ikoma range in Nara Prefecture. Yamato Province is now Nara Prefecture; Kōchi is part of Ōsaka City. This poem appears in *The Tales of Ise*, 23, with similar circumstances of composition.

995 • *Topic unknown.*

ta ga misogi	whose cock adorned with
yūtsukedori ka	purification ribbons
kara koromo	crows incessantly
tatsuta no yama ni	on bright Tatsuta Mountain
orihaete naku	colorful as Chinese robes

Anonymous

"Misogi" refers to a ritual purification in the stream in front of the Tatsuta Shrine. "Kara koromo" (Chinese robe) is a makurakotoba for the kakekotoba "tatsu" (to cut out)/"tatsuta." For Tatsuta Mountain, see 994.

996 • *Topic unknown.*

wasuraren	as a remembrance
toki shinobe to zo	for the time when I have been
hama chidori	forgotten I leave
yukue mo shiranu	these runes varied as plovers'
ato o todomuru	random prints along the shore

Anonymous

The author's handwriting is compared to the haphazard prints of plovers.

997 • *Composed and presented to the Mikado in the Jōgan era when he asked, "When was the Man'yōshū compiled?"*

kannazuki	these are the ancient
shigure furiokeru	songs of the capital which
nara no ha no	bears the name of the
na ni ou miyako no	Nara tree on whose leaves the
furu goto zo kore	cold rains of the Tenth Month fall

Funya no Arisue

Seiwa and Yōzei tennō reigned during the Jōgan era, 859–877. Presumably it was Seiwa whose question prompted this poem. Kannazuki, the Godless Month, was the Tenth Month. The nara (oak), also called the hahaso, grows prolifically in the Nara area. This is the oldest reference to the compilation of the *Man'yōshū*, but a textual variant makes the dating questionable: "nara no miyako" (the Nara capital) was the capital from 710 to 794; but if the fourth line reads "nara no mikado" (the Nara Mikado), it refers to Heizei tennō, who reigned from 806 to 809.

Kokinshū

998 • *Presented with other poems to the Mikado in the Kanpyō era.*

ashitazu no	a single reed crane
hitori okurete	left behind by his fellows
naku koe wa	raises his sad voice
kumo no ue made	hoping his cries will carry
kikoetsu ganan	beyond the celestial clouds

Ōe no Chisato

For the Kanpyō era, see 177. The poem is a veiled reproach to the Mikado for having left Chisato behind in the rounds of promotions that elevated his contemporaries.

999 • *Presented with other poems to the Mikado in the Kanpyō era.*

hito shirezu	may the secret wish
omou kokoro wa	hidden within my heart where
harugasumi	no one can know rise
tachi idete kimi ga	now and drift like the spring mists
me ni mo mienan	before the eyes of my lord

Fujiwara no Kachion

"Harugasumi" (spring mists) is a makurakotoba for "tachi" (rising). This poem, too, is a veiled request for promotion.

1000 • *Written at the end of a manuscript presented when the Mikado was gathering poems.*

yamagawa no	distant rumors reach
oto ni mono kiku	me like the murmurs of an
momoshiki o	unseen mountain stream
mio haya nagara	how I wish I could see the
miru yoshi mo gana	palace fences as before

Ise

If this poem concludes the collection of Ise's poems that include her elegies for the Consort Onshi (d. 907), it is among those that establish the date of compilation of the *Kokinshū* as post-905. "Yamagawa no" (of the mountain stream) is a makurakotoba for "oto" (sound; rumors). "Mio" (body; river channel) is also a kakekotoba. "Haya" (swift) and "yamagawa" are engo.

BOOK XIX

Miscellaneous Forms

TANKA

IOOI • *Topic unknown.*

au koto no
mare naru iro ni
omoisome
waga mi wa tsune ni
5   amagumo no
haruru toki nake
fuji no ne no
moetsutsu to wa ni
omoedomo
10 au koto katashi
nani shi ka mo
hito o uramin
watatsumi no
oki o fukamete
15   omoiteshi
omoi wa ima wa
itazura ni
narinu beranari
yuku mizu no
20 tayuru toki naku
kaku nawa ni
omoimidarete
furu yuki no
kenaba kenubeku
25   omoedomo
ebu no mi nareba

as seldom seen as
some rare hue is the one for
   whom love stains my heart
within   my heart is bleak   dark
   as cloud-laden skies
that neither brighten nor clear
   like the molten core
of Fuji   my love will burn
   undying   I know
we can never rendezvous
   but   why should I feel
resentment or reproach her
   the longings I've felt
unfathomable as the
   deep waters of the
offing   are in vain
   I cannot hope to
quench the fires within my heart
   like running water
which never ceases to flow
   my yearnings pour forth
entangled as Chinese sweets
   if I must vanish
with as little trace as the
   snowflakes   so be it
a being of this transient

338

nao yamazu	world am I and thus
omoi wa fukashi	my endless longings run deep
ashihiki no	through the foothills of
30 yama shita mizu	the lonely mountains flows a
ko kakurete	stream hidden within
tagitsu kokoro o	the dark sheltering forest
tare ni ka mo	to whom may I speak
aikatarawan	of the turbulence in my heart
35 iro ni ideba	if it should push to
hito shirinubemi	the surface others would know
sumizome no	when night comes at last
yūbe ni nareba	quiet night dyed inky black
hitori ite	I am all alone
40 aware aware to	and I sigh and sigh again
nageki amari	as grief overflows
sen sube nami ni	there is only the solace
niwa ni idete	of entering my
tachiyasuraeba	garden and wandering through
45 shirotae no	its stillness thinking
koromo no sode ni	if I must vanish with as
oku tsuyu no	little trace as the
kenaba kenu beku	dew that settles on my robe's
omoedomo	white sleeves so be it
50 nao nagekarenu	still my sighs grow in number
harugasumi	for I long to see my
yoso ni mo hito ni	love even from afar as
awan to omoeba	we view the distant spring mists

Anonymous

The poems labeled here as tanka (short poems) are actually chōka (long poems of alternating five- and seven-syllable lines, concluding with an extra seven-syllable line).

Lines 1–5: "Au" means both "to meet" and "to deepen a color with lye" in dyeing cloth. "Iro" (color; love) and "some" (dying; beginning) are both kakekotoba and engo. "Hi" (fire) in "omo(h)i" (longings) may also function as engo.

Lines 11–15: "Fukamete" (deepening) functions as a pivot, linking the images of the sea and thoughts of love.

Lines 24–30: "Ebu" is the Japanese version of the Sanskrit Jambudvīpa, the transient human world of suffering.

Lines 31–35: Lines 29–32 are the same as the first four lines of XI, 491, an anonymous love poem.

Lines 36–40: "Sumizome no" (ink-dyed) is a makurakotoba for "yūbe" (night).

Lines 41–45: "Shirotae no" (white hempen) is a makurakotoba for "koromo" (robe).

Lines 51–53: "Harugasumi" (spring mist) is a makurakotoba for "yoso" (far off).

1002 • *A catalogue in the form of a long poem prepared on presenting the old poems to the Mikado.*

chihayaburu	since the age of the
kami no miyo yori	awesome gods never ceasing
kuretake no	during reigns profuse
yoyo ni mo taezu	as the joints of black bamboo
5 amabiko no	men have sung with thoughts
otowa no yama no	entangled by the spring mists
harugasumi	that drift over Mount
omoimidarete	Otowa where echoes sound
samidare no	unable to sleep
10 sora mo todoro ni	when awakened by the late
sayo fukete	night cries of mountain
yama hototogisu	hototogisu echoing
naku goto ni	through skies rumbling with
tare mo nezamete	early summer thunderstorms
15 kara nishiki	gazing lovingly
tatsuta no yama no	upon the bright brocade of
momijiba o	autumn leaves scattered
mite nomi shinobu	upon Tatsuta Mountain
kannazuki	when like the Tenth Month
20 shigure shigurete	showers chill winter's portent
fuyu no yo no	like the snow that falls
niwa mo hadare ni	in patches on the garden
furu yuki no	during winter nights
nao kiekaeri	they felt their hearts melt and fade
25 toshi goto ni	when as the cycle
toki ni tsuketsutsu	of the year passed once more or
aware chō	when especially
koto o iitsutsu	moved to express their feelings
kimi o nomi	they wished their lords a
30 chiyo ni to iwau	lifespan of one thousand years
yo no hito no	the burning desires
omoi suruga no	of the people of this world
fuji no ne no	smoldering like the
moyuru omoi mo	molten core of Mount Fuji

35	akazu shite	in far Suruga
	wakaruru namida	the tears of those who part too
	fujigoromo	soon the strands of grief
	oreru kokoro mo	that bind hearts like skeins of fine
	yachi kusa no	wisteria boughs
40	koto no ha goto ni	these words abundant as the
	suberagi no	leaves of eight thousand
	ōse kashikomi	grasses upon the meadows
	maki maki no	humbly receiving
	naka ni tsukusu to	that imperial command
45	ise no umi no	in scroll upon scroll
	ura no shiogai	I gathered selecting them
	hiroiatsume	as one collects shells
	toreri to suredo	by the waters of Ise still
	tama no o no	my heart's measure was
50	mijikaki kokoro	insufficient to embrace
	omoiaezu	the jewels I'd found
	nao aratama no	each year I greet the New Year
	toshi o hete	having spent the old
	ōmiya ni nomi	entirely in the palace
55	hisakata no	in the service of
	hiru yoru wakazu	my lord working day and night
	tsukau tote	'neath skies light and dark
	kaerimi mo senu	never looking back upon
	waga yado no	my own beloved home
60	shinobugusa ouru	where grasses of longing grow
	itama arami	through widening cracks
	furu harusame no	do spring rains seep through
	mori ya shi nuramu	while verses yet elude me

Ki no Tsurayuki

The "old poems" catalogued are the poems presented to Daigo tennō in the form of the *Kokinshū*.

Lines 1–5: "Chihayaburu" is a makurakotoba for "kami" (gods). "Kuretake no" (of the black bamboo) is a makurakotoba modifying "yoyo" in line 4, which refers both to the segments of the bamboo and to generations.

Lines 6–10: For Otowa Mountain, see 142. Lines 5–8 are the spring segment of this catalogue of poetic topics.

Lines 11–15: Lines 9–14 present summer subjects. "Kara nishiki" (Chinese brocade) is a makurakotoba for "tatsu" (to cut out)/Tatsuta (place name).

Lines 16–20: For Tatsuta Mountain, see 108.

Lines 21–25: Lines 15–18 describe autumn, and lines 19–24 treat the topic of winter.

Lines 26–30: Lines 25–30 treat congratulatory subjects.

Lines 31–34: "Suru" (to do)/Suruga (place name) is a kakekotoba. "Omo(h)i" (longings) contains the word "hi" (fire). For Suruga, see 534. "Fuji no ne no" (of the base of Fuji) is a makurakotoba for "moyuru" (burning). Lines 31–34 represent love poetry.

Lines 35–40: Lines 35 and 36 represent poems of parting and travel. For fuji-goromo (wisteria robe), see 654. Lines 37 and 38 represent the poems of grief. Lines 39 and 40 represent the miscellaneous poems and conclude the catalogue. The last lines tell of the difficulties endured by the compilers.

Lines 45–50: Lines 45 and 46 (the salty shells of the bay of the sea of Ise) are a jo linked to "hiroiatsume" (gathering up). "Tama no o no" (of the jewels' string) is a makurakotoba for "mijikaki" (short)

Lines 50–54: "Aratama no" (of rough jewels; or newly minted[?]) is a makurakotoba for "toshi" (year). "Ōmiya" (the palace) in line 54 refers to the palace building in which the work of compiling the *Kokinshū* was carried out.

Lines 55–59: "Hisakata no" is here a makurakotoba for "hiru" (daytime).

Lines 60–64: "Furu harusame no" (the falling spring rain) is a jo linked to the kakekotoba "mori" (seeping; being omitted).

1003 • *A long poem presented along with the old poems.*

kuretake no	were it not for the
yoyo no furugoto	poems of past generations
nakariseba	numerous as black
ikaho no numa no	bamboo how would we tell each
5 ika ni shite	other of the thoughts
omou kokoro o	within our hearts silent as
nobaemashi	Ikaho Marsh yes
aware mukashibe	how fortunate we are how
ariki chō	we rejoice that once
10 hitomaro koso wa	long ago there was a man
ureshikere	called Hitomaro
mi wa shimo nagara	though a lowly man still he
koto no ha o	raised his songs and made
amatsu sora made	them heard within the palace
15 kikoeage	distant as the skies
sue no yo made no	made them proper models for
ato to nashi	songs of days to come
ima mo ōse no	now I too am asked for the
kudareru wa	songs piled about me
20 chiri ni tsuge to ya	and though unworthy I must
chiri no mi ni	obey those commands
tsumoreru koto o	to follow the footsteps of
towaru ran	that poet of old

kore o omoeba	when I realize all this
25　inishie ni	my feelings are those
kusuri kekaseru	of that animal of long
kedamono no	ago who lapped up
kumo ni hoeken	the elixer and howled from
kokochi shite	the clouds far above
30　chiji no nasake mo	all my many sorrows and
omōezu	joys are put aside
hitotsu kokoro zo	and my heart is set upon
hokorashiki	only this proud task
kaku wa aredomo	yet while this is so　I who
35　teru hikari	once was a trusted
chikaki mamori no	guard who was posted near to
mi narishi o	that shining presence
tare ka wa aki no	was deceived by someone and
kuru kata ni	transfered to the west
40　azamuki idete	the region from which autumn
mikaki yori	comes　did ever I
to no e moru mi no	think I would long remain guard
mikaki mori	of these outer gates
osaosashiku mo	sentry of the far precincts
45　omōezu	of our shining lord
kokono kasane no	within the noble ninefold
naka ni te wa	enclosure I lived
arashi no kaze mo	and never heard the shrill winds
kikazarike	of the raging storms
50　ima wa no yama shi	now　because of the nearness
chikakereba	of fields and mountains
haru wa kasumi ni	I walk enshrouded　muffled
tanabikare	in thick mists of spring
natsu wa utsusemi	crying throughout the summer
55　nakikurashi	like a cicada
aki wa shigure ni	wiping the autumn drizzle
sode o kashi	with my sodden sleeves
fuyu wa shimo ni zo	ravaged by the harsh winter's
semeraruru	merciless frosts　as
60　kakaru wabishiki	I live in this misery
mi nagara ni	I reckon all the
tsumoreru toshi o	years　years which piled one upon
shirusereba	another　and I
itsutsu no mutsu ni	find they have numbered six times

65	narinikeri	five thirty in all
	kore ni sowareru	and added to all those years
	watakushi no	of public service
	oi no kazu sae	my private years my lifetime
	yayokereba	spans numerous days
70	mi wa iyashikute	so while my status is low
	toshi takaki	my store of years is
	koto no kurushisa	high a painful fact to me
	kakushitsutsu	I must continue
	nagara no hashi no	hiding living out my span
75	nagaraete	like Nagara Bridge
	naniwa no ura ni	sodden wrinkles trembling like
	tatsu nami no	the waves which rise row
	nami no shiwa ni ya	upon uneven row in
	obōren	Naniwa's fair bay
80	sasuga ni inochi	even so my life is dear
	oshikereba	I cling to my life
	koshi no kuni naru	though my hair has turned as white
	shira yama no	as the peak of famed
	kashira wa shiroku	White Mountain in the distant
85	narinu tomo	Province of Koshi
	otowa no taki no	I long for that elixir
	oto ni kiku	they tell of whispering
	oizu shinazu no	soft as the rushing waters
	kusuri mo ga	that keeps one ever
90	kimi ga yachiyo o	young so that I too might see
	wakaetsutsu min	my lord's eight-thousand-year reign

Mibu no Tadamine

Lines 1–5: "Yoyo" is a kakekotoba meaning both "segments of bamboo" and "generations." "Ikaho no numa no" (of Ikaho Marsh) is a makurakotoba linked to "ika ni" (how) in line 5 by the sound repetition. Ikaho Marsh may be Haruna Lake in Gunma Prefecture.

Lines 20–24: "Chiri ni tsuge" (dust after chariot wheels) suggests "second best," "following the precedent of Hitomaro." The phrase also appears in the Chinese Preface to the *Kokinshū*. "Tsumoreru" (heaped up) is an engo for "chiri" (dust). The suggestion of the preface that former sovereigns sought their ministers' opinions in verse is reflected in these lines.

Lines 25–29: Lines 25–28 refer to a story in the *Shen hsien ch'uan* 神仙伝 that tells of a dog and rooster consuming an elixer prepared by Liu-an 劉安, King of Huainan, and rising, howling and crowing, into the cloudy heavens. Lines 25 and 26 have been added to the *Kokinshū* texts from the version of this poem found in the *Tadamine Collection* (*Tadamine shū*).

Lines 35–39: Line 36 refers to Tadamine's one-time position as head of the Imperial Guards. He was tranferred to the Right Guards, which were quartered to the west, the direction associated with autumn, and where he guarded the perimeters of the imperial compound rather than the sovereign's own person and rooms.

Lines 70–74: "Nagara no hashi no" (of the Nagara Bridge) is a jo linked to "nagaraete" (lengthening; living on) by the repetition of sounds. For Nagara Bridge, see 826.

Lines 75–79: For Naniwa Bay, see 604. Lines 77 and 78 contain another repetition: that of the phrase "nami no" (like waves). "Obōren" (shall drown) is an engo for "nami" (waves).

Lines 80–84: For Shira yama, see 383.

Lines 85–89: Lines 86 and 87 contain another sound repetition: Otowa Falls and "oto" (sound). For Otowa Falls, see 928.

1004 • *Envoy to 1003.*

kimi ga yo ni	born in my lord's reign
ōsaka yama ni	to live as I thought unknown—
iwashimizu	hidden as the springs
kogakuretari to	whose pure rockbound waters flow
omoikeru kana	deep in Mount Ōsaka's forests

Mibu no Tadamine

One or more envoys in tanka form are often appended to chōka. Au (to meet)/Ōsaka is a kakekotoba. For Ōsaka, see 374.

1005 • *A long poem on winter.*

chihayaburu	October the month
kannazuki to ya	when the awesome gods retreat
kesa yori wa	has come suddenly
kumori mo aezu	this morning the clouds gathered
5 katsu shigure	to shed the first cold
momiji to tomo ni	rain of winter together
furusato no	with the colored leaves
yoshino no yama no	on our old hamlet deep in
yama arashi mo	Yoshino Mountain
10 samuku hi goto ni	raging storms sweep down the slopes
nariyukeba	each day grows more chill
tama no o tokete	the pearl necklace is untied
kokichirashi	its jewels stripped and
arare midarete	scattered as wildly falling

15 shimo kōri	hail frost crystals freeze
iya katamareru	on the now rock-hard surface
niwa no omo ni	of my ravaged garden
mura mura miyuru	where brown hillocks and mounds of
fuyu kusa no	withered grasses stand
20 ue ni furishiku	soft snows settle there and spread
shiragumo no	drifting from the thick
tsumori tsumorite	white clouds that blanket the sky
aratama no	ah how many new
toshi o amata mo	years unformed as rough-cut gems
25 sugushitsuru kana	have I lived to see pass by

Ōshikōchi no Mitsune

Lines 1–5: "Chihayaburu" (awesome) is a makurakotoba for Kannazuki (the Godless Month, the tenth lunar month).
    Lines 6–10: "Furu" (to fall)/"furusato" (home town) functions as a kakekotoba. For Yoshino, see 3.
    Lines 21–25 "Aratama no" is a makurakotoba for "toshi" (year).

1006 • *Composed after the death of the Seventh Ward Consort.*

okitsu nami	I too who now fish
are nomi masaru	the wide waters of Ise
miya no uchi wa	lived for years on end
toshi hete sumishi	within that palace now grown
5 ise no ama mo	desolate and still
fune magashitaru	like a ship adrift in rough
kokochi shite	waves in the offing
yoran katanaku	no mooring can I find no
kanashiki ni	solace for my grief
10 namida no iro no	the tears which stain our faces
kurenai wa	have turned a blood-red
warera ga naka no	as they fall among us like
shigure nite	melancholy rains
aki no momiji to	because all the others have
15 hitobito wa	scattered to their homes
ono ga chirijiri	drifting away like colored
wakarenaba	leaves of late autumn
tanomu kagenaku	we have been abandoned here
narihatete	with no sheltering
20 tomaru mono to wa	shade of those who remain here

hanasusuki	only the blooming
kimi naki niwa ni	plume grass standing in clusters
mure tachite	in the garden you
sora o manekaba	visit no more beckons to
25 hatsu kari no	the sky where the first
nakiwataritsutsu	geese cry on their long journey
yoso ni koso mime	no longer will this be home

Ise

For the Seventh Ward Consort, see 968.

Lines 1–5: "Okitsu nami" (waves of the offing) is a makurakotoba for "are" (rough).

Lines 16–20: "Chirijiri" (scattering) is an engo for "momiji" (colored leaves), line 14, as is "kage" (shade, shelter), line 18.

Lines 25–27: "Hatsu kari no" (of the first wild geese) is a makurakotoba for "nakiwataritsutsu" (crying and crossing).

Ise refers both to the author of this poem and to the Ise Sea.

SEDŌKA

1007 • *Topic unknown.*

uchiwatasu	I would ask of you
ochikatabito ni	you who are so far away
mono mōsu ware	as far as my eyes can see
sono soko ni	what is that flower
shiroku sakeru wa	that blooms so fair and white
nani no hana zo mo	upon those distant meadows

Anonymous

Poems 1007–1010 are sedōka, poems with six lines of 5/7/7/5/7/7 syllables.

1008 • *Reply.*

haru sareba	when we welcome spring
nobe ni mazu saku	this is the flower that first
miredo akanu hana	clothes the fields the blossom we
mainashi ni	behold tenderly
tada nanoru beki	is this then a bloom whose name
hana no na nare ya	should be spoken lightly

Anonymous

hatsuse gawa	Hatsuse River
furu kawa nobe ni	there by those ancient waters
futamoto aru sugi	towering two-trunked cedar
toshi o hete	after years have passed
mata mo aimin	once more we'll meet you and I
futamoto aru sugi	towering two-trunked cedar

Anonymous

The Hatsuse River flows through Nara Prefecture. It is unclear whether "furu kawa" means "ancient river" and refers to the Hatsuse, as translated here, or whether it is a proper name, or whether it refers to the upper reaches of the Hatsuse and means "the river that runs through Furu."

1010 • *Topic unknown.*

kimi ga sasu	broad as my lord's an
mikasa no yama no	umbrella of clouds stretches
momijiba no iro	above Mikasa Mountain
kannazuki	the brilliant autumn
shigure no ame no	leaves have been dyed in harvest
someru narikeri	colors by the early winter drizzle

Ki no Tsurayuki

"Kimi ga sasu" (which my lord carries) is a makurakotoba for Mikasa, which is a place name (see 406) and also means "umbrella." "Mi" is a decorative prefix.

HAIKAI POEMS

1011 • *Topic unknown.*

ume no hana	I came here only
mi ni koso kitsure	to gaze upon plum blossoms
uguisu no	but still the wood thrush
hitoku hitoku to	laments hitoku hitoku
itoi shi mo oru	a man has come man has come

Anonymous

Poems 1011–1068 are haikai (humorous) poems, a term borrowed from Chinese essays on poetry. These poems may contain expressions not ordinarily considered suitable for waka, unusual engo and kakekotoba, or personifications, but many are not markedly different from poems found in other books of the *Kokinshū*. "Hitoku" (a person comes) represents the sound of the cry of the uguisu (mountain thrush). The next ten poems are arranged in the order of the seasons.

1012 • *Topic unknown.*

yamabuki no
hana iro goromo
  nushi ya tare
toedo kotaezu
kuchinashi ni shite

who owns this garment
bright yellow as the lovely
  wild mountain roses
I ask   yet no reply comes
cape jasmine dye cannot speak

Sosei

The yamabuki is a yellow wild rose, *Kerria japonica*; the kuchinashi (no-mouth) is a cape jasmine, *Gardenia florida*.

1013 • *Topic unknown.*

ikubaku no
ta o tsukureba ka
  hototogisu
shide no taosa o
asa na asa na yobu

hototogisu
foreman of the netherworld
  how many fields must
ploughshares till   as you call out
each morning at planting time

Fujiwara no Toshiyuki

The cry of the hototogisu (nightingale) was said to be "shide no taosa" (field foreman of the underworld).

1014 • *A poem about Tanabata, composed on the sixth day of the Seventh Month.*

itsu shika to
mataku kokoro o
  hagi ni agete
ama no kawara o
kyō ya wataran

impatiently he
stands there   cloak raised to his knees
  eager to straddle
heaven's river   wondering
if today he will cross it

Fujiwara no Kanesuke

The poem describes the herdsman on the day before Tanabata, the day he is permitted to cross the river of heaven to meet the weaver maid. See 173.

1015 • *Topic unknown.*

mutsugoto mo
mada tsukinaku ni
  akenu meri

their sweet words of love
are not yet exhausted   but
  already day has

izura wa aki no   dawned   where are those autumn nights

nagashi chō yo wa   those hours they say are so long

Ōshikōchi no Mitsune

1016 • *Topic unknown.*

aki no no ni   flirtatiously they

namameki tateru   sway in the fields of autumn

ominaeshi   fair maiden flowers

ana kashigamashi   competing loudly for my gaze—

hana mo hitotoki   your blossoms too are short-lived

Henjō

For ominaeshi, see 226. The image continues for three poems.

1017 • *Topic unknown.*

aki kureba   when autumn arrives

nobe ni tawaruru   and lovely maiden flowers

ominaeshi   frolic in the fields

izure no hito ka   who can resist them   who can

tsumade miru beki   just look and not pluck their blooms

Anonymous

1018 • *Topic unknown.*

akigiri no   as the autumn mists

harete kumoreba   clear and then cover the fields

ominaeshi   the maiden flowers'

hana no sugata zo   lovely colors too   appear

miekakure suru   and then disappear once more

Anonymous

"Hana" means both "flower" and "beautiful."

1019 • *Topic unknown.*

hana to mite   seeing their lovely

oran to sureba   blossoms   I reached out my hand

ominaeshi   to pluck one   only

| utata aru sama no | to recall their name   maiden |
| na ni koso arikere | flowers   I must resist |

Anonymous

Again, "hana" means both "flower" and "beautiful."

1020 • *A poem from the poetry contest held at the residence of the Consort in the Kanpyō era.*

aki kaze ni	unraveled and torn
hokorobinu rashi	apart by the autumn winds
fujibakama	purple trousers of
tsuzurisase chō	the fields sew up their seams
kirigirisu naku	the cicadas loudly cry

Ariwara no Muneyana

For fujibakama, see 239. The kirigirisu, a kind of cricket, was said to cry "tsuzuri sase" (prick and sew); see 196.

1021 • *A poem sent to the neighboring house on seeing that the wind had blown snow over from the neighbor's garden on the day before the first day of spring.*

fuyu nagara	still winter and yet
haru no tonari no	its neighbor spring must be near
chikakereba	for over the fence
nakagaki yori zo	between our gardens fragile
hana wa chirikeru	snow-white petals are falling

Kiyowara no Fukayabu

1022 • *Topic unknown.*

isonokami	a long-ago love
furinishi koi no	became a ghostly spirit
kamusabite	who haunts me now at
tataru ni ware wa	Isonokami where I
i zo ne kanetsuru	can no longer sleep in peace

Anonymous

The place name Isonokami is a makurakotoba for "furinishi" (aged) because of the similarity of the first two syllables to the place name Furu; see 144.

1023 • *Topic unknown.*

makura yori
ato yori koi no
  semekureba
senkata nami zo
toko naka ni oru

when from my pillow
and from the foot of my bed
  thoughts of love rise to
inflict their pain   I simply
cower here in the middle

Anonymous

The next group of haikai poems treat the topic of love.

1024 • *Topic unknown.*

koishiki ga
kata mo kata koso
  ari to kike
tatere oredomo
naki kokoshi kana

in love   they tell me
there are established forms
  certain conventions
but   whether I sit down or
stand up   I feel no order

Anonymous

1025 • *Topic unknown.*

arinu ya to
kokoromi gatera
  aimineba
tawabure nikuki
made zo koishiki

to test my heart I
decide to stay away   to
  see if I can live
with separation   but my
love is too strong to play with

Anonymous

1026 • *Topic unknown.*

miminashi no
yama no kuchinashi
  eteshi gana
omoi no iro no
shitazome ni sen

if only I could
secure blooms of the silent
  gardenias that grow
upon Earless Mountain   to
dye my robe with love's scarlet

Anonymous

Miminashi (Earless) Mountain in Nara Prefecture was known for kuchinashi ("no-mouth"; cape jasmine or *Gardenia florida*). "Omo(h)i" (longings) contains the word "hi" (scarlet), the color of the kuchinashi.

1027 • *Topic unknown.*

ashihiki no	ah so even you
yama ta no sōzu	you clumsy scarecrow of the
onore sae	rugged mountain fields—
ware o hoshi to iu	want me to become your wife—
urewashiki koto	what a lamentable lot

Anonymous

"Ashihiki no" is a makurakotoba for "yama" (mountain).

1028 • *Topic unknown.*

fuji no ne no	ah burn brightly then
naranu omoi ni	bitter fires of hopeless love
moeba moe	hot as Fuji's flames—
kami dani ketanu	not even the gods would quench
munashi keburi o	these unavailing smoke clouds

Ki no Menoto

"Omo(h)i" (longings) contains the word "hi" (fire) and functions as a kakekotoba.

1029 • *Topic unknown.*

aimimaku	innumerable
hoshi wa kazu naku	as the stars are my longings
arinagara	to meet my love but
hito ni tsuki nami	I am lost unable to
madoi koso sure	see her in the moonless night

Ki no Aritomo

"Hoshi" (desire; star) is a kakekotoba, as is "tsuki" (moon; opportunity).

1030 • *Topic unknown.*

hito ni awan	no moon lights the night
tsuki no naki ni wa	nor can I meet my lover
omoi okite	my blazing passion
mune hashiribi ni	wakens me my pounding heart
kokoro yakeori	shoots flame then turns to cinders

Ono no Komachi

"Tsuki" (moon; opportunity); "omo(h)i" (longings)/"hi" (fire); "okite" (waking; blazing up); "hashiri" (pounding)/"hashiribi" (shooting sparks); and "yakeori" (is burned; is anxious) are all kakekotoba. "Hi" (fire), "okite" (blazing up), "hashiribi" (shooting sparks), and "yakeori" (is burned) are engo.

1031 • *A poem from the poetry contest held at the residence of the Consort in the Kanpyō era.*

harugasumi	if for a time I
tanabiku nobe no	could become a fresh young shoot
wakana ni mo	upon the meadows
narimite shi gana	where the spring mists softly trail
hito mo tsun ya to	would someone bend to pluck me

Fujiwara no Okikaze

1032 • *Topic unknown.*

omoedomo	truly I love but
nao utomarenu	we never grow intimate—
harugasumi	unfaithful mists of
kakaranu yama no	spring are there any mountain
araji to omoeba	peaks where you do not linger

Anonymous

"Kakaranu" (does not hang; does not have a relationship) is a kakekotoba.

1033 • *Topic unknown.*

haru no no no	from the shelter of
shigeki kusaba no	spring meadows' luxuriant
tsuma koi ni	green grass the pheasant
tobi tatsu kiji no	yearning for his mate flutters
hororo to zo naku	up with sobbing throbbing wings

Taira no Sadafun

Lines 1 and 2 (of the thick leaves of grass of the fields of spring) are a jo linked to "tsuma" (stalks; wife). "Hororo" is the sound made by the pheasants' wings as well as the sound of human sobbing.

1034 • *Topic unknown.*

aki no no ni	for years in autumn
tsuma naki shika no	fields the mateless stag has belled

toshi o hete
nazo waga koi no
kaiyo to zo naku

his mournful complaint
crying that his misery
is the fault of love alone

Ki no Yoshihito

"Kaiyo," the cry of the mateless deer, contains the word "kai" (result).

1035 • *Topic unknown.*

semi no ha no
hitoe ni usuki
  natsu goromo
nareba yorinan
mono ni ya wa aran

as unlined summer
robes   fragile as cicadas'
  filmy wings   soften
and ripple   so your heart will
yield   relent   when you know me

Ōshikōchi no Mitsune

"Hitoe ni" means both "in a single layer" and "extremely." Lines 1–3 (summer robe, unlined and thin as the cicadas' wings) are a jo linked to the kakekotoba "nareba yorinan" (when wilted, will wrinkle; when accustomed to, will approach).

1036 • *Topic unknown.*

kakurenu no
shita yori ouru
  nenunawa no
nenu na wa tateji
kuru na itoi so

I'll come so there will
be no rumors that I sleep
  alone   lonely as
the water weeds deep in the
hidden marsh   receive me well

Mibu no Tadamine

Nenunawa (now called junsai) is the water weed called watershield, *Brasenia purpurea.* Lines 1–3 (growing from the bottom of the hidden marsh) are a jo linked to "nenu na" (rumor that one does not sleep) in line 4 by the repetition of sounds. "Kuru" (to come; to reel) is an engo for "nawa" (rope).

1037 • *Topic unknown.*

koto naraba
omowazu to ya wa
  iihatenu
nazo yo no naka no
tamadasuki naru

if things have come to
this   why not simply say that
  you no longer love
that our union has broken
like bright jeweled suspenders

Anonymous

"Tama" (jeweled) is a poetic prefix for an object of beauty.

1038 • *Topic unknown.*

omou chō
hito no kokoro no
  kuma goto ni
tachikakuretsutsu
miru yoshi mo gana

ah for a way to
hide myself and peer into
  each secret recess
within the mysterious
heart of one who claims he loves

Anonymous

1039 • *Topic unknown.*

omoedomo
omowazu to nomi
  iu nareba
ima ya omowaji
omou kai nashi

although I love him
he only says he does not
  love me   ah no   I
must not go on loving   for
my love is unavailing

Anonymous

1040 • *Topic unknown.*

ware o nomi
omou to iwaba
  arubeki o
ide ya kokoro wa
ōnusa ni shite

if he would but say
that he loves me only   then
  I could be at peace
ah   but like the votive strips
his heart is touched by many

Anonymous

Ōnusa (votive strips) were strips of cloth attached to sticks for use during the Great Purification Ceremony

1041 • *Topic unknown.*

ware o omou
hito o omowanu
  mukui ni ya
waga omou hito no
ware o omowanu

I did not love the
one who set his heart for me—
  is it fate's revenge
is it retribution   the
one I love does not love me

Anonymous

1042 • *Topic unknown.*

omoiken	that one who might
hito o zo tomo ni	have loved me if only I
omowamashi	could have loved him too—
masashi ya mukui	for in truth has there not been
nakarikeri ya wa	retribution for my sin

Father of Kiyohara no Fukayabu

Some texts attribute this to Kiyohara no Fukayabu.

1043 • *Topic unknown.*

idete yukan	I cannot detain
hito o todomen	him here my love who would
yoshinaki ni	depart and not one
tonari no kata ni	of my neighbors will deter
hana mo hinu kana	him with a timely sneeze

Anonymous

A sneeze was taken as a bad omen; presumably a sneeze would have persuaded a lover that the safest course would be to stay where he was.

1044 • *Topic unknown.*

kurenai ni	I shall not rely
someshi kokoro mo	even on that heart dyed with
tanomarezu	love deep as scarlet
hito o aku ni wa	for a lye can bleach and fade
utsuru chō nari	hearts as quickly as colors

Anonymous

"Aku" means both "to tire of" and "lye." "Utsuru" (to change, fade) is an engo for "kurenai" (scarlet) and "someshi" (dyed).

1045 • *Topic unknown.*

itowaruru	rejected am I
waga mi wa haru no	abandoned have I become
koma nare ya	an unwanted foal

| nogai gatera ni | to be set loose to forage |
| hanachisutetsuru | in the grasses of spring fields |

Anonymous

"Ito haruru" (very clear)/"itowaruru" (hated) is a kakekotoba. "Ito haruru" (very clear), "haru no koma" (spring colt), and "nogai" (raised in the field) are engo.

I046 • *Topic unknown.*

uguisu no	am I too to be
kozo no yadori no	abandoned cast off as the
furusu to ya	wood thrush's year-old nest
ware ni wa hito no	how indifferently he treats
tsure nakaru ran	me how cold he has become

Anonymous

"Furusu" (grown old, castoff nest) is a kakekotoba.

I047 • *Topic unknown.*

sakashira ni	slender bamboo leaves
natsu wa hitomane	which wisely slept apart like
sasa no ha no	us in summer's heat
sayagu shimo yo o	now whisper together these
waga hitori nuru	frosty nights I sleep alone

Anonymous

"Hitomane" (imitating; sleeping alone) is a kakekotoba.

I048 • *Topic unknown.*

au koto no	rarely can we meet—
ima wa hatsuka ni	no opportunity do
narinureba	we find the moon of
yoru fukakarade wa	the twentieth does not shine
tsuki nakarikeri	for this night is still too young

Taira no Nakaki

"Hatsuka ni" (rarely; the twentieth day) is a kakekotoba, as is "tsuki" (moon; opportunity).

1049 • *Topic unknown.*

morokoshi no	although you retreat
yoshino no yama ni	deep within the Yoshino
komoru tomo	Mountains distant as
okuren to omou	far Cathay I am not one
ware naranaku ni	who will be left behind here

Fujiwara no Tokihira

"Morokoshi" (Cathay) suggests physical distance; the Yoshino Mountains were known as a place of retreat, or social and psychological distance, from the capital and secular society.

1050 • *Topic unknown.*

kumo harenu	capricious as
asama no yama no	smoke clouds that constantly spread
asamashi ya	above Asama
hito no kokoro o	Mountain are you look into
mite koso yamame	my heart then drift if you must

Taira no Nakaki

Asama Mountain is a volcanic mountain on the border of Nagano and Gunma Prefectures. Lines 1 and 2 (like Asama Mountain where the clouds never clear) are a jo linked to "asamashi ya" (capricious).

1051 • *Topic unknown.*

naniwa naru	they say the bridge of
nagara no hashi mo	Nagara in Naniwa
tsukuru nari	will be repaired and
ima wa waga mi o	then to what shall I compare
nani ni tatoen	this time-worn body of mine

Ise

For Naniwa, see 604. For Nagara Bridge, see 826. "Tsukuru" (to be rebuilt) could also mean "to collapse."

1052 • *Topic unknown.*

mame naredo	I may be faithful
nani zo wa yokeku	but what good does it do me—

karu kaya no
midarete aredo
ashi keku mo nashi

though entanglements
be as snarled as piles of cut
reeds   what is the consequence

Anonymous

"Karu kaya no" (like the reaped reeds) is a makurakotoba for "midarete" (scattered in confusion).

1053 • *Topic unknown.*

nani ka sono
na no tatsu koto no
    oshikaran
shirite madou wa
ware hitori ka wa

why should I regret
these rumors that carry my
    name far and wide   am
I alone in wandering
confused   through mazes I foresaw

Fujiwara no Okikaze

1054 • *Written when people whispered that she had wedded her cousin.*

yoso nagara
waga mi ni ito no
    yoru to ieba
tada itsuwari ni
sugubakari nari

we are not kindred—
those who claim my cousin and
    I are close as thread
and needle are spinning lies—
twisting the truth like fine yarns

Kuso

"Ito" (thread) suggests the word "itoko" (cousin). "Yoru" (to spin) also means "to approach." "Itsuwari ni sugu" (exaggerating, telling lies to excess) contains the phrase "hari ni sugu" (to thread a needle).

1055 • *Topic unknown.*

negi goto o
sa nomi kikiken
    yashiro koso
hate wa nageki no
mori to naru rame

this holy precinct
where it seems prayers have been
    lavishly answered
will surely become at last
an arbor of repentance

Sanuki

"Nageki" (entreaty) contains the word "ki" (tree). "Arbor of repentance" probably is a reference to the Ebisu Shrine in Aira District of Kagoshima Prefecture.

1056 • *Topic unknown.*

nageki koru	my loud sighs rise as
yama to shi takaku	high as the mountain where
narinureba	woodcutters fell trees
tsurazue nomi zo	as I sit melancholy—
mazu tsukarekeru	holding my head in my hands

Taifu

"Nageki koru" (absorbed in sorrows) includes the phrase "ki koru" (felling trees). "Tsurazue" (head on hands) includes the word "tsue" (staff), which calls mountain climbing to mind.

1057 • *Topic unknown.*

nageki oba	supplication trees
kori nomi tsumite	he fells heaping one upon
ashihiki no	another till they
yama no kainaku	mount and fill the ravine as
narinu beranari	his hopeless sighs multiply

Anonymous

"Nageki oba kori" (given over to sighs) contains the phrase "ki oba kori" (felling trees). "Ashihiki no" is a makurakotoba for "yama" (mountain). "Kai" (ravine; result) is a kakekotoba.

1058 • *Topic unknown.*

hito kouru	his yearning love he
koto o omo ni to	bears like a heavy burden
ninai mote	on his shoulders like
augo naki koso	a porter without a pole—
wabishikarikere	no meeting eases his lot

Anonymous

"Augo" (meeting time; carrying pole) is a kakekotoba.

1059 • *Topic unknown.*

yoi no ma ni	when the three-day moon
idete irinuru	climbs into the dark expanse
mikazuki no	of night sky my heart

warete mono omou   too becomes diminished and
koro ni mo aru kana   shadowed with melancholy

Anonymous

Lines 1–3 (like the three-day moon that comes out into the night) are a jo linked to "warete" (broken).

1060 • *Topic unknown.*

soe ni tote   when I say I'll do
to sureba kakari   this   it turns out that   when I
kaku sureba   say I'll do that   the
ana iishirazu   result is this   what can I
au sa kiru sa ni   say   it's all misunderstanding

Anonymous

1061 • *Topic unknown.*

yo no naka no   if in this sad world
uki tabi goto ni   each time someone met with grief
mi o nageba   he cast himself from
fukaki tani koso   the highest cliff   even deep
asaku nariname   valleys would become shallow

Anonymous

1062 • *Topic unknown.*

yo no naka wa   so many angry
ika ni kurushi to   people bitterly blaming
omou ran   it   how painful it
kokora no hito ni   must be for this sad world of
uramirarureba   ours to see such resentment

Ariwara no Motokata

1063 • *Topic unknown.*

nani o shite   what was I doing
mi no itazura ni   growing old so heedlessly—
oinu ran   no accomplishments—

toshi no omowan   I am embarrassed by what
koto zo yasashiki   my past years must think of me

Anonymous

1064 • *Topic unknown.*

 mi wa sutetsu   I'll abandon my
kokoro o dani mo   body   but I'll not discard
 hōrasaji   this watchful heart
tsui ni wa ikaga   for   in the end   I must know
naru to shiru beku   just what will become of me

Fujiwara no Okikaze

1065 • *Topic unknown.*

 shirayuki no   as steadily as
tomo ni waga mi wa   the white snows of winter fall
 furinuredo   my age has grown   but
kokoro wa kienu   my youthful heart endures while
mono ni zo arikeru   evanescent drifts vanish

Ōe no Chisato

"Furi" (falling; aging) is a kakekotoba. "Furi" (falling) and "kienu" (not vanishing) are engo for "yuki" (snow).

1066 • *Topic unknown.*

 ume no hana   unpalatable
sakite no nochi no   as the sour fruit that forms once
 mi nareba ya   the plum blossoms have
sukimono to nomi   fallen   is this false gossip
hito no iu ran   about my wanderlust

Anonymous

"Mi" (body; fruit) and "sukimono" (sour thing; amorous person) are kakekotoba.

1067 • *Commanded to write a poem on the topic "monkeys howling in the mountain ravine" on the day the tonsured Mikado traveled to the West River.*

 wabishira ni   ah monkeys   do not
mashira na naki so   cry so forlornly   deep in

ashihiki no
yama no kai aru
kyō ni ya wa aranu

the valleys of the
rugged mountains   is there not
some reason to live today

Ōshikōchi no Mitsune

For the tonsured Mikado and this excursion, see 919. "Ashihiki no" is a makura-kotoba for "yama" (mountain). The first three-and-one-half lines (monkeys of the rugged mountains, do not cry so forlornly) are a jo linked to the kakekotoba "kai" (ravine; result).

1068 • *Topic unknown.*

yo o itoi
ko no moto goto ni
tachiyorite
utsubushizome no
asa no kinu nari

this is the hempen
robe   dyed with hollow galls   of
one who rejected
the world   and lies down to rest
at the foot of each tree he sees

Anonymous

"Utsubushizome" (lie prone; dyed by hollow oak galls) functions as a kakekotoba.

BOOK XX

Court Poetry

1069 • *A poem for Great Naobi*

atarashiki	at the beginning
toshi no hajime ni	of this auspicious new year
kakushi koso	we anticipate
chitose o kanete	the joys of a thousand years
tanoshiki o tsume	by piling stacks of firewood

In the Nihongi, *the last two lines are*

tsukaematsurame
yorozu yo made ni

Anonymous

The god Naobi transformed bad events to good; he was said to have been born when Izanagi cleansed himself after returning from the underworld. "Tanoshiki" (enjoyment) contains the word "ki" (tree, wood), a reference to the firewood that was piled in the palace garden during the festival of Naobi. The *Zoku Nihongi* includes the variant lines (in this way we will worship until a thousand years have passed) in a description of a banquet held at the court of Shōmu tennō (r. 724–749) in 742.

1070 • *An old song from the Yamato dances.*

shimo to yū	love is as constant
kazuraki yama ni	as the dense never-ending
furu yuki no	snows that fall upon
ma naku toki naku	Kazuraki Mountain where
omōyuru kana	I bundle kindling with vines

Anonymous

The Yamato dances, which originated in the Yamato area (central Honshū), were performed at the Services for the Dead at court and at worship ceremonies at various shrines. "Shimo to yū" (bundling as kindling) is a makurakotoba for the kakekotoba "kazu" (ivy)/Kazuraki. Kazuraki Mountain is on the border of Ōsaka City and Nara Prefecture. The first three lines (of the snow falling on Kazuraki Mountain where we bind twigs with vines) are a jo linked to "ma naku" (without interval).

1071 • *An Ōmi song.*

ōmi yori	I rose and set out
asa tachikureba	from Ōmi before daybreak—
une no no ni	as cranes cried over
tazu zo naku naru	the meadows of Une the
akenu kono yo wa	long dark night quietly dawned

Anonymous

This and the next two songs, named after words appearing in their first lines, were collected by the Poetry Bureau at court. Une Meadow, now called Gamo Meadow, is in Shiga Prefecture (formerly Ōmi Province).

1072 • *A Mizukuki song.*

mizukuki no	ah the bitter frosts
oka no yakata ni	settling at daybreak as
imo to are to	she and I sleep in
nete no asake no	this temporary hut at
shimo no furi wa mo	Oka of the tender stalks

Anonymous

"Mizukuki no" (of the tender stalks) is a makurakotoba for Oka. Oka (slope) may refer to Ashiya City in Onga District of Fukuoka Prefecture, or it may be a common noun.

1073 • *A Shihatsu Mountain song.*

shihatsu yama	coming from behind
uchiidete mireba	Shihatsu Mountain I see
kasayui no	rowing off to hide
shima kogi kakuru	beyond Kasayui Isle
tana nashi obune	a dory without side rails

Anonymous

The location of Shihatsu Mountain and Kasayui Island have not been determined.

SONGS FOR SHINTŌ CEREMONIES

1074 • *Poems 1074 through 1079 are "torimono" songs.*

kamikaki no	fragrant sakaki
mimuro no yama no	growing luxuriantly
sakakiba wa	encircles the shrine
kami no mimae ni	the sanctuary of the
shigeriainikeri	gods on this holy mountain

Anonymous

This and the next five songs are about objects the dancers hold (torimono)—a sakaki branch, wreathes of leaves, a bow, a gourd dipper. "Mimuro" is a common noun; it refers to any holy mountain where the gods are believed to reside. Sakaki is a fragrant evergreen tree, *Cleyera japonica*.

1075 •

shimo ya tabi	like the hardy leaves
okedo karesenu	of the fragrant sakaki
sakakiba no	which do not wither
tachisakayu beki	under eightfold frosts maids who
kami no kine ka mo	serve the gods remain youthful

Anonymous

"Ya" (eight) is used to mean "numerous." For sakaki, see 1074. Lines 1–3 (like the sakaki leaves, which do not wither although the frost settles on them eight times) are a jo linked to "tachisakayu" (will flourish).

1076 •

makimoku no	bedeck yourselves with
anashi no yama no	wreathes of mountain leaves until
yamahito to	all see you as one
hito mo miru ga ni	who dwells on Mount Anaji
yama kazura seyo	deep within Makimoku

Anonymous

The place names Makimoku (Makimuki) and Anashi remain in Sakurai City in Nara Prefecture.

1077 •

miyama ni wa	surely now the hail
arare furu rashi	is falling deep in the fair

toyama naru
masaki no kazura
irozukinikeri

mountains　for on
nearby slopes　the creeping vines
are tinged with autumn's colors

Anonymous

1078 •

michinoku no
adachi no mayumi
　waga hikaba
sue sae yoriko
shinobi shinobi ni

from Adachi in
far Michinoku comes this
　spindle bow　as its
tips draw together　silently
come to me　now and always

Anonymous

For Michinoku, see 380. Adachi City is in present-day Fukushima Prefecture, Adachi District. It was famous for the manufacture of mayumi (spindle-tree bows). Lines 1 and 2 (spindle bow of Adachi of the Far North) are a jo linked to "waga hikaba" (if I pull; if I invite). "Sue" (tip) and "yori" (approaching) are engo for "yumi" (bow). "Sue" also means "future."

1079 •

waga kado no
itai no shimizu
　sato tōmi
hito shi kumaneba
mikusa oinikeri

so distant from the
village are the pure waters
　of my wooden-walled
well　that none come to dip here
and water grasses flourish

Anonymous

1080 • *A Hirume song.*

sasa no kuma
hinokuma kawa ni
　koma tomete
shibashi mizu kae
kage o dani min

Sasanokuma—
by the Cypress-shade River
　rein in your steed and
let him drink the waters　that
I may gaze after you a while

Hirume is another name for the goddess Amaterasu ōmikami, whom this poem celebrates. Sasa may be a scribal error for Sahi, which appears in *Man'yōshū* 1109 and 3097. "Sasa(hi)no kuma" (pure Sanokuma) is a makurakotoba for Hinokuma (Cypress-shade) River, a small stream that flows through Asuka Village in Nara Prefecture.

1081 • *A "changing" song.*

aoyagi o	twisting slender green
kata ito ni yorite	willow tendrils into floss
uguisu no	the trilling mountain
nū chō kasa wa	thrush weaves a sun hat they say—
ume no hanagasa	delicate plum blossom shade

This is a Saibara song in which the mode changes from minor to major.

1082 •

makane fuku	a sash girt about
kibi no naka yama	Naka Mountain in Kibi
obi ni seru	where they smelt iron—
hoso tanigawa no	how clear the splashing of that
oto no sayakesa	narrow rill that circles it

Anonymous

This is a Kibi Provinces song for the Jōwa Great Thanksgiving festival.

"Makane fuku" (smelting iron) is a makurakotoba for Kibi (the provinces of Bizen, Bitchū, Bingo, and Mimasaka; now Okayama and eastern Hiroshima Prefectures), where iron was mined. Naka Mountain was on the border of Bizen and Bitchū. *Man'yōshū* 1102 is a similar poem about Mount Mikasa. The Great Thanksgiving festival (Daijōsai) was held following the enthronement of a Mikado. Two provinces were selected to contribute new rice for offerings to the gods. The Jōwa festival celebrated the enthronement of Ninmyō; Bitchū was one of the provinces that offered rice.

1083 •

mimasaka ya	in Mimasaka
kume no sara yama	Sara Mountain of Kume
sarasara ni	towers but never
waga na wa tateji	in ten thousand long years will
yorozu yo made ni	I ever let my name rise

Anonymous

This is a Mimasaka Province song for the Great Thanksgiving festival held at Mizunō.

"Mimasaka ya" (in Mimasaka Province) is a makurakotoba for Kume, a city in Okayama Prefecture. Lines 1 and 2 (Sara Mountain in Kume, Mimasaka) are a jo linked by sound to "sarasara ni" (not at all). The Great Thanksgiving festival held at Mizunō, now in Sakyō-ku, Kyōto, celebrated the enthronement of Seiwa.

1084 •

mino o kuni	ceaseless is the flow
seki no fuji kawa	of the Fuji River at
taezu shite	the barrier of
kimi ni tsukaen	Mino I will serve my lord
yorozu yo made ni	until ten thousand years pass

Anonymous

This is a Mino Province song for the Gangyō Great Thanksgiving festival.

Fuji River flows through Gifu Prefecture (Mino Province), near the Fuwa barrier. Lines 1 and 2 (the Fuji River at the barrier in Mino Province) are a jo linked to "taezu" (ceaseless). The Gangyō ceremony celebrated the enthronement of Yōzei.

1085 •

kimi ga yo wa	no number shall be
kagiri mo araji	put to the limitless years
nagahama no	of my lord's life not
masago no kazu wa	even if we count each grain
yomitsukusu tomo	of sand on Nagahama

Anonymous

This is an Ise Province song for the Ninna Great Thanksgiving festival.

Nagahama may refer to the shore in Inabe District of Mie Prefecture (Ise Province). The Ninna Great Thanksgiving festival celebrated the enthronement of Kōkō tennō.

1086 •

ōmi no ya	because in Ōmi
kagami no yama o	a brilliant Mirror
tatetareba	Mountain has been raised
kanete zo miyuru	we can see reflected there
kimi ga chitose wa	the thousand years our lord will live

Anonymous

This is an Ōmi Province song for the Great Thanksgiving festival of the present Mikado.

Ōmi Province is part of modern Shiga Prefecture. For Kagami Mountain, see 899. The "present Mikado" was Daigo.

EASTERN SONGS

1087 • *Poems 1087 to 1093 are songs from the Far North.*

abukuma ni	the mists spread over
kiri tachiwatari	the Abukuma but though
akenu tomo	dawn has come I will
kimi oba yaraji	not send him away for to
mateba sube nashi	have to wait is too painful

The rest of the poems in this book are Azuma uta, songs from the areas east of Ise Province, including Michinoku, the Far North (see 368). Abukuma River flows through Fukushima and Miyazaki Prefectures.

1088 •

michinoku wa	Northern Provinces
izuku wa aredo	lovely wherever you go—
shiogama no	spellbinding are the
ura kogu fune no	men towing the ships which will
tsunade kanashi mo	sail across Shiogama

Anonymous

For Shiogama Bay, see 852.

1089 •

waga seko o	when my beloved
miyako ni yarite	is in the far capital—
shiogama no	on Magaki Isle
magaki no shima no	in Shiogama I wait
matsu zo koishiki	pining 'neath the evergreens

Anonymous

For Shiogama, see 852. Lines 3 and 4 (of Magaki Isle in Shiogama) are a jo linked to the kakekotoba "matsu" (pine; to wait).

1090 •

oguro saki	if those three little
mitsu no kojima no	islands along Oguro

hito naraba
miyako no tsuto ni
iza to iwamashi o

Cape were people   I
would invite them back to the
capital as fond keepsakes

Anonymous

The location of Oguro Cape is unknown.

1091 •

misaburai
mikasa to mōse
  miyagi no no
ko no shita tsuyu wa
ame ni masareri

oh guardsman   remind
your master to wear his hat—
    here on Miyagi
Moor the dewdrops fall from the
trees more heavily than rain

Anonymous

For Miyagi Moor, see 694.

1092 •

mogami gawa
noboreba kudaru
  inabune no
ina ni wa arazu
kono tsuki bakari

as the rice boats ply
the Mogami River   they
    pole upstream and back—
you too should come again   it's
only this month I say "no"

Anonymous

Mogami River flows through central Yamagata Prefecture to empty into the Japan
Sea. Lines 1–3 (of the rice boats that row up and come back down the Mogami
River) are a jo linked to the kakekotoba "ina" (rice; no).

1093 •

kimi o okite
adashi gokoro o
  waga motaba
suenomatsu yama
nami mo koenan

if ever I should
change my mind   and banish you
    from my heart   then would
great ocean waves rise and cross
Suenomatsu Mountain

Anonymous

For Suenomatsu Mountain, see 326.

372

1094 •

koyorogi no	do not splash these young
iso tachinarashi	girls who run upon rocky
isona tsumu	Koyorogi Beach
mezashi nurasu na	gathering the sea bracken
oki ni ore nami	ah waves break in the offing

Anonymous

Sagami Province corresponds to present-day Kanagawa Prefecture. For Koyorogi, see 874.

1095 • *A Hitachi song.*

tsukubane no	on Tsukubane
kono mo kano mo ni	cooling shade is found beneath
kage wa aredo	each and every tree
kimi ga mikage ni	yet nowhere is there shelter
masu kage wa nashi	like the refuge of my lord

Anonymous

Hitachi Province corresponds to present-day Ibaraki Prefecture. For Tsukubane, see 966. "Kage" is used in two senses in this poem: "shade" and "protection, shelter."

1096 • *A Hitachi song.*

tsukubane no	drifting and falling
mine no momijiba	like the bright autumn leaves on
ochitsumori	Tsukubane peak
shiru mo shiranu mo	how pitiful all these men
nabete kanashi no	both those I know and strangers

Anonymous

For Tsukubane, see 966.

1097 • *A Kai song.*

kai ga ne o	how I wish I could
saya ni mo mishi ga	clearly see the mountains of
kekere naku	Kai heartlessly
yoko hori fuseru	it stretches before my eyes
sayanonaka yama	Sayanonaka Mountain

Anonymous

Kai Province, the origin of this and the next song, is now Yamanashi Prefecture. "Kekere" is believed to be the eastern dialectal equivalent of standard Japanese "kokoro" (heart). For Sayanonaka Mountain, see 594.

1098 • *A Kai song.*

kai ga ne o	the blowing wind which
ne koshi yama koshi	crosses the peaks and ridges
fuku kaze o	of Kai Mountain
hito ni mo ga mo ya	if it were but mortal it
kotozute yaran	could become my messenger

Anonymous

1099 • *An Ise song.*

ofu no ura ni	the ripening pears
katae sashi ōi	on the side branches shelter
naru nashi no	us along Ofu
nari mo narazu mo	Bay let us recline and talk
nete katarawan	of our love's maturation

Anonymous

Ise Province is part of present-day Mie Prefecture. The location of Ofu Bay is unclear. Lines 1–3 (the pears ripening and hanging over the water of Ofu Bay) are a jo linked by sound to "nari" (materializing; consummating).

1100 • *A song from the winter Kamo festival.*

chihayaburu	cherished pines before
kamo no yashiro no	the shrine of the awesome gods
hime komatsu	at Kamo surely
yorozu yo fu tomo	their color will never change
iro wa kawaraji	though ten thousand years may pass

Anonymous

The winter Kamo festival was an irregularly held festival celebrated at the Kamo Shrine in the Eleventh Month. It was begun by Uda tennō in 889. "Chihayaburu" is a makurakotoba that modifies the gods or, as here, something related to them (Kamo Shrine).

The following poems were inked out of the so-called Critical Text compiled from various texts to which they had been added.

1101 • *Higurashi (cicada).*

somabito wa	the woodcutters must
miyagi *hiku rashi*	be pulling out the trees for
ashihiki no	the Shrine for in the
yama no yamabiko	rugged mountains echoes sound
yobi to yomu nari	endless as cicadas' cries

Anonymous

This poem came after the "hototogisu" poem (423) and before the "utsusemi" poem (424).

The last eleven poems are poems Fujiwara Teika (Sadaie) (1162–1241) restored to the Shunzei text, copied by his father, Eujiwara Shunzei (Toshinari) (1114–1204). The topic "higurashi" (cicada) is hidden in line 2, "hiku rashi" (it seems they pull). "Ashihiki no" is a makurakotoba for "yama" (mountain).

1102 • *Ogatama no ki (an evergreen).*

kakeritemo	the spirit now soars
nani *o ka tama no*	above why would we ever
kite mo min	hear of its return—
kara wa hono to	for the body it once knew
nari ni shi mono o	has been turned to flying sparks

Anonymous

This poem came after the "ogatama no ki" poem by Tomonori (431).

"Ogatama no ki" (an evergreen tree) is hidden in lines 2 and 3, "nani o ka tama no kite" (why will the spirit return?).

1103 • *Kureno-omo (fennel).*

koshi toki to	at the hour when he
koi tsutsu oreba	used to visit me I long
yūgure no	for him still but now
*omo*kage ni nomi	it is only his image
miewataru kana	that comes to me at twilight

Anonymous

This poem came after the "shinobugusa" poem by Toshisada (446).

The topic kureno-omo (fennel) is hidden in lines 3 and 4, "yūgure no omokage" (image in the evening).

1104 • *Okinoi, Miyakojima.*

okinoite	more painful than the
mi o yaku yori mo	searing touch of flames against
kanashiki wa	my flesh is the great
*miyako shima*be no	distance between this isle and
wakare narikeri	the beloved capital

Anonymous

This poem came after the "karakoto" poem by Kiyoyuki (456).

The topics Okinoi and Miyakojima are place names, but their location is unknown. The topics are hidden in line 1, "okinoite" (flaring up), and line 4, "miyako shimabe" (capital and islands).

1105 • *Somedono, Awata.*

ukime oba	after these painful
yo*so me to no*mi zo	events I'll flee to a place
nogare yuku	where I can put them
kumo no *awa ta*tsu	behind to the skirts of the
yama no fumoto ni	far mountains where dense clouds rise

Anonymous

This poem was composed on the occasion of the Mizuno-o Mikado's moving from the Somedono to Awata. It came after the "katsura no miya" poem (463).

For Somedono, see 52. Awata is part of Sakyō-ku, Kyōto. The Awata-in, the residence of Fujiwara no Mototsune, was located there. Somedono is hidden in line 2, "yoso me to nomi" (only from eyes of others); Awata, in line 4, "awatatsu" (meaning unclear; it may mean "rise thickly")

1106 • *Poems 1106 and 1107 came after the poem "okuyama no suga no ne shinogifuru yuki no" (551).*

kyō hito o	the tumult in my
kouru kokoro wa	heart today yearning for the
ōi gawa	one I hold so dear
nagaruru mizu ni	is no less frenzied than the
otorazarikeri	Ōi River current

Anonymous

For Ōi River, see 312. Ōi is a kakekotoba, also meaning "numerous."

1107 •

wagi mo ko ni	my passion shall stay
ōsaka yama no	hidden as the unopened
shino susuki	buds of plume grasses
ho ni wa idezu mo	on the Ōsaka slopes
koiwataru kana	where I met my beloved

Anonymous

Au (to meet)/Ōsaka (see 374) is a kakekotoba. The first three lines (unopened plume grass of Ōsaka slope where I meet my love) are a jo linked to the kakekotoba "ho ni" (in ears; openly). This poem is nearly the same as *Man'yōshū* 2283; "shino susuki" has replaced "hadasusuki."

1108 • *After the poem "koishiku wa shita ni o omoe murasaki no" (652).*

inugami no	Name-taking River
tokono yama naru	of Tokono Mountain in
natori gawa	Inukami please
ise to kotae yo	answer that you do not know—
waga na morasu na	do not let my name leak out

Anonymous

Some say this poem was sent to a serving maid from Ōmi by a Mikado.

Inugami is in Shiga Prefecture (formerly Ōmi Province). Tokono Mountain is said to be present-day Shōhōji Mountain in Hikone City, Shiga Prefecture. For Natori River, see 628. *Man'yōshū* 2710 is the same poem with Isaya River substituted for Natori River. Other *Kokinshū* texts have Isaya or Isara River. Isaya river flows at the foot of Shōhōji Mountain. The sound is repeated in line 4 of these variant poems, "isa ya" (well then) replacing "ise to".

1109 • *Reply.*

yamashina no	shall my love be known
otowa no taki no	to all by the prattling of
oto ni dani	gossip whispering
hito no shirubeku	echoing like Sound of Wings
waga koime ya mo	Rapids in Yamashina

A serving maid

For Otowa Falls, see 928. This poem is almost the same as 664. It followed 1108 in its position after 652 in the Shunzei text.

1 1 1 0 • *This poem came after the poem "omou chō koto no ha nomi ya aki o hete" (688). When she was alone, Princess Sotōri sent this to the Mikado to tell him of her love.*

waga seko ga	this is the night when
kubeki yoi nari	my beloved will come to me—
sasagani no	already I know
kumo no furu mai	for the spiders are weaving
kanete shirushi mo	the webs that will seize his heart

Princess Sotōri

Princess Sotōri was a Consort (kisai) of Ingyō tennō (412?–453) and sister of Princess Oshisaka no Onaka, who was Ingyō's concubine (kōgō). "Sasagani no" (of the spider[?]) is a makurakotoba for kumo (spider). In both China and Japan it was believed that a spider's weaving a web attached to one's garment was an omen that the one awaited would come.

1 1 1 1 • *This poem came after "koishi to wa ta ga nazukeken iinaran" by the father of Fukayabu (698).*

michi shiraba	if I knew the road
tsumi no mo yukan	I would go there to gather
suminoe no	those grasses of love's
kishi ni ou chō	forgetfulness they tell me
koi wasuregusa	grow on Suminoe's shores

Ki no Tsurayuki

For Suminoe, see 360. For wasuregusa, see 765. This poem is similar to *Man'yōshū* 1147.

MANAJO

THE CHINESE PREFACE

by Ki no Yoshimochi

translated by Leonard Grzanka

Japanese poetry[1] takes root in the soil of one's heart and blossoms forth in the forest of words. While a man is in the world, he cannot be inactive. His thoughts and concerns easily shift, his joy and sorrow change in turn. Emotion is born of intent; song takes shape in words. Therefore, when a person is pleased, his voice is happy, and when frustrated, his sighs are sad. He is able to set forth his feelings to express his indignation. To move heaven and earth, to affect the gods and demons, to transform human relations, or to harmonize husband and wife, there is nothing more suitable than Japanese poetry.

Japanese poetry embodies six principles.[2] The first is the Suasive, the second is Narration, the third is Analogy, the fourth is the principle of Evocative Imagery, the fifth is the principle exemplified in the Elegantia, and the sixth is the principle exemplified in the Eulogies.

It is like an oriole[3] in spring warbling among the flowers, or like a cicada in autumn humming high in a tree. Though they are neither harassed nor disturbed, each one puts forth its song. That all things have a song is a principle of nature.

But in the Seven Generations of the Age of the Gods the times were unsophisticated and people were simple. The realm of emotions was not

---

[1] The two probable models for the opening statement, the *Mao-shih cheng-i* preface and the "Major Preface" to the *Classic of Songs*, both begin simply with the word "poetry." "Japanese poetry" is used here and throughout this preface in a general sense of poetry of all kinds in Japanese as opposed to poetry written by Japanese in Chinese.

[2] For discussion of these principles see Chinese Influences on the *Kokinshū* Prefaces.

[3] The bird mentioned in this passage is the ying, a different bird from the uguisu, the Japanese reading of the character.

distinguished and Japanese poetry had yet to arise.[4] Later, when the god
Susano-o arrived at Izumo, the thirty-one syllable song first appeared.[5] This
was the creation of the modern hanka.[6] After this, though it be the Grandson
of the Heavenly Gods, or the Daughter of the God of the Sea, no one would
convey what he felt without using Japanese poetry.[7]

Later, in the Age of Man, this practice flourished tremendously.[8] With
such types as the chōka, tanka, the sedōka, and konpon, the diverse forms
were of more than one kind, and the lines of development gradually grew
profuse.[9] This is like a cloud-scraping tree which grew out of a fog of one-

[4] The chronological framework of Yoshimochi's literary history of waka follows events
portrayed in the official histories, the *Nihon shoki* and the *Kojiki* (see W. B. Aston, *Nihongi:
Chronicles of Japan from the Earliest Times to AD 697* [New York: Paragon, 1956], pp. 7–9, and
D. L. Philippi, *Kojiki* [Princeton: Princeton University Press, 1969], p. 48), and the conflicting,
problematical statement accords well in both meaning and Taoist overtones with the opening
statement of the preface to the *Kojiki*: "When the primeval matter had congealed but breath and
form had not yet appeared, there were no names and no action."

[5] The poem appears as the first song in both the *Nihon shoki* (an interlinear note) and *Kojiki*. It
is admittedly old, but due to structural considerations many songs in both works appear older.

[6] The poem is not a hanka in the standard sense of the term, an envoy in tanka form appended
to the body of a long poem (chōka). The tanka is referred to in the following section within a list
of genres which Yoshimochi, erroneously applying to the Japanese tradition a Chinese concept
of development of forms from one or two predecessors, states to have developed later than the
hanka. Perhaps in this section Yoshimochi is referring to the hanka as an early, primitive form
out of which later forms developed.

[7] This alludes to the story of the Grandson of the Heavenly Gods, Hiko-hoho-demi no
Mikoto, and the Daughter of the God of the Sea, Toyo-tama-hime, which is found in both the
Nihon shoki and the *Kojiki*. After their marriage Toyo-tama-hime warned Hiko-hoho-demi not
to look at her during chidbirth. He disregarded her warning and watched her transform into a
sea-creature and became frightened and fled. She was angered by his actions and returned to
the sea. The exchange of poems differs in the two books, but for the purposes of this allusion, it is
important that in both versions they communicate in poetry. See Aston, *Nihongi*, pp. 104–8,
and Philippi, *Kojiki*, pp. 156–158.

[8] It is interesting to note how closely the preface follows the chronology of the official
histories. The last allusion was to the episode of the Grandson of the Heavenly Gods and the
Daughter of the God of the Sea, which is the final episode of "The Age of the Gods" in both the
Nihon shoki and *Kojiki*. This next section opens with "The Age of Man," alluding to the
beginning of the next major section of the histories, the reign of Jimmu tennō and the later
sovereigns.

[9] Yoshimochi states that the forms of poetry increased as the practice of writing it flourished.
Hisamatsu Sen'ichi, in *Nihon bungaku hyōron shi* (Tōkyō: Shibundō, 1970), pp. 40–56, has
shown convincingly that the process was not one of expansion into several forms, but rather a
consolidation of the various forms found in the *Man'yōshū* into the tanka as dominant form in
the *Kokinshū* period. This consolidation was so thorough that there is controversy over the exact
structure of one of the forms Yoshimochi proposes to have evolved from the hanka, the
konpon. This is the first appearance of this term in Japanese literature. That it is a poetic form is
obvious from context, but what it actually refers to is uncertain. Among the various theories

inch sprouts, or like a wave cresting into the sky which arose from a single drop of dew.

Later, as in the eulogy "naniwazu," which was offered up to the sovereign [Nintoku], or the poem "tominōgawa" in requital of the Crown Prince [Shōtoku Taishi], either the circumstances concern the miraculous, or the inspiration delves into the abstruse.[10] But if we consider the poems of high antiquity, most maintain antique simplicity. They had yet to become amusements of the eye and ear, serving only as sources of moral edification.[11]

On each fine day of a beautiful season, the sovereigns of antiquity would summon their ministers and have the officials taking part in the banquet offer up Japanese poetry. The feelings between sovereign and subject could be seen by this, and the qualities of virtue and stupidity were then distinguished one from the other. This is how one may accord with the desires of the people, and select talent from among the courtiers.

Since the time when Prince Ōtsu[12] introduced the composition of the

---

presented are (1) that it is a six-line form either the same as or similar to the sedōka; (2) that it is a four-line form in the meter 5/7/5/7; or (3) that it is a katauta or "half-poem." Here again it would seem that Yoshimochi is following a Chinese model that does not correspond to the Japanese tradition: this was the concept in Chinese poetics that certain later poetic forms evolved from the four-syllable-line meter found in the *Classic of Songs*.

[10] Just as the previous portion of the preface dealt with the development of poetic forms, this following section deals with the development of content. As the forms proliferated, the content became more varied and complex. For the "naniwazu" poem, see The Japanese Preface. The story alluded to in the reference to the "tominōgawa" poem is found in the *Nihon shoki* (Aston, *Nihongi*, II, pp. 144–145) without the poem, and the story with the poem may be found in the *Nihon ryōiki* (compiled ca. 787) or as the headnotes and last two poems (1350–51) of the *Shūishū*. The story is an encomium of the Prince Regent, who gave his cloak to a sick beggar by the roadside, yet did not hesitate to don it again later when it was found hanging from a branch. When the beggar died, he left this poem at the door of the tomb built for him by the Prince Regent:

Only when the Tominogawa
In Ikaruga runs dry
Only then could the name
Of my lord be forgotten.

The term translated here as "abstruse" is the first appearance of the word "yūgen" in Japanese literary criticism or aesthetics (Ozawa, *Kokinwakashū*, p. 415, n. 14).

[11] The statement should not be construed as pejorative. In the Chinese tradition flamboyant verse was frowned upon and didactic writing was prized.

[12] Prince Ōtsu was the third son of Tenmu tennō, the fortieth sovereign. Actually it was Kōbun tennō, whose poems are found first in the *Kaifūsō*, who chronologically may have composed the first Chinese poems, and who is traditionally considered to be the first to compose Chinese verse in Japan.

lyric and rhyme-prose,[13] poets and men of ability admired this practice and followed in his wake. They imported the writing of China and transformed the customs of Japan. The ways of the people were changed entirely, and Japanese poetry gradually declined. Yet we still had the Illustrious Master Kakinomoto,[14] who exalted thoughts of the miraculous and who was unrivaled between ancient and modern times. (There was Yamabe no Akahito,[15] who was also an immortal of poetry.)[16] The remaining composers of Japanese poetry continued uninterrupted.

Then when the times shifted into decline and men revered the lustful, frivolous words arose like clouds, and a current of ostentatiousness bubbled up like a spring.[17] The fruit had all fallen and only the flower bloomed. Later the licentious used poetry as the messenger of flowers and birds,[18] and beggarly guests used it as a means of existence. Because of this, it became half the handmaid of women and was embrassing to present before gentlemen.

In modern times there were only two or three persons who maintained the practices of old.[19] But their strengths and weaknesses were not the same, and they will be discussed so that these may be distinguished. The High Priest of Buddhism from Kazan[20] is especially proficient in poetic form,[21] but his

[13] Shih and fu.

[14] "Illustrious" translates "taifu," which may refer to those of the Fifth Rank or, as here, be a general term of respect.

[15] Yamabe no Akahito (d. 736?) was a great poet of the *Man'yōshū* period.

[16] This passage seems to be an interpolated commentary that found its way into the text. Three of the manuscripts collated by Kyūsojin Hitaka (*Kokinwakashū seiritsuron*. Tōkyō: Kazama shobō, 1950) have the phrase as a commentary outside the main body of the text, and two of these also set off a later phrase which has been found to be an interpolated commentary. However, the corresponding passage in the kanajo also contains the reference to Akahito.

[17] Through its reference to Hitomaro and Akahito we may place the previous section in the *Man'yōshū* period. The next section may be said to discuss the state of poetry from after the *Man'yōshū* period to slightly before *Kokinshū* times.

[18] The term "messenger of flowers and birds" was used during the K'ai yüan reign period of the T'ang dynasty in China (713–741) to refer to the envoy dispatched yearly to select beauties across the empire for service as consorts of the Emperor. Later the term came to designate, as it does here, a go-between or messenger of love. (Morohashi Tetsuji, *Dai Kan-Wa jiten* [Tōkyō: Daishūkan shoten, 1955–1959], 9/30734:394.)

[19] Yoshimochi brings his history of Japanese verse to the period just prior to his time with a discussion and evaluation of six modern poets. Here again the influence of models in the Chinese tradition of poetic criticism may be found, but Ozawa Masao ("*Kokinshū* jo to *Shihin*" in *Heian bungaku kenkyū*, vol. 19 [Dec. 1958], pp. 12–13) feels that the concepts in the criticism are indigenous and based on the intellectual climate of the time in Japan. Nevertheless, the criticism seems too comprehensive and systematic to have appeared without prior development.

[20] Sōjō Henjō (816–890).

[21] It appears that "form" refers to so intangible a quality as the "decorum" of the poem, or how well it conformed to Heian sensibilities and tastes.

expression is flowery[22] and has little substance.[23] This is like a picture painted of a beautiful woman which arouses the feelings of man in vain. In the poetry of Middle Counselor Ariwara[24] there exists an abundance of feeling but the expression is insufficient. This is like a withered flower which, though it has little color, still retains a sweet fragrance. Bunrin[25] is skillful at poems composed on set topics but his form approaches the vulgar. This is like a peddler dressed in elegant robes. With the Buddhist priest Kisen[26] from Mount Uji the expression is beautiful and florid, but there is a torpid quality in the overall sense of his poetry. The poetry of Ono no Komachi[27] is of the school of Princess Sotōri of antiquity, but it is seductive and spiritless. This is like a sick woman wearing cosmetics. The poetry of Ōtomo no Kuronushi[28] follows that of the Illustrious Sarumaru. Many of his poems rise above the mundane but the form is extremely rustic. This is like a field hand resting before flowers.

The others with names of wide repute could not possibly be numbered. The majority of them all consider sensuousness to be essential, but they do

[22] In Chinese criticism, the term "flowery" is usually applied as a pejorative to extravagent, lush imagery, and it has appeared previously in the preface as a pejorative in the phrase "the fruit [substance of the poem] had all fallen and only the flower [outward display] bloomed." This may imply that Henjō attempts to dazzle us with his virtuosity without paying heed to content.

[23] The "lack of substance" in the poetry may refer to the lack of reality or truth due to the frequent use of hyperbole.

[24] Ariwara no Narihira (825–880). The phrase "abundance of feeling" would appear to refer to the highly subjective nature of his poetry and the frequent use of subjective, emotional diction and verb aspects. His most frequent themes, unrequited love and the ephemerality of life, add to the subjective, highly emotional character of his poetry. The criticism of his expression as "insufficient" may suggest that many of his poems are misleading or unintelligible without explanatory headnotes. Being overly emotional or being too sparse in diction at first glance appear to be derogatory notices. Yet the metaphor applied to his poetry can be seen as complimentary. Yoshimochi may be showing that even though Narihira approached the art in an unconventional manner, his poetry succeeds.

[25] Fun'ya no Yasuhide (fl. ca. 870) is here referred to in Chinese fashion: Bun is an abbreviation of his family name and Rin is his style, or literary name. To say that one is "skillful" is pejorative in the Chinese tradition, and to say that his form "approaches the vulgar" is not mild. The lesson to be learned here may be to avoid artificiality and to vary the style of your compositions lest you become overly mechanical.

[26] The only poem by Kisen in the Kokinshū is XVIII, 983, in which Kisen makes three related statements which, although having a slight charm in their wordplay, seem to be three false starts and the game is over.

[27] To say that Komachi (fl. ca. 850) is in the stream of Sotōri (a legendary beauty and wife of Ingyō tennō) suggests that she is writing sensual poetry. The statement that she "lacks power," while not the highest of praise, may be taken as an expression of admiration in a culture in which helplessness and fragility exhibited in a framework of sensuality were appreciated.

[28] Ōtomo no Kuronushi (fl. ca. 860) has only three poems in the Kokinshū. Little is known of Sarumaru, to whom he is said to show similarities.

383

not recognize the soul of Japanese poetry. The vulgar contend for profit and fame, and have no need to compose Japanese poetry. How sad! How sad! Although one may be honored by being both a minister and general, and though his wealth may be a bounty of gold and coin, still, before his bones can rot in the dirt, his fame has already disappeared from the world. Only composers of Japanese poetry are recognized by posterity. Why is this? When their words approach men's ears, the meaning conveys[29] their spirit.[30]

In former times Heizei tennō summoned his ministers and commissioned the compilation of the *Man'yōshū*.[31] From that time up to the present, we have spanned ten reign periods and have numbered more than one hundred years. In that time Japanese poetry was discarded and was not compiled. Even if their works were as elegant as those of the Minister Ono,[32] or as refined[33] as those of the Counselor Ariwara,[34] they were all noted for other talents[35] and it was not because of this path that they gained fame.

(Prostrating myself before you, I solemnly consider that)[36] In the nine years up to the present in which Your Majesty[37] has ruled the world, your benevolence has flowed outside the Region of Harvests[38] and your kindness has flourished overshadowing Mount Tsukuba.[39] The lament of the abyss

[29] The variant "t'ung" has been translated here, instead of "kuan," which is the character in the text.

[30] The translation of 神明 as "spirit" follows Morohashi 8/24673 : 507 (#2). There are other interpretations; Bonneau, Kubota, and Ozawa take the phrase as "conveying the will of the gods." The translator feels the sentence is explaining why "only composers of Japanese verse are recognized by posterity": when a poet's words are heard, they convey the spirit of the man to the hearer.

[31] In this section Yoshimochi attempts to create a historical precedent for the rulers' patronage of Japanese verse. There is no evidence this legend is true.

[32] Ono no Takamura (802–852) was exiled because he refused to go as an envoy to T'ang China.

[33] The translation follows Kubota and Ozawa in reading the variant "refined" instead of the "frivolous emotions" of the text.

[34] Ariwara no Yukihira (818–893), brother of Narihira.

[35] That is, the composition of Chinese verse.

[36] These words are found in many manuscripts, but the phrase may have been added by later scribes. This is the beginning of the final major division of the preface, the statement of formal presentation, including a statement of praise of the sovereign, the description of the receipt of the sovereign's commission and the compilation process, and the statement disclaiming any ability on the part of the compilers.

[37] Daigo tennō.

[38] Akitsushima is an ancient name for Japan, which also became a makurakotoba for Yamato, another name for Japan. There are four orthographies and a variety of interpretations of the term; this translation follows Aston.

[39] A reference to *Kokinshū* XX, 1095.

changing into shallows[40] is silent, no longer spoken,[41] and the eulogy of a pebble growing into a rock[42] swells up and fills the ears.

Your Majesty considered continuing the practice which had been abandoned and desired to resurrect the path which had been discontinued for so long. Therefore, Your Majesty commissioned Senior Private Secretary Ki no Tomonori, Chief of the Documents Section Ki no Tsurayuki, Former Junior Clerk for the Province of Kai Ōshikochi no Mitsune, and Lieutenant of the Headquarters of the Outer Palace Guards, Right Division, Mibu no Tadamine, and had each offer up his private collection of poetry together with poems from antiquity. (This was called the *Man'yōshū Continued*.)[43] They were further ordered to classify and arrange the poems that they had presented. These were arranged in twenty scrolls and named *The Collection of Ancient and Modern Japanese Poetry*.[44]

These words of your humble servants have less luster than the flowers of spring, and their fame is shallower[45] than the length of an autumn night. Need we say how we come forward fearing the ridicule of the world, and retire ashamed of our lack of talent? If there should happen to be a revival of Japanese poetry, we would delight in the resurrection of our path. Alas! Hitomaro has died! But is not the art of Japanese poetry contained here?

On the fifteenth day of the Fourth Month of the Fifth Year of the Engi Reign Period,[46] the year-star[47] lodging in the sign of Younger Wood and Ox, your servant Tsurayuki[48] and others humbly offer up this preface.

---

[40] *Kokinshū* XVIII, 933.

[41] This is a slight deviation from the original, which may be rendered literally as "quiet and still, mouths are closed."

[42] *Kokinshū* VII, 343.

[43] *Shoku Man'yōshū*. Kyūsojin Hitaka states that this is an interpolation (*Kokinwakashū seiritsuron* [Tōkyō: Kazama shobō, 1950], vol. 1, p. 260).

[44] *Kokinwakashū*.

[45] The usual sense of this verb is "to steal" and the traditional interpretation of this passage is "though their fame has stolen the length of an autumn night," but the word is also used to mean "shallow" (Morohashi 8/25713) and the latter meaning has been chosen here.

[46] May 21, 905.

[47] Jupiter.

[48] Although this sounds as if Tsurayuki wrote the preface, "the last words of the Chinese preface cannot be taken to disprove Yoshimochi's authorship: Tsurayuki's name was formally used as that of the main compiler of the anthology ..." (E. B. Ceadel, "The Two Prefaces of the Kokinshu," *Asia Major*, N.S. 7 [1959], pp. 40–51).

CHINESE INFLUENCES ON
THE *KOKINSHŪ* PREFACES

by John Timothy Wixted

In what respects is early Japanese critical theory dependent on Chinese models?[1] Considerable light can be thrown on Japanese literature—at least the Japanese poetic tradition—by delving into this question. Chinese critical theory was adopted by early Japanese critics in such a way that the expressive function of literature was stressed. Chinese critical discourse, sometimes in truncated form, was used to give intellectual legitimization to the unprecedented undertaking of an anthology of poetry in Japanese being compiled by imperial commission. At the same time, much of the critical vocabulary used to characterize Japanese poets, unlike the theory that was propounded, was decidedly non-Chinese in cast.

This essay will discuss the two prefaces to the *Kokinshū* (completed between A.D. 905 and 917),[2] the one in Chinese, the manajo, attributed to Ki no Yoshimochi, the other in Japanese, the kanajo, by Ki no Tsurayuki. In examining the Chinese sources for and influences on these prefaces, one must look to the corpus of Chinese critical opinion familiar to a ninth-century Japanese educated in Chinese. Such works would include the following:

---

[1] The text of this chapter is a shortened version of an article by the author entitled "The *Kokinshū* Prefaces: Another Perspective," *Harvard Journal of Asiatic Studies* 43.1 (June 1983), pp. 215–38. Please consult that article for considerably fuller bibliographical citation of relevant secondary scholarship, especially Western-language articles, on the texts and themes treated in this chapter.

Discussion of critical theory here follows the terminology devised by M. H. Abrams to distinguish orientations of literary theory. The expressive, pragmatic, mimetic, and objective refer respectively to theories concerned with the artist, the audience, the subject (or universe), and the work itself; see *The Mirror and the Lamp: Romantic Theory and the Critical Tradition* (1953; rpt. London, Oxford, New York, 1976), pp. 3–29. (The didactic, although subsumed under the pragmatic, is noted so as to stress that area of pragmatic concern.)

[2] See discussion in the Introduction.

The "Major Preface" to the *Book of Songs*, formerly attributed to Pu Shang, but in
   more likelihood written by Wei Hung in the first century A.D.
The "Essay on Literature" written by Ts'ao P'i early in the third century
The "Rhymeprose on Literature" by Lu Chi, composed nearly a century later
And a series of works composed in the first half of the sixth century:
Poetry Gradings by Chung Hung. Its three prefaces offer comments on literary theory
   and outline the history of Chinese poetry; the body contains characterizations and
   evaluations of more than 120 earlier poets, ranking them according to categories
   roughly equivalent to A, A−/B+, and B gradings.
The preface to the *Wen hsüan*, or *Literary Selections*, by Hsiao T'ung. It is clear that this
   anthology was popular in Japan. It contains all the above-mentioned works on
   criticism, except *Poetry Gradings*.
The preface to the *New Songs from the Tower of Jade*, written by Hsü Ling.

One is tempted to add to this list the greatest work of Chinese criticism,
one also written in the sixth century, the *Wen-hsin tiao-lung*, or *The Heart of
Literature: Elaborations*, by Liu Hsieh.[3] However, that work seems to have
been overlooked in Japan, just as it was in China for over eight hundred
years, even though short passages from it do appear in the *Bunkyō hifuron* (A
Literary Mirror: Discussions of Its Secret Store) by Kūkai (774–835).

Critical concepts introduced in the *Kokinshū* prefaces become clearer
when explicated in terms of antecedent Chinese models. The Chinese
preface opens as follows:

Japanese poetry takes root in the soil of one's heart, and blossoms forth in the forest of
words. While a man is in the world, he cannot be inactive. His thoughts and concerns
easily shift, his joy and sorrow change in turn. Emotion is born of intent; song takes
shape in words. Therefore, when a person is pleased, his voice is happy, and when
frustrated, his sighs are sad. He is able to set forth his feelings to express his
indignation. To move heaven and earth, to affect the gods and demons, to transform
human relations, or to harmonize husband and wife, there is nothing more suitable
than Japanese poetry[4]

Poetry is said to find its origin in the heart. The source for this statement is
the "Record of Music" chapter of the *Book of Rites*:

Emotion stirs within, then takes form in sound.... Poetry gives words to one's
intent. Songs give music to one's voice. Dance gives movement to one's manner, and
all three originate from the heart.[5]

In the "Major Preface" to the *Book of Songs*, poetry is described in similar
terms:

[3] This work may be more familiar by its translated title, *The Literary Mind and the Carving of
Dragons* (Vincent Yu-cheng Shih, tr.), New York 1959.

[4] This and other citations from the Chinese preface to the *Kokinshū* are from the translation
by Leonard Grzanka.

[5] Unpublished translation by Donald Gibbs (cited with permission here and elsewhere in this
chapter).

Poetry is the outcome of intent. In the mind it is intent; expressed in words, it becomes poetry. Emotion stirs within and forms into words. As the words are inadequate, one sighs them. As the sighing is inadequate, one sings it aloud. As the singing is inadequate, without knowing it, the hands start to dance, and the feet beat in time.[6]

The Chinese preface to the *Kokinshū* combines elements that are pragmatic (poetry can move heaven and earth, affect gods and demons, transform human relations, and harmonize husband and wife), as well as expressive (the poet sets forth his feelings and expresses his excitement). What is stated as simple fact by Ki no Yoshimochi concerning the pragmatic end of literature is presented in a more carefully argued form in the "Major Preface" to the *Book of Songs*. There, as noted above, emotion is said to be expressed in sound: in sighing, humming, and the dancing of hands and feet. Wei Hung develops his argument from this point:

When sounds are accomplished with artistry, they become a theme. The theme heard in a well-ordered time is one of contentment, whereby joy is expressed at the government being in harmony. The theme heard in a disordered time is one of resentment.... The theme heard in a state of ruin is mournful.... Therefore, to give proper recognition to success and failure, to move the powers of Heaven and Earth, to promote responses amongst ghosts and supernatural spirits, there is nothing like poetry.[7]

Here the implication is that a poet responding to external stimuli cannot but reflect those stimuli; he cannot but reflect the environment in his poetry. (It was for this reason that the *Book of Songs* is said to have been collected, as a record or mirroring of the feelings and concerns of the people.) A good environment produces songs of contentment, just as elsewhere in early Chinese critical theory it is stated that the music of a disordered state expresses disaffection and anger.

The further implication, unstated in the "Major Preface," but found in the *Book of Changes*, and beautifully elaborated in the opening chapter of *The Heart of Literature: Elaborations*, "On Tracing the Tao," is that patterned words, i.e. poetry or literature, are a manifestation or correlate of a cosmic Tao (or Way), a correlate that acts in sympathetic harmony, or mutual resonance, with the cosmos. Hence the "Major Preface" states there is nothing like poetry to give proper recognition to success and failure, to move the powers of heaven and earth, and to promote responses among ghosts and supernatural spirits.

[6] Translation by Donald Gibbs, "M. H. Abrams' Four Artistic Co-ordinates Applied to Literary Theory in Early China," *Comparative Literature Today: Theory and Practice*, Proceedings of the 7th Congress of the International Comparative Literature Association, Montreal and Ottawa, 1973 (Budapest, 1979), p. 678 (with modifications).

[7] Translation by Donald Gibbs, "M. H. Abrams' Four Artistic Co-ordinates," p. 678.

Chung Hung in the opening section of *Poetry Gradings* presents a similar formula:

Life-breath (ch'i) moves the external world, and the external world moves us. Our sensibilities, once stirred, manifest themselves in dance and song. This manifestation illumines heaven, earth, and man and makes resplendent the whole of creation.

That is to say, poetry, the extension of song and dance, is a cosmic correlate that reflects and adumbrates the manifold glory of the cosmos.

Heavenly and earthly spirits depend on it to receive oblation, and ghosts of darkness depend on it for secular reports.

Poetry is said to be an instrument whereby man communes with his two complements in the universe, heaven and earth. He does this by deferentially reflecting their manifold interworkings in his poetry; in so doing, he communicates with the supernatural, just as in the "Great Preface" eulogies are said to be a "means whereby successes are reported to supernatural intelligences."[8] To this, Chung Hung then adds:

For moving heaven and earth and for stirring ghosts and spirits, there is nothing better than poetry.[9]

Heaven and earth, and the spirits, each in turn, react to literary patternings in sympathetic harmony.

These sources—the "Record of Music," the "Major Preface," the *Book of Changes*, and *Poetry Gradings*—form the background to Ki no Yoshimochi's statement:

To move heaven and earth, to affect the gods and demons, to transform human relations, or to harmonize husband and wife, there is nothing more suitable than Japanese verse.

Interestingly enough, of the functions of poetry that he enumerates, the latter pair, the transforming of human relationships and the harmonizing of husband and wife, are more indebted to the didactic/pragmatic attitude toward literature found in Confucius' *Analects* than to the "Major Preface." Ki no Tsurayuki in his kana version of the preface adds an interesting twist to the formula:

It is poetry which, without effort, moves heaven and earth, stirs the feelings of the invisible gods and spirits, smooths the relations of men and women, and calms the hearts of fierce warriors.[10]

[8] Unpublished translation by Donald Gibbs.

[9] Ch'en Yen-chieh, *Shih-p'in chu* (1927; rpts. Peking, 1958, Taipei, 1960), p. 1.

[10] This and other citations from The Japanese Preface are from the translation by Laurel Rasplica Rodd.

The concept that poetry is able to calm fierce warriors' hearts, one might add, is quite un-Chinese.

E. B. Ceadel argues the Chinese preface to the *Kokinshū* was written before and served as the basis for the Japanese preface.[11] Pointing to several passages from Chinese critical sources that appear in the *Kokinshū* prefaces, with but slight modification in the Chinese version and with greater change in the Japanese text, he argues that Tsurayuki wrote the kana version by modifying the manajo text (the latter being the mediator of Chinese critical principles). This view is open to question. Tsurayuki himself wrote a Chinese preface of his own to the *Shinsen wakashū* (*An Anthology of Japanese Poems, Newly Selected*). Although he was not the master in the writing of Chinese prose that Yoshimochi was, it is likely they were both familiar with the same Chinese sources. Moreover, there is one passage in particular that appears in the Japanese preface to the *Kokinshū* (with no counterpart in the Chinese preface) and seems clearly indebted to a Chinese model. I refer to the listing (virtually a litany, in a nonreligious sense) of circumstances under which the anthology's poets are said to have expressed themselves; the opening paragraph in the following passage from the kanajo has its equivalent in the manajo,[12] but not the listing that follows:

> Whenever there were blossoms at dawn in spring or moonlit autumn nights, the generations of sovereigns of old summoned their attendants to compose poetry inspired by these beauties. Sometimes the poet wandered through untraveled places to use the image of the blossoms; sometimes he went to dark unknown wilderness lands to write of the moon. The sovereigns surely read these and distinguished the wise from the foolish.
>
> Not only at such times, but on other occasions as well:
>
> the poet might make comparison to pebbles
> or appeal to his lord by referring to Tsukuba Mountain;
> joy overflowing, his heart might be filled with delight;
> he could compare his smoldering love to the smoke rising from Fuji,
> turn his thoughts to friends when he heard the voice of the pining cricket,
> think of the pine trees of Takasago and Suminoe as having grown up with
>   him,
> recall the olden days of Otoko Mountain,
> or protest the swift passage of the maiden flowers' beauty;
> seeing the blossoms fall on a spring morn, hearing the leaves fall on an autumn
>   evening, he sighed to see the drifts of snow and ripples in the mirror increase
>   with each passing year;
> he was startled to realize the brevity of his life when he saw the dew on the
>   grass or the foam on the waters;
> he who yesterday had prospered lost his influence;

[11] "The Two Prefaces to the Kokinshū," *Asia Major* N.S. 7 (1959), pp. 40–51.
[12] Cf. The Chinese Preface.

falling in the world, he became estranged from those he had loved;
he might invoke the waves on Matsuyama,
dip water from the meadow spring,
gaze upon the underleaves of the autumn bush clover,
count the flutterings of the wings of the snipe at dawn,
or bemoan the sad lengths of the black bamboo;
alluding to the Yoshino River, he complained of the ways of the world of love;
or he might hear that there was no smoke rising from Mount Fuji
or that the Nagara Bridge had been rebuilt—

At such times, it was only through poetry that his heart was soothed.

Each of the circumstances mentioned above refers to a specific poem or group of poems in the *Kokinshū*.[13] There is no such listing by Yoshimochi in the Chinese preface.

Chung Hung in *Poetry Gradings*, after making a somewhat different prefatory statement, had provided a similar listing of circumstances prompting poetic expression:

Vernal breezes and springtime birds, the autumn moon and cicadas in the fall, summer clouds and sultry rains, the winter moon and fierce cold—these are what in the four seasons inspire poetic feeling. At an agreeable banquet, through poetry one can make friendship dearer. When parting, one can put one's chagrin into verse.

When a Ch'u official is banished;
When a Han consort must leave the palace;
When white bones are strewn across the northern plain,
    And souls go chasing tumbleweed;
When arms are borne in frontier camps,
    And a savage spirit overflows the border;
When the frontier traveler has but thin clothing,
    And in the widow's chambers all tears are spent;
When, divested of the ornaments of office, one leaves the court,
    Gone, no thought of return;
When by raising an eyebrow a woman wins imperial favor,
    And with a second glance topples the state—

These situations all stir the heart and move the soul. If not expressed in poetry, how can such sentiments be presented? If not expanded in song, how can these emotions be vented?[14]

Although Chung Hung's work was not an anthology, each of the situations he describes, beginning with "When a Ch'u official is banished," refers to a specific poet or group of poems that he treats in his critical scheme.[15] What

[13] For references, see footnotes to The Japanese Preface.

[14] *Shih-p'in chu*, pp. 4–5.

[15] For the putative poets being referred to here, see this passage as quoted by J. T. Wixted, "The Nature of Evaluation in the *Shih-p'in* (Gradings of Poets) by Chung Hung (A.D. 469–518)," in *Theories of the Arts in China*, ed. Susan Bush and Christian Murck (Princeton, 1983), sect. IV.

makes this so unmistakably the source of Tsurayuki's list is the latter's tag at the end: "At such times, it was only through poetry that his heart was soothed." He speaks of the same expressive catharsis referred to by Chung Hung at the end of his listing.

Both *Kokinshū* prefaces contain an important passage from the "Major Preface" to the *Book of Songs* which is incomprehensible without discussion of early Chinese critical theory. The excerpt is only slightly reworded in the Japanese preface (with sample poems appended), while being cited virtually verbatim in the Chinese preface:

Japanese verse embodies six principles. The first is the Suasive (feng 風) [principle of the Airs (feng) (of the States) section of the *Book of Songs*], the second is Description (fu 賦), the third is Comparison (pi 比), the fourth is Evocative Image (hsing 興), and the fifth and sixth are the principles exemplified in the Elegantia (ya 雅) and Eulogies (sung 頌) [sections of the *Book of Songs*].

Of the six terms, three refer to aspects or principles of poetry. Hsing, pi, and fu—Evocative Image, Comparison, and Description—are best thought of as specifying three rhetorical modes. Chung Hung in his work expounds succinctly on them:

Poetry has three aspects: Evocative Image (hsing), Comparison (pi), and Description (fu). When meaning lingers on, though writing has come to an end, this is an Evocative Image. When an object is used to express a sentiment, this is Comparison. And when affairs are recorded directly, the objective world being put into words, this is Description. If one expands these three aspects and uses them judiciously, backing them up with lively force and lending them beauty of coloration so that those who read from one's work find it inexhaustible and those who hear it are moved, this is the perfect poetry.

If only Comparison and Evocative Image are used, writing will suffer from density of thought; and when ideas are dense, expression stumbles. If only Description is employed, writing will suffer from superficiality; and when thought is superficial, language becomes diffuse. Further, if one carelessly drifts back and forth among these, his writing will be without anchoring and will suffer from prolixity.[16]

The other three terms—feng, ya, and sung, here translated as the Suasive principle of the "Airs of the States" section and the principles exemplified in the "Elegantia" and "Eulogies" of the *Book of Songs*—had a different import before the writing of the "Major Preface" and are sometimes understood differently by later Chinese critics as well. As they appear in their earliest usage, in the *Rites of Chou*,[17] these terms refer to music, where they differentiate melodic tempos, and by extension, poetic rhythms.[18] In the

---

[16] *Shih-p'in chu*, p. 4.

[17] *Chou li* (Shih-san-ching chu-su ed. [Nanchang, 1815; rpt. Taipei, n.d.]) 23.13a & 18b.

[18] C. H. Wang, *The Bell and the Drum: Shih Ching as Formulaic Poetry in an Oral Tradition* (Berkeley, Los Angeles, London, 1974), p. 3.

"Major Preface," however, they are used to stress primarily the pragmatic, and secondarily the mimetic, functions of literature. The aim of the Suasive is oblique criticism: "the one who speaks out does so without incriminating himself, and the one who is criticized hears enough to be warned." The Elegantia songs serve the mimetic and didactic purposes of "tell[ing] of the causes for the decay or the rise of the Royal Government." And the Eulogies are also mimetic and pragmatic, for they "are descriptions of flourishing virtue and are the means whereby successes are reported to supernatural intelligences."[19]

If these latter three terms are taken in their original sense of melodic tempos and hence poetic rhythms, all six terms form a nuclear technical vocabulary for poetry—one according with a technical orientation that is objective (or work oriented). Three of the terms, in any case, are so oriented. Alternatively, the other three can be seen to serve more pragmatic/didactic ends—a view which is to be preferred, for that is the way they were traditionally understood.

An attempt at the application of these critical terms was made by Yoshimochi and Tsurayuki. Variously interpreted and inconsistently applied by Chinese commentators to the *Book of Songs*, the terms had become a formula which, being sacrosanct, was invoked for the purposes of legitimizing one's stand. Yoshimochi and Tsurayuki employed them in much the same way.

There is another theme in the *Kokinshū* prefaces that deserves attention because of its Chinese model: the view that it is literature that brings one immortality. As Yoshimochi writes:

The vulgar contend for profit and fame, and have no need to compose Japanese poetry. How sad! How sad! Although one may be honored by being both a minister and general, and though his wealth may be a bounty of gold and coin, still, before his bones can rot in the dirt, his fame has already disappeared from the world. Only composers of Japanese poetry are recognized by posterity.

The same theme is developed by Tsurayuki in his preface.

The celebrated locus classicus in Chinese criticism for discussion of the immortality of letters is the "Essay on Literature" by Ts'ao P'i (187–226), in which he says:

Our life must have an end and all our glory, all our joy will end with it. Life and glory last only for a limited time, unlike literature (wen-chang) which endures for ever. That is why ancient authors devoted themselves, body and soul, to ink and brush and set forth their ideas in books. They had no need to have their biographies written by

[19] Unpublished translation by Donald Gibbs.

good historians or to depend upon the power and influence of the rich and mighty: their fame transmitted itself to posterity.[20]

There are other areas in which comparison between the *Kokinshū* prefaces and antecedent Chinese critical works may be fruitful. One is the general structuring of the works. If one compares the prefaces by Yoshimochi and Tsurayuki with those by Chung Hung, in each of these essays a few general formulations of critical theory are stated, a history of antecedent poetry is outlined, and each (including Chung Hung's first preface) ends with a beautifully worded but rather forced encomium for the reigning Chinese or Japanese sovereign.

Another interesting similarity lies in the nature of the critiques of individual poets. In the *Kokinshū* prefaces, as in Chung Hung's work, writers are given a pedigree that is forced and formulaic: "The poetry of Ono no Komachi is of the school of Princess Sotōri of antiquity,"[21] or "The poetry of Ōtomo no Kuronushi follows that of the Illustrious Sarumaru."[22] This is like Chung Hung's saying that "Hsieh Ling-yün's poetic origins go back to Ts'ao Chih,"[23] or "T'ao Ch'ien's poetry derives from that of Ying Chü."[24]

Furthermore, in both of the *Kokinshū* prefaces and in Chung Hung's *Poetry Gradings*, a writer's style is often first described in a short, terse phrase that is then sometimes followed by a concrete analogy meant to sum up the writer's work. For example, Ono no Komachi's poetry is first said to be "seductive and spiritless";[25] to this is added the analogy that it "is like a sick woman wearing cosmetics." The form of Ōtomo no Kuronushi's poetry is said to be "extremely rustic"; it is "like a field hand resting before flowers."[26] And of Fun'ya on Yasuhide it is said, he "used words skillfully, but the expression does not suit the content. His poetry is like a tradesman attired in elegant robes."[27] Compare Chung Hung's description of Fan Yün and Ch'iu Ch'ih: "Fan Yün's poems are bracingly nimble and smooth-turning, like a flowing breeze swirling snow. Ch'iu Ch'ih's poems are quilted patches charmingly bright, like fallen petals lying on the grass."[28]

Another area of similarity between these works is their authors' penchant

---

[20] Translation by Donald Holzman, "Literary Criticism in China in the Early Third Century A.D.," *Asiatische Studien/Etudes Asiatiques* 28.2 (1974), p. 131.

[21] From the manajo; cf. the kanajo.

[22] From the manajo.

[23] *Shih-p'in chu*, p. 17.

[24] *Shih-p'in chu*, p. 25.

[25] From the manajo; cf. the kanajo.

[26] From the manajo; cf. the kanajo.

[27] From the kanajo.

[28] *Shih-p'in chu*, p. 29.

for setting up a hierarchy of greats. Thus, Tsurayuki calls Hitomaro the "sage of poetry," which is like Chung Hung's terming Ts'ao Chih and Liu Chen "the sages of literature." [29]

Women writers fare poorly in these critical treatises. Speaking of Li Ling and Lady Pan, Chung Hung states that "together they spanned roughly a century; but discounting the [one as a] woman, there was only one poet for the period." [30] When Yoshimochi describes the decline of earlier Japanese poetry, he states pejoratively, "it became half the handmaid of women, and was embarrassing to present before gentlemen." And Tsurayuki says of Ono no Komachi, "Her poetry is like a noble lady who is suffering from a sickness, but the weakness is natural to a woman's poetry."

It had been common in the Chinese critical tradition to make the "fruit" (or substance) of literature stand in opposition to its "flower" (or beauty of expression). Yoshimochi adopted the terminology whole, using it to decry the decline of poetry after Hitomaro, "who was unrivaled in ancient and modern times":

Then when the times shifted into decline and men revered the lustful, frivolous words arose like clouds, and a current of ostentatiousness bubbled up like a spring. The fruit had all fallen and only the flower bloomed.

The idea of decline (especially in recent times) from some antique ideal is a pervasive one in Chinese thought. It had been used by Chung Hung,[31] and is echoed in the *Kokinshū* prefaces. In the following passage, Tsurayuki uses somewhat different language to couch the thought expressed above by Yoshimochi:

Nowadays because people are concerned with gorgeous appearances and their hearts admire ostentation, poems poor in content and related only to the circumstances of their composition have appeared.

The critical orientations of the *Kokinshū* prefaces differ in emphasis. Yoshimochi's Chinese preface is more explicitly pragmatic than is Tsurayuki's kana piece. Both prefaces supply a similar listing of the pragmatic functions of poetry (those of moving heaven and earth, transforming human relations, etc.), and both prefaces state that it is through poetry that the feelings of sovereign and subject can be seen, the qualities of virtue and stupidity distinguished, and so forth. But Yoshimochi has an additional passage unparalleled in the Japanese preface. He says approvingly of the poems of high antiquity: "They had yet to become amusements of the eye and ear, serving only as sources of moral edification."

[29] *Shih-p'in chu*, p. 8.
[30] *Shih-p'in chu*, p. 2.
[31] *Shih-p'in chu*, p. 5.

More significantly, there is no counterpart in the Chinese preface to Tsurayuki's list of the circumstances which give occasion to the writing of poetry in general and which, in fact, gave rise to specific *Kokinshū* poems. The expressive orientation of the Japanese preface is explicit here;[32] when Tsurayuki delineates pragmatic ends, he does so more to illustrate poetry's hallowed origins than to prescribe its goals.

Both authors supply additional kindred statements about the expressive nature of poetry. Yoshimochi says of Japanese verse:

> It is like an oriole in spring warbling among the flowers, or like a cicada in autumn humming high in a tree. Though they are neither harassed nor disturbed, each one puts forth its song. That all things have a song is a principle of nature.

And there are the similar opening words of Tsurayuki's preface:

> The seeds of Japanese poetry lie in the human heart and grow into leaves of ten thousand words. Many things happen to the people of this world, and all that they think and feel is given expression in description of things they see and hear. When we hear the warbling of the mountain thrush in the blossoms or the voice of the frog in the water, we know every living being has its song.

But the expressive orientation of Tsurayuki's view is underscored by other passages of a sort which do not appear in the Chinese preface. After ascribing the beginning of thirty-one syllable verse to Susano-o no mikoto, he remarks:

> Since then many poems have been composed when people were attracted by the blossoms or admired the birds, when they were moved by the haze or regretted the swift passage of the dew, and both inspiration and forms of expression have become diverse.

And Tsurayuki says of the poems being anthologized:

> We have chosen poems on wearing garlands of plum blossoms, poems on hearing the nightingale, on breaking off branches of autumn leaves, on seeing the snow. We have also chosen poems on wishing one's lord the lifespan of the crane and tortoise, on congratulating someone, on yearning for one's wife when one sees the autumn bush

---

[32] Although inspired by the example of the *Shih-p'in*, Tsurayuki's list differs from its model in that it omits reference to the *Analects* quotation (17/8) which immediately follows the long passage by Chung Hung cited above: "Poetry teaches the art of sociability; it shows how to regulate feelings of resentment" (translation by James Legge, *Confucian Analects*, in *The Chinese Classics*, vol. 1 [rev. ed. Oxford, 1893; rpt. Hong Kong, 1960], p. 323). The *Analects* citation modifies the expressive thrust of the original statement by Chung Hung.

Both Tsurayuki and Chung Hung couch their arguments in terms of the affective (and hence pragmatic) benefit that the expression of feeling has on the one giving such expression. Thus, both speak of poetry in terms which are genetic (i.e. the occasions that prompt it) and affective (i.e. the effect at least on the author), as well as expressive.

clover or the grasses of summer, on offering prayer strips on Ōsaka Hill, on seeing someone off on a journey, and on miscellaneous topics that cannot be categorized by season.

What one should note in reference to these two passages, as well as the important list cited earlier, is that the writing of poetry is linked to an occasion. This suggests much about Japanese attitudes toward the social function of poetry. An occasion which initially may have prompted poetry of an expressive nature became a *de rigueur* demand for versification serving the more pragmatic end of social display. Notwithstanding the development of this tendency in the Japanese poetic tradition, it is important to keep in mind that Tsurayuki's words came to be taken as the classic statement legitimizing the expressive nature of poetry. The earliest critical statement written in Japanese, the kanajo later served as the revered source for this view of poetry.

If Tsurayuki's approach is more obviously expressive, Yoshimochi's is more subtly or circuitously so. One can point to the fact that Yoshimochi makes more references to the pragmatic ends (including the didactic) of literature, or that he offers no counterpart to Tsurayuki's list of occasions that prompt poetic expression, but Yoshimochi, like Tsurayuki, was writing a statement to introduce and justify an anthology of poetry written in Japanese—not poetry written by Japanese in Chinese, as had been the vogue.

A preface like the manajo, written in Chinese out of regard for the custom in Japan of writing prefaces to important works in that language, could scarcely avoid the accrued referential baggage of classical Chinese. Its argument is couched in terms of Chinese cultural values; Yoshimochi says all the right things about the nature and function of poetry, as he understood the Chinese critical tradition. But for which poets does he express the highest admiration in his preface? They are Hitomaro and Akahito,[33] authors said to be without peer in all poetic history. Their work scarcely embodies the pragmatic ends of literature repeatedly paid lip service in the manajo.

And what of Yoshimochi's discussion of poets of modern times? He echoes a Chinese view of history: alas! poetry has fallen from an earlier ideal state. Yoshimochi enumerates poets' strengths and weaknesses in pithy fashion, but, interestingly enough, not in terms of the abstract normative statements about the nature and functions of poetry made elsewhere in his preface. Bunrin, Ono no Komachi, and Ōtomo no Kuronushi, he says, are among the few who understand the poetry of the past. They may not be perfect, but they are acceptable.

---

[33] There is some question as to whether the inclusion of Akahito here is a later interpolation. See notes to The Chinese Preface.

Although Yoshimochi earnestly repeats Chinese views (be they of literature or of the nature of things), in the final analysis the message behind his words is that Japanese poetry not only has its sages, but a few greats as well. All of them partake in the immortality that goes with outstanding writing. Ultimately, the Chinese preface is an exercise in verbal bowing to venerable Chinese concepts, and a polite statement of collective self-deprecation for imperfect, yet immortal, Japanese verse. The message is clear: "Only composers of Japanese poetry are recognized by posterity.... Alas! Hitomaro has died! But is not the art of Japanese poetry contained here?"

In terms of critical theory, the expressive elements of literature are stressed in Japan, the pragmatic/didactic elements being given a place that is definitely secondary. Chinese theorists of the third through sixth centuries who were seriously interested in literature, such as Ts'ao P'i, Lu Chi, Chung Hung, and Liu Hsieh, were far more concerned with grounding that interest in a theoretical framework that encompassed the universe and legitimized a pursuit that still seemed to serious-minded men perilously close to being frivolous. The backdrop to all Chinese consideration of literature, from earliest times until today, has been the primacy of its pragmatic ends. In contrast with this, the *Kokinshū* prefaces, especially the Japanese preface, while paying homage to pragmatic ends, pointed the direction to a more expressively oriented literature. These in turn became the classic earliest source for later Japanese views of poetry. With such a venerable authority as the Japanese preface behind them—its recondite Chinese references misunderstood or ignored—later Japanese writers and theorists (unlike their Chinese counterparts) were spared having to concern themselves with justifying the expressive/lyrical function of literature. This has had profound implication for the later course of Japanese literature.

Notwithstanding their borrowings from Chinese models, the *Kokinshū* prefaces have a remarkable integrity of their own. The creative part of the Japanese transformation of the Chinese critical tradition, however, lies in the area of a different sensibility, a different way of looking at the world, which is reflected in the ways critical views are expressed in concrete language.

One example is the analogies devised by Yoshimochi and Tsurayuki to embody, as it were, the work of the writers they were commenting upon. It is curious how little overlap there is with the Chinese tradition in this regard. Chung Hung, for example, quotes with approval the characterization of two writers: "Hsieh Ling-yün's poetry is like lotus flowers coming out of the water; Yen Yen-chih's is like a mix of colors with inlays of gold." [34] Yoshimochi, on the other hand, could say of Ōtomo no Kuronushi's poetry that it "is like a field hand resting before flowers." And Tsurayuki said of the

---

[34] *Shih-p'in chu*, p. 26.

same poet's songs: "they are like a mountaineer with a bundle of firewood on his back resting in the shade of the blossoms."[35] There are simply no similar analogies used in earlier Chinese criticism. And few earlier Chinese metaphors characterizing writing are adopted by the Japanese, even in the Chinese-language preface by Yoshimochi. The same difference in sensibility is apparent in the lists of contrastive examples used by Tsurayuki and Chung Hung to make concrete the circumstances or occasions that prompt poetic composition.

In sum, one can say there is no new critical theory in the *Kokinshū* prefaces; it is all based on Chinese models, but with an emphasis that highlights the expressive function of literature. Fundamentally, Chinese critical discourse is used to legitimize in intellectual terms the compilation of an imperially sponsored anthology of poetry in Japanese. At the same time, the concrete vocabulary used to characterize Japanese verse is decidedly non-Chinese in cast—a subject one might delve into, the better to understand the contrast between Chinese and Japanese perceptions of both the written word and the world.

[35] Note the two additional examples cited above.

APPENDIX

Texts of the Kokinshū

Textual studies of the *Kokinshū* have reached voluminous proportions. The most important studies by Japanese scholars include *Kokinshū no denbon no kenkyū* by Nishishita Kyōichi (Meiji shoin, 1954) and *Kokinwakashū seiritsu ron* by Kusogami Hitaku (Kazama shobō, 1960–61). Their findings and those of other scholars are summarized in *Kokinshū Shinkokinshū* edited by Nishishita Kyōichi and Jitsukata Kiyoshi (Sanseidō, 1977).

Copying of the *Kokinshū* evidently began immediately after, or probably even during, the compilation of the text, and today about forty fragments of Heian manuscripts of the *Kokinshū* survive. However, the earliest work which can be regarded as a textual study is a collation in 1035 by Fujiwara no Yorimichi (992–1074) of the "Hanayama hōō shinkan" text with a manuscript in Tsurayuki's own hand. This manuscript was eventually inherited by Fujiwara no Shunzei (1114–1204), who collated it with a number of others and handed it on to his son Teika (1162–1241).

Among the other early lines of texts was the "Ono no kōtaigō no miya bon," said to be a copy made from one in Tsurayuki's hand. A collation with other manuscripts then in circulation is known as the Michimune text, after the editor, the twelfth-century scholar Fujiwara no Michimune. At about the same time Fujiwara no Sadazane made several copies of the *Kokinshū*, of which the Gen'ei text, copied in the Seventh Month of 1120, is the oldest complete copy of the *Kokinshū* extant.

A third line of texts is known as the Sutokuin (or Shin'in). Lectures based on it were given at the court in the late Heian and Kamakura periods, so it was copied by many different people. One of these copies, made by Asukai Masatsune (1170–1221) in the 1190s, is the second-oldest complete text extant.

Fujiwara no Kiyosuke (1104–1177) not only copied the Sutokuin text but also collated it with the Michimune text mentioned above, and then revised it using a "Yōmeimonin" text said to be in the hand of Fujiwara no Teika.

This collated version came to be known as the Kiyosuke text and was also recopied many times.

Another scholar and poet to copy the Sutokuin text was Fujiwara no Shunzei. In 1138 he became a pupil of Fujiwara no Mototoshi (1056–1142), and from him Shunzei received the early collation of the Hanayama hoō and Tsurayuki texts. A new collation and edition of all these is known as the Shunzei text, copies of which are extant in Shunzei's hand.

Teika inherited these texts from his father Shunzei and collated and edited them again, creating the Teika text. The Jōō 2 (1223) 7/22 version, inherited by the Nijō family, became so widespread that a reference to the *Kokinshū* came to mean this text. The version completed in Karoku 2 (1226) 4/9 was also widespread. The Jōō version includes the manajo but omits the "asa-kayama" poem from the kanajo, while the Karoku 2 version does the reverse. Both include the final "supplement" of poems that had been inked out by Shunzei. Most texts extant today descend from the Teika line.

WESTERN-LANGUAGE SOURCES

See also the footnotes to "Chinese Influences on the Kokinshū *Prefaces" by John Timothy Wixted.*

Bonneau, Georges. "Introduction au *Kokinshū*," *Bulletin de la Maison Franco-Japonaise*, Vol. V (1933).

―――. *Le Monument poétique de Heian: le Kokinshū*. Paris: Libraire Orientaliste Paul Guenther, 1933–35.

Brower, Robert and Earl Miner. *Japanese Court Poetry*. Stanford: Stanford University Press, 1961.

Ceadel, E. B. "The Ōi River Poems and Preface." *Asia Major*, 3 (1952), pp. 65–106.

―――. "Tadamine's Preface to the Ōi River Poems." *Bulletin of the School of Oriental and African Studies*, 18 (1956), pp. 331–43.

Cranston, Edwin A. "The Dark Path: Images of Longing in Japanese Love Poetry." *Harvard Journal of Asiatic Studies*, 35 (1975), pp. 60–100.

―――. "Five Poetic Sequences from the *Man'yōshū*." *Journal of the Association of Teachers of Japanese*, 13 (April 1980), pp. 5–40.

―――. *The Izumi Shikibu Diary*. Cambridge: Harvard University Press, 1969.

Harries, Phillip T. "Personal Poetry Collections: Their Origin and Development Through the Heian Period." *Monumenta Nipponica*, 35 (Autumn 1980), pp. 299–317.

Hightower, James R. "The *Wen hsüan* and Genre Theory." *Harvard Journal of Asiatic Studies*, 20 (1957), pp. 512–33.

Honda, H. H., trans. *The Kokin waka-shu: the 10th century anthology edited by the Imperial edict*. Tōkyō: Hokuseido, 1970.

Konishi Jin'ichi. "The Genesis of the *Kokinshū* Style." Trans. Helen C. McCullough. *Harvard Journal of Asiatic Studies*, 38 (1978), pp. 61–170. Originally published as "Kokinshū-teki hyōgen no seiritsu" in *Nihon gakushūin kiyō* 7:3, pp. 163–98, and reprinted in *Kokinwakashū*, ed. Nihon bungaku kenkyū shiryō kankōkai (Tōkyō: Yūseido, 1976).

―――, Robert H. Brower and Earl Miner. "Association and Progression: Principles of Integration in Anthologies and Sequences of Japanese Court

Poetry, A.D. 900–1350." *Harvard Journal of Asiatic Studies*, 21 (1958), pp. 67–127.

McCullough, Helen Craig. *Tales of Ise: Lyrical Episodes from Tenth-Century Japan*. Stanford: Stanford University Press, 1968.

McCullough, William H. and Helen Craig. *A Tale of Flowering Fortunes*. 2 vols. Stanford: Stanford University Press, 1980.

Miller, Roy Andrew. *"The Footprints of the Buddha": An Eighth-Century Old Japanese Poetic Sequence*. New Haven: American Oriental Society, 1975.

———. "The Lost Poetic Sequence of the Priest Manzei." *Monumenta Nipponica*, 36 (Summer 1981), pp. 133–72.

Miner, Earl. *Japanese Poetic Diaries*. Berkeley: University of California Press, 1969.

———. "Toward a New Conception of Classical Japanese Poetics." In *Studies on Japanese Culture* (Tokyo, 1973), pp. 99–113.

Owen, Stephen. *The Great Age of Chinese Poetry: The High T'ang*. New Haven: Yale University Press, 1981.

———. *The Poetry of Early T'ang*. New Haven: Yale University Press, 1977.

Reischauer, Robert Karl. *Early Japanese History*. 2 vols. Gloucester, Mass.: Peter Smith, 1967. Originally published 1937.

Sato, Hiroaki and Burton Watson, eds. and trans. *From the Country of Eight Islands*. Seattle: University of Washington Press, 1981.

Schafer, Edward H. *The Golden Peaches of Samarkand: A Study of T'ang Exotics*. Berkeley: the University of California Press, 1963.

Tahara, Mildred, trans. *Tales of Yamato*. Honolulu: University Press of Hawaii, 1980.

Teele, Nicholas J. "The Love Poems of the 'Kokinshu': A Translation, with Commentary and Study of the Influence of Chinese and Earlier Japanese Poetry." Ph.D. dissertation: University of Texas at Austin, 1980.

———. "Rules for Poetic Elegance: Fujiwara no Kintō's *Shinsen Zuinō* and *Waka Kuhon*." *Monumenta Nipponica*, 31 (1976), pp. 145–64.

Wakameda, T. *Early Japanese Poets*. Tōkyō: Yūhōdō, 1929.

Walker, Janet. "Conventions of Love Poetry in Japan and the West." *Journal of the Association of Teachers of Japanese*, 14:1, pp. 31–65.

———. "Poetic Ideal and Fictional Reality in the *Izumi Shikibu Nikki*." *Harvard Journal of Asiatic Studies*, 37 (1977), pp. 135–82.

Wixted, John Timothy. "The *Kokinshū* Prefaces: Another Perspective." *Harvard Journal of Asiatic Studies* 43 (June 1983), pp. 215–38.

———. "*The Nature of Evaluation in the Shih-p'in (Gradings of Poets)* by Chung Hung (A.D. 469–518)." In *Theories of the Arts in China*, ed. Susan Bush and Christian Murck (Princeton: Princeton University Press, 1983), Section IV.

JAPANESE AND CHINESE

REFERENCES

Hisamatsu Sen'ichi 久松潜一. *Kodai waka shi* 古代和歌史. Tōkyō: Tōkyōdō, 1960.

———, ed. *Shinpan Nihon bungaku shi* 新版日本文学史. Vol 2: Chūko. Tōkyō: Shibundō, 1971.

Kadokawa shoten 角川書店, ed. *Nihon bungaku chizu sakuin* 日本文学地図索引. Tōkyō: Kadokawa shoten, 1968.

Kaneko Takeo 金子武雄. *Tatoekotoba, makurakotoba, jokotoba no kenkyū* 称詞・枕詞・序詞の研究. Tōkyō: Kōronsha, 1977.

Kubota Utsubo 窪田空穗, ed. *Kokinwakashū hyōshaku* 評釈. 2nd ed., 3 vols. Tōkyō: Tōkyōdō, 1960.

Matsuda Osamu 松田修. *Manyō no hana* 萬葉の花. Tōkyō: Unsōdō, 1972.

Matsuda Takeo 松田武夫. *Kokinshū no kōzō ni kansuru kenkyū* 古今集の構造に関する研究. Tōkyō: Kazama shobō, 1965.

Nihon bungaku kenkyū shiryō kankōkai, ed. *Kokinwakashū*. Nihon bungaku kenkyū shiryō sōsho. Tōkyō: Yūseidō, 1976.

Nishishita Kyōichi 西下経一 and Sanekata Kiyoshi 実方清. *Kokinshū Shinkokinshū* 古今集新古今集. Zōhō kokugo kokubungaku kenkyūshi taisei, Vol. VII. Tōkyō: Sanseidō, 1977.

——— and Takizawa Sadao 滝沢貞夫. *Kokinshū kōhon* 古今集校本. Tōkyō: Kasama shoin, 1977.

Okumura Tsuneya 奥村恒哉. *Kokinshū Gosenshū no shomondai* 古今集・後撰集の諸問題. Tōkyō: Kazama shobō, 1971.

———, ed. *Kokinwakashū*. (Shinchō Nihon koten shūsei). Tōkyō: Shinchōsha, 1978.

Ozawa Masao 小沢正夫. *Kokin Shinkokin to sono shūhen* 古今新古今とその周辺. Kyōto: Daigakudō shoten, 1972.

———. *Kokinwakashū*. Nihon koten bungaku zenshū, Vol. VII. Tōkyō: Shōgakukan, 1971.

Saeki Umetomo 佐伯梅友, ed. *Kokinwakashū*. Nihon koten bungaku taikei, Vol. VIII. Tōkyō: Iwanami shoten, 1958.

Takeoka Masao 竹岡正夫. *Kokinwakashū zenhyōshaku* 全評釈. Tōkyō: Yūbunshoin, 1976.

AUTHOR INDEX AND BRIEF

BIOGRAPHIES

Numbers following each biography refer to the numbers of Kokinshū *poems by that author.*

ABE NO KIYOYUKI 安倍清行, 825–900.
Father of Sanuki 讃岐, the poetess. Graduated in 836 from the university (Monjōshō 文章生), and in 871 was appointed Governor of Suo Province. Thereafter, held various official posts and governorships in Iyo 伊予, Harima 播磨, Mutsu 陸奥, and Sanuki 讃岐. *456, 556*

ABE NO NAKAMARO 安倍仲麿, 698–770.
Was chosen as an envoy to China in 716; departed in 717 with Kibi no Makibi 吉備真備 and Genbō 玄昉. While serving with Hsüan-tsung 玄宗, he became known for his writing and associated with such Chinese poets as Li Po 李白 and Wang Wei 王維. Attempted to return to Japan with the party of Fujiwara no Kiyokawa 藤原清河 in 753. (Unfortunately, the party drifted off course, landed in Vietnam, and suffered casualties in a rebellion there. Nakamaro was able to return to China, where he died.) *406*

ABO NO TSUNEMI 阿保経覧, d. 912.
Appointed Clerk of the Bureau of Computation (Kazue gon no shō sakan 主計権少属) in 893. Thereafter, held several posts, one of which was Director of the Tax Bureau (Shuzei no kami 主税頭). *458*

AMANEIKO 洽子, late ninth century.
Daughter of Haruzumi no Yoshinawa 春澄善縄. Served as a palace attendant (Naishi no suke 典侍). *107*

ARIWARA NO MOTOKATA 在原元方, fl. ca. 900.
Son of Muneyana 棟梁, Governor of Chikuzen 筑前. Became the foster child (yūshi 猶子) of Major Counsellor Fujiwara no Kunitsune 国経 upon his sister's marriage to Kunitsune. *1, 103, 130, 195, 206, 261, 339, 473, 474, 480, 626, 630, 751, 1062*

ARIWARA NO MUNEYANA (Munehari) 在原棟梁, d. 898.
Eldest son of Narihira 業平. Served Seiwa 清和, Yōzei 陽成, Kōkō 光孝, Uda 宇多, and possibly Daigo 醍醐 tennō. *15, 243, 902, 1020*

ARIWARA NO NARIHIRA 在原業平, 825–880.
Fifth son of Prince Abo 阿保, son of Heizei tennō, and Princess Ito 伊登, daughter of Kanmu 桓武 tennō. In 826 he and his brothers were made commoners and given their surname. The *Sandai jitsuroku* 三代実録 describes Narihira as "Handsome of face and figure. Negligent and self-indulgent regardless. Talent and schooling abbreviated. Skillful at composing Japanese poetry." Central character of the *Tales of Ise* (*Ise monogatari* 伊勢物語). One of the "six poetic geniuses." *53, 63, 133, 268, 294, 349, 410, 411, 418, 476, 616, 618, 622, 632, 644, 646, 705, 707, 747, 785, 861, 868, 871, 879, 884, 901, 923, 969, 970, 971*

ARIWARA NO NARIHIRA'S MOTHER, d. 861.
Princess Ito, daughter of Kanmu tennō. *900*

ARIWARA NO SHIGEHARU 在原滋春, d. 905?
Second son of Narihira. *355, 372, 424, 451, 465, 862*

ARIWARA NO YUKIHIRA 在原行平, 818–893.
Narihira's brother. Held various court posts. *23, 365, 922, 962*

AYAMOCHI あやもち.
1105

FUJIWARA NO KACHION (KACHIOMU) 藤原勝臣, fl. ca. 890.
255, 472, 999, 1102

FUJIWARA NO KANEMOCHI 藤原兼茂, d. 923.
Brother of Kanesuke 兼輔. In 923 appointed Consultant (Sangi 参議) and Head of the Left Guards (Sa hyōe no kami 左兵衛督). *385, 389*

FUJIWARA NO KANESUKE 藤原兼輔, 877–933.
Brother of Kanemochi, great-grandfather of Murasaki Shikibu 紫式部. Achieved the post of Middle Counsellor (Chūnagon 中納言) in 927. Called Tsutsumi Chūnagon after the location of his residence along the Kamo River banks (tsutsumi). This mansion was the site of many literary gatherings. *391, 417, 749, 1014*

FUJIWARA NO KOREMOTO 藤原惟幹. *860*

FUJIWARA NO KOTONAO 藤原言直, fl. ca. 900. *10*

FUJIWARA NO KUNITSUNE 藤原国経, 827–908.
Rose to become Major Counsellor (Dainagon 大納言) in 902.   *638*

FUJIWARA NO NAKAHIRA 藤原仲平, 875–945.
Son of Mototsune 基経 and a daughter of Prince Hitoyasu 人康; brother of
Tokihira 時平. Rose to position of Minister of the Left (Sadaijin 左大臣) in
937. Known as Biwa no Otodo 枇杷大臣.   *748*

FUJIWARA NO NAOIKO 藤原直子, fl. ca. 900.   *807*

FUJIWARA NO NOCHIKAGE 藤原後蔭, fl. ca 919.
Appointed Provisional Governor-General of Bizen 備前権守 in 919. (See
the headnote to poem 385.)   *108*

FUJIWARA NO OKIKAZE 藤原興風, fl. ca. 900.
Son of Michinari 道成. Renowned musician. Wrote the screen poems for
the celebration of the fiftieth birthday of the Consort of Prince Sadayasu
貞保 in 891.   *101, 102, 131, 178, 301, 310, 326, 351, 567, 568, 569, 745, 814, 909,
1031, 1053, 1064*

FUJIWARA NO SADAKATA 藤原定方, 876 (869?)–932.
Son of Takafuji 高藤. Appointed Minister of the Right (Udaijin 右大臣)
and in 924 Captain of the Right Guards (Ukon no taishō 右近大将).   *231*

FUJIWARA NO SEKIO 藤原関雄, 815–853.
Retired from court offices because of illness. Was called Gentleman of
Higashiyama 東山進士 because he shunned secular affairs and lived in
retirement in Higashiyama. Noted for this koto playing and cursive calligraphy.   *282, 291*

FUJIWARA NO SUGANE 藤原菅根, 855–908.
A scholar, who lectured on the *Classic of History* (*Shih Chi* 史記). Became
Consultant (Sangi) in 908.   *212*

FUJIWARA NO TADAFUSA 藤原忠房, d. 928.
Held various court offices and governorships from 893. Famous for his skill
on the flute.   *196, 576, 914, 993*

FUJIWARA NO TADAYUKI 藤原忠行, d. 906.
Held various offices from 887. Became Governor of Wakasa 若狭 in
906.   *680*

FUJIWARA NO TOKIHIRA 藤原時平, d. 909.
Became Minister of the Left in 899.   *230, 1049*

FUJIWARA NO TOSHIYUKI 藤原敏行, d. 901 (907?).
Held various offices from 866 and rose to Head of the Right Military Guards
(Uhyōe no kami 右兵衛督) in 897.   *169, 197, 218, 228, 239, 257, 269, 295,
422, 423, 558, 559, 578, 617, 639, 874, 903, 1013, 1100*

FUJIWARA NO YORUKA 藤原因香, fl. ca. 875.
Daughter of the nun Kyoshin 敬信. Appointed to the court ranks beginning
in 871 and probably became a palace attendant.   *80, 364, 736, 738*

FUJIWARA NO YOSHIFUSA 藤原良房, 804–860.
Son of Fujiwara Fuyutsugu 冬嗣. Held various offices and in 857 reached the
position of Chancellor (Dajōdaijin).   *52*

FUJIWARA NO YOSHIKAZE 藤原好風 (or 良風), fl. ca. 900.
Appointed to court ranks in 898 and 911.   *85*

FUNYA NO ARISUE 文屋有季.
997

FUNYA NO ASAYASU 文屋朝康, fl. ca. 900.
Son of Yasuhide 康秀. Became Secretary (jō 掾) of Suruga 駿河 Province
in 892 and in 902 was appointed Senior Secretary of the Imperial Attendants
(Ōtoneri daijō 大舎人大允).   *225*

FUNYA NO YASUHIDE 文屋康秀, fl. ca. 860.
One of the "six poetic geniuses."   *8, 249, 250, 445, 846*

FURU NO IMAMICHI 布留今道, fl. ca. 860–900.
Appointed to various offices in 861, 882, 898.   *227, 870, 946*

HARUMICHI NO TSURAKI 春道列樹, d. 920.
Graduated from the university in 910. Appointed Governor of Iki 壱岐 in
920, but died before taking office.   *303, 341, 610*

HENJŌ 遍照 (or 遍昭), 816–890.
Born Yoshimine no Munesada 良岑宗貞. One of the "six poetic geniuses."
Grandson of Kanmu tennō. Held court offices from 844 until 850, when he
took Buddhist orders after the death of Ninmyō 仁明 tennō. Rose rapidly in
the ecclesiastical hierarchy; was given the Urin'in 雲林院 in 869. Became
Assistant High Priest (Gon no sōjō 権僧正) in 879. Became High Priest
(Sōjō 僧正) in 885. During the 860s established the Gangyōji 元慶寺 in
Kazan and became Chief Priest (Zasu 座主). Also known as Kazan no Sōjō.
27, 91, 119, 165, 226, 248, 292, 348, 392, 394, 435, 770, 771, 847, 872, 985, 1016

HYŌE 兵衛, fl. ca. 900.
Wife of Fujiwara no Tadafusa.   *455, 789*

IKAGO NO ATSUYUKI 伊香子淳行.
373

INABA 因幡, fl. ca. 900.
Daughter of Motoyo no ōkimi 基世王, who was appointed Provisional Governor of Inaba in 889. *808*

ISE 伊勢.
Daughter of Fujiwara no Tsugukage, who was Governor of Ise from 885 to 890. Served the Consort, Onshi. After an unhappy love affair with Fujiwara no Nakahira, she became an attendant of Uda tennō and bore him a son. After Uda's abdication, she lived in the Fifth Ward of the capital and had a daughter, Nakatsukasa 中務, by Prince Atsuyoshi 敦慶. *31, 43, 44, 61, 68, 138, 459, 676, 681, 733, 741, 756, 780, 791, 810, 920, 926, 968, 990, 1000, 1006, 1051*

KAGENORI NO ŌKIMI 景式王, fl. ca. 897.
Son of Prince Koreeda 惟条. Appointed to court rank in 897. *452, 786*

KAMUTSUKE NO MINEO 上野岑雄.
The *Index to the Kokinshū* (*Kokin wakashū mokuroku* 古今和歌集目録) describes him as active during the Shōwa 承和 era (834–848), but since he composed a poem on the death of Fujiwara no Mototsune in 891, he was of a later generation. *832*

KANEMI NO ŌKIMI 兼覧王, d. 932.
Son of Prince Koretaka 惟喬. Held various court offices and governorships from 886. *237, 298, 398, 457, 779*

KAN'IN 閑院, fl. ca. early 900s.
Noblewoman. *740, 837*

KAN'IN NO GO NO MIKO 閑院の五の御子.
857

KENGEI 兼芸, fl. ca. 875–885.
A priest believed to have been from Shirogami 城上 District in Yamato 大和 Province. *396, 768, 803, 875*

KI NO AKIMINE 紀秋岑, fl. ca. 890.
Sixth Rank. *158, 324*

KI NO ARITOMO 紀有朋, d. 880.
Father of Tomonori 友則. Held various offices from 844. *66, 1029*

KI NO ARITSUNE 紀有常, 815–877.
Son of Natora 名虎. Held various offices and governorships beginning in

843. Appears in the *Tale of Ise*. His daughter became Consort of Montoku tennō and mother of Prince Koretaka. *419, 784* (also attributed to Aritsune's daughter)

KI NO KOREOKA 紀惟岳, fl. ca. 860–885.
Sixth Rank? *350*

KI NO MENOTO 紀乳母, fl. ca. 880s.
Wet nurse of Yozei tennō. *454, 1028*

KI NO TOMONORI 紀友則, d. 906?
One of the *Kokinshū* compilers; died before its completion. Held various offices from 897. *13, 38, 57, 60, 84, 142, 153, 154, 177, 207, 265, 270, 274, 275, 337, 359, 405, 431, 437, 438, 440, 442, 561, 562, 563, 564, 565, 593, 594, 595, 596, 607, 615, 661, 667, 668, 684, 715, 753, 787, 792, 827, 833, 854, 876, 991*

KI NO TOSHISADA 紀利貞, d. 881.
Held various offices beginning in 875 *136, 369, 370, 446*

KI NO TSURAYUKI 紀貫之, d. 945?
One of the *Kokinshū* compilers and author of the Japanese preface. (See Introduction.) *2, 9, 22, 25, 26, 39, 42, 45, 49, 58, 59, 78, 79, 82, 83, 87, 89, 94, 115, 116, 117, 118, 124, 128, 156, 160, 162, 170, 232, 240, 256, 260, 262, 276, 280, 297, 299, 311, 312, 323, 331, 336, 342, 352, 363, 371, 380, 381, 384, 390, 397, 404, 415, 427, 428, 436, 439, 460, 461, 471, 475, 479, 482, 572, 573, 574, 579, 583, 587, 588, 589, 597, 598, 599, 604, 605, 606, 633, 679, 697, 729, 734, 804, 834, 838, 842, 849, 851, 852, 880, 881, 915, 916, 918, 919, 931, 980, 1002, 1010, 1101, 1103, 1111.*

KI NO YOSHIHITO 紀淑人, fl. ca. 900–910.
Brother of Yoshimochi 淑望. Served as Governor of Kawachi 河内, Iyo, and Tanba 丹波. *1034*

KI NO YOSHIMOCHI 紀淑望, d. 919.
Brother of Yoshihito. Chinese scholar, said to be the author of the Chinese preface to the *Kokinshū*. Graduated from the university in 896; then became head of the university. Appointed Provisional Vice-Governor of Shinano 信濃 in 913. *251*

KISEN 喜撰.
A priest. One of the "six poetic geniuses." Known by his poetry to have lived in Uji 宇治. *983*

KIYOHARA NO FUKAYABU 清原深養父, fl. ca. 910.
Appointed Secretary of the Bureau of Artisans (Takumi no jo 内匠允) in 908,

and Secretary of the Palace Storehouse Bureau (Kura no daijō 内蔵大允) in 923. Rose to Junior Fifth Rank, Lower Grade. *129, 166, 300, 330, 318, 429, 449, 581, 585, 603, 613, 665, 685, 698, 967, 1021, 1042*

KORETAKA NO MIKO 惟喬親王, 844–897.
Son of Montoku tennō. Because his mother was of the Ki family, he was not chosen Crown Prince. After serving in various minor court offices, he took Buddhist vows in 872 and moved to Ono 小野 Village. Also known as Prince Ono. *74, 945*

KUSO 久曽.
Daughter of Minamoto no Tsukuru 源作 (or possibly of Abe no Kiyoyuki). *1054*

KYOSHIN 敬信.
Mother of Fujiwara no Yoruka. This is her religious name. *885*

MIBU NO TADAMINE 壬生忠岑, fl. ca. 920.
One of the compilers of the *Kokinshū*. Held various offices but never rose above Sixth Rank. Said to be the author of *Waka tai jusshū* 和歌体十種. *11, 157, 163, 183, 194, 214, 235, 236, 258, 263, 296, 306, 327, 328, 361, 425, 462, 478, 566, 586, 592, 601, 602, 609, 625, 628, 835, 836, 839, 841, 843, 917, 928, 1003, 1004, 1036*

MICHINOKU 陸奥.
Daughter of Tachibana no Kuzunao 橘葛直. *992*

MIHARU NO ARISUKE 御春有助, fl. ca. 900.
A retainer of Fujiwara no Toshiyuki; said to be from Kawachi Province. *629, 853*

MIKUNI NO MACHI 三国町.
Daughter of Ki no Natora? Imperial concubine (kōi 更衣) of Ninmyō tennō. *152*

MINAMOTO NO HODOKOSU 源忠(恵), d. 931.
Held various provincial governorships. *463*

MINAMOTO NO MASAZUMI 源当純, fl. ca. 905.
Appointed Minor Counsellor (Shōnagon 少納言) in 903 and in 907 raised to Junior Fifth Rank, Upper Grade. *12*

MINAMOTO NO MUNEYUKI 源宗于, d. 939.
Grandson of Kōkō tennō. Given the Minamoto surname in 894. *24, 182, 315, 624, 788, 801*

MINAMOTO NO SANE 源実, d. 900.
Appointed Governor of Shinano in 899. *388*

MINAMOTO NO TOKIWA 源常, d. 844.
Son of Saga tennō. Became Minister of the Right in 840. *36*

MINAMOTO NO TŌRU 源融, 822–895.
Served as Governor of Sagami, Ōmi, Mimasaka 美作, and Ise, and as Consultant (Sangi) and Inspector (Azechi 按察使). Also known as Kawara no Hidari no Ōimauchigimi 河原左大臣. *724, 873*

MINAMOTO NO YOSHIARI 源能有, 845–897.
The Kon'in Minister of the Right. Son of Montoku tennō. *737, 848, 869*

MIYAJI NO KIYOKI 宮道潔興, fl. ca. 900. *966*

MIYAKO NO YOSHIKA 都良香, 834–879.
Graduated from the university in 860, and later became Doctor of Literature. One of the compilers of the *Montoku Jitsuroku* 文徳実録. His Chinese poems appear in *Wakan roeishū* 和漢朗詠集 and *Shinsen* 新撰 *roei shū*. *466.*

MONONOBE NO YOSHINA 物部吉名. *955*

MUNEOKA NO ŌYORI 宗岳大頼.
Doctor of Divination. *591, 979*

NANIWA NO YOROZUO 難波万雄. *374*

NARA NO MIKADO 奈良帝, 774–824.
Heizei 平城 tennō. Reigned 806–809. *90*

NARIHIRA NO ASON NO HAHA 業平朝臣母, d. 861.
Princess Ito, daughter of Kanmu tennō. Mother of Narihira; wife of Prince Abo. *900*

NIJŌ 二條.
Daughter of Minamoto Itaru 源至. *986*

NIJŌ NO KISAKI 二條后, 842–910.
Takaiko, Consort of Seiwa tennō. Mother of Yōzei tennō. *4*

NINNA NO MIKADO 仁和帝, 831–887.
Kōkō tennō, reigned 884–887. *21, 347*

ŌE NO CHISATO 大江千里, fl. ca. 900.
Appointed Junior Secretary of the Ministry of Central Affairs (Nakatsukasa shōjō 中務少丞) in 901. Punished once by imprisonment, but eventually

rose to office of Provisional Vice-Governor of Iyo. Confucian scholar. Produced a poetry collection, *Ōe no Chisato shū* (Kudai waka), in 894.   *14, 155, 193, 271, 467, 577, 643, 859, 998, 1065*

ONO NO CHIFURU GA HAHA 小野千古母. Daughter of Ono no Michikaze 小野道風? Mother of Chifuru.   *368*

ONO NO HARUKAZE 小野春風. Named Junior Lieutenant of the Right Military Guards (Uemon no shōjō 右衛門少尉) in 854 and rose to Provisional Governor of Sanuki. Appointed to the Senior Fifth Rank, Lower Grade, in 898. Famous as a military commander.   *653, 963*

ONO NO KOMACHI 小野小町, ninth century. One of the "six poetic geniuses."   *113, 552, 553, 554, 557, 623, 635, 656, 657, 658, 727, 782, 797, 822, 938, 939, 1030, 1104*

ONO NO KOMACHI GA ANE 小野小町姉, ninth century. Elder sister of Komachi.   *790*

ONO NO SADAKI 小野貞樹. Appointed Junior Secretary (Shoshin 少進) of the Palace of the Crown Prince (tōgū 春宮) in 849. In 860 became Governor of Higo 肥後.   *783, 937*

ONO NO SHIGEKAGE 小野滋蔭, d. 896. In 888 received first appointment as Junior Secretary of the Government Storehouse (Ōkura shōjō 大蔵少丞) and rose to Head of the Bureau of Housekeeping (Kamon no kami 掃部頭) in 893.   *430*

ONO NO TAKAMURA 小野篁, 802–852. Graduated from the university in 821. Appointed envoy to China in 834, but did not go and was exiled to the island of Oki 隠岐 until 840. In 847 appointed Consultant (Sangi); in 852, Left Major Controller (Sadaiben 左大弁). Famous for his Chinese verse.   *335, 407, 829, 845, 936, 961*

ONO NO YOSHIKI 小野美材, d. 902. Takamura's grandson. Graduate of the university. Rose to position of Provisional Assistant Governor (Gon no suke) of Shinano.   *229, 560*

ŌSHIKŌCHI NO MITSUNE 凡河内躬恒, fl. ca. 900–920. One of the *Kokinshū* compilers. Appointed Junior Clerk (Shōsakan 少目) of Kai 甲斐 in 894; rose to a minor position in Izumi Province. Accompanied Uda tennō on his excursion to Ōigawa 大堰川 in 907, composing waka with Tsurayuki, Sakanoue no Korenori 坂上是則, Mibu no Tadamine, and others. Also joined excursions to Ishiyamadera 石山寺 in 916 and to Kasuga Shrine 春日社 in 921. Known to have composed screen poems on various occasions. *30, 40, 41, 67, 86, 104, 110, 120, 127, 132, 134, 161, 164, 167, 168, 179, 180, 190, 213, 219, 233, 234, 277, 304, 305, 313, 329, 338, 358, 360, 382, 383, 399, 414, 416, 481, 580, 584, 600, 608, 611, 612, 614, 636, 662, 663, 686, 750, 794, 840, 929, 956, 957, 976, 977, 978, 1005, 1015, 1035, 1067*

OTO 乙, late ninth to tenth centuries.
Daughter of Mibu no Yoshinari 壬生益成, who became Assistant Governor of Tōtōmi 遠江 in 887. *413*

ŌTOMO NO KURONUSHI 大伴(友)黒主, 830?–923?
One of the "six poetic geniuses." Member of a provincial family descended from the imperial line. Participated in the "Chūjō no Miyasundokoro no ie Poetry Contest" 中将の御息所の家の歌合 of 887. Composed poetry for the accession of Daigo tennō (897), and wrote a poem in 917 during the excursion of Uda tennō to Ishiyamadera. *88, 735, 1086*

SADA NO NOBORU 貞登, ca. 834–894.
Son of Ninmyō tennō; brother of Kōkō tennō. Took Buddhist orders; later returned to secular life. Held governorships and assistant governorships in Tosa 土佐, Bitchū 備中, Etchū 越中, and Kii 紀伊. *769*

SAKAI NO HITOZANE 酒井人真, d. 917.
Appointed Provisional Senior Clerk (Gon no dai sakan 権大目) of Bizen in 889; rose to become Governor of Tosa. *743*

SAKANOUE NO KORENORI 坂上是則, fl. ca. 905–925.
Became Provisional Junior Secretary (Gon no shōjō) of Yamato in 908; in 924 rose to post of Assistant Governor (Suke 介) of Kaga 加賀. *267, 302, 325, 332, 362, 590, 826, 932*

SANJŌ NO MACHI 三条町.
Shizuko, daughter of Ki no Natora. Imperial concubine of Montoku tennō. Mother of Prince Koretaka. *930*

SANUKI 讃岐, late ninth to tenth centuries.
Daughter of Abe no Kiyoyuki. *1055*

SHIMOTSUKE NO OMUNE 下野雄宗. *728*

SHINSEI 真静.
A priest from Kawachi Province. *453, 921*

SHINTAI 神退.
A priest from Shiga in Ōmi 近江 Province.   *925*

SHIROME 白女.
A woman entertainer (yūjo 遊女) from Eguchi 江口 in Settsu 摂津.   *387*

SHŌEN 勝延, 827–901.
Monk at the Enryakuji 延暦寺. Became Junior Assistant High Priest (Shōsōzu 少僧都) in 898.   *831*

SHŌHŌ 聖宝, d. 909.
Intendant (Bettō 別当) at Tōdaiji, appointed High Priest (Sōjō) in 902.   *468*

SOSEI, PRIEST 素性, d. ca. 909.
Son of Henjō. Secular name: Yoshimine no Harutoshi 良岑玄利. Lived at the Urin'in. Appointed Provisional Master of Asceticism (Gon no Risshi) in 896. In 898, joined Uda tennō's Yoshino Waterfall Excursion and presented waka. Later composed many series of screen poems.   *6, 37, 47, 55, 56, 76, 92, 95, 96, 109, 114, 126, 143, 144, 181, 241, 244, 273, 293, 309, 353, 354, 356, 357, 421, 470, 555, 575, 691, 714, 722, 799, 802, 830, 947, 1012*

SOTŌRI HIME, 衣通姫.
Sister of the Consort of Ingyō 允恭 tennō (r. ca. 438–454). Lived in Fujiwara; later moved to Chinu 茅渟 in Kawachi.   *1110*

SUGANO NO TADAON 菅野忠臣, fl. ca. 877–898?   *809*

SUGANO NO TAKAYO 菅野高世, fl. ca. 810.   *81*

SUGAWARA NO MICHIZANE 菅原道真, 845–903.
Graduated from the university in 862, and completed the graduate program (tokugyōshō 得業生) the following year. Appointed to various posts by Uda and Daigo tennō to counter the power of the Fujiwara clan. Appointed Ambassador to China, but petitioned and had the order rescinded. In 899 became Minister of the Right (Udaijin) and in 901 was raised to Second Rank, Junior Grade, but was slandered and demoted to Provisional Governor-General (sotsu 帥) of Dazaifu 大宰府. Author of the poetry collections *Kankebunsō* 菅家文草, *Kankekōsō* 菅家後草, *Shinsen Manyōshū* 新撰万葉集, and the histories *Nihon sandai jitsuroku* 日本三代実録 and *Ruijū kokushi* 類聚国史. Posthumously appointed Chancellor (Daijōdaijin 大政大臣), First Rank, Senior Grade.   *272, 420*

TACHIBANA NO KIYOKI 橘清樹, d. 899.
Appointed Junior Secretary (Shōjō 少監) of Dazaifu in 877, Governor of Awa 阿波 in 896.   *655*

TACHIBANA NO NAGAMORI 橘長盛.
First appointed to court office in 897; rose to become Governor of Nagato 長門. *927*

TAIFU 大輔, ca. 880–920?
Daughter of Minamoto no Tasuku 源弼. *1056*

TAIRA NO ATSUYUKI 平篤行, d. 910.
Graduated from the university in 893. Became Governor of Kaga and Governor of Chikuzen *cum* Assistant Governor-General (shōni 少弐) of Dazaifu. *447*

TAIRA NO MOTONORI 平元規, d. 908.
Granted the privilege of attending the imperial court (shōden 昇殿) in 897; in 908 raised to Fifth Rank, Junior Grade. *386*

TAIRA NO NAKAKI 平中興, d. 930.
Became Chamberlain (Kurōdo 蔵人) in 898; Provisional Governor of Mino 美濃 in 922. *1048, 1050*

TAIRA NO SADAFUN 平貞文 (or 定文), 871?–931.
Rose from palace attendant (utoneri 内舎人) to Provisional Assistant Governor of Mikawa 三河. Central character in the *Heichū monogatari* 平中物語. *238, 242, 279, 666, 670, 823, 964, 965, 1033*

TAKAMUKO NO TOSHIHARU 高向利春, fl. ca. 890–930.
Became Secretary of the Ministry of Justice (Gyōbu no jō 刑部丞) in 890; Governor of Kai in 928. *450*

UNEME 采女.
A serving woman (uneme) from Ōmi. *1109*

URIN'IN NO MIKO 雲林院親王, d. 869.
Tsuneyasu 常康, son of Ninmyō tennō and a daughter of Ki no Natora 名虎. Took Buddhist orders after Ninmyō's death and took up residence at the Urin'in. (After his death, Henjō and Sosei lived at the Urin'in.) *781*

UTSUKU 寵.
376, 640, 742

YATABE NO NAZANE 矢田部名実, d. 900.
Graduated from the university in 884. Became Senior Private Secretary (Dainaiki 大内記) in 899. *444*

YOSHIMINE NO HIDEOKA 良岑秀崇, fl. ca. 879–896.
Graduated from the university in 879. Became Governor of Hōki 伯耆 in 896. *379*

YOSHIMINE NO MUNESADA. 良岑宗貞.
(See Henjō.)

YŪSEN 幽仙 (or 幽仁), 836–900.
A Buddhist priest who rose to the rank of Master of Asceticism (risshi 律師).
393, 395

INDEX OF FIRST LINES

Numbers refer to the number of the poem in which the line appears. Where first lines are identical, the second lines are given below.

abukuma ni 1087
adanari to 62
aimimaku 1029
aimineba 760
aiminu mo 808
aimizuba 678
ai ni aite 756
ajikinashi 455
akade koso 717
akanaku ni 884
akatsuki no 761
akazarishi 992
akazu shite
  tsuki no kakururu 883
  wakaruru namida 396
  wakaruru sode no 400
akenu tote
  ima wa no kokoro 638
  kaeru michi ni wa 639
aketateba 543
aki chikō 440
akigiri no
  harete kumoreba 1018
  haruru toki aki 580
  tomo ni tachiidete 386
akigiri wa 266
aki hagi mo 198
aki hagi ni 216
aki hagi no
  furu e ni sakeru 219
  hana oba ame ni 397
  hana sakinikeri 218
  shitaba irozuka 220
aki hagi o 217
aki kaze ni

aezu chirinuru 286
au tanomi koso 822
hatsukari ga ne zo 207
hokorobinu rashi 1020
kaki nasu koto no 586
koe o ho ni agete 212
yama no ko no ha no 714
aki kaze no
  fukiage ni tateru 272
  fukinishi hi yori
    hisakata no 173
    otowa yama 256
  fuki to fukinuru 821
  fukiuragaesu 823
  mi ni samukereba 555
aki kaze wa 787
aki kinu to 169
aki kureba 1017
aki kuredo
  iro mo kawaranu 362
  tsuki no katsura no 463
aki narade
  au koto kataki 231
  oku shiratsuyu wa 757
aki nareba 582
aki no kiku 276
aki no no ni
  hito matsumushi no 202
  michi mo madoinu 201
  midarete sakeru 583
  namameki tateru 1016
  oku shiratsuyu wa 225
  sasa wakeshi asa no 622
  tsuma naki shika no 1034
  yadori wa subeshi 228

420

aki no no no
    kusa no tamoto ka 243
    obana ni majiri 497
aki no ta no
    ho ni koso hito o 547
    ho no ue o terasu 548
    ine chō koto mo 803
aki no tsuki 289
aki no tsuyu 259
aki no yama 299
aki no yo mo 635
aki no yo no
    akuru mo shirazu 197
    tsuki no hikarishi 195
    tsuyu oba tsuyu to 258
aki no yo wa 199
aki o okite 279
aki to ieba 824
aki wa kinu
    ima yamagaki no 432
    momiji wa yado ni 287
amabiko no 963
ama kumo no 784
ama no hara
    furisake mireba 701
    fumitodorokashi 406
ama no karu 807
ama no kawa
    asase shiranami 177
    kumo no mio nite 882
    momiji o hashi ni 175
ama no sumu 727
amatsu kaze 872
ame fureba 263
ame furedo 261
ame ni yori 918
ana koishi 695
ana u me ni 426
aoyagi no 26
aoyagi o 1081
aozora wa 743
ara ota o 817
aratama no 339
arenikeri 984
ariake no 625
arihatenu 965
arinu ya to 1025
ariso umi no 818
ari to mite 443

asaborake 332
asajiu no 505
asamidori 27
asami koso 618
asana asana 513
asa nake ni 376
asa tsuyu no 842
asa tsuyu o 438
ashibe yori 819
ashigamo no 533
ashihiki no
    yamabe ni ima wa 844
    yamabe ni oreba 461
    yama hototogisu
        orihaete 150
        waga goto ya 499
    yama no mani mani 953
    yamashita mizu no 491
    yamatachi hanare 430
    yama ta no sōzu 1027
ashitazu no
    hitori okurete 998
    tateru kawabe o 919
asuka gawa
    fuchi ni mo aranu 990
    fuchi wa se ni naru 687
atarashiki 1069
au kara mo 429
au koto no
    ima wa hatsuka ni 1048
    mare naru iro ni 1001
    mohara taeruru 812
    nagisa ni shi yoru 626
au koto o 826
au koto wa
    kumoi haruka ni 482
    tama no o bakari 673
au made no
    katami mo ware wa 744
    katami to te koso 745
awanu yo no 621
aware chō
    koto dani naku wa 502
    koto koso utate 939
    koto no ha goto ni 940
    koto o amata ni 136
aware tomo 805
awayuki no 550
awazu shite 624

ayanakute 629
azumaji no 594
azusayumi
    haru no yamabe o 115
    haru tachishi yori 127
    hikeba moto sue 610
    hikino no tsuzura 702
    isobe no komatsu 907
    oshite harusame 20

chidori naku 361
chigiriken 178
chihayaburu
    kami no igaki ni 262
    kami no miyo yori 1002
    kami ya kiriken 348
    kamiyo mo kikazu 294
    kamo no yashiro no
        hime komatsu 1100
        yū tasuki 487
    kannabi yama no 254
    kannazuki to ya 1005
    uji no hashimori 904
chiji no iro ni 726
chi no namida 830
chiranedomo 264
chirinu tomo 48
chirinureba
    kouredo shirushi 64
    nochi wa akuta ni 435
chiri o dani 167
chiru hana no 107
chiru hana o 112
chiru to mite 47

eda yori mo 81
ezo shiranu 337

fujigoromo 841
fuji no ne no 1028
fukakusa no 832
fukimayou 781
fuku kara ni 249
fuku kaze ni 99
fuku kaze no 290
fuku kaze o 106
fuku kaze to 118
fumiwakete 288
furihaete 441

furusato ni 741
furusato to 90
furusato wa
    mishi goto mo arazu 991
    yoshino no yama shi 321
furu yuki wa 319
fushite omoi 354
futatsu naki 881
fuyugare no 791
fuyugomori 331
fuyu kawa no 591
fuyu nagara
    haru no tonari no 1021
    sora yori hara no 330
fuyu no ike ni 662

hachisuba no 165
hagi ga hana 224
hagi no tsuyu 222
hakanakute 575
hana chirasu 76
hana chireru 129
hanagatami 754
hana goto ni 464
hana mireba 104
hana mitsutsu 274
hana ni akade 238
hana no chiru 108
hana no goto 98
hana no iro wa
    kasumi ni komete 91
    tada hito sakari 450
    utsurinikeri na 113
    yuki ni majirite 335
hana no ka o 13
hana no ki mo 92
hana no ki ni 445
hana no naka 468
hana susuki
    ho ni idete koiba 653
    ware koso shita ni 748
hana to mite 1019
hana yori mo 850
harugasumi
    iro no chigusa ni 102
    kasumite inishi 210
    naka shi kayoiji 465
    nani kakusu ran 79
    tanabiku nobe no 1031

tanabiku yama no
  sakurabana
    miredomo akanu 684
    utsurowan to ya 69
tateru ya izuko 3
tatsu o misutete 31
haru goto ni
  hana no sakari wa 97
  nagaruru kawa o 43
haru kaze wa 85
haru kinu to 11
haru kureba
  kari kaeru nari 30
  yado ni mazu saku 352
haru no hi o 8
haru no iro no 93
haru no kuru 23
haru no no ni 116
haru no no no 1033
haru no yo no 41
harusame ni 122
harusame no 88
haru sareba 1008
haru tateba
  hana to ya miran 6
  kiyuru kōri no 542
haru tatedo 15
haru ya toki 10
hatsukari no
  hatsuka ni koe o 481
  naki koso watare 804
hatsuse gawa 1009
hayaki se ni 531
higurashi no
  nakitsuru nae ni 204
  naku yamazato no 205
hikari naki 967
hi no hikari 870
hisakata no
  ama no kawara no 174
  amatsu sora ni mo 751
  hikari nodokeki 84
  kumo no ue nite 269
  naka nioitaru 968
  tsuki no katsura mo 194
hisashiku mo 778
hito furusu 986
hito kouru 1058
hitome mishi 78

hitome moru 549
hitome yue 434
hito moto to 275
hito ni awan 1030
hito no mi mo 518
hito no miru 235
hito o omou
  kokoro ko no ha ni 783
  kokoro wa kari ni 585
  kokoro wa ware ni 523
hitori neru 188
hitori nomi
  nagame furu ya no 769
  nagamuru yori wa 236
hitori shite 584
hito shirenu
  omoi nomi koso 606
  omoi o tsune ni 534
  omoi ya nazo to 506
  waga kayoiji to 632
hito shirezu
  omoeba kurushi 496
  omou kokoro wa 999
  taenamashikaba 810
hitotose ni 419
hito wa isa
  kokoro mo shirazu 42
  ware wa nakina no 630
hito yari no 388
ho ni mo idenu 307
honobono to 409
horie kogu 732
hototogisu
  hatsu koe kikeba 143
  hito matsu yama ni 162
  kesa naku koe ni 849
  koe mo kikoezu 161
  mine no kumo ni ya 447
  naganaku sato no 147
  naku koe kikeba 146
  naku ya satsuki no 469
  ware to wa nashi ni 164
  yume ka utsutsu ka 641

ide hito wa 711
idete yukan 1043
ide ware o 508
ika naran 952
ike ni sumu 672

ikubaku no 1013
iku yo shi mo 934
ima iku ka 428
ima kon to
  iishi bakari ni 691
  iite wakareshi 771
ima koso are 889
ima mo kamo 121
ima sara ni
  nani oiizuran 957
  tou beki hito mo 975
  yama e kaeru na 151
ima shi wa to 773
ima wa haya 613
ima wa koji to 774
ima wa tote
  kaesu koto no wa 737
  kimi ga karenaba 800
  waga mi shigure ni 782
  wakaruru toki wa 182
ima yori wa
  tsugite furanan 318
  uete dani miji 242
ima zo shiru 969
inishie ni
  ariki arazu wa 353
  nao tachikaeru 734
inishie no
  no naka no shimizu 887
  shizu no odamaki 888
inochi dani 387
inochi ni mo 609
inochi tote 451
inochi ya wa 615
inugami no 1108
iro kawaru 278
iro miede 797
iro mo ka mo
  mukashi no kosa ni 851
  onaji mukashi ni 57
iro mo naki 729
iro nashi to 869
iro yori mo 33
isasame ni 454
ise no ama no 683
ise no umi ni 509
ise no umi no 510
ishi hashiru 54
ishima yuku 682

isonokami
  furininishi koi no 1022
  furu kara ono no 886
  furuki miyako no 144
  furu no nakamichi 679
itazura ni
  suguru tsukihi wa 351
  yukite wa kinuru 620
ito haya mo 209
ito ni yoru 415
ito semete 554
itowaruru 1045
itsu made ka 90
itsu no ma ni 140
itsu shika to 1014
itsu to te mo 546
itsuwari no
  naki yo nariseba 712
  namida nariseba 576
itsuwari to 713
itsu wa to wa 189
iza koko ni 981
iza kyō wa 95
iza sakura 77
izuku ni ka 947

kaeru yama
  ari to wa kikedo 370
  nani zo wa arite 382
kagami yama 899
kagaribi ni 529
kagaribi no 530
kagerō no 731
kagiri naki
  kimi ga tame ni to 866
  kumoi no yoso ni 367
  omoi no mama ni 657
kagiri naku 401
kai ga ne o
  ne koshi yama koshi 1098
  saya ni momiji ga 1097
kaji ni ataru 457
kakeritemo 1102
kakikurashi
  furu shirayuki no 566
  koto wa furanan 402
kakikurasu 646
kaku bakari
  au hi no mare ni 433

oshi to omou yo o 190
kaku koin 700
kakurenu no 1036
kaku shitsutsu
  to ni mo kaku ni mo 347
  yo o ya tsukusan 908
kameno o no 350
kamikaki no 1074
kanete yori 627
kannabi no
  mimuro no yama o 296
  yama o sugiyuku 300
kannazuki
  shigure furiokeru 997
  shigure mo imaga 253
  shigure ni nururu 840
kano kata ni 458
kara koromo
  himo yūgure ni 515
  kitsutsu narenishi 410
  nareba mi ni koso 786
  tatsu hi wa kikaji 375
karehaten 686
kareru ta ni 308
karigomo no 485
karikurashi 418
kari no kuru 935
karisome no 862
karite hosu 932
kasuga no ni 357
kasuga no no
  tobuhi no nomori 18
  wakana tsumi ni ya 22
  yukima o wakete 478
kasuga no wa 17
kasumi tachi 9
kasumi tatsu 103
katachi koso 875
kataito o 483
katami koso 746
katsu koete 390
katsu miredo 880
kawa kaze no 170
kawa no se ni 565
kawazu naku 125
kaze fukeba
  okitsu shiranami 994
  otsuru momijiba 304
  mine ni wakaruru 601

nami utsu kishi no 671
kaze fukedo 929
kaze no ue ni 989
kazoureba 893
kazukazu ni
  omoi omowazu 705
  ware o wasurenu 857
kazukedomo 427
keburi tachi 453
kenu ga ue ni 333
kesa kinaki 141
kesa wa shimo 643
kiehatsuru 414
kimi ga na mo 649
kimi ga omoi 978
kimi ga sasu 1010
kimi ga ueshi 853
kimi ga tame 21
kimi ga yo ni 1004
kimi ga yo wa 1085
kimi ga yuki 391
kimi kouru
  namida no toko ni 567
  namida shi naku wa 572
kimi kozuba 693
kimi masade 852
kimi narade 38
kimi ni yori 675
kimi o nomi
  omoi koshiji no 979
  omoine ni neshi 608
kimi o okite 1093
kimi o omoi 914
kimi shinobu 200
kimi to ieba 680
kimi ya kon 670
kimi ya koshi 645
ki ni mo arazu 959
kinō koso 172
kinō to ii 341
kirigirisu 196
kiri tachite 252
kita e yuku 412
kiyotaki no 925
koenu ma wa 588
koe o dani 858
koe taezu 131
koe wa shite 149
koikoite

au yo wa koyoi 176
mare ni koyoi zo 634
koiseji to 501
koishiki ga 1024
koishiki ni
inochi o kouru 517
wabite tamashii 571
koishikuba 652
koishiku wa 285
koishinaba 603
koishine to 526
koishi to wa 698
koi sureba 528
koiwabite 558
kokichirasu 922
kokoro ate ni 277
kokorogae 540
kokoro kara 422
kokoro koso 796
kokoro o zo 685
kokorozashi 7
koma namete 111
kome ya to wa 772
kono kawa ni 320
ko no ma yori 184
kono sato ni 72
kono tabi wa 420
konu hito o 777
kon yo ni mo 520
korizuma ni 631
koshi toki to 1103
koto naraba
kimi tomaru beku 395
koto no ha sae mo 854
omowazu to ya wa 1037
sakazu ya wa aranu 82
koto ni idete 607
kotoshi yori 49
kouredomo 766
koyoi kon 181
koyorogi no 1094
kozo no natsu 159
kozutaeba 109
kubeki hodo 423
kumo harenu 1050
kumoi ni mo 378
kumo mo naku 753
kumoribi no 728
kurenai ni 1044

kurenai no
furiidetsutsu naku 598
hatsuhanazome no 723
iro ni wa ideji 661
kuretake no 1003
kururu ka to 157
kuru to aku to 45
kusa fukaki 846
kusa mo ki mo 250
kyō hito o 1106
kyō kozuba 63
kyō nomi to 134
kyō wakare 369
kyō yori wa 183

makane fuku 1082
makimoku no 1076
makomo karu 587
makura yori
ato yori koi no 1023
mata shiru hito mo 670
mame naredo 1052
mate to iu ni 70
mate to iwaba 739
matsu hito mo 100
matsu hito ni 206
mesu shiranu 838
mezurashiki
hito o min to ya 730
koe naranaku ni 359
michinoku ni 628
michinoku no
adachi no mayumi 1078
asaka no numa no 677
shinobu mojizuri 724
michinoku wa 1088
michi shiraba
tazune mo yukan 313
tsumi ni mo yukan 1111
midori naru 245
mimasaka ya 1083
miminashi no 1026
mina hito wa 847
minase gawa 793
mine takaki 364
mino o kuni 1084
mi o sutete 977
mi o ushi to 806
miru hito mo

naki yamazato no 68
nakute chirinuru 297
mirume naki 623
misaburai 1091
mite mo mata 752
mite nomi ya 55
mitsu shio no 665
miwa no yama 780
mi wa sutetsu 1064
miwataseba 56
miwa yama o 94
miyagino no 694
miyakobito 937
miyako idete 408
miyako made 921
miyama ni wa
    arare furu rashi 1077
    matsu no yuki dani 19
miyama yori 310
miyoshino no
    ōkawa nobe no 699
    yamabe ni sakeru 60
    yama no anata ni 950
    yama no shirayuki
        fumiwakete 327
        tsumoru rashi 325
    yoshino no taki ni 431
mizukuki no 1072
mizu mo arazu 476
mizu no awa no 792
mizu no omo ni
    ouru satsuki no 976
    shizuku hana no iro 845
mizu no ue ni 920
mogami gawa 1092
momijiba no
    nagarete tomaru 293
    nagarezariseba 302
    chirite tsumoreru 203
momijiba o 859
momijiba wa 309
momijisenu 251
momochidori 28
momo kusa no 246
monogoto ni 187
morokoshi mo 768
morokoshi no 1049
morotomo ni 385
mukashihe ya 163
muradori no 674

murasaki no
    hitomoto yue ni 867
    iro koki toki wa 868
mushi no goto 581
musubu te no 404
mutsugoto mo 1015

nagara izuru 466
nagarete wa 828
nagashi tomo 636
nageki koru 1056
nageki oba 1057
naki hito no 855
nakikouru 655
naki tomuru 128
naki wataru 221
naku namida 829
namidagawa
    makura nagaruru 527
    nani minakami o 511
nami no hana 459
nami no oto 456
nami no utsu 424
nanihito ka 239
nani ka sono 1053
na ni medete 226
nani o shite 1063
na ni shi owaba 411
naniwagata
    ouru tamamo o 916
    shio michikurashi 913
    uramu beki ma mo 974
naniwa naru 1051
natori gawa 650
natsubiki no 703
natsugusa no 462
natsu mushi no 544
natsu mushi o 600
natsu nareba 500
natsu no yo no 156
natsu no yo wa 166
natsu to aki to 168
natsu yama ni
    koishiki hito ya 158
    naku hototogisu 145
nayotake no 993
negi goto o 1055
ne ni nakite 577
nenuru yo no 644

neru ga uchi ni 835
nete mo miyu 833
nobe chikaku 16
nochimaki no 467
nokorinaku 71
no to naraba 972
nukimidaru 923
nurete hosu 273
nuretsutsu zo 133
nushi nakute 927
nushi shiranu 241
nushi ya tare 873

ōaraki no 892
ochikochi no 29
ochitagitsu 928
ofu no ura ni 1099
ogura yama 439
oguro saki 1090
ōhara ya 871
oinureba 900
oinu to te 903
oiraku no 895
ōkata no 185
ōkata wa
   tsuki o mo medeji 879
   waga na mo minato 669
oki e ni mo 532
oki mo sezu 616
okinoite 1104
okitsu nami
   are nomi masaru 1006
   takashi no hama no 915
okuyama ni 215
okuyama no
   iwagaki momiji 282
   suga no ne shinogi 551
ominaeshi
   aki no nokaze ni 230
   fukisugite kuru 234
   ōkaru nobe ni 229
   ushirometaku mo 237
   ushi to mitsutsu zo 227
ōmi no ya 1086
ōmi yori 1071
omoedomo
   hitome tsutsumi no 659
   mi o shi wakereba 373
   nao utomarenu 1032

omowazu to nomi 1039
omoiidete 735
omoiizuru
   tokiwa no yama no
     hototogisu 148
   iwatsutsuji 495
omoiken 1042
omoiki ya 961
omoiseku 930
omoitsutsu 552
omoiyaru
   koshi no shira yama 980
   sakai haruka ni 524
omou chō
   hito no kokoro no 1038
   koto no ha nomi ya 688
omoudochi
   haru no yamabe ni 126
   hitoribitori ga 654
   mataisenu yo wa 864
omou ni wa 503
omou tomo
   karenan hito o 799
   kou tomo awan 507
omou yori 725
onaji e o 255
ōnusa no 706
ōnusa to 707
orite miba 223
oritoraba 65
oritsureba 32
oroka naru 557
ōsaka no
   arashi no kaze wa 988
   seki ni nagaruru 537
   seki shi masashiki 374
   yūtsukedori mo 536
   yūtsukedori ni 740
oshimedomo 130
oshimu kara 371
oshimu ran 398
oshiteru ya 894
oshi to omou 114
osoku izuru 877
oto ni nomi 470
otowa yama
   kesa koe kureba 142
   kodakaku nakite 384
   oto ni kikitsutsu 473

ōzora no 316
ōzora o 885

saho yama no
  hahaso no iro wa 267
  hahaso no momiji 281
sakasama ni 896
sakashira ni 1047
sakidatanu 837
sakisomeshi
  toki yori nochi wa 931
  yado shi kawareba 280
saku hana wa 101
sakurabana
  chiraba chiranan 74
  chiri kai kumore 349
  chirinuru kaze no 89
  haru kuwawareru 61
  sakinikerashi na 59
  toku chirinu tomo 83
sakura chiru 75
sakura iro ni 66
samidare ni 153
samidare no 160
samushiro ni 689
sasa no ha ni
  furitsumu yuki no 891
  oki hatsu shimo no 663
  oku shimo yori mo 563
sasa no kuma 1080
satobito no 704
sato wa arete 248
satsuki koba 138
satsuki matsu
  hana tachibana no 139
  yama hototogisu 137
satsuki yama 579
sayo fukete
  ama no to wataru 648
  nakabatake yuku 452
sayonaka to 192
semi no ha no
  hitoe ni usuki 1035
  yoru no koromo wa 876
semi no koe 715
se o sekeba 836
shide no yama 789
shiguretsutsu 820
shihatsu yama 1073

shiite yuku 403
shikari tote 936
shikishima no 697
shikitae no 595
shimo no tate 291
shimo to yū 1070
shimo ya tabi 1075
shinobureba 519
shinoburedo 633
shinonome no
  hogara hogara to 637
  wakare o oshimi 640
shinuru inochi 568
shio no yama 345
shiragumo ni 191
shira kawa no 666
shirakumo no
  konata kanata ni 379
  taezu tanabiku 945
  yae ni kasanaru 380
shiranami ni 301
shiranami no 472
shiratama to 599
shiratsuyu mo 260
shiratsuyu no 257
shiratsuyu o 437
shirayuki no
  furite tsumoreru 328
  furushiku toki wa 363
  tokoro mo wakazu 324
  tomo ni waga mi wa 1065
  yae furishikeru 902
shiriniken 946
shirushi naki 110
shiru shiranu 477
shiru to ieba 676
shita ni nomi 667
shita no obi no 405
shitawarete 389
sode hijite 2
soe ni tote 1060
sokoi naki 722
somabito wa 1101
sore o dani 811
sugaru naku 366
suma no ama no
  shio yaki koro mo 758
  shio yaku keburi 708
suminoe no

kishi ni yoru nami 559
kishi no hime matsu 906
matsu hodo hisa ni 779
matsu o aki kaze 360
sumiyoshi no 906
sumiyoshi to 917
sumizome no 843
suruga naru 489

tachidomari 305
tachikaeri 474
tachinuwanu 926
tachiwakare 365
taezu yuku 720
ta ga aki ni 232
ta ga misogi 995
ta ga sato ni 710
ta ga tame ni 924
ta ga tame no 265
tagitsu se ni 592
tagitsu se no
    hayaki kokoro o 660
    naka ni mo yodo wa 493
tamaboko no 738
tamadare no 874
tamakazura
    hau ki amata ni 709
    ima wa tayu to ya 762
tamakushige 642
tamoto yori 425
tamuke ni wa 421
tanabata ni 180
tane shi areba 512
tani kaze ni 12
tanomekoshi 736
tanometsutsu 614
tarachine no 368
tarekomete 80
tare miyo to 856
tare o ka mo 909
tare shi ka mo 58
tatsuta gawa
    nishiki orikaku 314
    momijiba nagaru 284
    momiji midarete 283
tatsutahime 298
tayori ni mo 480
te mo furede 605
tobu tori no 535

todomeaezu 898
todomu beki 132
toki shi mo are 839
toki sugite 790
tokiwa naru 24
toritomuru 897
toshi fureba 52
toshi goto ni
    au to wa suredo 179
    momijiba nagasu 311
toshi no uchi ni 1
toshi o hete
    hana no kagami to 44
    kienu omoi wa 596
    sumikoshi sato o 971
tsui ni yuku 861
tsukigusa ni 247
tsuki kage ni 602
tsuki mireba 193
tsuki ya aranu 747
tsuki yo ni wa
    konu hito mataru 775
    sore to mo miezu 40
tsuki yo yoshi 692
tsukubane no
    kono mo kano mo ni 1095
    ko no moto goto ni 966
    mine no momijiba 1096
tsuma kouru 233
tsu no kuni no
    naniwa no ashi no 604
    naniwa omowazu 696
tsure mo naki
    hito o kou tote 521
    hito o ya netaku 486
tsuremonaku 788
tsurenaki o 809
tsurezure o 617
tsuru kamo mo 355
tsutsumedomo 556
tsuyu nagara 270
tsuyu naranu 589
tsuyu o nado 860

ubatama no
    waga kurokami ya 460
    yami no utsutsu wa 647
    yume ni nani ka wa 449
uchitsuke ni

koshi to ya hana no 444
sabishiku mo aru ka 848
uchiwabite 539
uchiwatasu 1007
ueshi toki 271
ueshi ueba 268
uete inishi 776
uguisu no
  kasa ni nū to yū 36
  kozo no yadori no 1046
  naku nobe goto ni 105
  tani yori izuru 14
ukigusa no 538
uki koto o 213
ukime nomi 755
ukime oba 1105
ukinagara 827
ukiyo ni wa 964
ume ga eda ni 5
ume ga ka o 46
ume no hana
  mi ni koso kitsure 1011
  niou harube wa 39
  sakite no nochi no 1066
  sore to mo miezu 334
  tachiyoru bakari 35
ume no ka no 336
ura chikaku 326
uramite mo 814
ureshiki o 865
utatane ni 553
utsusemi no
  kara wa ki goto ni 448
  yo ni mo nitaru ka 73
  yo no hito goto yo 716
utsusemi wa 831
utsutsu ni wa 656

wabibito no
  sumu beki yado to 985
  wakite tachiyoru 292
wabihatsuru 813
wabinureba
  mi o ukigusa no 938
  shiite wasuren to 569
wabishira ni 1067
waga gotoku
  mono ya kanashiki 578
  ware o omowan 750

waga io wa
  miwa no yamamoto 982
  miyako no tatsumi 983
waga kado ni 208
waga kado no 1079
waga kimi wa 343
waga kitsuru 295
waga koi ni 590
waga koi o 668
waga koi wa
  hito shiru rame ya 504
  miyamagakure no 560
  munashiki sora ni 488
  shiranu yamaji ni 597
  yukue mo shirazu 611
waga kokoro 878
waga matanu 338
waga mi kara 960
waga seko ga
  koromo harusame 25
  koromo no suso o 171
  kubeki yoi nari 1110
waga seko o 1089
waga sode ni 763
waga sono no 498
waga tame ni 186
waga ue ni 863
waga yado ni 120
waga yado no
  hana fumishidaku 442
  hanami gatera ni 67
  ike no fujinami 135
  kiku no kakine ni 564
waga yado wa
  michi no naki made 770
  yuki furishikite 322
waga yowai 346
wagi mo ko ni 1107
wakare chō 381
wakare oba 393
wakarete wa 372
wakaruredo 399
wakuraba ni 962
ware mite mo 905
ware nomi ya
  aware to omowan 244
  yo o uguisu to 798
ware nomi zo 612
ware o kimi 973

ware o nomi 1040
ware o omou 1041
ware wa kesa 436
warinaku mo 570
wasuraren 996
wasuraruru
  mi o ujibashi no 825
  toki shi nakereba 514
wasuregusa
  kare mo ya suru to 801
  nani o ka tane 50 802
  tane toramashi o 765
wasurenan 719
wasurenan to 718
wasurete wa 970
wata no hara
  yaso shima kakete 407
  yosekuru nami no 912
watatsumi no
  kazashi ni saseru 911
  okitsu shioai ni 910
  waga mi kosu nami 816
watatsumi to 733
watatsu umi no 344

yado chikaku 34
yadori seshi
  hana tachibana mo 155
  hito no katami ka 240
yadori shite 117
yamabuki no 1012
yamabuki wa 123
yamagatsu no 742
yamagawa ni 303
yamagawa no 1000
yama kakusu 413
yama kaze ni 394
yama no i no 764
yamashina no
  otowa no taki no 1109
  otowa no yama no 664
yamashiro no 759
yama takami
  hito mo susamenu 50
  kumoi ni miyuru 358
  mitsutsu waga koshi 87
  shitayuku mizu no 494
  tsune ni arashi no 446
yama ta moru 306

yamazakura
  kasumi no ma yori 479
  waga mi ni kureba 51
yamazato wa
  aki koso koto ni 214
  fuyu zo sabishisa 315
  mono no wabishiki 944
ya yo ya mate 152
yodo gawa no 721
yoi no ma mo 561
yoi no ma ni 1059
yoi yoi ni
  makura sadamen 516
  nugite waga nuru 593
yo ni fureba
  koto no ha shigeki 958
  usa koso masare 951
yo no naka ni
  furinaru mono wa 890
  izura waga mi no 943
  saranu wakare no 901
  taete sakura no 53
yo no naka no
  hito no kokoro wa 795
  ukeku ni akinu 954
  uki mo tsuraki mo 941
  uki tabi goto ni 1061
yo no naka o 949
yo no naka wa
  ika ni kurushi to 1062
  izure ka sashite 987
  kaku koso arikere 475
  mukashi yori ya wa 948
  nani ka tsune naru 933
  yume ka utsutsu ka 942
yo no ukime 955
yo o itoi 1068
yo o samumi
  koromo kari ga ne 211
  oku hatsu shimo o 416
yo o sutete 956
yorozuyo o 356
yorube nami 619
yoshino gawa
  iwakiri tōshi 492
  iwanami takaku 471
  kishi no yamabuki 124
  mizu no kokoro wa 651
  yoshi ya hito koso 794

yoso nagara 1054
yoso ni mite 119
yoso ni nomi
　aware to zo mishi 37
　kikamashi mono o 749
　koi ya wataran 383
yoso ni shite 541
yo to tomo ni 573
yo ya kuraki 154
yūgure no 392
yūgure wa 484
yuki fureba
　fuyugomori seru 323
　ki goto ni wa nazo 337
yuki furite
　hito mo kayowanu 329
　toshi no kurenuru 340
yukikaeri 785
yuki no uchi ni 4

yuki to nomi 86
yuku mizu ni 522
yuku toshi no 342
yumeji ni mo 574
yumeji ni wa 658
yume ni dani
　au koto kataku 767
　miyu to wa mieji 681
yume no uchi ni 525
yume to koso 834
yū sareba
　hito naki toko o 815
　hotaru yorike ni 562
　itodo higataki 545
　koromode samushi 317
yūzuku yo
　obotsukanaki o 417
　ogura no yama ni 312
　sasu ya okabe no 490

SUBJECT INDEX

Abe no Nakamaro, 15
Abrams, M. H., and four artistic
    coordinates, 386n, 389n
Adachi City, 368
aesthetic of reading the anthology, 24–34
aesthetics of *Kokinshū* waka, 13–15
Age of Man, 380, 380n
Age of the Gods, 36, 36n, 379, 380n
"Airs of the States" (feng, soeuta), 23, 37,
    37n, 393. *See also* suasion
Akashi Bay, 165
Akirakeiko (Somedono Consort), 64, 304
Akitsushima, 384n
allusive variation, 59, 98, 144
Amanogawa, 168
Amaterasu ūmikami, 36, 368
Amewaka, Prince, 36
Analects, 37n, 144, 390, 397
Ankō tennō, 89
anonymous poems, 15, 23, 46n, 50
Anthology of Japanese Poems, Newly Selected,
    9, 391
antithesis in waka, 134
Ariwara no Narihira, 8, 44, 383, 383n
Ariwara no Tokiharu, 149
Ariwara no Yukihira, 8, 9, 18, 384
arrangement: and interpretation, 24; of
    anthologies, 4, 19–24, 34; of poems in the
    Kokinshū, 19–34
Asaka Marsh, 244
Asama Mountain, 359
association of imagery, 20, 34
Asuka (capital), 139
Asuka River, 47, 129, 144
Asukai no Masatsune, 401
Atsunori, Prince, 295
Atsuyoshi, Prince, 314
authorship of the Prefaces, 385n

Awa Province, 328
Awaji Island, 311
Awata, 376
Azuma, 154
Azuma uta, 23, 34, 371

balance of subject and object, 19
Book of Changes, 389, 390
Book of Rites, 49, 52, 388
Book of Songs, 23, 53, 379n, 388, 389, 393,
    394
books of the *Kokinshū*, 4, 21
Buddhism: and politics, 6; in waka, 7, 16,
    34, 112, 176, 198, 235, 324, 339
Bunkashūreishū, 3n
Bunkyō hirfuron, 388
Bunrin. *See* Fun'ya no Yasuhide
byōbu-uta, *see* screen poems

calendar, vii, 49, 96, 97, 120, 137, 186, 248;
    and imagery, 85, 87; and intercalery
    months, 66
Ceadel, E. B., 391
celebratory poems, 22
ceremonies and ritual, 34, 156, 185, 189,
    252, 300, 356, 365, 367, 369, 374
Ch'ang-an, 6
cherry blossoms, 63
chidori, 150
Chinese characters used in Japan, 5
Chinese criticism, 382n, 383, 387–400
Chinese influence on *Kokinshū* prefaces,
    387–400
Chinese language, 3
Chinese legends, 98, 334
Chinese literary theory, 387–400
Chinese poetry: as model, 5–8, 381, 382n;
    written by Japanese, 3, 3n, 5, 8, 9, 381n

Chinese Preface, 3, 344, 379–386, 387–400
passim; and date of compilation, 11;
authorship of, 385n. *See also* manajo
Ch'iu Ch'ih, 395
chōka, 7n, 23, 34, 338, 339, 380, 380n; form,
15; included in *Kokinshū*, 15
chokusenshū, 55. *See also* imperial
anthologies
Chou Li, 393
Chrysanthemum Festival, 125
chūjitsu, 17
Chung Hung, 388, 390, 392, 393, 395, 396,
397n, 399, 400
Classic of Songs. See *Book of Songs*
comparison, principle of (pi, nazuraeuta),
38, 38n, 393
compilation: of *Man'yōshū*, 20; of the
Kokinshū, 3, 9, 10–13
compilers of the *Kokinshū*, 3, 9, 10–13. *See
also* Ki no Tomonori, Ki no Tsurayuki,
Mibu no Tadamine, Ōshikōchi no
Mitsune
Confucius, 390
court poetry, 3, 6, 8–10, 23; rules of, 15–19
court rank and office, viii, 94, 300, 319

daiei, 15, 26
Daigo tennō, viii, 43n, 55, 144, 151, 161,
300, 341, 371; and commissioning of the
Kokinshū, 11, 46, 46n; and occasions for
poetry, 9; and screen poems, 10
Daijōsai, 369, 370
dating: of *Kokinshū* compilation, 11, 337; of
Kokinshū poems, 5, 15, 16; of *Kokinshū*
Prefaces, 391
decline of Japanese poetry, 40
decorative prefix, 17, 50
decorum, 382n; in T'ang poetry, 14; of
Kokinshū waka, 14, 15, 23; of poetic
topics, 15
descriptive principle (fu, kazoeuta), 38, 38n,
381, 393
diction: in waka, 14, 15; of *Kokinshū*, 17, 18;
of *Man'yōshū*, 16, 17, 18
didactic theory, 386n, 390, 394, 398, 399

eastern songs, 23, 34, 371
elegant confusion, 27, 50, 142, 151; and

Fujiwara style, 18
"Elegantia," principle of (ya, tadagotouta),
23, 38, 39, 39n, 379, 393
engo (word association), 18, 23
Enryakuji, 74, 292
enthronement, 369, 370
envoys to chōka, 345
"Essay on Literature," 388, 394
"Eulogies," principle of (sung, iwaiuta), 23,
39, 39n, 379, 393
evocative image, principle of (hsing,
tatoeuta), 38, 38n, 379, 393
expressive theory, 38n, 389, 393, 397–99

Fan Yün, 395
feng, 23, 37n, 393
fictionalized autobiographies, 3
Fifth Ward Consort (Junshi), 264
figurative language, 7, 15, 16
folk songs, 15, 138, 369
formal poetry, 21
forms of poetry, 15, 36, 339, 347, 380,
380n
fu, 38, 38n, 381, 393
fu (poetic form), 382n
Fuji, 40, 41, 41n
fujibakama, 116
fujigoromo, 290
Fujiwara family, 8, 151; Junshi, 264; Kintō,
12, 36n, 68; Kiyosuke, 11, 401; Meishi, 8;
Michiko (Manshi), 149; Michimune, 401;
Mototoshi, 402; Mototsune, 147,
288; Nakazane, 11; Onshi, 9, 151, 300,
327, 337; Sadakuni, 13, 149; Sadazane,
401; Sekio, 18; Shunzei, 375, 401, 402;
Sokushi, 304; Takaiko, 10, 50, 51, 148;
Teika, vii, 12n, 61, 74, 142, 229, 375;
Tokihira, 13; Yorimichi, 401; Yoshifusa,
8, 51, 64
Fujiwara style, 18
"Fujiwara Takaiko gobyōbu-uta," 10
Fukakusa, 292, 328
Fukakusa Mikado, 292. *See also* Ninmyō
tennō
Fukiage, 125
Fun'ya no Yasuhide, 44, 383, 383n, 395
Furu Falls, 118
Fushimi, 331
Futami, 168

Gain, 72
gejitsu, 18
Godless Month (Kannazuki), 137, 336
Gosechi dancers, 300
Gosenshū, 8, 12n, 230
Goshūishū, 12
Great Thanksgiving Festival, 369, 370
Great Western Temple, 57

hagi, 105, 110
haikai poems, 23, 34, 348
hana, 63
hanka, 380n
Hatsuse, 61
Hatsuse River, 348
headnotes, 15
Heart of Literature: Elaborations, 388, 389
Heian: beliefs, 247, 301, 316, 357, 365, 378;
    capital, 6, 65; customs, 54, 58, 145, 185,
    236, 237, 263, 290, 298; legends, 33, 98,
    104, 168; poetry, 3–10, 20; ranks and
    offices, viii, 94, 300, 319
Heian society, 20; and literature, 3, 4; and
    love, 23, 101; and travel, 22, 164
Heijō, 140, 331
Heizei tennō, viii, 42, 42n, 43n, 74, 111,
    128, 336; and compilation of the
    Man'yōshū, 384
Henjō, 8, 43, 70, 382
Henjō Collection (Henjō shū), 44n
Hiei, Mount, 74, 160, 292
Higashiyama, 128
higurashi, 106
Hinokuma River, 368
Hitachi Province, 155, 373
honkadori (allusive variation), 59, 98, 144
Horikawa Chancellor, 288
hototogisu, 87, 88, 349
Hsiao T'ung, 388
Hsieh Ling-yün, 395, 399
hsing, 38, 38n, 379, 393
Hsü Ling, 388
hua (literary flower), 383n, 396
human affairs in waka, 7, 19, 20
Hyakunin isshū, 12n, 61, 109

I Ching, 389, 390
Ide, 84
Ikaga, Cape, 179

Ikaho Marsh, 344
imagery: and arrangement of the Kokinshū,
    21–33; in waka, 27
immortality of literature, 394, 399
imperial anthologies, 3, 12, 13, 55
imperial palace, 72, 94, 103, 120, 121, 125,
    180, 185
Inaba, 152
incense, 58
Index to the Kokinshū, 11
influence of the Kokinshū, 34
Ingyō tennō, 45n, 378
inspiration for Japanese poetry, 35, 36, 40
integrating of waka sequences, 19–34
intensifying prefix, 17
interpolated commentary, dating of, 39n
interpretation of poems, 24
Inugami, 377
Ise, 314
Ise Bay, 194
Ise monogatari, 4, 35n, 54; See also Tales of
    Ise
Ise Province, 234, 374
Ise shū (Ise Collection), 61
Ishiyama Temple, 121
Isonokami Temple, 89, 113
Itō, Princess, 308
iwaiuta, 39n. See also "Eulogies"
Izumi Province, 312
Izumi River, 165

Japanese literary theory, 382n, 387–400
Japanese poetic, 14
Japanese poetry: as art, 14; decline of, 40;
    forms of, 15, 36, 339, 347, 380, 380n;
    inspiration for, 35, 36, 40, 379; origins of,
    35–37, 40, 41, 380, 381; power of, 35
Japanese Preface, 3, 13–14, 35–47, 387–400
    passim; and date of compilation, 11; and
    distinction between kotoba and kokoro,
    14; and Man'yōshū, 103, 163
jo, 17
jōjitsu, 17
Junna tennō, viii, 3n, 6, 70

Kagami Mountain, 308
Kagawa Keiki, 12n
Kai Province, 296, 319, 374
Kaifūsō, 381n

kakekotoba (pivot word), 18, 23
Kakinomoto no Hitomaro, 87, 108, 142,
    382n, 385, 396, 399; as model, 47, 382; as
    poet, 41, 42, 398; compared with
    Tsurayuki, 12
kakitsubata, 165
Kameno-o Mountain, 147
Kamiya River, 180
Kamo festival, 374
Kamo Priestess, 304
Kamo River, 97
Kamo Shrine, 189, 374
kanajo, 3, 35–47, 386. *See also* Japanese
    Preface
Kanmu tennō, viii, 181, 308, 325
Kannabi, 159
Kannarinotsubo, 103
Kannazuki, 137, 336
"Kanpyō no ontoki kisai no miya no
    utaawase," 9, 102
Kara, Cape, 180
Karakoto, 179
Kasatori Mountain, 122
Kase Mountain, 165
Kasuga, Mount, 151
Kasuga Meadow, 54, 186
Kasuga Shrine, 164, 186
Katano City, 181
Kataoka, 120
katauta, 380n
katsura, 104, 327
Katsura River, 314
Katsura Village, 327
Kawara Minister, 292
Kazan Temple, 82
kazoeuta, 38n. *See also* descriptive principle
Kazuraki Mountain, 366
Keikokushū, 3n
Ki family, 8
Ki no Aritsune, 8
Ki no Tomonori, 11, 13, 46, 385
Ki no Tsurayuki, 3, 9, 12n, 12, 24, 387–400
    passim; and compilation of the *Kokinshū*,
    8, 11, 46, 38; and the Japanese Preface, 3,
    12, 386; as critic, 14, 397n; as poet, 12, 15,
    17, 18, 26, 61
Ki no Yoshimochi, 3, 382n, 387–400 *passim*
Kibi, 369
kin (lute), 333

kinuginu poem, 101
Kin'yōshū, 12
kirigirisu, 104, 351
Kisen, 45, 383, 383n
Kitayama, 76, 132, 135
Kiyohara no Fukayabu, 357
Kiyotaki River, 315
Kizu River, 165
Kōbun tennō, 381n
Kōchi, 335
kochū (old commentary), 36n
Kojiki, 380n
Kokindenjū, 107, 172, 177
Kokinrokujō, 76
Kokinshū as literary model, 4
Kokinwakashū mokuroku, 11
Kokinwakashū seigi, 12n
Kōkō tennō, viii, 8, 55, 102, 118, 146, 370
kokoro, 12, 14, 18, 36n
Komachi Collection (Komachi shū), 101
konpon, 380, 380n
"Koresada no miko no ie no utaawase," 9
Koresada, Prince, 9, 102
Koretaka, Prince, 8, 64, 70, 168, 303, 321,
    328
Koshi, 58
koto, 7n
kotoba, 12, 14, 18, 36n
Koyorogi, 301
kuchinashi, 349, 352
kudaishi, 7
kudaiwaka, 7
Kudaiwaka, 7n, 101
Kujō residence, 147
Kūkai, 7, 388
Kume City, 369
kuo-feng, 23. *See also* "Airs of the States"
Kurabu, Mount, 60
Kurōdo-dokoro, 113
kutsukanmuri, 182
kuzu, 123
Kyōto. *See* Heian

Lady Ise, 15
Lady Murasaki, 3
Lady of the Bedchamber (miyasundokoro),
    79
Lady Pan, 396
Li Chi, 49, 52, 388

Li Ling, 396
literary flower (hua), 383n, 396
literary fruit (chih), 383n, 396
Literary Mind and the Carving of Dragons (Heart of Literature), 388, 389
Literary Mirror: Discussions of Its Secret Store, 388
Literary Selections, 7, 21, 388
literary style, 395
literary theory, 387–400 *passim*; didactic, 386n, 390, 394, 398, 399; expressive, 386n, 389, 393, 397, 398, 399; mimetic, 386n, 394; objective, 386n, 394; pragmatic, 386n, 389, 390, 394, 396–99
Literature: Elaborations, 389
Liu Chen, 396
Liu Hsieh, 388
Lotus Sutra, 95, 209
love as poetic topic, 21, 29–34
Lu Chi, 388, 399
"Lun Wen," 388, 394
Lun yü (Analects of Confucius), 37n, 144, 390, 397
lunar calendar. *See* calendar
lyric, 382
lyrical function of literature. *See* literary theory, expressive

"Maiden Flower Contest at the Suzakuin," 113
"Major Preface" (*Book of Songs*), 388, 389, 390, 393, 394
Makura no sōshi, 3, 193
makurakotoba, 16
manajo, 3, 36n, 40n, 379–86. *See also* Chinese Preface.
Man'yōshū, 19, 380n; allusions to, 75, 138, 145, 163, 188, 189, 190, 192, 193, 199, 206, 207, 208, 209, 235, 248, 249, 250, 256, 297, 312, 336, 369, 377, 378; arrangement of, 20; as predecessor of *Kokinshū*, 3, 6, 43, 110; compilation of 20, 41n, 384; era, 382n; poems excluded from *Kokinshū*, 11, 46; poems in *Kokinshū*, 46n; rhetoric compared with *Kokinshū*, 16, 17; scholarship, 12n; style, 49; travel poems in, 22
Man'yōshū Continued, 385, 385n
Mao-shih cheng-i, 379n

Masaoka Shiki, 12, 49
matsumushi, 105
Matsuyama, 41
mayumi, 222
Mibu no Tadamine, 11, 13, 15, 46, 345, 385
Michinoku, 153, 156
Mika Meadow, 165
Mikado, vii, 369. *See also* tennō
Mikasa Mountain, 164
Mikawa Province, 319
mimetic theory, 386n, 394
Miminashi Mountain, 352
Minamoto no Noboru, 11
Minamoto no Tōru, 292
Minase River, 223
Mitsune Collection (Mitsune shū), 12n, 84
Miwa, Mount, 75, 273
Miyagi Moor, 249
Montoku tennō, 10, 64, 168, 304, 317
Morokoshi, 270, 359
Moru Mountain, 122
Motoyasu, Prince, 148
mountain thrush, 50, 52
Murakami tennō, 8, 9
murasaki, 236
Musashi Plain, 284
Musashi Province, 159
music, 393
mysteries of the *Kokinshū*, 57, 107, 172, 176

nadeshiko, 117
Nagara Bridge, 41, 41n, 285
Nagisa villa, 64
Naka Mountain, 369
Nakatsukasa, 314
Naniwa, 222
Naobi, 365
Nara, 6, 15, 41, 41n, 74, 336
Nara Mikado, 42; *see* Heizei tennō
Narihira Collection (Narihira shū), 166
narration, 379
natural world in poetry, 7, 19
nature in *Kokinshū* waka, 19, 29
nazuraeuta, 38n. *See also* comparison
nenunawa, 355
New Songs from the Tower of Jade, 388
next morning poem, 101
Nihon ryōiki, 381n
Nihon sandai jitsuroku, 146

Nihon shoki, 380n, 381n
Nijō Consort (Takaiko), 50
nikki bungaku, 3
Ningyō tennō, 45n
Ninken tennō, 89
Ninmyō tennō, viii, 8, 76, 148, 264, 292, 369
Ninna Mikado, 55, 118, 146, 147. *See also* Kōkō tennō
Ninnaji, 127
Nintoku tennō, 37n
Nishi no Ōtera, 57
Nunohiki Falls, 315

Obasute Mountain, 302
objective theory, 386n, 394
obliqueness in poetry, 7
occasional poetry, 15, 398
Ōe no Chisato, 7n, 101
Ōgura Mountain, 136
Ōharano Shrine, 299
Ōi River, 11, 136, 147, 314
Ōi River Excursion, 9
"Ōigawa gyōkō waka no jo," 12
Ōjin tennō, 37n
Oki, 164
Okitsu, 312
Ōmi, 153, 154
Ōmi Province, 240
ominaeshi, 112
One Hundred Poems by One Hundred Poets, 12n, 61, 109
Ono, 133, 321
Ono no Komachi, 45, 383, 383n, 395, 396, 398
Ono no Takamura, 18, 164, 384, 384n
oral songs, 46n
origins of Japanese poetry, 35–37, 40, 41, 380, 381
oriku, 166, 174
Ōsaka, 231
Ōsaka Barrier, 89, 154
Ōsaka Hill, 47
Ōsawa Pond, 126
Ōshikōchi no Mitsune, 11, 13, 15, 46, 385
Otoko Mountain, 41, 113
Ōtomo no Kuronushi, 46, 383, 383n, 395, 398, 399
Ōtomo Yakamochi, 20

Otowa Falls, 316
Otowa Mountain, 89
Otowa River, 265
Ōtsu, Prince, 381n
Ōutadokoro, 23

paintings on screens, 10
pattern of courtly love, 22, 22n
personal poetry collections, 3
personification, 19
pi, 38, 38n, 393. *See also* comparison
Pillow Book, 3, 193
pillow word, viii, 16
pivot word, viii, 18
place names, 10
Po Chü-i, 36n, 101, 109, 205
poem tales, 3
poetic sequences, 20
poetic vocabulary, 4
poetry: as art, 5; as private communication, 5; forms of, 15, 36, 339, 347, 380, 380n; integrated into other texts, 20; social use of, 15, 20, 398
Poetry Bureau, 11, 366
poetry competitions, records of, 3, 4, 9, 62
"Poetry Contest at the House of Prince Koresada," 9, 12
"Poetry Contest at the House of the Minister of Popular Affairs," 9
"Poetry Contest Held at the Residence of the Consort in the Kanpyō Era," 102
"Poetry Contest Held by the Consort in the Kanpyō Era," 9, 12
"Poetry Contest of Teijinoin," 11
"Poetry Contest of the Second Prince of the Ninna Era," 102
Poetry Gradings, 388, 390, 392, 392n, 395
power of Japanese poetry, 35
pragmatic theory, 386n, 389, 390, 394, 396–99
prayer strips (nusa), 156, 252, 356
preface (jo), 17
Prefaces, order of composition, 13. *See also* Chinese Preface, Japanese Preface, kanajo, manajo
private poetry, 21
progression of topics, 20, 24, 34
"Prose-poem on the Goddess," 198
Pu Shang, 388

reading the anthology 24–34
reasoning in poetry, 7, 49
"Record of Music," 388, 390
records of poetry contests, 3, 4, 9, 62
reigns of tennō, viii
rhetorical modes, 393
rhetorical techniques, 7, 15, 16
rhymeprose, 382
"Rhymeprose on Literature," 388
rhythm of waka, 16
rikugi. See six poetic principles
Rites of Chou, 393
rokkasen, 43n. See also six poetic geniuses
rule of taste, 4
rules of court poetry, 14, 15–19
Ryōkiden, 121
Ryōunshū, 3n
Ryūmon Temple, 316

Sadatoki, Prince, 147
Sadayasu, Prince, 148
Saga Meadow, 44, 115
Saga tennō, 3, 6, 74, 84, 325
Saho Mountain, 123
Saho River, 150
saibara, 7n, 369
Saichō, 7
saigū, 234
sakaki, 367
sakura, 63
sama, 14
Sandai jitsuroku, 299
Sanjō no machi, 10
Sarashina, 302
Sarumaru Dayū, 109
Sayononaka Mountain, 219
screen poems, 55, 131, 149, 279; and artistic
    presentation of waka, 5, 10
seasonal imagery, 10, 21, 24–29
sedōka, 15, 23, 34, 347, 380, 380n
Sei Shōnagon, 3
Seiwa tennō, 8, 50, 64, 121, 146, 147, 148,
    336, 370
Senzaishū, 12
set topics, 15, 26
Shen hsien ch'uan, 344
Shide Mountain, 275
Shiga Pass, 81
Shiga Temple, 82

shih (literary fruit), 383n, 396
Shih Ching, 23, 53, 379n, 388, 389, 393, 394
Shih-p'in, 388, 392n, 397
Shikashū, 12
shikashū, 3
Shimōsa, 166
Shimotsu Izumo Temple, 209
Shinkokinshū, 63, 66
shinobu, 105, 257
Shinsen Man'yōshū, 9, 21, 391
Shinsen wakashū, 391
Shintō ceremonies, 23, 185, 189, 300, 367
Shiogama, 293
Shira Mountain, 157
Shira River, 240
Shitateru, Princess, 35, 36
Shoku Man'yōshū, 385, 385n
Shūishū, 12, 381n
Six Dynasties, 6–8, 14, 18
six poetic geniuses, 15, 43n, 382; criticized,
    43; in the Japanese preface, 13; poetic
    techniques, 18. See also Ariwara no
    Narihira, Fun'ya no Yasuhide, Henjō,
    Kisen, Ono no Komachi, Ōtomo no
    Kuronushi
six poetic principles, 34, 37, 40, 40n, 379,
    393. See also "Airs of the States"
    (suasion), comparison, descriptive,
    "Elegantia," "Eulogies," evocative image
social use of poetry, 15, 20, 398
soeuta. See suasion
Somedone Consort (Meishi), 8
Somedono, 8, 64
Sosei Collection (Sosei shū), 69, 71
Sotōri, Princess, 15, 45, 45n, 378, 383, 395
sovereign. See tennō
Spring Palace, 51
style of Kokinshū waka, 8
Suasion, principle of, 37, 37n, 39, 379. See
    also "Airs of the States"
subject nouns, location of, 18
Sugawara District, 331
Sugawara Michizane, 9, 21
Suma, 253, 326
Sumida River, 166
Suminoe (Sumiyoshi), 41, 150
sung, 23, 39, 39n, 379, 393
Sung Yü, 198
Suruga, 202

Susano-o no mikoto, 35, 36, 397
susuki, 116
Suzakuin, 113, 169
"Suzukuin no ominaeshi awase," 113

"Ta hsü." *See* "Major Preface"
tachibana, 83
Tachibana Isle, 83
Tachibana no Kiyotomo, 84
tadagotouta. *See* "Elegantia"
Tadamine Collection (Tadamine shū), 13, 344
Tadamine juttei, 13
Tago Bay, 189
Tai K'ai-chih, 325
Taira no Kanemori, 39n
Tajima, 168
Takasago Peak, 110
Takashi, 312
Takatsu, Princess, 325
Tale of Genji, 3
Tales of Ise, 54, 64, 66, 124, 165, 168, 185,
    199, 226, 228, 231, 234, 252, 263, 264,
    274, 280, 296, 298, 315, 328, 332, 335;
    allusions to, 86, 88, 90; use of poems in,
    24
Tales of Yamato, 13, 24, 42n, 124, 185
Tamatsushima Mountain, 311
Tamino Island, 311
Tamura, 317
Tamura Mikako, 304. *See also* Montoku
    tennō
Tanabata, 98, 168, 297, 349
T'ang dynasty, 5, 6, 382, 382n
tanka, 338. *See also* waka
tao, 389
T'ao Ch'ien, 395
tatoeuta. *See* evocative imagery
Tatsuta, Princess, 132
Tatsuta Mountain, 79, 335
Tatsuta River, 42, 128
Teiji villa, 68
"Teijinoin Maiden Flower Contest," 113
"Teijinoin no utaawase," 11, 68
"Teijinoin ominaeshi awase," 113
Teika text of the *Kokinshū*, 402
Ten Principles of Japanese Poetry, 13
tennō, 43n; and imperial anthologies, 55;
    and poetry anthologies, 3; in history, vii
    viii, 1; Yōzei, 51, 336, 370

texts of the *Kokinshū*, 74, 382n, 401
thirty-six poetic geniuses, 11
Thousand Character Classic, 37n
time: and arrangement of the *Kokinshū*, 20,
    28; in waka, 7, 19, 26
Tobuhi field, 54
Tokiwa Mountain, 90
tokonatsu, 95
Tokono Mountain, 377
tomeuta, 39, 39n
tone of Heian waka, 7, 14
topical organization, 23, 24, 34
topics, 34; dai, 7, 15, 26; of Japanese court
    poetry, 4; of *Kokinshū*, 21; of spring
    poems, 25
torimono, 367
Tosa Diary, 12, 167
Toyora, 139
Ts'ao Chih, 395, 396
Ts'ao P'i, 388, 394, 399
Tsu Province, 222
tsukigusa, 118
Tsukuba Mountain, 40, 46, 327
Tsukushi, 158
Tsuneyasu, Prince, 8, 76, 160
Tsurayuki Shū (Tsurayuki Collection), 12n

Uda tennō, viii, 99, 115, 125, 127, 279, 295,
    300, 309, 327, 374; and occasions for
    poetry, 9–10, 12, 314; and screen poems,
    10, 279; and Suzakuin, 113, 169; and the
    Teiji villa, 68
uguisu (mountain thrush), 50
Uji Mountains, 332
Uji River, 83, 247, 309
Une Meadow, 366
uneme, 37n
unohana, 94
Urin'in, 70, 76
ushin, 98
uta makura, 10
utaawase, 5, 9
utamonogatari, 3

vocabulary of waka, 15
votive strips, 252, 356

waka: as an art, 9; formal characteristics,
    viii, 3, 18; images, viii; influences on, 6;
    rhetorical devices, viii

"Waka from the Sovereign's Excursion to the Ōi River," 12
Wakan rōei shū, 145
Wakatei jusshu, 13
Wani, 37, 37n
wasuregusa, 269
Watari River, 287
We-hsin tiao-lung, 388
Wei Hung, 388, 389
Wen hsüan, 7, 21, 388
"Wen-fu," 388
women writers, 396
word association, 18
word play in waka, 22, 37n, 38, 166, 170, 324

ya, 23, 38, 39, 39n, 379, 393
yaemugura, 330
Yamabe no Akahito, 42, 382, 382n, 398
yamabuki, 349
Yamashina, 240
Yamashiro Province, 154, 249
Yamato, 250
Yamato dances, 365

Yamato monogatari, 13, 24, 42n, 124, 185
Yamato Province, 335
Yamato uta, 35n
yamato-e, 10
Yamazaki, 158
Yasuakira, Prince, 72, 151
year-periods, vii, viii
Yen Yen-chih, 399
Ying Chu, 395
Yodo Marsh, 217
Yodo River, 113, 159, 165, 180
yōen, 229
Yoshino Mountain, 41, 42, 50, 66, 83, 151, 359
Yoshino River, 83, 286
Yōzei tennō, viii, 51, 336, 370
yūgen, 381n
Yü-t'ai hsin-yung, 388
Yüeh chih, 388, 390

"Zai minbukyō no ie no utaawase," 9
Zenrinji, 128
Zenyu, 50
Zoku Nihongi, 365